Communities, Development, and Sustainability across Canada

The Sustainability and the Environment series provides a comprehensive, independent, and critical evaluation of environmental and sustainability issues affecting Canada and the world today.

SUSTAINABILITY
AND THE
ENVIRONMENT

Edited by John T. Pierce and Ann Dale

Communities, Development, and Sustainability across Canada

A project of the Sustainable Development Research Institute

UBCPress / Vancouver

Printed in Canada on acid-free paper ∞

ISBN 0-7748-0722-9 (hardcover)
ISBN 0-7748-0723-7 (paperback)

Canadian Cataloguing in Publication Data
 Main entry under title:

 Communities, development, and sustainability across Canada

 (Sustainability and the environment, ISSN 1196-8575)
 Includes bibliographical references and index.
 ISBN 0-7748-0722-9 (bound)
 ISBN 0-7748-0723-7 (pbk.)

 1. Community development – Canada. 2. Sustainable development – Canada. I. Pierce, J.T. II. Dale, Ann, 1948- III. Series.
 HC120.E5C6382 1999   307.1′4′0971   C99-910425-X

UBC Press gratefully acknowledges the ongoing support to its publishing program from the Canada Council for the Arts and the British Columbia Arts Council. We also wish to acknowledge the financial support of the government of Canada through the Book Publishing Industry Development Program (BPIDP) for our publishing activities.

Canadä

Set in Stone by Val Speidel
Copy editor: Dallas Harrison
Proofreader: Joanne Richardson
Indexer: Annette Lorek
Printed and bound in Canada by Friesens

UBC Press
University of British Columbia
6344 Memorial Road
Vancouver, BC V6T 1Z2
(604) 822-5959   Fax: 1-800-668-0821
E-mail: info@ubcpress.ubc.ca
www.ubcpress.ubc.ca

In memory of my beloved son, Daniel James Frazer
September 19, 1966 – May 10, 1998

Some people when they are on Earth occupy only
the space of a tree, but when they leave, they leave
the space of a forest.

Ann Dale

Contents

Preface:
The Importance of Community

Hon. Clifford Lincoln, MP

Sustainable development will be impossible to achieve without neighbourliness, which makes us aware of the connections between us, both locally and globally. Neighbourliness, however, is manifested in many different ways in our complex modern societies. Robert D. Putnam (1996), for example, explains that it is common in North American society for people to talk on a daily basis electronically to people as far away as Australia or Thailand, but not to know the name of the next-door neighbour.

Communities now exist on many different levels, and our increasing global interdependence means that our sense of community is becoming far more fluid. Globally, equity dictates that Canada, a country blessed with space and natural resources beyond compare, should act as a caring global citizen, a good neighbour to the countries with which it shares this planet.

Consider the issue of climate change. Are we caring global citizens when, despite our immense comparative advantages, we are the runners-up in the international championship of per capita energy use and of carbon emissions into the atmosphere that we share with other countries with far less capacity and poorer than our own? The actions of Canadian citizens, in their choices of where they live, how they travel, and when they travel, affect people everywhere. McLuhan's global village will become even more of a reality in the twenty-first century.

Governments can play a key role in facilitating the movement toward sustainable communities, especially because one of the fundamental features of sustainable development is a strong and vibrant civil society. There are immense difficulties in Canada, however, because the current federal-provincial constitutional arrangements and political boundaries are not structured in ways that encourage sustainable development. Fragmented and competing jurisdictions, overlapping mandates, and unclear accountabilities result in what Holling (1993) refers to as increasingly brittle and rigid bureaucracies incapable of dealing with current realities.

We need to look at ways to strengthen our communities through mechanisms that go beyond devolution, to subsidiarity, to municipal/regional round tables and enlarged decision-making contexts that bring together bureaucrats, researchers, community planners, and activists with business to realize sustainable goals. As Dale and Hill (1996) argue, it is only through the dynamic and "untidy" interface of pluralistic decision-making forums such as this that the most innovative and effective solutions for sustainable development will emerge. By fostering "communicative rationality" in addition to "technical rationality," citizen participation in the planning process can result in broader support for the recommendations within those plans and, in turn, in a greater commitment from policymakers to address community sustainability (May et al. 1996). These kinds of citizen-based forums are better positioned to influence elected officials to develop more cooperative intergovernmental regimes that actively facilitate the implementation of sustainable development.

In addition, from my own perspective as a parliamentarian, our immense societal difficulties in initiating, let alone coordinating, collective action toward sustainable development stem in no small measure from a significant lack of vision and resolve in looking at, and planning for, the long term. It is obvious that the current electoral cycle works against the kind of long-term planning and thinking that is so necessary for sustainable development.

In saying this, my intent is not to lay blame on this party or that, or on this government or the other. Rather, it is to note that for far too long our governments have moved from one five-year mandate to another, planning from one election to the next, without enough attention to the paramount need for coalescing the energies and actions of civil society toward a truly sustainable way of life.

Given that Canadians value equity and neighbourliness, as well as health and environment, four of the key prerequisites for the building of sustainable communities, why have our efforts and results been so scattered and so uneven across the country? Why, given these key preoccupations in Canadians, is it so difficult for us to coalesce action among our governments and civil society to foster sustainability as a central concept for a lasting future?

Communities need to pressure and convince our governments to adopt sustainability as their tool of governance but can only do so if the citizens who elect these governments become solidly convinced in their individual lives and actions that it is the only way of building a lasting future for themselves and future generations. It is not sufficient for us to hold dear certain essential values, unless we are prepared to filter them holistically into our daily lives and make them a real and an integral part of ourselves. Only then can we choose and fashion governments that will be faithful reflections of ourselves and of our sustainable living.

The conundrum is that, in the absence of the generational concept and ideal in government, and therefore leadership from government that will inspire and guide us, we must turn the tables on government and, in a way, force it to learn and to lead. If today the efforts and achievements of civil society are so scattered and uneven, then it is because civil society sees sustainable development with a myriad of eyes and minds.

One way to transcend fragmentation, competing jurisdictions, overlapping mandates, and the plurality of eyes and minds is through catalyzing local community decision making. One very successful example of the kinds of pluralistic decision-making forums we need is the Salmon River Watershed Round Table, created in 1993, with 130 members – representing industry, government, First Nations, environmentalists, and landowners – dedicated to being a catalyst in achieving and maintaining a healthy Salmon River watershed through coordinated management of all resources, respect for all concerns, and cooperative positive action. As one of the First Nations participants stated, "We want to see the river back the way it was when our forefathers were here." This local round table has adopted an approach that involves building understanding of the watershed as a whole, developing a watershed-wide stewardship plan to guide future activities, and initiating on-the-ground actions that are clearly desirable no matter what their future management plan might be. First Nations have formed the Salmon River Restoration Committee. The watershed now has the kind of community involvement in decision making that ensures that future actions will be sustainable.

I believe that this kind of grassroots driven community collaboration, based on strategic planning combined with immediate concrete actions, is a key to implementing effective sustainable development decision making. In British Columbia, for example, over forty-five community round tables are now active. They are based to varying degrees on the principles of equality, community building, cooperation, interdependence, participation, living within ecological limits, self-reliance, community control, diversity, and developing appropriate indicators.

Another key to solving the problem is widespread community awareness and education to gradually and systematically convince Canadians to transform their deeply felt values and concerns for the future into a regular and ingrained pattern of sustainable living – and in so doing forge between them the necessary holistic connections around the common objective of sustainability.

Twenty-five years ago, Canadians started to become aware of their health and that of their children. Yet few were those who translated the concern into physical activity and properly balanced nutrition. Through a massive program of community and public awareness, made possible through a remarkable partnership of all sectors of society, including government, a quiet health revolution came about. As a result of the ParticipACTION program, cycling, jogging, power-walking, and gymnasiums were suddenly discovered and took hold. Canadians started to watch what they ate and drank and to transmit their newly acquired healthier-living habits to their children. The trends today are irreversible: summer and winter alike, Canadians enjoy exercise and fitness in record numbers – and monitor their nutrition and eating habits in increasing numbers.

What we desperately need today to motivate civil society toward sustainable living is a comprehensive and ongoing program of public awareness and education that will reach into our schools and colleges, into our boardrooms and businesses, into our government offices and our homes. Through messages and examples, it will show that sustainable development and thus a sustainable society are healthier, more economically prosperous and stable, and more peaceful and enjoyable than their short-term and piecemeal counterparts.

If today we have so readily accepted and promoted recycling within our communities, and now take it for granted as part of our lives, then it is because we have understood that it makes both environmental and economic sense. It would not take long to convince Canadians of the need for sustainable use of energy, water, and land. Once convinced, we can strive for this common ideal and goal.

Yet throughout our country, and despite the hurdles and the lack of leadership from government, a host of deeply committed and courageous Canadians continues to participate in the promotion of sustainable development values within our communities, at all levels. The more we persevere in our efforts, the more surely our message will spread and influence others.

Nature has a formidable capacity to heal and restore itself, but it can do so only if we, in total partnership and communion with nature, have the wisdom, foresight, and resolve to heal ourselves and to choose the path of sustainability. We have no other choice. The question now is whether strengthening civil society means hiring more police officers, or encouraging people to know the next-door neighbour's name (Putnam 1996).

References

Dale, A., and S.B. Hill. 1996. "Biodiversity Conservation: A Decision-Making Context." In A. Dale and J.B. Robinson, eds., *Achieving Sustainable Development*, 97-118. Vancouver: UBC Press.

Holling, C.S. 1993. An Ecologist's View of the Malthusian Conflict. Paper presented at the Population-Environment-Development Lecture Series, the Royal Swedish Academy of Sciences, Stockholm.

May, P.J., R.J. Burby, N.J. Ericksen, J.W. Handmer, J.E. Dixon, S. Michaels, and D.I. Smith. 1996. *Environmental Management and Governance: Intergovernmental Approaches to Hazards and Sustainability*. London: Routledge.

Putnam, Robert D. 1996. "The Decline of Civil Society: How Come? So What?" The 1996 John L. Manion Lecture. *Optimum: The Journal of Public Sector Management* 27, 2: 27-42.

Introduction

Ann Dale

Books in the Sustainable Development Research Institute (SDRI) series grew out of a number of discussions between the general series editors, Ann Dale and John Robinson, in 1993 about three things. First, we recognized the need to move from rhetoric to action in achieving sustainable development. Although Canada is internationally renowned for its contributions to global sustainable development, it seemed to us that most of this activity reflected the standard Canadian achievement of being very innovative and progressive in issues of process but much less so in integrating substance into process.

Second, it was clear that, although more research was needed on a whole range of issues, analysts and researchers knew enough about the causes and possible consequences of problems of unsustainability to support strong actions in the policy arena. Furthermore, given the interlocutory and interactive effects of most sustainable development issues, incomplete knowledge and imprecise information were inherent to the problematic. Lack of knowledge and the need for further analysis and study were no longer valid reasons for lack of action in many areas.

Third, there was no regular vehicle for conveying information to the relevant policy communities or to interested Canadians in a timely fashion. Although there was no lack of research, analysis, opinion, and background information on sustainable development issues in Canada, much of it was not in an easily accessible form or one that spoke easily to senior policy analysts. There existed no Canadian equivalent of the various publication series of the WorldWatch Institute or the World Resources Institute.

Thus, it appeared that the research and policy analysis community could make some contribution toward solving these problems by initiating a series of regular publications that brought together the findings of the research community, based on the premise that it was time to move from analysis to action. The focus of the SDRI series is therefore deliberately prescriptive, with the goal of not simply describing the problems but also of proposing some solutions to the problems.

The idea for this volume came from a meeting of the coeditors based on two distinctive but complementary experiences that reinforced the need to better understand the challenges of sustainable local development. Over five years ago, Ann Dale had a discussion with Bill Irving, mayor of Ucluelet on Vancouver Island. At that time, Ann was researching the CORE process, and during a discussion with Bill he asked, "What is a sustainable community?" He added that, if he had any "real" information on the meaning of a sustainable community, then he could take this information to his town council and begin to talk about how to make their community more sustainable. A quick review of the literature at that time revealed considerable discussion about the macro and theoretical issues involved with sustainable development but little micro-level analysis and few practical case studies that would be helpful to people trying to implement the theories. We are indebted to Bill Irving for those observations.

In a similar vein, John Pierce in the early 1990s was researching structural change in resource-dependent communities and had recently assumed the directorship of the Community Economic Development Centre at Simon Fraser University, a position that brought him in contact with a wide range of communities seeking alternative and more sustainable forms of development. It quickly became apparent that communities, although at the base of the development chain, had become the missing link in efforts to refashion relations between environment and economy. These experiences, along with the supportive comments from the Canadian Consortium for Sustainable Development Research (CCSDR), provided the genesis for this book.

It attempts to highlight the importance of community as a critical link in achieving sustainable development. We hope that this contribution to the evolving debate on the theory and practice of sustainable development distinguishes itself from other contributions by recognizing that, although the scale of development and the globalization of economies and societies are the forces recasting and perhaps imperilling the future, we need to invert the proverbial telescope to emphasize that many of the sources of our problems and the solutions to them are embedded locally. Toward this end, *Communities, Development, and Sustainability across Canada* will provide readers with both retrospective and prospective analyses – the former dealing with the decline in community, symbolically and structurally, and continuing threats to its survival ecologically, socially, and economically; and the latter addressing what can be done to strengthen the ability of communities to support sustainable development locally.

Each SDRI volume is divided into four parts. The first part, "Vision," includes papers describing significant Canadian initiatives in some aspect of creating a sustainable society for Canada. The second part, "Connections," represents an attempt to reach beyond the field of sustainable development as conventionally defined. In this section, we address topics and include authors from other fields asking in each case for connections to be drawn to the field of sustainable development. In this way, we hope to contribute to a broadening of the field. The third part, "Action," is the heart of the volume. It contains papers on various sustainable development topics, always with the premise that we know enough to take action. Authors are encouraged to make concrete proposals for action. Finally, the fourth part, "Assessing Progress," provides information on how we are doing and whether we are getting closer to or farther from our sustainable development goals.

The "Vision" section of this volume contains a paper by Marcia Nozick, who looks at community solutions to global problems. She offers a practical model of how to begin building sustainable communities through economic self-reliance grounded in the life experiences of the people who live in them.

In the "Connections" section, Robert Woollard and William Rees examine the policy and social implications of changing to sustainable urban systems. Although these authors are no strangers to the sustainable development debate, they make important contributions to our understanding of the link between the physical growth in throughput and the change in the size of the "ecological footprint."

The "Action" section contains eight papers, including far-ranging and in-depth case studies and theoretical accounts of community change and adaptation. The first paper, by Rosemary Ommer and Peter Sinclair, offers a history of the Newfoundland outport in terms of formal (merchant) and informal (settler) economies and how their subsequent separation has been one of the factors leading to the systemic crisis. The second paper, by Christopher Bryant, explores the patterns of planned community change in Canada and develops a theoretical basis for a set of actions at the community level aimed at sustainable community development. The next three chapters offer critical profiles of communities dependent on a resource sector and the prospects and possibilities for models of alternative development: Timothy McTiernan's paper on northern communities, Michael Gertler's paper on sustainable agriculture on the Prairies, and Richard Schwindt's paper on communities and the Pacific salmon fishery. In the final three chapters, Alison Gill and Maureen Reed look at incorporating postproductivist values into community processes, Mark Roseland discusses the meaning of natural and social capital for sustainable community development, and Bryan Massam and Jill Dickinson interrogate the meaning of the civic state and civil society in relation to sustainable development.

The fourth section, "Assessing Progress," contains a paper by Thomas Meredith that examines how the concepts of socioecosystem and of critical environmental zones can help us to explore the critical questions of where (or who) we are and where we want to go.

The conclusion, by John Pierce, synthesizes the key arguments, concepts, and issues according to the ecological, social, and economic imperatives of sustainable development.

Vision

1

Sustainable Development Begins at Home: Community Solutions to Global Problems

Marcia Nozick

I remember hearing an economics professor being interviewed on TV. He was saying that we have to accept the disappearance of "uneconomic communities" as a fact of modern life; a fishing village or a rural town is a thing of the past. Governments, he stated, should be putting more resources not into saving places but into *moving people* away from their communities to other economic growth centres. The argument appeared sound, yet something about it disturbed me deeply ... an underlying assumption. The expert on TV was expressing a prevalent view among politicians and economists – that economic globalization is an inevitable process and that where capital flows people must follow. In other words, the dictates of our global economy take precedence over people, local culture, and history. *Community* is not seen as having any inherent value worth saving apart from economics. Furthermore, there is no recognition that people *have* resources and means within their communities and regions to meet many or most of their needs.

People, history, and place become leftovers or waste by-products in the process of globalization. The more we direct our attention "out there," the more we lose sight of what is going on "in here," at home, in our communities. The more we are consumed by the idea of turning our particular city into a World-Class City like Los Angeles or New York, the more we lose touch with our local traditions. And the more we focus on integrating our local economies into the global economy, the more we lose control over how our communities will develop. In the race to become globally competitive, valuable resources are being diverted away from meeting community needs.

The most serious crisis that we face today, along with environmental destruction, is the disappearance of community, both as an idea and as a physical form. Once-vibrant farm towns are dying as rural populations dwindle and the local farm economy is replaced by large-scale agribusiness. Single-resource towns have become ghost towns as industries shut down or moved to other countries for bigger tax breaks. At the same time, inner-city neighbourhoods are being ravaged from within by the destructive effects of poverty, alienation, and violence.

These are not random occurrences but the results of complex global forces working to dismantle the structures of community life and the social relationships of family and friends that for thousands of years have been a source of genuine support and identity for people. Rootlessness and dispossession are the inevitable fallout of an economic system based on free mobility of capital and global competition. People move to find jobs, corporations move to find cheaper labour, and even the food we eat, which we once produced ourselves, now comes to us from thousands of miles away – like the modern tomato, industrially bred not for improved taste or nutrition but for efficiency of transport: thick skinned, square, and waterless.

In the last two decades, we have seen the emergence of a global economic restructuring based on the precept that the world is no longer made up of neighbourhoods, cities, regions, or even nations; there is now a single world order dominated by transnational corporations, free trade, global competition, unfettered growth, harmonization of social programs, and the decline of the nation-state. In the last two decades, industries have become global in size and control world markets. Corporations continue to expand, accumulate, and concentrate huge amounts of capital into fewer and fewer hands by merging, buying out, and putting out of business their large and small competitors, including local producers. As a result, hundreds of neighbourhoods, towns, cities, and entire regions are being marginalized, written off as bad investments.

Rootlessness, transitoriness, and dispossession are the fallout of an increasing trend toward global competition. In the process of globalization, corporations are dissociated from identification with a local place and abstracted from responsibility to a local community. Dissociation takes on another face in the global marketplace, where money itself has become a commodity, the object of speculation and trade for profit detached from the actual production of goods and services. And production has become separated from employment as computers and machines have replaced the work carried out by men and women. These global forces have meant death to community life, which is based on an attachment to place, to work, and to people in social relationships with one another.

Communities across North America are in major crisis. They are breaking apart under the strain of centrifugal forces of global development. There are six major stress points of community breakdown:

1   declining local economies due to deindustrialization and the draining of wealth out of communities by large, outside-owned corporations
2   loss of citizen control as decisions affecting the future of a community

are made by higher levels of government and corporations that have no personal stake in the community

3 environmental degradation as local supplies of water, air, and soil are poisoned by industrial and consumer waste and auto pollution

4 social degradation and neglect of human needs as increasing numbers of people are abandoned to homelessness, joblessness, and unsafe living conditions

5 erosion of local identity and community cohesiveness as people increasingly identify with the images of mass consumer culture

6 dissociation of corporate identity with place, resulting in a loss of responsibility to communities.

In order to regenerate our communities, we must deal with all of these related aspects of community breakdown. We have to address the whole picture at once. Currently, we are just dealing with the parts, and the parts often conflict. For example, if we chase after outside investment, we increase a community's vulnerability to outside interference. At the same time, if we try to alleviate poverty by simply expanding welfare services, we do not empower people to become self-sufficient or provide them with the opportunity to give something back to the community. Likewise, it is not enough to impose environmental restrictions on industries. We need to create entire communities that are ecologically, socially, and economically sustainable, where people can walk or bicycle to work and work at life-enhancing as opposed to life-destroying activities.

What is needed is an *integrated* approach that addresses economic, ecological, political, and cultural development as part of a strategy to reclaim and restore community as a focal point in people's lives and an essential life-support system. We need to build communities that (1) can sustain and regenerate themselves through economic self-reliance, increased community control, and environmentally sound development, and (2) are worth preserving because they are grounded both in the life experiences of people who live in them and in the natural histories of specific regions. This calls for the revival of local culture and the meeting of people's needs.

The remainder of this chapter presents a model of how to begin this process. There are five major action areas that, taken together, provide a framework for an integrated development strategy designed to address the stress points of community breakdown. These action areas are:

1 enhancing local wealth through economic self-reliance
2 gaining community control over local resources
3 becoming ecologically sustainable
4 meeting the needs of individuals
5 building a community culture.

Following is a brief discussion of each of the five action areas.

Enhancing Local Wealth through Economic Self-Reliance

Economic self-reliance begins with the notion of producing the things that you need yourself rather than getting them through exchange. The process begins with the individual and moves outward to household, community, city, region, nation, and finally planet. At every level, self-sufficiency is the goal.

Pursuing self-reliance is a major step toward unhooking from the tentacles of a global economy. Whereas a global economy is built on imports and exports, and on mass production and consumption, the self-reliant economy is built on local markets, gears its production to serve community needs, and works to recapture and retain the wealth produced by the community. It is an approach that looks inward rather than outward, building on internal strengths and resources.

Self-reliance can work collectively as well. Because few communities will ever achieve self-sufficiency, there will always be the need for trade. *Collective self-reliance* is a trading strategy that avoids exploitation and the domination of one party over another. It is a strategy of exchange between equal partners for the purpose of building collective strength among a block of cooperating communities. Examples might include intentional trading between interlinked cooperatives, such as we find in Mondragon, Spain, between community businesses that share a similar social ethic, or between businesses belonging to a particular ethnic or social community, such as within the Aboriginal community.

What is often not recognized is that people do have resources and means within their communities to meet many of their basic needs. Every community in Canada, even the poorest, has income, skills, and physical resources. It is how we put these resources to use that makes the difference. There are several strategies that can be used to create or enhance community wealth. For example, communities generate new wealth by:

1   making more with less – maximizing the use of existing resources
2   making the money go around – circulating dollars within a community
3   making things for themselves – import replacement
4   making something new – creating a new product.

New wealth is created when an economy can produce more using the same or less amount of energy and the same or fewer number of resources – by stretching existing resources further through conservation and recycling. In this way, economic growth is tied to ecological sustainability. Substantial savings are derived from the efficient use of resources. Energy conservation is a good example. In the town of Osage, Iowa, population

4,000, the municipal hydro company helped people to save electricity and gas in their homes through inexpensive technologies. It saved an average of about $1,000 per year per household in energy costs – money that could be spent in the local economy, making it more prosperous. The bank saw an increase in deposits of 10 percent per year, of which 10 percent was attributed directly to energy savings. The result over ten years was that the utility saved so much money that it paid off all of its debts and held an interest-bearing surplus; it cut the rates five times in five years and thereby attracted two new industries to the town (Lovins 1994).

In land-use planning, it is far more economically and ecologically efficient to concentrate development in older neighbourhoods that are already serviced than to promote suburban sprawl, which eats up land, energy used in transportation, and money spent to service these areas. Thus, the revitalization of inner-city neighbourhoods contributes to sustainable development (economically, ecologically, and socially, in terms of preserving community history and identity). Likewise, the integrated planning of cities, such that work, recreation, shopping, and living are within close distances of each other (called "proximity planning"), is another way to conserve energy and reduce the high costs of infrastructure (roads, bridges, sewer lines). A study in Portland, Oregon, showed that, by reviving neighbourhood grocery stores, 5 percent of the city's energy consumption spent driving to shopping centres for small items could be saved (Morris 1982, 139). Both the City of Vancouver, in its 1990 *Clouds of Change* report, and the City of Ottawa, in its 1991 *Official Plan,* promote proximity planning as well as other initiatives directed at energy conservation (Nawaz 1993). The benefits are both environmental and economic.

Every time a dollar changes hands, it becomes a new dollar for somebody else to spend. In this way, dollars that circulate multiply. As long as money circulates within a self-contained system, it generates wealth within that system, but when money leaves the system the multiplier effect stops. In a healthy economy, a dollar gets spent six to eight times before it leaves a community; in an unhealthy economy, money falls out of circulation almost immediately. As a step toward self-reliance, a community needs to plug the leakage of dollars from the local economy. To do so, it has to identify the holes in its bucket.

In poor inner-city neighbourhoods, rent paid to absentee landlords accounts for a major outflow of capital. Information obtained from the 1991 census data shows rent paid out by residents in one inner-city neighbourhood of Winnipeg amounted to $20 million in one year. Given that 75 percent of rental properties are owned by absentee landlords, that means between $15 million and $18 million left the neighbourhood. As one community organizer from upstate New York put it, "We're all of us paying one way and another to own a home. Question is, whose home are we paying

for, ours or our landlord's?" Government programs and nonprofit development groups that assist residents to own, either cooperatively or privately,
their own homes help to stem the outflow of capital from a neighbourhood. Housing is big business. When communities get involved in developing local housing, it has proven to be one of the most effective tools for
accumulating capital in poorer inner-city neighbourhoods.

Neighbourhood revitalization involves more than the upgrading of
houses. It involves people. Housing and restoration help to create jobs for
local residents, promote training and skills development, organize the
community (resident associations, co-ops, etc.) to empower people to participate in decisions that affect their neighbourhood, spin off commercial
developments (more jobs) as the neighbourhood improves, and build pride
in the community and self-esteem among the residents. The Project for
Pride in Living (PPL) is a community development corporation in the
poorest inner-city neighbourhood of Minneapolis. Over its twenty-year
history, PPL has operated with donations from corporations, foundations,
and individuals, as well as with government cooperation and volunteer
assistance. Starting off small, rehabilitating only a handful of houses at a
time, PPL has grown into a multimillion-dollar enterprise that has rebuilt
and renovated over 700 housing units and established 162 co-ops; it manages 333 units of rental housing co-ops and runs a tool-lending library, a
neighbourhood general store, and a home- and office-surplus store that
trains and employs "hard-to-employ" neighbourhood residents. It has
increased the tax base for the city by $21.7 million and has reversed the
outflow of population from the inner-city neighbourhood. Most important, PPL has managed to maintain its grassroots connections and self-help
orientation, employing minority groups, giving people tools to fix their
homes, and training residents in life and work skills to ease them off welfare and chemical dependencies. Neighbourhood revitalization, implemented as a *community development process*, can accumulate wealth for a
neighbourhood and, at the same time, meet people's needs and build individual self-worth and community pride.

Bank savings and imports are two primary sources of money leaks out of
a community. Money put into savings is money taken out of circulation.
Bank savings would not damage a local economy if a significant portion of
this money was reinvested locally, but Canadian banks have taken billions
of dollars in deposits out of our communities and even our country, investing in foreign loans and international money markets. To recapture some
of this outflow of wealth, we could enact legislation such as exists in the
United States, where a Community Reinvestment Act requires banks to
lend at least 16 percent of their loan portfolios to projects aimed at revital-
izing decaying inner-city neighbourhoods. Alternatively, we can work with
our local credit unions, where members hold voting power, to establish

community investment accounts and community loan funds. VanCity in Vancouver and Assiniboine Credit Union in Winnipeg are examples.

Consumption of imports is another major source of money leakage. The counterstrategy is *import replacement* – making things ourselves. One of the keys to successful import replacement is setting up local markets for local products through matchmaking, brokering, and prearranged agreements. Governments can be effective catalysts in community renewal through their own targeted local spending. On the Prairies, with the demise of the Crow rate subsidy for grain transportation, a group of farmers banded together to invest collectively in a large hog operation and a local seed-processing plant to create new local markets for their grain, thus cutting down on the need for and the cost of shipping grain out of the region. In another example, in Eugene, Oregon, ten different businesses were analyzed to find what they bought from outside the region and then put in touch with local suppliers who could do the job more cheaply. One hotel was importing order forms from Boston when local printers could provide the same product for 40 percent cheaper. Another business, which made airline meals, was importing chicken broth from Arkansas. As part of a community economic development project in Eugene, a consultant was able to strike a deal with local poultry producers, the airline company, and the bank that resulted in setting up a new company to produce chicken broth locally. Eighty-five local jobs were directly created plus hundreds more in the building and installing of equipment. A neighbourhood clearing house was established in Eugene to act as a broker to match local buyers and sellers and to help set up new neighbourhood enterprises. These examples show how, with coordinated effort and strategic planning, a community can create new businesses and generate new wealth through import replacement – keeping dollars circulating locally, intensifying the level of exchange between local producers and consumers, and stemming the outflow of local dollars.

In the end, entrepreneurial inventiveness and diversification are the most important human resources in creating new wealth for communities. Through invention, we can learn how to extract more from the resources that we already have and, in this sense, create new wealth. Through creativity, we learn to improvise with and adapt the materials at hand to make new products and to reduce our dependency on imports. We can make something new. The Tall Grass Prairie Bread Company in Winnipeg is an example of local inventiveness. This worker–co-op bakery discovered that, by owning and operating its own small flour mill (eight inches in diameter), it could buy wheat directly from local organic farmers and grind the grain at the bakery, as opposed to purchasing flour from large transnational milling companies. The little flour mill has enabled the bakery to cut its production costs to such an extent that it can pay local organic farmers more than double the price of what wheat is selling for on the market and still make a profit. The bakery has become a local success story, with a steady flow of customers for its fresh organic bread and delicious baking. More important, the bakery has helped to form direct links between local farmers and urban consumers by bypassing the corporate milling companies. In this way, it can support local organic growers and offer quality food to the public at affordable prices. In addition, the bakery has created seven new full-time jobs for the neighbourhood.

Gaining Community Control over Local Resources

The long-term welfare of a community depends on its ability to shape its own future. A decentralized, community power base is needed to support a community-based economy, the same way that centralized power is used to support national and global economic interests. Because power in today's society is concentrated at the top, the conditions for local control will require a transformation from centralized to decentralized power, from bureaucracy to grassroots management, from outside ownership and control of capital to local ownership and control of capital, and from hierarchical to nonhierarchical structures to allow for the maximum participation by community members in the development process.

Gaining community control and decision-making power over the allocation and use of local resources – land, capital, industry, and human resources (delivery of community services) – is essential to building sustainable communities. Various organizational structures can help to redistribute power and control from the top to the community level. In particular, community development corporations, community land trusts, community loan funds, cooperatives, and neighbourhood councils stand out as models for community control and self-management.

Gaining Control over Capital

Community projects and businesses require capital. Gaining access to capital can be a major stumbling block for those who are poor, who have few material possessions that they can use as collateral to get a bank loan. Banks do not lend money to "high-risk" (low-income) borrowers. To fill the gap left by traditional lending institutions, many community-based nonprofit groups have set up revolving loan funds of their own to lend capital to high-risk clients, who may want to start a business or local initiative. The pool of capital for the revolving loan fund usually comes from a variety of sources such as public and private foundations, unions, individuals, corporations, governments, and churches. Money is either donated or lent to the organization at reduced interest rates for a specified time period. The structure of the community loan fund may vary, but the basic concept remains the same: to finance enterprises that are beneficial to a community but that would otherwise be blocked from access to mainstream financing. In a sense, a community loan fund is like a small-scale community bank.

SEED Winnipeg is a non-profit organization that attempts to alleviate poverty through community economic development strategies. It operates a community loan fund and provides technical assistance to low-income individuals wanting to start or expand a business. SEED was set up with the assistance of a local credit union that donated $100,000 to start it off. Behind the setting up of SEED is another story of community power. A local Winnipeg social-action group called CHO!CES set the ball in motion. After identifying the need for a community investment fund, the group decided that it needed to gain some decision-making control over the Assiniboine Credit Union (the largest credit union in the city), which had been operating for years like a traditional bank, investing in foreign money markets while ignoring the need for investment in the inner city. CHO!CES organized its dozens of members to join the credit union and vote for a slate of board members who supported community economic development. One of the first actions of the new board was to help set up SEED Winnipeg. Programming began in 1993. By the end of 1996, SEED had helped to start eighty-nine new businesses and twenty-two expansions of existing businesses, accounting for approximately $350,000 worth of loans. All of the clients were on low income. Success rates after about four years are comparable to those in the traditional small-business community, with about two-thirds of the businesses still operating.

Gaining Control over Land Use and Housing

Private ownership of land plays a determining role in the development of communities and the provision of housing. Land is a market commodity, to be bought and sold to the highest bidder. Some communities have become "overinvested" with speculators, developers, and homeowners, who push up land costs by buying and selling properties to make profits on inflated land values. As the price of land skyrockets, so does the cost of housing, forcing low-income and longtime residents to leave the community. The result is a loss of affordable housing in the inner city and the breakup of longtime, stable, lower-income communities. By contrast, other communities are suffering from the opposite extreme, being "disinvested" of capital, with businesses and families (who can afford to) fleeing to the suburbs. Once the cycle of disinvestment begins, a neighbourhood quickly degenerates: houses and apartments are allowed to deteriorate by absentee landlords, buildings are abandoned, and more businesses and families move away, leaving only the poorest of the poor, the homeless, criminals, and drug dealers.

The community land trust (CLT) has solutions for both disinvestment and overinvestment. A CLT is a private nonprofit corporation set up to acquire property in a neighbourhood and to hold it in trust in perpetuity for the use and benefit of local residents and future generations. The essence of a CLT is the separation of ownership of land and buildings. The trust leases its land to private homeowners, co-ops, and community businesses on ninety-nine-year leases. Individuals own the buildings, but the community retains ownership of the land under the buildings and thus gains control over how the land is used and over the cost of housing in a neighbourhood. A CLT does many things: it reduces the cost of housing, makes owning a home possible for the poor, guarantees that housing will remain affordable for future generations, and infuses a neighbourhood with new capital resources and community energy, all of which help to build and stabilize communities.

The United Hands Community Land Trust in Philadelphia, for example, has helped to restore hundreds of rundown houses into affordable and comfortable homes and to create a safe, caring community – a kind of oasis in the midst of a neighbourhood otherwise characterized by crime, drug deals, and abandoned buildings. The families in the land trust work together, meeting every Saturday to construct or rehabilitate their future homes and those of their neighbours. Their work counts as a sweat-equity downpayment on a future house. Workshops teach homeowners about repairs and managing finances. And finally, with the completion of each house, there is a street celebration to welcome in the new family. The United Hands CLT, run by the residents themselves, is a vehicle for people to make decisions and work together, get to know one another, and build supportive community relationships. In this way, bit by bit, block by block, a neighbourhood is being restored to health.

Self-Governance

There are various organizations that allow residents to democratically participate in the planning and development of their community. Neighbourhood associations and councils bring residents together to discuss community issues and work out community solutions to community problems. Community development corporations (CDCs) take on the role of community developer. Working together, a neighbourhood council plans development and the CDC executes the plans, building and managing needed housing, social services, and new businesses and industries. The West Bank neighbourhood in Minneapolis, which has planned and developed the Cedar Riverside neighbourhood over the past twenty years, operates in this self-determining fashion, with a neighbourhood planning group directing the activities of the CDC. The Downtown Eastside Residents Association in Vancouver has played a similar role for the neighbourhood, building and upgrading housing, developing a library/community centre, and making the neighbourhood a safer place to live through a variety of actions and programs.

Gaining Control over Local Industry

Cooperatives can play a significant role in helping to redistribute power to the grassroots through a structure of collective ownership of local industries and services. In a co-op, every member has one vote. Profits are distributed equally among a collective membership in the form of reduced prices (consumer co-ops) or improved services (service co-ops) or are paid out in dividends, reinvestment capital, or a raise in salaries (worker co-ops), depending on the type of enterprise. The co-op model bridges the adversarial split between worker, owner, manager, and consumer by integrating all of these functions into a single body represented by its collective membership. As a member of a food co-op, I am not only a consumer but also have a say in how the business is run and in what is sold at what price. As a member of a producer/worker co-op, I not only have a job as a worker but also have a say, as a part-owner, in the conditions of my work, what I want to produce, and how to reinvest profits. As a member of a housing co-op, I am not only a tenant but also a co-owner protected against rent increases by landlords wanting to make a profit. The features of worker control, user participation, and equalized distribution of surplus wealth among members make the co-op especially attractive for community development. Some communities have built up a complex network of linked co-ops that mutually support each other through their purchases of goods and services (collective self-reliance).

In all of the above organizational models – be it the cooperative, community land trust, community development corporation, neighbourhood association, or community loan fund – the community acts in its own self-interest. The community *is* the developer, banker, landlord, and government, controlling decisions about the use of land, housing, capital, and industry, which are the community's resources.

Yet, in the end, it takes more than structures to empower a community – it takes community will and vision. Summoning a community's will, motivating people to care about their community, is far more difficult than setting up an organization. To build a community power base, we have to start with people and the issues that concern them. We need to acknowledge their capacities and gifts and provide them with the needed supports to unleash their hidden talents and potential. Whereas traditional power is based on a few people exerting control over the many, community power is the opposite – it gains strength by *sharing* power between as many people as possible. That means building coalitions, connecting diverse groups, networking, creating partnerships, community organizing. It means setting up community organizations that encourage democratic decision making and, finally, when the groundwork is done and the community's will is focused on a vision, setting up appropriate structures to ensure long-term community control over neighbourhood resources, such as those described in this section.

Becoming Ecologically Sustainable

Ecology teaches us that our world is a dynamic system of relationships of which we are all a living part. Ecology is about more than just "resources" – trees, air, water – it is about processes, relationships, and natural systems of integration that encompass all of human and nonhuman development. Nature is made up of an integrated network of self-contained systems related to other systems. This complex web of "systems within systems" is like a human body, in which each cell operates as an entity on its own, actively processing its own food, energy, and waste, yet is not isolated from but connected to other cells that make up larger systems of the body. All the different parts of our social and natural world make up our *diversity*; taken together, they make up our *unity*. The principle of "unity in diversity" leads to an understanding that the health of the planet depends on the health and integrity of the smallest community and that the health of the community depends on the health and integrity of each individual.

From the study of ecology, we can derive certain organizational principles for restructuring our social and economic relationships, for changing how we live in and relate to the world around us. For example, an economy is like an ecosystem. Its health is dependent on a diversity of local enterprises as a way to achieve long-term sustainability and to protect against the kind of sweeping disaster that occurs when a community depends on a single industry and that industry shuts down or moves away. As Jane Jacobs has pointed out, a truly vibrant and self-sustaining economy is built upon a complex web of interchange between a multitude of different local producers and consumers. Diversity, ingenuity, and flexible entrepreneurship are the cornerstones of economic regeneration (Jacobs 1984). They must be nurtured and made ongoing parts of a living economy.

Ecology teaches us that development is a *process*, not a product. It focuses our attention on means as opposed to ends. Do the processes of human production and consumption respect the limits of nature? Do production methods empower people? Are work relationships cooperative or dominating? Does development improve our quality of life and learning?

Finally, ecology teaches us that all things, from the individual to the community to the region and upward, are interconnected. Although we always need to respect the autonomy of each individual or community, we must also see each person or community as fitting into a larger social and natural ecosystem of which it is a part. The emphasis of ecology is on building relationships between the various parts that make up a healthy, diverse community and on establishing connections between communities and regions. How we work together to strengthen the mutual relationships between the various parts that make up the whole is key to building healthy communities.

The Royal Commission on the Future of the Toronto Waterfront (see

Crombie 1990) began as an inquiry into a specific area of the city, its harbourfront, but soon grew into a study of the entire Greater Toronto Bioregion, stretching forty miles east and west of Toronto and inland thirty miles. This area is fed by sixteen rivers whose waters eventually end up in the Toronto harbour. It became impossible to separate the lakefront from the rivers flowing into it or from the human activities that affect the water's quality. The commission recommended an ecosystem approach to planning that would bring together thirty municipalities and six regions included in the watershed to work in partnership for the sake of the whole. Some of the contributing factors to environmental stress include water and sewer systems, dispersed settlement, lack of landfill sites, consumer waste, commuter use of automobiles, and pollution by 600 industries. To solve the problems of the environment, each community must transcend narrow self-interest and see its part in a greater ecosystem.

From an ecological perspective, the solution to human-created environmental problems requires a fundamental rethinking and restructuring of human processes. The *Clouds of Change* report by Vancouver's Task Force on Atmospheric Change concluded with the statement, "Atmospheric change means *we* have to change" (City of Vancouver 1990, 69). What we have to change are our patterns of living. The *Clouds of Change* report included recommendations such as:

1   decentralize work back into the home using telecommunications
2   introduce energy-efficient land-use policies by creating self-contained communities where social services, shopping, working, recreation, and housing are within walking or bicycling distance of each other
3   intensify residential neighbourhoods, thereby reducing urban sprawl
4   implement an urban reforestation program
5   set up community councils to develop ecological neighbourhood plans
6   give incentives to ecological enterprises
7   implement an energy conservation by-law for new and existing buildings
8   institute a composting program at schools and community centres
9   expand programs for recycling and reducing solid waste.

In building an ecological community, we could add other things to the list:

• promoting urban food production, using converted warehouses, greenhouses, and empty lots
• employing a system of ecological treatment of waste at the neighbourhood level
• creating wildlife habitats in the city
• restoring local rivers and the watershed so that they can be used safely for drinking, swimming, and fishing.

There are hundreds of community projects that can help to build an ecocity in small bits. Community supported agriculture (CSA) is one example of an ecological initiative. In 1992, Shared Farming was started up in Winnipeg by a group of organic farmers and some city residents. City people collectively purchase shares in local farm operations. Each family puts up about $140 to $200 at the beginning of the growing season, an amount that pays for the farmers to grow organic vegetables that are then harvested, divided among the community membership, and delivered to the city on a weekly basis throughout the summer months. CSA enables the small farmer to raise capital in the spring when it is most needed without having to take out a bank loan, and it guarantees a local market for the produce, meaning that he or she can bypass the large wholesalers and retailers. In return, city families receive a steady supply of organic vegetables during growing season. In the first year, over 200 families joined the program. Shared Farming is more than just a food source – it is a process of community building that links city and country, food producer and food consumer. People from the city go out to the farms to help with seeding, weeding, and harvesting. The farm families hold large picnics for the city families that they provision. And the CSA group meets regularly to plan and organize their project. Through shared farming, urban consumers of food become partners with rural producers of food, sharing directly in the real costs and risks of food production. The project builds awareness and community and supports organic growers in a way that is mutually beneficial for everyone.

Another ecological project is the Habitat Re-Store in Winnipeg, an arm of Habitat for Humanity. Habitat for Humanity is a worldwide organization run by locally based chapters. Its purpose is to build homes for families on low income by attracting hundreds of volunteers from all walks of life who participate in a work camp where, armed with hammer and nail, they literally raise houses from basement to roof in a few days. The experience is that of a big building bee infused with a magnificent energy of celebration. Because of the work of volunteers and all the donations it receives from businesses, Habitat for Humanity can make the price of a new home affordable for a low-income family. The house is sold at cost, and Habitat for Humanity assumes the mortgage – interest free.

In Winnipeg, Habitat for Humanity was inundated with offers of donations of used building materials, windows, and doors; however, because Habitat houses are built with new construction materials, it had to refuse them. Then it came up with the idea of the Habitat Re-Store. Started in 1991, it is a warehouse of recycled building materials. It accepts used materials from individuals and institutions. Pickup is free of charge, and Habitat Re-Store sells the materials to the public at nominal prices. It also collects materials through salvage projects. This spin-off business was the first of its kind in North America and is now used as a model to start similar projects elsewhere. The business, in 1996, was highly successful, with revenues in excess of $300,000. It has nine paid employees and about 2,000 hours a month of volunteer labour. The Habitat Re-Store has several goals: to help people renovate and upgrade their homes at affordable costs; to keep building materials from ending up in garbage dumps (discarded building materials comprise 16 percent of dump sites); to create a new community business; and, finally, to raise capital for the Habitat for Humanity project. It donates $100,000 a year, the profit after operating expenses, to the Habitat revolving loan fund to build new houses each year for the poor.

Meeting the Needs of Individuals
Sustainable development was defined in 1987 by the UN Commission on the Environment and Development as meeting "the needs of the present without compromising the ability of future generations to meet their own needs" (Brundtland 1987, 8). Any discussion of building sustainable communities has to begin with the questions "What is it that we need?" and "How can we best meet our needs in a way that will provide a legacy of hope for our grandchildren?"

People everywhere have the same basic needs: health, safety, security, continuity, identity, meaning, and a feeling of connection and belonging. All of these needs are met by supportive communities. In a healthy community, there is an interdependent relationship between the individual and the collective – individuals give to a community through working, participating in community life, and helping and caring for others; in exchange, a community provides the individual with security, opportunities for meaningful work, a sense of identity, and self-fulfilment. The community and the individual mutually reinforce each other.

Yet, as a by-product of modern development, we have witnessed the breakdown of this social contract and the demise of community. Increasing numbers of people are being marginalized and abandoned to suffer the debilitating effects of alienation, stress, discrimination, hunger, homelessness, violence, and low self-esteem. This situation is costing our system dearly, because a community is only as strong as its individuals. When children are abused or go hungry, their performance in school suffers, and they are blocked from developing their potential as healthy, contributing adults. The entire community pays the price socially, economically, and spiritually.

The road to recovery lies in building healthier neighbourhoods where people know and trust each other, work together, support one another, and participate in the process of meeting their own basic needs. The problem is that institutions have replaced communities as providers – the market system provides jobs, housing, food, and consumer goods; when it fails, government provides social services and programs to compensate. People, instead of growing their food, repairing their cars or appliances, caring for their children or parents, have become passive receivers of consumer goods and public services, which they have come not only to expect but also to require. Social relationships are depersonalized, and individuals are devalued, in a process that creates further feelings of alienation, frustration, and low self-worth manifesting as social/communal problems.

People need to feel needed, to know that they have gifts (not just deficiencies), and to have a place to offer their gifts to the community where they will be affirmed and appreciated. We need every person's gifts. In Toronto, a group of homeless people were able to plan, help to build, and manage their own housing in a project called Street City. It is a small "town" comprised of seventy-two residents (half women, half men), complete with houses, streets, trees, and recreation areas, all built inside the vacant shell of a large Canada Post building that had skylights added to it spanning the length of the ceiling. The adaptive design for reuse of this vacant building won an award. But more important is the social and personal development of the residents in the project. All of the people living at Street City came directly from the street (alcoholics, drug addicts, schizophrenics, etc.). The residents make up their own rules for living together (unlike in shelters, which treat their residents like children) and work out their own conflicts through mediation. They hold town hall meetings, run by two mayors (one male, one female), to decide on issues. At Street City, the community residents started up their own small grocery store, banking service, maintenance business, recycling, and bicycle repair business. On Sundays, they collectively prepare a dinner for other street people at a charge of $1.25. With the security of a place to call home and a mutual support network, residents are taking steps to integrate into society. Some have gone back to school, others to jobs. Some are working with other homeless people at a new Street City being planned elsewhere. Street City is an outstanding example of how, in providing shelter, we can also meet people's needs for belonging, security, income, participation in decision making, and self-worth.

When building community is the goal, *how* we organize to provide shelter, food, health, and safety is as important as what we provide. Self-help processes empower people to become self-sufficient (as opposed to relying on charity, which leads to greater dependency). There are hundreds of other examples like Street City where communities are turning to self-help and mutual aid, such as neighbourhood safety projects, in which residents of a city block get together to deal with safety issues and enhance their neighbourhood, or community kitchens, where women meet once or twice a week to plan and cook a week's worth of meals and thereby reduce food costs while getting to know one another. These types of self-help projects build trusting relationships and personal self-esteem.

Social change works from the inside out, beginning with self-healing and self-development, which affect relationships with family and friends, eventually transforming community relationships and institutions. A community can play a pivotal role in creating environments that nurture personal development through its support of community-based literacy programs, abuse treatment, adult education, and self-help organizations of all types. Most of all, changed social attitudes demonstrating respect for those who have been devalued by society (women, children, minority groups, the handicapped) help to validate the worth of individuals. When we realize that people – not things – matter most, we can adopt a whole new perspective on development and human services. From this starting point, we need to ask of each development activity and program "Do the processes encourage self-actualization, self-determination? Do they help to integrate individuals into a community?"

Building a Community Culture

Communities are able to sustain themselves over generations not just on the basis of material wealth or power but also on the basis of something deeper and more intangible – a common identity, purpose, and culture that bind people together. Just as an individual has an identity, so too does a community. A community has a heart – a source of feeling and spirit. Its lifeblood is its culture – the ways in which people do things together, local traditions, a geographic landscape, shared experiences of the past, and people's dreams and hopes for a future. These things cannot be bought or manufactured, but they can be nurtured by development. Modern development has been a process of *disconnecting* people from the land, alienating them from each other, dissociating them from their past and their future, and cutting them off from their deeper selves. A community culture, in contrast, has the potential to restore and *reconnect* people to the land, to each other, and to their past and their future; they can rediscover themselves in their collective roots.

Many things shape a community's identity: the collective/social history of a place, the geographic or natural history of a place, the values that people share, and the ways that people live, work, and play together.

The social history of a community is often embodied in many of its older neighbourhoods. Heritage conservation thus has the potential to make the past a living part of a community's identity. Heritage does not have to be limited to artifacts in a museum, monuments, or designated buildings. It can mean reviving and maintaining the character of older neighbourhoods – houses, streets, parks, shops, markets. It is an effective tool to revitalize older inner-city neighbourhoods. The saving of the Milton Park community in Montreal was a heritage restoration project initiated by residents and spearheaded by Heritage Montreal, which renovated and upgraded 600 units of housing. Most importantly, the project brought people in the neighbourhood together for a common purpose, fuelled their spirit, and laid the foundation for cooperative community living for years to come.

Heritage preservation can mean preserving *a way of life* for a community. Toronto's famous Kensington Market, covering several city blocks, attracts visitors from all over to its crowded narrow streets filled with stalls and exotic smells. At one time threatened with demolition as part of a redevelopment plan for the neighbourhood, today it is a cultural heritage resource for the city. Yet the market still functions to meet the needs of and to preserve a way of life for the new immigrants in the neighbourhood, who use the market daily to buy, sell, or bargain for fresh foods at affordable prices.

By discovering and developing what is unique about each neighbourhood and town, we create a sense of meaning attached to place. One of the keys to building community identity is to discover and celebrate the inherent and historic meanings of *special places*. Every city, town, and neighbourhood has them. Montreal has its famous Mount Royal, which identifies the city. Winnipeg has the Forks, a 100-acre parcel of land in the heart of the city where the Assiniboine River meets the Red River. The site was publicly reclaimed in 1989 from Canadian National Railways. The Forks is a special place imbued with natural beauty, symbolic meaning, and historic significance, being the birthplace of western Canada, the site of five forts, the location of a Hudson's Bay Company trading post, and the meeting place for Aboriginal people for over 6,000 years. Thousands of people visit the site, walk beside the rivers, go to the farmers' market, and attend open-air cultural events. But to what extent will the Forks be developed? There are different visions. Over the last five years, there has been an attempt to build an arena at the site, and there have been discussions of housing, trade towers, and other commercial developments, whereas others have spoken out to save the site for use as a cultural and historic park, in keeping with its status as a special place.

The natural history of a place is also important in shaping a community's identity. Where we live includes the local streams, indigenous plants and animals, and special geographical features such as woodlands, hills, and gorges. People become very attached to the particular trees, birds, flowers, and rivers in their community. Projects that restore and protect natural areas are a way to combine environmental stewardship with the building of community identity.

In downtown Toronto, there is a plan under way to restore the historic Garrison Creek Ravine, once one of Toronto's most distinctive natural landforms, which provided water for Fort York. By the early 1900s, however, the creek had become polluted and was filled in and finally consumed by housing. Brown and Story Architects have completed a mapping project that lays the original creek and landforms over the existing urban structures and creates a strategic plan to connect the present network of parks and public spaces to begin the restoration project. Because the path of the creek crosses the wards of seven city councillors and many neighbourhoods, the project will require the cooperation of many players and different jurisdictions. The Garrison Creek Community Group hopes to generate new projects at the community level to begin the incremental process of reclaiming the historic creek.

In another example, Sudbury has taken on a project to regreen a mountain and to protect it for use as a park by local residents. The mountain is located in the older, working-class neighbourhood of Donovan and Flour Mill and has been a place where children have played for years. Yet encroaching development is threatening to destroy (literally level) the mountain and remove it from community use. The restoration program involves children and their parents planting indigenous trees and grasses as well as mapping out all the green spaces in their neighbourhood. In this way, people are getting together to participate in the reclamation of their own community landscapes and learning about the history, geography, and politics of their neighbourhood. The process helps to build a sustainable community in that it encourages people to envision a future for their neighbourhood, gets them to participate in the stewardship of the natural environment, and creates a common activity that bonds people together over time.

Other community restoration projects include the reclaiming of vacant city lots for use as community gardens. In Winnipeg, EarthCorp brought hundreds of local residents together in 1995, both as paid workers and as volunteers, to build and plant community gardens in the inner city. The project helped to build community relationships, provided food for people, and restored green space to otherwise derelict and garbage-strewn empty lots.

Finally, community culture evolves out of the thousands of interactions between people. Empty places on a map do not constitute communities. People need to rub shoulders with each other, so there have to be reasons to get together. These "reasons" are all around us when building community is the goal. We can establish a community newspaper, start a popular theatre group, pick an issue that matters to people and fight a battle together, plant a garden, put on a community festival with local performers, paint a mural, write a history of the neighbourhood. It is the interactive life in a community that will define its personality and identity over time.

Many social and economic barriers stem from fear of differences. Yet sometimes all that is needed is for people to get to know each other face to face. Here is a story that illustrates the point. In Ottawa, there is an organization called West End Community Ventures that works to develop skills, community businesses, and jobs in a low-income neighbourhood, populated mainly by new immigrants and single-parent families. In one project, women were trained to run much-needed home day cares. However, once training was completed and day cares were set up, mothers were unwilling to leave their children at day care homes of women from different cultural backgrounds. They were afraid, for instance, of what food their children would eat – afraid of differences. To deal with this problem, West End Community Ventures began to hold regular luncheon get-togethers where each time a different immigrant woman would prepare food from her ethnic background, dress in traditional clothes, and give a presentation about her country of origin. For many, it was the first time that they spoke of their countries of origin since coming to Canada. People spoke to each other from their hearts and got to know one another. Understanding and trust came to replace ignorance and fear, and the day care problem was soon solved.

Conclusion

This chapter has identified an underlying conceptual framework for building sustainable communities based on five themes: self-reliance, community control, ecological sustainability, individual needs, and local culture. Together they provide an integrated model of development. The themes are interrelated. A self-reliant economy, because it relies on local markets, is more responsive to the needs of individuals in a community. Local production and consumption reduce long-distance transport of goods and are thus more ecological in terms of energy use and pollution reduction. A community culture, grounded in the appreciation of a particular landscape and history of a place, is a protector of local environments. As people in neighbourhoods are drawn into more direct dealings with one another, they come to know and trust each other, which adds to the safety and security of a neighbourhood and builds community culture. These five components are essential to building sustainable communities.

It is only by rebuilding community – which calls for restructuring our social and economic relationships and our relationship to the Earth – that we can build a sustainable future for everyone in the world. It is at the level closest to home that we can work with each other to undertake actions that will protect a community's heritage and shape its future. At home, *we* are the experts. We know our children, streets, buildings, community history, trees, and rivers. More importantly, we are the ones who *care* about the quality of air, water, safety, and life in our communities because we are directly affected.

Sustainable development has often been viewed as an exercise in top-down resource management. But a hierarchical approach to sustainable development cannot provide the plurality of solutions or the grassroots political will needed to deal with location-specific problems that communities in crisis are facing today. Instead, what we need are sustainable *communities*. In the final analysis, we need to shift from thinking that we have "global" problems that require "global" solutions. What we really have is a multiplicity of local problems, and our best solutions will come out of local actions.

References

Brundtland, Gro Harlem, chair. 1987. *Our Common Future*. The World Commission on Environment and Development. Oxford: Oxford University Press.

City of Vancouver Task Force on Atmospheric Change. 1990. *Final Report*. Vol. 1 of *Clouds of Change*.

Crombie, David. 1990. *Watershed*. Royal Commission on the Future of the Toronto Waterfront.

Jacobs, Jane. 1984. *Cities and the Wealth of Nations: Principles of Economic Life*. New York: Random House.

Lovins, Amory. 1991. "First Put in the Plug." *City Magazine* 12,2: 34-5.

Morris, David. 1982. *Self-Reliant Cities: Energy and the Transformation of Urban America*. San Francisco: Sierra Club Books.

Nawaz, Rasheda. 1993. "An Official 'Green' Plan for the City of Ottawa." *City Magazine* 14,1: 41-3.

Connections

2
Social Evolution and Urban Systems: Directions for Sustainability
Robert Woollard and William Rees

> Over the past several decades, there has been a marked shift in systems thinking from optimization of ideal systems with well-defined objectives to emphasis on systemic processes of learning related to problems or issues with ill-defined objectives. This shift has facilitated the use of systems thinking in analysis of complex, ill-defined, real situations. The difficult issue of assessing progress towards sustainability falls well within the bounds of this latter category of problems. (Hodge 1996, 267)

The above observation was made in *Achieving Sustainable Development*. It is an important point of departure for this chapter. The literature on sustainability increasingly contains studies in two general areas: first, those that address the "optimization of ideal systems with well-defined objectives" (these studies tend to foster increasingly complex models that do not have an obvious application in the rather ill-defined area of policy development); second, in-depth reports of particular biological, social, and/or economic subsystems – both "ill-defined" and "real" – that are unconnected to broad policy development at a scale beyond the system under study.

The stated intent of the SDRI series of books is to influence the policy community. This volume accents community and its role in enhancing sustainability. This chapter seeks to straddle the above two "themes" and to provide a synthesis useful to the assessment of progress toward sustainability within current urban systems. Straddling is required because any urban system is embedded in and interconnected with other systems. It is not possible, even in principle, to isolate any given urban system from its many related systems and still have anything worthy of serious analysis regarding sustainability. For example, Vancouver is nested in a regional structure of governance that in turn is nested within a provincial, federal, and (to some extent) international hierarchy of formal policy systems. In another dimension, it exists in a bioregional, hemispheric, and global hierarchy of nested ecosystems. Serious analysis of the prospect for a sustainable Vancouver must therefore simultaneously address the particular and the general, the individual and the systemic. On the one hand, it is fruitless to articulate and idealize once again the community in harmonic balance both socially and ecologically. On the other hand, ongoing reports of local studies that are not drawn together within a conceptual framework may be of marginal utility to policy makers except in dealing with specific choices. To attempt such a synthesis in such a short space runs the risk of being insufficiently particular about the general and insufficiently general about the particular. We thus ground this chapter in the broader framework of "evolution" and especially in some of the newer concepts in the biological expression of the term. This approach can be justified on the basis that the term "sustainability," as it applies to human activities (with their attendant policies), must at minimum consider the persistence of humanity over time and humanity's adaptation to changing circumstances.

Any approach to the study of complex adaptive systems must be prepared to put forth concepts that frame the principal issues of the system under discussion. In this chapter, we seek to articulate the foundations of sustainability, identify specific patterns of action, and outline some of the policy directions that might reasonably derive therefrom.

If sustainability is to have any meaning in reference to humans, then it seems fundamental that human populations must *persist* over time. Because the Earth has undergone dramatic changes over time and will continue to do so, such persistence will only occur if humans are able to *adapt* to changing circumstances. Although long-term survival may require biological adaptation, it is unlikely (notwithstanding Hollywood's hopes) that it will be rapid enough to be useful in present circumstances. Therefore, our efforts should focus on social adaptation (or maladaptation) and the policy implications of our studies.

If persistence and adaptation are central characteristics of sustainability, then, first, we might usefully assess their presence in current social and political structures. Second, we might consider what potential our contemporary arrangements have for future persistence and adaptation.

Let's look at some of the more recent insights into evolutionary change and adaptation. The original and unadorned Darwinian concept of "the survival of the fittest" might imply that pressures of selection for survival would shift urban systems toward increasingly perfect and effective systems with the dying of the "less fit." The view from the secure upper- and middle-class enclaves in our wealthier cities may be that this is in fact what is happening. However, it is increasingly obvious in the spectrum from Kinshasa to Los Angeles that the continued healthy existence of even wealthy enclaves is increasingly tenuous. Urban systems must be seen in their entirety. Talk of the sustainability of wealthy suburbs in the absence of the health of the overall city is tantamount to discussing the future evolution of the peacock's tail while the body that supports it is dying.

To talk about the sustainability of the human species is to talk about the health and viability of urban systems. This is not only because half the human population will soon live in urban environments but also because cities are the primary sources of the massive adverse effects that the human species is having on the rest of the ecosphere. To the extent that survival becomes impossible when such sustaining ecosystems are damaged beyond utility, we have to take seriously our impact on them. If, as noted above, we take a simple view of Darwinian selection, then we might end up looking for cases of urban systems that are perfectly adapted to their surrounding environments and bring them forward as examples of the highest evolutionary achievement. We might then suggest that other communities should emulate these cities such that the world would be populated by thousands of similar, well-functioning utopian systems. We might even take into account that the variety of climatic zones would lead to some delightful variations on a fundamentally similar theme. In the same way that, until the last few decades, most writing on evolution focused on the elegant successes of particular adaptations, much of the writing on urban systems has sought to outline notable successes in particular urban ecological "niches." More recent work in the field of evolution popularized by Stephen Jay Gould (1996) takes a radically different tack on the understanding of the evolution of species and their successful adaptation to changing environmental conditions. Various authors argue that specific adaptation to particular conditions (e.g., specific flowers requiring an exclusive species of insect pollinators) leads to increasing vulnerability rather than evolutionary robustness.

These authors argue that subtle forces are at work in the development of the rich array of successful species that are now threatened by human activities. We might usefully apply some of their insights to those activities. Any predator species that is so successful as to exterminate its prey can be seen as an example of hunting success and evolutionary failure. Our current urban systems can be seen as teetering on the edge of such an evolutionary outcome. Indeed, the short-term "success" of wealthy North American cities such as Vancouver may simply presage a rapid and even catastrophic decline if the elaborate systems for extracting and retaining wealth from other parts of the province and the world are threatened. Like the predator that is too successful, we might rapidly find ourselves incapable of digesting alternatives to our present diet if we destroy the basis for replenishment of the only "food" (material consumption) that we have adapted ourselves to use. Continued studies of our entrails without consideration of dramatically alternative ways of being in the world are unlikely to be useful if we overshoot the world's carrying capacity by our current style of life. As demonstrated in this chapter, there is little doubt that we have already done so. We might, therefore, look to the newer ideas in evolutionary biology to see which lessons we might adapt.

Three ideas of obvious utility are worth exploring briefly. They are the factors of *latent potential with quirky shifts*, *redundancy*, and *selective flexibility* (Gould 1996). Space does not permit an extensive discussion of each of these somewhat self-explanatory concepts. A wide variety of urban forms and arrangements coupled with the variety of neighbourhood functions within any given urban area provides a latent potential for reducing rather than exacerbating automobile dependency. This is but one obvious example. Gould cites the example of making sandals out of worn tires in the Nairobi recycling market. He states that "Durability for sandals is a latent potential of auto tires, and the production of such sandals defines a quirky functional shift. Evolution works like the Nairobi market, not like the throwaway society of the wealthy West. You can evolve further only by using what you have in new and interesting ways" (1996). The degree of latent potential within the world's urban systems is attested by their variety and by the number of experiments that already exist whereby communities have attempted to behave more sustainably (Alexander 1994; Rabinovitch and Leitman 1996; Roseland 1992). Not so clear is how this latent potential can be manifested in a way that enhances the persistence and adaptation of particular urban centres.

As to the second factor, redundancy, we demonstrate in this chapter that current consumption patterns exceed by a factor of ten that which may be necessary and desirable for sustainability. This might indicate that our material and energy systems have tremendous reserves of redundancy when looked at from the perspective of sustainability. We must make a distinction between abundance and redundancy. The volume of material and energy throughput in our present economy denotes a dramatic abundance, even if it is maldistributed. Properly managed, we can use this abundance to create a number of alternative ways to accomplish similar ends – hence redundancy. If, on the other hand, much of this abundant throughput is concentrated on a single strategy such as urban systems based on automobiles, then we can have the opposite of redundancy – that is, vulnerability. Theoretically, we could use our fortunate circumstances to explore an array of alternatives. The selection of which forms of consumption might be the most useful in long-term survival is another matter.

This brings us to selective flexibility, the third factor in our discussion. Latent potential and redundancy help to provide flexibility against the tendency for a natural system to evolve toward an excellent but rigid fit within its environment such that any change in the environment would compromise long-term survival. The current evolution of urban systems toward a high-consumption, automobile-dependent design is a wonderful example of this rigidity and vulnerability. The principle of selective flexibility would imply that the human species, by virtue of its highly developed brain and general delay in reaching maturity, is potentially capable of exercising its flexibility and hence its survival through the selection of alternative ways of organizing and adapting. The challenge therefore becomes recognizing the latent potential and redundancy within our urban systems and selecting those aspects that would help us to evolve in a more sustainable fashion.

The UBC Task Force on Healthy and Sustainable Communities has established a four-year working relationship with the City of Richmond, British Columbia. In the course of that relationship, we have explored ways in which the community might sense relevant threats and opportunities within its external and internal environments such that it can adapt in the direction of sustainability. One of the overriding external threats to the sustainability of Richmond is common to every other major urban centre in the "developed" world. This is the problem of acknowledging that overconsumption is central to the sustainability of its urban system.

Overconsumption has a moral dimension, but for our purposes it is a profoundly practical issue and can be understood in relation to the overall carrying capacity within which consumption takes place.

On Human Carrying Capacity

It is a central premise of this chapter that human carrying capacity is at the heart of the sustainability crisis. This premise is controversial. Carrying capacity is usually defined as the maximum population of a given species that can be supported indefinitely in a defined habitat without destroying that habitat. However, conventional economists and planners argue that this concept is irrelevant because we humans can continuously increase our own carrying capacity by eliminating competing species, by importing locally scarce resources, and through technology. As Daly (1986) critically observes, the prevailing vision assumes a world in which carrying capacity is infinitely expandable and in which the economy floats free of environmental constraints.

By contrast, ecologists argue that carrying capacity is (or should be) the fundamental basis for demographic accounting (Hardin 1991). From this perspective, humans are seen as biological entities and their economy as an inextricably embedded subsystem of the ecosphere. As such, the latter is constrained by real ecological limits (Rees 1990).

Our analysis of the Lower Mainland of British Columbia aligns us with Hardin. Using a new method to assess human resource requirements, we show that the population of any urban region (and even of whole countries) vastly exceeds the long-term carrying capacity of the geographic territory that it occupies. By extrapolation, it seems that the wealthy quarter of the world's population has already appropriated the entire long-term productive capacity of the Earth. This result poses a direct challenge to any local or global strategies of sustainability based on sheer economic growth.

Ecological Footprints: Measuring Human Load
The issues at hand become clearer if we define human carrying capacity not as a maximum population but as the maximum "load" that can safely be imposed on the environment by people. Human load is clearly a function not only of population but also of average per capita consumption. Significantly, the latter is increasing even more rapidly than the former due – ironically – to expanding trade, advancing technology, and rising incomes. As Catton (1986) observes, "The world is being required to accommodate not just more people, but effectively 'larger' people." In 1790, for example, the estimated average daily energy consumption by Americans was 11,000 kcal per capita. By 1980, this amount had increased almost twentyfold to 210,000 kcal per day (Catton 1986). As a result of such trends, load pressure relative to carrying capacity is rising much faster than is implied by mere population increases.

By inverting the standard carrying capacity ratio and extending the concept of load, this study advances a new tool for assessing carrying capacity. The critical issue becomes not what population a particular region can support sustainably but how large an area of productive land is needed to sustain a defined population indefinitely, *wherever on Earth that land is located*. In the language of the previous paragraph, we ask how much of the Earth's surface is appropriated to support the load imposed by the referent population, whatever its dependence on trade or its level of technological sophistication.

Now, because most forms of natural income (resource and service flows from nature) are produced by terrestrial ecosystems and associated aquatic ones, it should be possible to estimate the area of land and water required to produce sustainably the quantities of various resources and ecological services used by a defined population at any level of technology. The sums of such calculations for significant categories of consumption would provide a conservative area-based estimate of the load imposed by that population on the Earth. We call this area the population's true "ecological footprint." Formally defined, *the ecological footprint (EF) is the total area of productive land and water required continuously to produce all the resources consumed, and to assimilate all the wastes produced, by a specified human population, wherever on Earth that land is located* (full details can be found in Rees 1996; Rees and Wackernagel [1994]; and Wackernagel and Rees [1995]).

Canada is one of the world's wealthiest countries. Its citizens enjoy high average material standards by any measure. Indeed, EF analysis shows that the total land required to support present levels of consumption by the average Canadian is *at least* 4.3 hectares, including 2.3 hectares for carbon dioxide assimilation alone (Wackernagel and Rees 1995). Thus, the per capita ecological footprint of Canadians is almost three times their "fair Earthshare" of 1.5 hectares. (There are only about 1.5 hectares of ecologically productive land for each human on Earth.)

The Ecological Footprint of Vancouver

Let's apply this result to the City of Vancouver. In 1991, Vancouver had a population of 472,000 and an area of 114 km2 (11,400 hectares). Assuming a per capita rate of land consumption of 4.3 hectares, the 472,000 people living in the city require, conservatively, 2 million hectares of land for their exclusive use to maintain their current patterns of consumption (assuming that such land is being managed sustainably). However, the area of the city is only about 11,400 hectares. This means that the city population appropriates the productive output of a land area *nearly 180 times larger than its political area* to support its present consumer lifestyles. If we add the city's marine footprint (about .7 hectare per capita for seafood consumption) to the terrestrial footprint, then the total area needed to support Vancouver's population is 2.36 million hectares (5.83 million acres) or more than 200 times the geographic area of the city.

Although these findings might seem extraordinary to the uninitiated, other researchers have obtained similar results for other modern cities. Using our methods, British researchers have estimated London's ecological footprint for food, forest products, and carbon assimilation to be 120 times the geographic area of the city proper (International Institute for Environment and Development 1995). Similarly, Folke, Larsson, and Sweitzer (1994) report that the aggregate consumption of wood, paper, fibre, and food (including seafood) by the inhabitants of twenty-nine cities in the Baltic Sea drainage basin appropriates an ecosystem 200 times larger than the area of the cities themselves. (Although this study includes a marine component for seafood production, it has no energy-land component.) The most recent analyses, incorporating additional ecosystems functions, suggest that urban metabolism may require from 500 to 1,000 times the built-up area actually occupied by cities.

There is little question that some cities are among the brightest stars in the constellation of human achievement. They also increasingly serve as the engines of national economic growth. However, from an ecological perspective, cities are also concentrated nodes of material consumption – entropic black holes – within an increasingly human-dominated global landscape. The rural landscape is actually the more productive and (at least) coequal component of the total system. (Whereas there can be no city without the countryside, the countryside can be viable without the city.)

The Lower Fraser River Basin

Let's extend EF analysis to the entire Lower Fraser River Basin, the urbanizing region within which Vancouver is located (population = 1.78 million; area = 5,500 km2). Although only 18 percent of the region is dominated by urban land use (i.e., most of the area is rural agricultural or forested land), consumption by its human population appropriates through trade and biogeochemical flows the ecological output and services of an extraterritorial land area about fourteen times larger than the region itself. In other words, the people of the Lower Fraser River Basin, in enjoying their consumer lifestyles, have "overshot" the terrestrial carrying capacity of their home territory by a factor of fourteen. In effect, however healthy its economy in monetary terms, the region is running a massive "ecological deficit" with the rest of Canada and the world. These results are summarized in Table 2.1.

Table 2.1

Estimated ecological footprints of Vancouver and the Lower Fraser Basin (terrestrial component only)

Geographic unit	Population	Land area (ha)	Ecological footprint (ha)	Overshoot factor
Vancouver city	472,000	11,400	2,029,600	178.0
Lower Fraser Basin	1,780,000	555,000	7,654,000	13.8

This analysis shows why sustainability is more difficult to achieve locally than is generally appreciated. In ecological terms, the human population of the Lower Fraser River Basin does not actually live in its home region! The people and their consumer habits are sustained largely by trade and biogeochemical exchanges with a vast "elsewhere" scattered all over the Earth. There are a number of relevant questions. Just how reliable are these vital material flows? Is the rest of the world being managed for sustainability? Have we as a "predator" species, focusing only on one strategy, outstripped our prey? It seems that, for long-term survival, thinking locally is not enough. No high-income city or region can achieve sustainability on its own. Sustainable development is a global affair.

The Global Context

EF analysis can be applied to entire countries. It turns out that most high-income nations run an ecological deficit about an order of magnitude larger than the sustainable natural income generated by the ecologically productive land within their political territories (Rees 1996; Wackernagel and Rees 1995). For example, Japan and the Netherlands boast positive trade and current account balances measured in monetary terms, and their populations are among the most prosperous on Earth. Densely populated yet relatively resource (natural capital) poor, these countries are regarded as stellar economic successes and held up as models for emulation by the developing world. At the same time, we estimate that Japan has a 2.5 hectare per capita and the Netherlands a 3.3 hectare per capita ecological footprint that yields national ecological footprints respectively about eight and fifteen times larger than their total domestic territories. In short, the prosperity of both economies is sustained by extraterritorial carrying capacity acquired through commercial trade or appropriated from the global commons.

These data could hardly be more damaging to prevailing national and international policies of development. Growth is widely promoted as the principal instrument of both social and environmental policy, yet it seems that even present rates of economic production and consumption are unsustainable. Ecological deficits are real deficits, and global sustainability cannot be deficit financed; simple physics dictates that *not all countries or regions can be net importers of biophysical capacity.* To make matters worse, our analysis shows that the wealthiest quarter of the world's population have already appropriated the entire long-term carrying capacity of the planet. This means that the levels of material consumption currently enjoyed in high-income countries simply cannot be extended sustainably to even today's world population using anything like prevailing technology. Achieving this relatively modest goal would require the equivalent of two additional planet Earths (Wackernagel and Rees 1995). Industrial civilization will have to discover all its latent potential and exploit whatever redundancy is available to it if we are to enjoy a smooth path to sustainability. Some possibilities are explored briefly below.

The Factor-10 Economy
There is no getting around the fact that material consumption is at the heart of the sustainability crisis. As noted, the aggregate ecological footprint of humanity is already larger than the Earth. The ecological challenge for sustainability, therefore, is how to accommodate both rising material expectations and a near-doubling of population over the next fifty years while actually *reducing* total throughput.

Most analysts seem to agree that, barring disaster, the reduction of throughput can be achieved in one of two ways: through an absolute reduction in average material standards of living or through a massive increase in material and energy efficiency (or some combination of the above). It is generally assumed that the increasingly ubiquitous cultural values implied by "consumerism" render the first approach politically unfeasible in developed countries. Certainly, too, it would justifiably be rejected by the impoverished quarter of the world's population living mostly in developing countries. Thus, many economists insist that global sustainability is achievable only through large increases in the consumption of goods and services in both poor and rich countries.

The bad news, then, is that growth is seen as the only politically and economically viable means to alleviate poverty and inequity both within countries and between rich and poor countries. The good news is that many advocates of this approach have at last accepted the fact of limits to *material* growth. A consensus is emerging that the needed increase in consumption will be sustainable only if there is a corresponding reduction in the material and energy intensity of goods and services (see Pearce 1994).

Numerous researchers and organizations are therefore exploring the policy implications of reducing the energy and material throughput of so-called advanced economies. Conscious of the need for growth, particularly in the developing world, they conclude that the material intensity of consumption in industrial countries should be reduced by a factor of up to ten to accommodate it (Business Council for Sustainable Development 1993; Ekins and Jacobs 1994; Rees 1995; RMNO 1994a, b; Young and Sachs 1994). Because markets do not reflect ecological reality, governments must create the necessary policy incentives to ensure that, as consumption rises, the material and energy content of that consumption falls apace. Achieving a "factor-10" economy will require major changes in industrial strategy, fiscal and taxation policy, and consumer-corporate relations. However, if managed properly, the net effect of this transformation should be not only less consumption and waste but also more jobs and increased regional self-reliance.

Ecology and Fiscal Reform: Taxing Our Way to Sustainability

It is an economic axiom that underpricing leads to overuse. Much of the sustainability crisis derives from the fact that today's prices do not reflect the resource depletion or pollution damage costs of economic goods and services. Ecological and economic sustainability requires the restructuring of economic incentives and taxation policy to encourage material and energy conservation and to increase the demand for labour. This sustainability can best be achieved by replacing present subsidies by a system of taxes on resource use and depletion and by (marketable?) quotas offset by corresponding reductions in other taxes, particularly on labour. By raising prices closer to the full social costs of goods and services, taxes on energy and resources create an incentive for industry to minimize material throughput; meanwhile, lower labour costs (further) increase workers' comparative advantage over capital.

Taxing Consumption not Labour

Ecological tax reform is ultimately likely to produce more economic gains than losses (Flaven and Lenssen 1990). Income, value-added, and similar taxes increase the upward pressure on wages and salaries. This upward pressure reinforces an already undesirable incentive for industry to replace labour with energy and machinery that, in turn, increase resource use, unemployment, and pressure on the environment. Resource taxes can reverse the incentives, helping to reduce consumption and to stimulate employment by enabling payroll tax reductions (Commission of the European Communities 1993; Pearce 1994). An analysis of just eight "green taxes" for the United States, covering items such as carbon emissions ($US 100/ton) and groundwater depletion ($US 50/acre-foot), suggested that these levies alone could raise $US 130 billion, allowing a reduction of 30 percent in personal income taxes (Brown, Flaven, and Postel 1991).

Reducing income and other taxes in proportion to resource taxes would make the latter revenue neutral, so ecological tax reform would not necessarily increase the average fiscal burden on taxpayers. Nor (unlike regulation or add-on pollution charges) would it jeopardize international competitiveness (von Weizsäcker 1994). On the contrary, those countries that act first to develop new energy- and material-efficient technologies and processes will gain the upper hand in marketing these products and services in a global market of enormous potential demand. Note that economies that retained or increased energy prices after the OPEC oil price shock of the 1970s have subsequently generally fared better than those that kept domestic energy prices low (Rechsteiner, cited in von Weizsäcker 1994).

There are additional advantages at the other end of the consumption stream. Because they reduce throughput, levies on resource use and depletion may be as effective at reducing pollution as are comparable existing pollution charges. Moreover, as a part of fundamental tax reform, ecological taxes can be fifty or even 100 times greater than the special environmental charges currently set in some jurisdictions. Greater ecological taxes may be both necessary and sufficient to bring about the rapid technological gains and fundamental restructuring of the economy required for sustainability.

As noted, ecological taxes should be increased gradually over a period of several decades to maintain a constant, predictable, and manageable pressure for innovation on industry. Increasing the initial tax on the most damaging input factors such as fossil fuels by 5 percent per year would double the tax cost in fourteen years. With indirect labour cost falling simultaneously, "It should gradually become more profitable to lay off kilowatt hours and barrels of oil than to lay off people" (von Weizsäcker 1994, 134). The factor-10 approach, then, may make a significant contribution to job creation and therefore to family and community sustainability.

The Social Factor in Sustainability

Despite the potential for job creation, achieving a factor-10 economy implies a mainly technical approach to sustainability. It relies on economic incentives to induce rapid gains in material and economic efficiency that will enable global society to remain solidly on the GDP growth track. Thus, there is no examination of the fundamental values and behaviours that produced the ecological crisis in the first place. In effect, it implies that we can eat our economic cake and have the environment too!

But is this really enough? Confronting the technological optimism of many mainstream analysts is a growing belief that sustainability will require a more profound paradigm shift than any society has been willing to contemplate to date. The time has come for us to reassess the role, impact, and presumed necessity of continuous material growth. Do we have the latent potential and the selective flexibility to reconsider this and other fundamental assumptions upon which industrial society is based?

One variation on this theme is to consider the implications and possible advantages of redirecting more of society's resources to investment in social capital. Can improved community life, more satisfying relationships, greater self-esteem, improved social infrastructure, et cetera substitute for people's present (manufactured) desire to accumulate material possessions? If so, then large reductions in consumption and in society's ecological footprint may be possible *even while maintaining or improving quality of life.*

There are at least two lines of evidence that encourage exploration of this hypothesis. The first is revealed in the relationship between income (consumption) and well-being. Available data show that life expectancy initially rises rapidly with per capita income but then levels off and is virtually flat beyond $10,000 per annum. It appears that 90 percent or more of the gain in life expectancy is "purchased" by the time that income reaches between $7,000 and $8,000 per annum (World Bank 1993, Fig. 1.9). Similar relationships hold for other objective health and social indicators: infant mortality rates, literacy, fecundity, et cetera. Even below this income level, several examples of outstanding performance occur – one at least (Alexander 1994) at a per capita GDP of less than $500 (see next section).

From $7,000 to $8,000 is only a third to a half of the per capita income of the world's wealthier countries. It seems, therefore, that substantial reductions in consumption by people in these countries might well be possible before there would be any significant deterioration in welfare as measured by standard objective indicators. We should also note that "happiness" or well-being is not correlated with income in the upper income range. Indeed, people's perceptions of their social and health status seem to be more a factor of relative social position than of absolute material wealth.

These data pose a serious challenge to conventional assumptions about the social need for continuous economic growth. They suggest that a healthy and sustainable society may in fact be possible at relatively modest income levels even without any dramatic restructuring of society or social relationships.

The Case of Kerala

A second argument for investing in social capital can be found in the state of Kerala, India. With an annual income per capita of only $US 350, Kerala has achieved a life expectancy of seventy-two years (the norm for states earning $5,000 or more per capita), a fertility rate of less than two, and a high school enrolment rate for female students of 93 percent. According to Alexander (1994), "extraordinary efficiencies in the use of the earth's resources characterize the high life quality behavior of the 29 million citizens of Kerala." Similarly, Ratcliffe (1978, 140) claims that Kerala refutes "the common thesis that high levels of social development cannot be achieved in the absence of high rates of economic growth ... Indeed, the Kerala experience demonstrates that high levels of social development – evaluated in terms of such quality of life measures as mortality rates and levels of life expectancy, education and literacy, and political participation – are consequences of public policies and strategies based not on economic growth considerations but, instead, on equity considerations" (including, in this case, an emphasis on social investment in public health and education).

The point here is not to suggest that Kerala, with its unique political and cultural history, is a precise model for other regions to follow. Rather, it is simply to emphasize that every society and culture is in part a social construction, not entirely a product of natural laws. In short, *there is nothing sanctified or inevitable about our high-throughput industrial culture.* In evolutionary terms, Kerala is an example of latent potential with a quirky shift that, when interpreted in light of the seeming redundancies in our own systems, demands a rethinking on our part toward selective adaptability. This is a profoundly practical, not an ideological, issue. Kerala shows that a high quality of life with minimal impact on the Earth is possible through the accumulation of social rather than manufactured capital. As such, it is a hopeful, contemporary, real-world illustration of the unexplored potential in us all.

Policy Implications

How should our emergent understanding of the new biophysical and social reality be reflected in local and global strategies for ecologically sustainable socioeconomic development? We should first acknowledge that many of the required policies (whether driven by technical or social analysis) are in conflict with those in effect today. The new policy directions will therefore be disturbing to some and rejected outright by others. However, if the foregoing analysis is correct, then it is the prevailing growth-bound model of "development" that leads to ecological collapse and sociopolitical chaos, the antithesis of sustainability. This *conventional* model should therefore be seen as bad news. The good news in this analysis is that, once we are aware of our present danger and the opportunity that it conceals, society at least has a chance to draw back from the brink. The following policy suggestions are consistent with this conclusion.

Questioning Growth

1   Governments should acknowledge that, to the extent that conventional economic growth fosters energy and resource consumption, it is antagonistic to sustainability. Policies that increase material throughput (aggregate consumption) can only exacerbate ecological decline and social instability.
2   Development policy should focus on improving the quality of life, not the quantity of goods.
3   No development proposal should leave the world ecologically worse off than before.
4   Taxation and pricing policies should be oriented to reducing the relevant per capita ecological footprints.
5   Monetary indicators of economic "health," such as GDP growth per capita, are potentially dangerous as indicators of sustainability. Governments should encourage the development of biophysical indices to monitor current status and progress toward sustainability. For example, it appears that female literacy and land ownership have a dramatic positive correlation with life expectancy and an equally dramatic negative correlation with infant mortality and fertility rates. This correlation is stronger than that related to per capita income and simultaneously addresses population control and quality of life.
6   Population influx to a high-consumption area such as Vancouver aggravates the ecological footprint – disproportionately so if the incoming population is converting from lower to higher material consumption. However, we must keep in mind that our ecological footprint is visible all over the globe, so merely keeping more for ourselves aggravates the global sustainability crisis even as it may give us a false sense of security.

Encouraging Technological Efficiency

1   Government intervention is required to create the necessary economic incentives for conservation – the current reliance on market forces is carrying us away from sustainability.

2   Ecological fiscal reform (material and energy taxes accompanied by declining payroll and income taxes) should be considered as a means to stimulate required gains in technological efficiency.

Reducing Trade, Increasing Self-Reliance

1   In a shrinking world, interregional dependency could be a stabilizing force. However, ecological footprinting suggests that, under circumstances of growing demand, shrinking supply, and heightened global competition, it is more likely to be destabilizing.
2   In the present regulatory environment, trade accelerates the depletion of natural capital, thereby reducing global carrying capacity. (The decline of forests, agricultural soils, and fish stocks in Canada has been driven largely by export demand.) Trade policies and incentives should be adjusted to ensure the enhancement of self-producing (renewable) natural capital stocks.
3   In a period of accelerating global change (e.g., incipient climatic change), development policy should discourage irreversible economic dependence on international trade.
4   Present circumstances warrant a shift toward policies that encourage greater regional self-reliance.

Protecting Life-Support Services

1   Land and resource policy should recognize that every hectare of ecologically productive land on Earth is already fully "in use" providing essential biophysical goods and services to urbanizing populations.
2   The discounted present value of unpriced biophysical goods and services produced by certain ecosystems may exceed the money value of marketable commodities obtained by destroying those systems. Environmental assessments of proposals for land or resource development should include total social cost accounting to prevent such "growth that impoverishes."
3   A system of resource taxes and (marketable?) quotas should be explored as means to finance the maintenance and enhancement of vital natural capital stocks. (This idea is compatible with well-established concepts such as "polluter pays" and full cost accounting.)
4   Local, provincial, and national sustainability has little meaning without a firm international commitment to the protection and enhancement of "common-pool" natural capital stocks (e.g., the ozone layer) and life-support services (e.g., climatic moderation).
5   The system of national and provincial accounts should be extended to enable monitoring of essential biophysical stocks and flows for the

management of ecological integrity. (Present approaches to revising environmental and economic accounts are inadequate for sustainability, because resource accounts are relegated to mere "satellite" status, and only those stocks that can be evaluated through market pricing are included.)

Sustainable Cities through Investing in Natural Capital

1   Policy and planning for truly sustainable urban regions must take into account the ecological resource base – natural capital – upon which cities depend. Indeed, perhaps the concept of "the city" should be redefined more comprehensively to incorporate essential ecological and biophysical systems and processes that heretofore have implicitly been taken for granted.

2   At a minimum, urban plans and planners should

- recognize the multifunctionality of green areas (e.g., aesthetics, carbon sink, climatic modification, food production, functions) both within and outside the city (Peterson 1996)
- integrate open-space planning with other policies to increase local self-reliance in terms of food production, forest products, water supply, carbon sinks, et cetera
- protect the integrity and the productivity of local ecosystems to reduce the ecological load imposed on distant systems and the global common pool
- ensure that any destruction of ecosystems and related biophysical systems due to urban growth in one area is compensated for by at least equivalent ecosystem rehabilitation in another area.

Investing in Social Capital

1   Meaningful social relationships and a supportive community infrastructure may be more effective than technology in reducing per capita consumption. Policy should encourage investigation of this "soft" alternative in the effort toward sustainability.

2   Government should reaffirm its legitimate role in maintaining redundant social safety nets and in assuring a more equitable distribution of wealth than can be achieved through the marketplace. Indeed, we need to explore proposals such as negative income taxation and other alternative forms of entitlement to ease the transition to sustainability by economically affected groups.

3   Special research programs should be funded to determine how to enhance "social caring capacity." Following are some relevant research

questions. Which formal and informal social relationships enhance people's sense of self-worth and personal security? Which of these personal relationships and community qualities reduce the compulsion to consume and to accumulate private capital (i.e., which forms of social capital can substitute for manufactured capital)? Which public policies would facilitate the development of these forms of social capital? In the answer to each question lies a measure of our capacity for selective adaptability.

Conclusion

This chapter started from the premise that urban systems, as currently constituted, provide both the greatest threats to and opportunities for sustainability. The sheer volume of their ecological impact gives urban areas a pivotal role, but the global distribution of cities effectively insulates them from the ecological consequences of their social and economic actions. In evolutionary terms, then, urbanization and trade have blunted our ability to detect and respond to threats to our continued existence. If ever a species deliberately designed an evolutionary cul de sac, then we are that species. The data summarized here, together with a growing consensus across many disciplines around the globe, show that our current pattern of growth and consumption is unsustainable. The question has clearly moved beyond *whether* we must change to *whither* we must go. Any discussion of sustainability must start from this central question.

In seeking sustainability, we must look to the human potential for selective adaptability. We cannot afford to maintain outmoded nineteenth-century views of the dominance and invincibility of technological "man." These views carry a quaint and dangerous hubris that implies the capacity to bend the world to the will of humans – an ability to control all and build the perfect society. It is increasingly apparent that this vision is flawed – there is no point in reflecting on and defining a "new Jerusalem." Success will be found and must be measured in terms of our ability to foster both urban and global systems of feedback that simultaneously detect and communicate threats to our ecological, social, and economic systems.

We have outlined a few of the ways in which policies might foster more effective connections between human activities and their ecological consequences. This is a minimal requirement for selective flexibility to operate. Any optimism about the long-term survival of humanity rests to a large extent on our social and institutional capacity to exploit the latent potential and the redundancy of modern urban systems. Aiding the advancement of systematic policies of sustainability at all levels of community, from the neighbourhood to the planet, is the urgent task of anyone reading this book.

References

Alexander, W. 1994. Humans Sharing the Bounty of the Earth: Hopeful Lessons from Kerala. Paper prepared for the International Congress on Kerala Studies, Kerala, India, 27-9 August.

Business Council for Sustainable Development (BCSD). 1993. *Getting Eco-Efficient.* Report of the First Antwerp Eco-Efficiency Workshop. Geneva: BCSD.

Brown, L., C. Flaven, and S. Postel. 1991. *Saving the Planet: How to Shape an Environmentally Sustainable Global Economy.* Washington, DC: Worldwatch Institute.

Commission of the European Communities (CEC). 1993. *Growth, Competitiveness, Employment: The Challenges and the Ways Forward into the 21st Century.* Brussels: CEC.

Catton, W. 1986. Carrying Capacity and the Limits to Freedom. Paper prepared for the Social Ecology Session 1, Eleventh World Congress of Sociology, New Delhi, India, 18 August.

Daly, H. 1986. Comments on "Population Growth and Economic Development." *Population and Development Review* 12: 583-5.

Ekins, P., and M. Jacobs. 1994. *Are Environmental Sustainability and Economic Growth Compatible?* Energy-Environment-Economy Modelling Discussion Paper 7. Cambridge: Department of Applied Economics, University of Cambridge.

Flaven, C., and N. Lenssen. 1990. *Beyond the Petroleum Age: Designing a Solar Economy.* Worldwatch Paper 100. Washington, DC: Worldwatch Institute.

Folke, C., J. Larsson, and J. Sweitzer. 1994. Renewable Resource Appropriation by Cities. Paper presented at Down to Earth: Practical Applications of Ecological Economics, Third International Meeting of the International Society for Ecological Economics, San Jose, Costa Rica, 24-8 October.

Gould, S.J. 1996. "Creating the Creators." *Discovery* 17,10.

Hardin, G. 1991. "Paramount Positions in Ecological Economics." In R. Costanza, ed., *Ecological Economics: The Science and Management of Sustainability* (47-57). New York: Columbia University Press.

Hodge, R.A. 1996. *A Systemic Approach to Assessing Progress towards Sustainability.* In A. Dale and J. Robinson, eds., *Achieving Sustainable Development* (267-92). Vancouver: UBC Press.

International Institute for Environment and Development (IIED). 1995. *Citizen Action to Lighten Britain's Ecological Footprints.* London: IIED.

Pearce, D. 1994. Sustainable Consumption through Economic Instruments. Paper prepared for the Government of Norway Symposium on Sustainable Consumption, Oslo, 19-20 January.

Peterson, Susan. 1996. Sustainability and the Urban Landscape. MA thesis, Institute for Resources and Environment, University of British Columbia.

Rabinovitch, J., and J. Leitman. 1996. "Urban Planning in Curitiba." *Scientific American,* August, 46-53.

Ratcliffe, J. 1978. "Social Justice and the Demographic Transition: Lessons from India's Kerala State." *International Journal of Health Services* 8,1.

Rees, W. 1990. "The Ecology of Sustainable Development." *The Ecologist* 20,1: 18-23.

–. 1995. "More Jobs, Less Damage: A Framework for Sustainability, Growth, and Employment." *Alternatives* 21,4: 24-30.

–. 1996. "Revisiting Carrying Capacity: Area-Based Indicators of Sustainability." *Population and Environment* 17,3: 195-215.

–. 1997. "Urban Ecosystems: The Human Dimension." *Urban Ecosystems* 1,1: 63-75.

Rees, W., and M. Wackernagel. 1994. "Ecological Footprints and Appropriated Carrying Capacity: Measuring the Natural Capital Requirements of the Human Economy." In A.-M. Jansson et al., eds., *Investing in Natural Capital: The Ecological Economics Approach to Sustainability* (362-90). Washington: Island Press.

RMNO. 1994a. *Sustainable Resource Management and Resource Use: Policy Questions and Research Needs.* Publication 97. Rijswijk, The Netherlands: Advisory Council for Research on Nature and Environment.

–. 1994b. *Toward Environmental Performance Indicators Based on the Notion of Environmental Space*. Publication 96. Rijswijk, The Netherlands: Advisory Council for Research on Nature and Environment.

Roseland, M. 1992. *Towards Sustainable Communities: A Resource Book for Municipal and Local Governments*. Ottawa: The National Roundtable on the Environment and the Economy.

von Weizsäcker, E.U. 1994. *Earth Politics*. London: Zed Books.

Wackernagel, M., and W. Rees. 1995. *Our Ecological Footprint: Reducing Human Impact on the Earth*. Philadelphia and Gabriola Island, BC: New Society Publishers.

World Bank. 1993. *World Development Report 1993: Investing in Health*. New York: Oxford University Press.

Young, J., and A. Sachs. 1994. *The Next Efficiency Revolution: Creating a Sustainable Materials Economy*. Worldwatch Paper 121. Washington, DC: Worldwatch Institute.

Action

3

Systemic Crisis in Rural Newfoundland: Can the Outports Survive?

Rosemary E. Ommer and Peter R. Sinclair

The history of the Newfoundland outport from settlement to the present can be thought of in terms of a formal economy and an informal economy interconnected to form two mutually sustaining subsystems of a larger New World whole. Based on the fishery as its commercial raison d'être, the typical outport operated on two levels – that of the people who fished (for the merchant) and lived off the land (for themselves), and that of the merchants who caught and/or traded fish in a formal international commercial system lubricated by the state.[1] The state in question changed over time from a colony of Great Britain, to Newfoundland as a British dominion, to a province of Canada in which federal and provincial jurisdictions had different roles. Increasingly, this history of the outport is becoming better known and documented, for various parts of the coast at various times (e.g., Cadigan 1995; Mannion 1977; Ommer 1989, 1990a, 1991, 1994; Thornton 1978), but the history of the sustainability of the outport, the settlers, or the environment has rarely been considered, never mind the relationship between them. That is, outports have been analyzed in terms of the formal economy (Alexander 1983, 66-7) and the informal economy (Ommer 1989), but the link from economic activity to sustaining the primary resource base and thus the outports has not been made until recently.

We propose to demonstrate that socioeconomic and environmental pressures are beginning to overwhelm rural Newfoundland's capacity to function. Prior to 1950 (the date is approximate), the interconnection of global and local, formal and informal, economic activities sustained life in the outports, though not without hardship and periodic local resource crises. However, we maintain that the rapid modernization of the fishing industry after 1950 fractured the relatively homogeneous social structure, and, in conjunction with foreign pressure on the stocks, this complex of events has contributed to current resource depletion and economic crisis. More specifically, we argue that the way in which people provided for themselves (the informal subsystem) became increasingly dependent on cash from earnings and transfer payments. Because of the fishery decline and the general withdrawal of the state from a generous program of income support, this older mode of adaptation is now threatened. Hence the systemic crisis in the outports: the old flexible socioeconomic structure cannot easily function, so the accordion-like pattern whereby informal economic activities could substitute for formal ones when the economy was in crisis (or be cut back during times of expansion) appears to be breaking down, perhaps irretrievably.

After considering briefly the general features of the two subsystems, we develop the analysis by surveying each period in general terms before drawing in more detail on our research on the Bonavista Peninsula, an important fishery-dependent area on the northeast coast of Newfoundland. In a single paper, we can only summarize and illustrate some of the results of collaboration with a large interdisciplinary team of researchers from Memorial University.[2] Thus, we will review the functioning of formal and informal subsystems before industrialization of the fishery, consider the impact of modernization after 1950, and examine the socioeconomic implications of the resource crisis of the 1990s. In a single paper, we cannot hope to review the diversity of practices at the local level or to discuss why systemic change did not occur at other times.

Informal and Formal Subsystems
When we talk about the outport in terms of sustainability, we enter an area of blurred concepts. What has been sustained? By whom? How? And then, of course, now what? In Newfoundland (and, indeed, in Canada), the historical continuum of human life in this cold coastal environment has been sustained – maintained – by peoples who have utilized resources in the context of a mercantile commercial economy underlaid by a subsistence settler way of life. The formal subsystem has always operated on an international scale through the exploitation of resources for export, the informal one through the utilization of resources for subsistence. The logic of commercial exploitation is very different than that of subsistence utilization, and there are two very different sets of implications – the former inherently intended to "maximize," the latter inherently intended to "satisfy." Both involved exchange, the former for profit, the latter for need. The history of rural Newfoundland plays out the stories of both subsystems, the dominance[3] of one and, later, the possible imminent destruction of both.

The first subsystem, that of people *utilizing* resources, was found at the levels of household, band, community, and extended kin group over historical and archeological time. It was pragmatic, based on trial and error, prone to flux, and usually able to accommodate change in the wide arena in which it was embedded. The *generic type* of this subsystem was location based, resource dependent, satisfaction oriented, kin organized, and a

small-scale society in which informal economic arrangements and an egalitarian ethic were commonplace and understood. Social scientists and
humanists recognize it in various manifestations (First World and beyond)
as a tribal (in some cases) or peasant (in others) society. It was based on the
weaving together of various seasonal economic activities into a complex
yearly round, a strategy that has been an adaptive device for the so-called
marginal economies of the North Atlantic rim from time immemorial (see,
e.g., Macpherson 1969).

There are, of course, variants. Nonetheless, whether it be the northern
reaches of Norway, the Highlands of Scotland, the Channel Islands, or rural
areas of Ireland (in the Old World) that are considered, or the Maritimes or
Newfoundland (in the New World), similar strategies can be identified over
a long period of time (Arensberg and Kimball 1968; Brox 1964; Mannion
1977; Ommer 1991; Thornton 1978). Geographical mobility has often
been a feature of such strategies – "transhumance," as in the *saeters* of
Norway or the *sheilings* (summer pasture grounds with rough huts for shep-
herds) of Scotland (Brox 1964; Macpherson 1969); temporary migration, as
in the West Country-Newfoundland migratory fishery (Matthews 1968;
Ommer 1991) appears to have been another feature.

The reasons for such patterns of behaviour were also shared to some
degree. At root, the seasonality of the resources of these economies forced
the amalgamation of several different resources into one interlinked economy. For the use of specific resources, each with its own distinctive ecological "niche," mobility was required. In some cases, population pressure also
encouraged the search for other forms of livelihood to supplement temporarily the resources of a community from a distance. Such was the case
with some seamen in the days of sail; today work on an oil rig is a similar
adaptive strategy.

The second subsystem, that of *exploiting* resources for profit, arose historically out of the first (utilizing resources) and has come to dominate it in our
modern world. From the perspective of European history, it is now
accepted as having its roots in the twelfth-century shift from gift[4] to profit
among ruling elites in feudal society – not the same thing as the age-old
search for profit among other sectors of society, because it signalled a
change in cultural values and has been seen, consequently, as the harbinger
of the modern capitalist state. By the seventeenth century, as the nation-
states of Western Europe intensified their search for wealth in the New
World, merchant capital was spearheading the penetration of these "new-
found-lands" to exploit their natural resources to fuel imperial economies
at home. Such endeavours, just because the places to be developed and
enriched were the mother countries, not the staple-producing regions, did
not take into account the environmental or cultural disruptions that
resulted: they must have been neither obvious nor even considered and

were not part of the logic of the mercantile system. The "natural products of the earth" were primary goods, raw materials, inputs for a complex process of exchange that generated incremental wealth for the mercantile firm and for (by extension) the state under whose auspices it functioned. Such was the basis of the functioning and wealth acquisition of staple firms – the Hudson's Bay Company, Charles Robin and Company, or the Ryans or Templemans of Bonavista are examples.

The Two Subsystems in Preindustrial Rural Newfoundland

In Newfoundland, early settlers, who were initially indentured over two summers and one winter, were brought to the shores of the colony to fish for the merchants. The fiscal logic of the migratory fishery slowly gave way to one in which a settled labour force made more sense, provided that labourers did not have to be paid year-round for work that was limited to a fishing season of perhaps four to six months. From that requirement came the occupational pluralism of the settlers and the truck system of the merchants, who operated in a cash-scarce frontierlike economy. Consumer goods that could not be derived through hunting, gathering, and "gardening" constituted essential inputs to the household; they were delivered by the merchant to the settler, who paid for them in fish.

The implication here is that traditional economies did have a commercial component; also, arguably, at least in the New World, some mercantile economies relied on the flexibility of the community and its seasonal exploitation of a range of resources to support an otherwise too expensive labour force. That is, the two subsystems (formal and informal, utilizers and exploiters) met at the interface of the commercial and survival needs of each. Thus, for example, merchant firms such as Job Brothers in Newfoundland could operate a business that dealt in a range of seasonal resources (cod, seals, salmon, and furs) obtained from different ecological niches at different seasons by people who then traded their produce to Job's for shipment to European markets.[5] This mercantile strategy was possible because local settlers had more than one component in their economy so that, when the cod season was over, they were still able to maintain a livelihood and thus to remain in their communities year-round (e.g., Ommer 1990b; Thornton 1977).

Diversity in products and flexibility in adjusting to the local resource base and to markets were hallmarks of both subsystems. Merchant account books show a range of purchases from settlers: codfish, potatoes, furs, berries, to name a few, would sell in the company store, St. John's, or a foreign market (Ommer 1989; Thornton 1978). For settlers, too, multiple resource exploitation was a means of survival. Thus, in Bonavista, pluralism meant animal husbandry, gardening, and fishing; in François (south coast), it meant harvesting herring, lobster, seal, and cod, there being no soil to speak of, whereas on the richer soils of the west coast, from Bonne Bay south, agriculture and timber alternated with herring and lobster fisheries but cod was less important. Ferryland, close to St. John's, had a mixed inshore and offshore fishery; Catalina was a centre of the northeast coast cod fishery; Greenspond focused on sealing; Forteau and Red Bay used the more northerly Labradorian resource mix; Burin concentrated on the historic banks fishery; and Bell Island was host to the first major industrial endeavour in Newfoundland – the exploitation of iron in a previously rural environment. In all these settlements, nonetheless, the *principle*, the founding structures, of rural life and culture remained the same regardless of location and regardless of date ... until Confederation in 1949.

That said, analysis of the censuses shows that many places were facing demographic decline for much of the first half of the twentieth century, with the exceptions of relatively new settlements on the west coast or industrial locations such as Bell Island, one of the few communities to experience significant in-migration during the first two decades of this century. By and large, communities had to balance high rates of out-migration with natural increases if they were to maintain their size, but the old English Shore[6] settlements lost population consistently, especially from the labour force age groups.[7] In some places, such as Harbour Grace, Red Bay, and Catalina, population decline was associated with falling birth rates early in the century.

The picture of the twentieth-century outport is one of general restraint in contrast to that of the period before the late nineteenth century when the population reached what David Alexander called its "limits of extensive growth" (1983, 66-7). We must now think of this period in terms of limits to sustainability beyond which the outport could not develop without some change somewhere in the structure. Several things need to be considered here: occupational structure, amount/value of production, main/supplementary sectors of each economy, and change over time. In almost all cases, the fishery was the mainstay of the economy, but there were exceptions. By Newfoundland standards, Bell Island had a strong agricultural base – farming was the dominant traditional sector in 1891 and 1921 – but with the advent of the mines the old basis of the economy was severely disturbed. Harbour Grace had a relatively weak dependence on the fishery and a concomitant diversification into artisan-style occupations. Places such as Ferryland and Bonavista had a joint fishing-farming base, and a commercial logging component was added to the economies of some west coast communities after Bowater's arrived in 1921. The southern half of the west coast evolved a genuinely "mixed" economy of fishing-farming in which cod was not necessarily the dominant resource, although important. Indeed, this area was more akin to a Gulf of St. Lawrence/Maritimes economy than to one that we think of as typical of Newfoundland.

Nonetheless, the combination of a variety of commercial and noncommercial resources worked by season is typical of the whole North Atlantic rim. The least diversified settlements, even at the subsistence level, were in the more remote northeast and southwest coastal areas, which depended more exclusively on the fishery. Only in Labrador does it appear that this mix was seriously restricted throughout the period, but the census statistics likely provide a picture of an economy more narrowly based than was actually the case (Thornton 1978).

Finally, a modern gloss is laid on this otherwise preindustrial picture with the diversification that grew around an artisanal base in the old English Shore settlement of Harbour Grace, in the commercial logging of the west coast as far north as Bonne Bay, and in the enclave economies of Buchans, Bell Island, St. Lawrence, Grand Falls, and Corner Brook. However, the demographic consequence of rapid industrialization or modernization (as in the case of areas close to the American bases near Stephenville and Argentia[8]) was population explosion and, along with it, the erosion of the traditional economy. This situation created problems that the government was aware of as early as 1933 and that have arisen many times since then. The Amulree Royal Commission of 1933, looking at new resource towns, saw an impending crisis clearly: "As at Grand Falls, the high birth-rate at Buchans gives rise to some anxiety. Indeed, the future of the town itself may be said to hang in the balance ... The problem of providing for the coming generation of Newfoundlanders is one to which we have referred elsewhere" (162). The report of the commission said specifically of Bell Island that:

> The miners and surfacemen in former years were engaged in two six-monthly shifts, the first comprising those who went fishing in the summer and worked in the mines in the winter, and the second those who worked in the woods in the winter and in the mines in the summer, but in recent years the men employed have adopted mining as a steady occupation and are now not equipped for fishing ... Under present conditions, the unemployed miner is unable to earn a livelihood either from the fishery or from work in the woods, and large numbers of men have therefore been forced to fall back on public relief. Their numbers, too, have been swollen by returning emigrants who have lost their employment abroad. (157)

The commission recommended that household production be seen by government as making an invaluable contribution to general welfare, a plea that was repeated by the 1986 Royal Commission on Employment and Unemployment in Newfoundland and Labrador, which was created to look at the crisis in the economy during the recession of the early 1980s:

"The whole social, economic and cultural history of Newfoundland is rooted in the community life of the outport. This Commission recognises the strength and value of the pluralist way of life ... recognises the survival value of this economy and seeks, not to destroy, but to strengthen it" (Newfoundland and Labrador, 112).

If, however, we also consider the evidence of other communities in our sample, Newfoundland settlements were clearly capable of maintaining what Thornton (1978) has called a "dynamic equilibrium" – capable of making demographic adjustments over time to changing economic conditions. What Bell Island demonstrates is that they could not cope with the impact of industrial decline driven by external markets. Initially, the mining industry led to a higher birth rate, but it also destroyed the capacity of the people and their resource base to support an expanding population by reverting to fishing and woods work when employment contracted. As elsewhere, historically, the new wage-labour economy seemed better than the old system as long as it was on an upswing. The problems only arose in a downswing when the loss of flexibility, a characteristic of the old system, often meant that people no longer had the skills or the opportunities to adapt to the loss. Economies, and cultures like those of the Newfoundland outports, are well equipped to handle a slow process of adjustment. However, the introduction of large-scale, capital-intensive enterprise – especially if of limited duration, such as the exploitation of a nonrenewable resource guarantees – inevitably severely disrupts the fragile complexities of these economies.

Bonavista in the Preindustrial Period

Turning now to Bonavista, a large settlement of some 3,500 to 4,000 people by 1891 and the focus of the eco-research project at Memorial University, we can see many of the same patterns described above for the more general Newfoundland case. Bonavista's mature population changed little demographically over the years, except for a slight aging and a minor shift in birth rates. Indeed, this community was more stable than others on the English Shore, although it did experience the loss of population in the labour force that seems to have been a feature of most Newfoundland fishing communities and a way of adjusting population size at the community level that allowed the community to maintain a state of dynamic equilibrium.

Although "agriculture" in Bonavista was not prominent in terms of output per household, this settlement was predominantly a fisher-cultivator community: indeed, by 1911 the amounts of acreage "held" and "improved" were identical. This is also, of course, an indication that the demographic carrying capacity of the settlement had been reached. The community showed a consistent subsistence backdrop of vegetable production and animal husbandry. Its great strength was the shore fishery: inshore cod and cod oil were the mainstays. It was a typical English Shore settlement: stable, mature, and able to adjust to short-term crises as they occurred. Such was its informal sector, as we have defined that term at the start of this chapter.

The formal sector in Bonavista can be represented by the mercantile firm of Philip Templeman Ltd. Established in the area about 1880, the firm developed branches in Trinity Bay, Bonavista Bay, and White Bay, and it supplied the Labrador fishery. By 1914, it was dealing in 50,000 quintals (112 lbs.) of dried cod per annum. It closed its doors about 1937 (Templeman 1918-28). It was a typical Newfoundland merchant firm in that its business was exporting fish and supplying fishers with the wherewithal for fishing and daily living. The business that Templeman conducted in Bonavista is perhaps best described as that of a general store operating on cash and credit, supplying all manner of goods to the local population either for cash or for fish as a means of exchange. Store goods ranged from nails and spruce boards through a wide variety of foodstuffs to clothing, furnishings, and even luxury items such as wristwatches. Two separate sets of accounts were kept. One dealt with wage employees and family members working for the firm, shipments, dealings with other firms, codfish accounts, and the like; the other dealt with fishers and other clients.

In a general sense, the books allow us to get a handle on the nature and scale of Templeman's operations and thus (by extension) to identify the nature of the mercantile economy in Newfoundland.[9] Templeman had an extensive local business network of suppliers, handling accounts ranging in value from nearly $200,000 to less than $10 and amounting to $600,000 total business in 1918. The company also sold goods to other Newfoundland businesses, such as Job Brothers and Reid Newfoundland.

Templeman exported codfish and cod oil. In 1918, codfish brought a gross return of $952,634.70, or about one-twentieth of the average value of annual exports of cod from Newfoundland over the period 1916-20 (Mackay 1946, Appendix, Table 10). The firm's collapse appears to have been linked to the more general collapse suffered by the old mercantile economy in the face of the world depression in the 1930s, when a bankrupt Newfoundland found its lines of credit choked off by banks that would not, or could not, sustain the losses that the old salt-fish trade sustained during those years (Alexander 1977; Ommer 1989; Wright 1997). Thereafter, the Second World War and the postwar years marked a hiatus, for the outport, between the old mercantile outport and the post-Confederation "modernization" of rural Newfoundland.

Social Transformation and Unsustainable Development
Confederation with Canada in 1949 marked a shift for Newfoundland toward a new kind of social and economic system. Confederation fractured

the symbiosis between two related subsystems and reduced them to one old and one new subsystem that failed to work well together. Thus, the years following Confederation brought crucial change through the imposition of rapid modernization[10] of the provincial economy and the addition of a series of "safety nets" for the informal sector through government pensions, welfare, baby-bonus cheques, and unemployment insurance, which, in effect, took the place of the old subsystem of merchant credit. Along with this shift came increased pressure on the fish stocks of the northwest Atlantic. When we examine the historical record to understand changes in the socioeconomic system, a number of things become clear.

First, there had been pressure on fish stocks for a long time. The work of Hutchings and Myers (1994, 1995) points to long-term decline from at least the 1840s, though we must use these statistics carefully (as the authors themselves emphasize) because they cannot tell us with certainty about specific stocks, the merchant cod fishery being such that fish were collected at fishing stations and then centralized in major merchant ports that could be at considerable distances. Harbour Grace, for example, processed and exported Labrador fish (Gentilcore 1993, plate 37). Cadigan (1996), moreover, drawing on sources such as the diaries of Bonavista merchants Slade and Kelson, in which observations of the availability of fish were systematically recorded, identifies problems as early as 1845: "there is growing evidence that, between 1845 and 1880, increased fishing was having a negative influence on marine resources. As early as the 1840s a significant public demand pressured government to regulate the use of new fishing gears to protect cod stocks ... With hindsight and late twentieth century awareness, we can now understand that frequent fishery failures and a necessary shift to more intensive technologies, when set beside rapid population increase and large fluctuations in Newfoundland salt cod and seal exports, combine to point to a likely ecological problem" (2-3).

Second, even prior to 1950, the roots of the changes in the formal subsystem can be traced to fisheries modernization, and those in the informal subsystem to cash inputs from both the formal economy and the state's expanding welfare net. What were these changes, and what impacts did they have on environment, economy, and social structure?

The formal subsystem was under stress for decades prior to 1950, and under Commission of Government the seeds of a new industrial structure were planted (Sinclair 1987, 22-35; Wright 1997). The natural resources commissioner[11] created a plan to centralize harvesting and processing in fifteen core ports. Commissioner Dunn's initial idea of directing the fishery through a single state company (Dunn was sceptical about the possibility of private companies taking the risk) was rejected by 1944 in favour of a small number of publicly subsidized private operators. It was thought that only a few districts were suitably prepared for development based on cooperatives. By the end of the Second World War, it seemed that the new policy was taking hold: there were eighteen frozen-fish plants and thirteen trawlers operating in 1945 (Sinclair 1987, 34). Still, the main thrust for change occurred during the Joey Smallwood years when the provincial government's drive for centralization of the outports and an industrial fishery coincided with the objectives of Canada's federal government. Recent work (Wright 1997) shows that the years around Confederation saw a collision between a model of cooperative development (along the lines of Moses Coady and the Antigonish movement) and a model of "top-down" industrial development, which was the wisdom of the day in central Canada and which won out. In the first twenty years after Confederation, the dominant technology shifted from the fixed-gear small boats and household processing of the salt-cod fishery to the mobile trawls, large steel draggers, and factory processing of the more diversified frozen-fish industry. Yet there has usually been a grassroots opposition speaking in favour of a different model, such as cooperatives of small producers. Indeed, certain state policies, especially the extension of unemployment insurance to fishers in 1957, by supporting small producers, worked in the opposite direction to that of modernization. Thus, the number of fishers increased after 1957. Although most politicians and bureaucrats favoured the new formal subsystem, they also faced pressure to hold back the process of change because of the inability of the local formal economy to absorb those displaced by the changes.

The result of the industrialization of fisheries was social fragmentation as outporters adapted in different ways to the pressures for change in the new formal subsystem. A large number of fishers, even as late as the 1980s, persisted with an inshore fishery by then propped up by state income and capital infusions, as well as indirectly by the paid labour of other household members in fish plants and service industries. These were the people, studied by social-anthropological researchers in the 1960s and early 1970s (Brox 1972; Chiaramonte 1971; Faris 1972; Firestone 1967; Nemec 1972; Philbrook 1966; Wadel 1969), who struggled to maintain what Sinclair (1985) has termed "domestic commodity production."[12] Increasingly, however, this type of fisher found it difficult to make a living, even with state income support. The reasons include a licensing policy that made it impossible to move flexibly from one species to another as availability and prices dictated, as well as the scarcity of cod inshore in many of the past thirty years. The flexibility of the earlier outport system was being destroyed.

At the same time, fisher-owned "longliners," capable of going far offshore and utilizing mobile gear, became a core part of the fishery in many areas, especially the northwest coast, where they ventured into shrimp fishing starting in 1970. Frequently, these enterprises departed from the inshore model of domestic commodity production as they approximated small capitalist firms in their social organization (Sinclair 1985). With a labour force less than 10 percent that of the small-boat sector, these vessels accounted for about one-third of the cod catch by the 1970s.

Deep-sea trawlers owned by fish-processing companies were organized as components in larger capitalist enterprises, although it took a strike in 1974 for trawlermen to be recognized as wage workers rather than "coadventurers." This deep-sea fleet took a growing share of the catch, initially concentrating on flatfish but increasingly focusing on cod to supply the frozen-fish plants on shore. By 1970, the landings by weight from offshore vessels far surpassed those from inshore boats, and cod processed in freezing plants greatly exceeded the share that was salted (Copes 1972, 199, 212). Over 1,000 men typically worked as wage labourers on these vessels, and many more people were employed in the plants. In those plants, the majority of workers were often women, now wage earners rather than exclusively unpaid household workers. By 1986, 45.3 percent of plant employees were women, up from only 18.6 percent in 1971 (Sinclair 1992, 87).

In the second period, outport people became more dependent on cash income from some source to supplement their well-developed informal sector of subsistence production and interhousehold cooperation. In fishing areas, the importance of unemployment insurance payments cannot be overstated. In the 1980s, the ratio of UI income to fishing income ranged from 0.53 to 1.19 and to plant-work income from 0.29 to 0.49 (Cashin 1993, 189). Often, but not always, cash came directly from fishery earnings. In this example from our research area, however, farming and construction work were significant. We will let Harold, our respondent from the Trinity area, describe a way of living that still retained many features of the first period:

> In 1946 [at age twenty-two] I moved back here and did some farming on a small scale, but enough to make a living at. Then I had four years [of] fishing, and back then, if your fishing year was bad, you could always move to something else in the off-season – like you [could] go to the lumber woods in the fall and winter, or you went away doing a bit a carpentry work somewhere. This changed a lot from today: you can't step into someone else's trade. Unions have done a lot of good, but there's a lot of hurt gone in there too. Today you're deprived of being free and able to do what you want.

Harold later talked about how government regulations had made it almost impossible for small sawmill operators like him to survive:

> So over the years that I lived here from 1946, like I say, I farmed and I fished and I worked with highways for a number of years – on the heavy

equipment, and [I was] general foreman for four or five years. Then I quit that and went on construction with the contractors, and I spent the rest of my days all over the island and Labrador. Somewhere in between there, in 1952, I started a sawmill. My family was all small then, so I was working alone, and whatever help you had to get you had to hire, and you couldn't make enough then to keep the family going.

Movement from job to job without regulation or demand for formal quali-fication allowed Harold to earn a modest living. After describing the wide variety of his work for cash, he pointed out the importance of his wife's labour and of exchanges between households:

There was times I was away then – one summer I was gone for six months before I got back again, from May to the latter part of November. If some-thing went wrong, well, if one of the children was big enough, they'd go down next door or go out to their grandmother's. She [Harold's wife] looked after the gardens and growed enough vegetables to keep us, the family, for the winter – plus we always had some sheep, and they were sheared before I went away anywhere, and the wool was shipped to Nova Scotia. They did up the wool and sent it back again. We had some done up for blankets and more done up for yarn for sweaters, socks, and mitts. So my wife done the knitting and sewing and made clothes for the little ones. She made all their clothes. Bell, my wife now, she done the same thing when hers was small – she made all their clothes.

A combination of wages, cooperation between households, and consider-able subsistence production allowed Harold and other outport residents a modest living:

You didn't earn much money then, but still you didn't need that much money. You operated on a much different way of life than you do today. For instance, if you went fishing during the summer, and you were doing alright, when you'd get settled up in the fall you'd have to buy enough, clear little knickknacks [extras that people could live without but preferred not to have to do so], and store it all in the house for the winter. You had flour, sugar, salt beef, pork, tea, and dried fruit [such as prunes and apples], and it was all stored away in the house, and you wouldn't go to the store anymore for the whole winter. When freeze-up time come, you'd kill a lamb, or if someone had a cow to kill the meat was shared. If someone had a cow to kill this year and you had a pig to kill next year, you'd exchange back and forth. You'd have to wait till the frost come before you could keep the meat by natural frost. You'd kept it hung up out in the shed, and you went out and sawed off a piece of meat whenever you needed it. In the spring then, there was always a few turrs [local sea birds] on the go, and seal. Everything was fresh that way.

In time, cash became increasingly important. If it was unavailable from the usual round of work, it had to be found by other means:

Back in the '30s to the '40s, if a family man went to the Labrador and made $300 or $400 for the summer, he was considered well away. But now, as the years went on, the price of everything keep going up, and the wages went up a little bit, and it cost more to live. Therefore, you had to earn more. Back in 1948-9, we were fishing, and one year we were down a bit, and my income for the season was $625. We had all the fish dried and shipped. We paid our bills to the merchant that we owed at the end of the summer, paid our doctor's fee, which was five dollars a year we had to pay to keep the doctor in the community, paid the church, and that year, when I had all bills paid off, I had about fifteen or twenty dollars left. Now what was I gonna do for the rest of the winter? So I stored up what wood I could for my wife and the children, and the fifteenth of December I went in the lumber woods and spent Christmas and stayed until just about the last of January. I went for to try to get $100 to get me over for the knickknacks. I didn't owe any money. So that's what I done. I come out of the woods with $110 to $120. I was safe then.

Coming on in the spring, things was starting to run out. So if you had a few dollars to go and buy the things you were runned out of, like tea, baking powder, or baking soda, you would be able to make it through what we used to call the long, hungry month of March. It was called this because by March month a lot of your winter supplies was starting to run out. In my time, we didn't have a wooden keg of molasses, but we had a earthen jar of gallon size – unless you were running off a drop of moonshine; then you'd have a bit extra. We made blueberry wine, dogberry wine, sarsaparilla wine, you name it. We'd [husband and wife] work together on that one since it was fairly time consuming, and the woman didn't have time to do it.

Modernization brought with it the logic of resettlement along with the increasing marginalization of the informal outport subsystem and its dependence on a structure of transfer payments for support instead of the old credit system. The flexibility and diversity associated with the first period were lost, hampered by a net of legislation and management structures that limited such strategies. The inshore fishery, the fishery of the outports, was seen more and more as inefficient, uneconomic, not "sustainable." In the south coast trawler ports and a few northeast locations such as Catalina, the fishery was year-round, and the old informal "economy" declined in importance as people became accustomed to buying much of what they needed, particularly food. Where the fishery remained seasonal and people had more "free" time, the informal sector thrived, although it now depended on cash inputs, not on merchant credit. Cash came from wages, UI benefits, and transfer payments. As Pahl (1984) argued for the Isle of Sheppey (southern England) and Felt and Sinclair (1992) for Newfoundland's Northern Peninsula, the informal sector does not function more extensively among the most deprived segments of the population because it needs those cash inputs, which make house construction possible and provide the snowmobiles, fuel, and saws to cut wood or the guns to hunt moose.

It is more difficult for the informal sector to meet people's expectations in the late twentieth century, because they are different than in the past. Many people are much better educated today than only a few decades ago and are less easily satisfied with the kinds of work available to them locally. The mass media that enter every household contribute to consumption requirements (e.g., electronic products) that can only be met through the formal economy and sometimes only by moving to larger centres. Living off the land and building one's own home are still attractive to many people (though mostly to men), but they would not likely be satisfied with what are now seen as the deprivations that earlier generations endured. In other words, modernization has been a source of cultural dislocation as well as economic stress to the old outport way of life.

Another problem is that the perception that land resources have been stretched too far by permitting open access for activities such as wood cutting has produced a series of rules that further limit the informal sector. A middle-aged Bonavista man made this point when asked about building his home:

Interviewer: Did you get your own lumber?
Respondent: Yeah.
Interviewer: Do you think there's still a fair bit of that on the go these days?
Respondent: Not as much as dere was. See, all that stuff is different now than it was when I started the house, when I came down here first ... We lived with the wife's parents. It was six or seven years before we had the house done enough that we could move in it; just did as much, a little, as I could afford it.
Interviewer: You guys didn't get a mortgage?
Respondent: Yep, we did afterwards. That was a mistake, should never had done it [laughs]; that's besides the point ... But, like I say, there's not as many people doin' that kind of a thing

> because, ... like everyt'ing else, that's gettin' harder to do.
> You know, you can't go and cut logs and dat like you used
> to be able to do. Like when I built that house, I could go
> anywhere and cut logs.

Interviewer: Is it just scarcer?

Respondent: Scarcer, and there's more restrictions on it.

This passage brings out not only the continuation of home construction
but also the necessity for substantial cash input (a mortgage) and the difficulty of obtaining a basic wood supply. Nevertheless, providing for one's
own household remained widespread in 1994, when our survey of 619
adults in 320 households indicated that most people live in households in
which some part of the basic food and fuel is supplied through subsistence
activities (see Table 3.1). Women are limited, with a few exceptions, to the
first three activities. Indeed, women, in both the past and the present, primarily undertake the informal work of running the household – domestic
labour and child care. Some women help outdoors, but men do most of the
outside labour.

Table 3.1

**Percentage of respondents living in households in which somebody
engages in selected subsistence tasks, Bonavista Peninsula** (N = 619)

Subsistence tasks	Percent
Picking berries (blueberries, partridge berries, bakeapples)	81.9
Making pickles or jam	85.9
Growing vegetables	48.9
Fishing for home use (including trout)	72.2
Hunting	63.0
Cutting wood	55.6

Systemic Crisis

Not only did the new formal subsystem have social, economic, and cultural implications, but it also brought the threat of environmental crisis,
even resource extinction unless carefully controlled. Although inshore
fishers may have overfished bay stocks in the past, offshore cod populations were not seriously depleted until the advent of the industrial fishery.
The first great resource crisis of the late 1960s to the early 1970s was primarily a result of foreign overfishing, but the second crisis of the early
1990s was due mainly to Canadian overfishing and mismanagement. It
appears that the northern cod populations were almost as severely overfished by 1974 as when the moratorium was declared in 1992, but the
problem was caught in time, and some rebuilding clearly took place with

the extension in 1977 of Canadian control to 200 miles offshore. Limited entry licensing and quota management might have prevented serious problems, but inappropriate data (trawler logs) and a questionable inter- pretative model led to serious overestimation of how much could safely be caught. Add various illegal fishing practices, discounted because they had no place in the model, and we have the recipe for ecological disaster.

In areas such as rural Newfoundland, where alternative employment on a scale that might absorb people displaced from fishing is absent, the fish resource crisis is necessarily one of the formal socioeconomic system. To the extent that public funds substitute for cash inputs from the fishing industry, the impact on the informal sector is mitigated or minimized. In the after- math of the cod moratorium, first the Northern Cod Adjustment and Recovery Program (NCARP) and then, in 1994, The Atlantic Groundfish Strategy (TAGS) served this need. TAGS has been properly criticized for the inequities that emerged in its implementation and for the ineffectiveness of its training programs, but it was successful in this critical sense. By promis- ing financial support for seven years (later reduced to six), TAGS protected the informal subsystem, and thus the possibility of maintaining an accept- able lifestyle, although this surely was not part of the TAGS plan.

In late 1998, with that support just ended, a double systemic crisis is nearly upon us as the ongoing problems of the formal subsystem appear likely to destroy the informal subsystem as well. Despite some success sto- ries, there has been little change in the occupational opportunities avail- able to people in areas highly dependent on groundfish – such as the Bonavista Peninsula. The landed value of fish is actually high, but most of this fishery is comprised of crab and shellfish caught by a restricted num- ber of vessels compared with the cod fishery and processed in relatively few plants. It is unlikely that a large cod fishery can be sustained. With nothing planned to replace TAGS, the informal subsystem will be unable to function for many people. Thus, both subsystems appear to be headed for crisis, and that is why many fear, finally, a major resettlement of the outports. In our general survey, 35 percent of those interviewed late in 1994 expected to be living elsewhere in five years.

Policy Implications

What should governments do in the face of the systemic crisis that we have identified? We offer several guidelines implied by our research and analysis. Clearly, government policy needs to focus urgently on helping to solve the cash deficit in the local economy if social life is to be sustained at a level approaching that of the past. If groundfish stocks can be rebuilt and then maintained, then doing so should be treated as a priority, as all levels of government formally acknowledge. This fishery should not be reopened until there is strong evidence of recovery. However, we must also recognize that there may not be a widespread recovery in the fishery. In any case, it is unwise for a region to be dependent on a single industry. Therefore, economic diversification should be a priority. This means small-scale, locally generated economic diversification that might include ecotourism, specialty products (e.g., the artisanal furniture and goat's cheese now produced by two Bonavista entrepreneurs), and local produce (e.g., blueberries). Needed is greater promotion of self-employment and small businesses, private and cooperative, as well as larger enterprises. Nevertheless, it will take many businesses of the kind that we have mentioned to compensate for the closure of a large fish plant such as Fishery Products International in Catalina.

As we have stated, the fishery needs to be protected and rebuilt. Considering that inadequate management was a major factor in the resource collapse that led to the cod moratorium, the management process should be adjusted to include serious consideration of local ecological knowledge. It is encouraging that the Department of Fisheries and Oceans is now more open to this possibility. Indeed, researchers from our eco-research project who have focused on fishers' knowledge were invited to give presentations to the DFO's stock-assessment workshops in 1996 and 1997. This type of initiative should be expanded, while acknowledging that it is a complicated matter to integrate information from diverse sources such as fishers' accounts and research vessel surveys.

Recognizing that so many residents draw on the local environment to maintain themselves, in part, government leaders should consider supplying more support to help people make the best use of the environment's resources in a way that will both contribute to subsistence and protect the resources. This support might include making available more advice and demonstrations for small-scale agriculture and woods work. Perhaps the area might become a testing ground for the environmentally safe technologies with which we must become increasingly concerned.

Finally, part of the systemic crisis derives from past reductions and impending cuts in various social support programs. Insofar as these cutbacks are financially driven, the evaluation of which programs should or should not be changed ought to take into account the full costs of relocating people who are ill equipped to live elsewhere without assistance compared with the costs of supporting them where they currently live. The combination of high adjustment costs and pressure on employment across the nation makes this a strong argument.

There is a strong case to be made for the historically central role of the nonindustrial economy in the development of coastal communities around the North Atlantic rim. There is also some evidence that this economy is not dead but has simply altered to meet the exigencies of this age. Thus, work on an oil rig is a present-day strategy similar to the nineteenth-century adaptation of going to the herring fishery (in the Old World) or to the seal fishery (in the New World); temporarily relocating to work in Alberta's oil industry, in Nova Scotia's apple industry, or in Toronto is another recent variation of historical responses to the pressures of highly seasonal resource bases and limited economic opportunities close to home.

The informal economic sector in Newfoundland, then, has a long history. Today it is often associated with the noncommercial activities of Newfoundlanders, but that association is as inaccurate now as it was in the past. The informal subsystem was first disrupted in the years when the economy began to take its first hesitant steps toward industrialization and when cash, in the form of transfer payments, altered existing balances of inputs and outputs, which had always been based on local needs and sensitivities. As expectations changed and cash transfers made the North American "good life" accessible, old balances were further disrupted. The altered expectations of both government and people pushed the formal-informal balance even further, and overfishing destroyed the resource on which the whole system had been based. The question now is whether it has been disrupted, altered, or destroyed.

Notes

1   We are describing something akin to the articulation of modes of production as set out by Marxist theorists of development in the 1970s. To suggest that fully separate systems operated in the outports is to suggest that each was, by definition, viable or self-sustaining.
2   *Sustainability in a Changing Cold Ocean Coastal Environment*, funded by Environment Canada through the Green Plan, administered by the SSHRCC, NSERC, and MRC. The project's final report was completed in August 1998.
3   Subsistence production (informal sector) cheapened the cost to the merchants of the fish that they purchased. Thus, the formal subsystem in a sense required the informal subsystem. Of course, the informal needed inputs from the formal to survive as well. See Ommer (1989, 189).
4   Gift; that is, distributed excess wealth into the community as part of noblesse oblige, as in the endowment of monasteries from an overlord's wealth.
5   Again, firms such as Charles Robin and Company of Jersey and Gaspé might concentrate on one resource (cod), but in a variety of locations, thereby extending their productive season to its widest annual extent.
6   The English Shore refers to the coast that was set aside for English settlement and use in contrast to the French Shore, which provided seasonal use but no settlement entitlement to French fishers.
7   For a detailed and insightful analysis of out-migration that compares Newfoundland and the Maritimes between 1871 and 1921, see Thornton (1988).
8   For population statistics, see Ommer and Hiller (1990), who detail demographic, economic, and social patterns for communities along the southwest coast.
9   The extension is legitimate in that all cod-firm records analyzed so far for the Atlantic region appear to have operated on the same general system. Local variations no doubt occurred, and they may prove significant; however, in the absence of other detailed research for Newfoundland to date, Templeman must stand as a surrogate for the mercantile economy at large.
10 We use the term "modernization" with some hesitation to refer to the development of industrial capitalism in the formal economy and to institutional changes such as mass

public education, democratic political representation, and urbanization. We do not wish to imply, as was common in the 1950s and 1960s, that "good," successfully developed, societies were those that became modern like the United States. The concept was also associated with a tendency to see social and economic systems in a dualist way – traditional and modern sectors with little interconnection (Oxaal, Barnett, and Booth 1975).
11 Commission of Government was the government put in place by Britain as caretaker when Newfoundland lost dominion status. The natural resources commissioner was the official who administered that sector.
12 The term refers to the production of goods for sale based on household ownership of the means of production and the utilization of household labour.

References
Alexander, David. 1977. *The Decay of Trade: An Economic History of the Newfoundland Salt-fish Trade 1935-1965*. St. John's: Institute of Social and Economic Research, Memorial University of Newfoundland.
–. 1983. "Economic Growth in the Atlantic Region 1880-1940." In Eric W. Sager, Lewis R. Fischer, and Stuart O. Pierson, eds., *Atlantic Canada and Confederation: Essays in Canadian Political Economy* (51-78). Toronto: University of Toronto Press.
Amulree Royal Commission (chaired by Lord Amulree). 1933. Report of the Newfoundland Royal Commission. St John's: Dominions Office.
Arensberg, Conrad W., and Solon T. Kimball. 1968. *Family and Community in Ireland*. 2nd ed. Cambridge: Harvard University Press.
Brox, Ottar. 1964. "Natural Conditions, Inheritance, and Marriage in a North Norwegian Fjord." *Folk* 6: 35-45.
–. 1972. *Newfoundland Fishermen in the Age of Industry*. St. John's: Institute of Social and Economic Research, Memorial University of Newfoundland.
Cadigan, Sean T. 1995. *Hope and Deception in Conception Bay*. Toronto: University of Toronto Press.
–. 1996. "The Sea Was Common and Every Man Had a Right to Fish in It": Failed Proposals for Fisheries Management and Conservation in Nfld, 1855-1880. Occasional paper, History/Eco-Research, Memorial University of Newfoundland.
Cashin, Richard (chair). 1993. *Charting a New Course: Towards the Fishery of the Future*. Task Force on Incomes and Adjustment in the Atlantic Fishery. Ottawa: Supply and Services Canada.
Chiaramonte, Louis J. 1971. *Craftsmen-Client Contracts: Interpersonal Relations in a Newfoundland Fishing Community*. St. John's: Institute of Social and Economic Research, Memorial University of Newfoundland.
Copes, Parzival. 1972. *The Resettlement of Fishing Communities in Newfoundland*. Ottawa: Canadian Council on Rural Development.
Faris, James. 1972. *Cat Harbour: A Newfoundland Fishing Settlement*. St. John's: Institute of Social and Economic Research, Memorial University of Newfoundland.
Felt, Lawrence R., and Peter R. Sinclair. 1992. "'Everyone Does It': Unpaid Work in a Rural Peripheral Region." *Work, Employment, and Society* 6,1: 43-64.
Firestone, Melvin M. 1967. *Brothers and Rivals: Patrilocality in Savage Cove*. St. John's: Institute of Social and Economic Research, Memorial University of Newfoundland.
Gentilcore, R. Louis, ed. 1993. *The Land Transformed*. Vol. 2 of *Historical Atlas of Canada*. Toronto: University of Toronto Press.
Hutchings, Jeffrey A., and Ransom A. Myers. 1994. "What Can Be Learned from the Collapse of a Renewable Resource? Atlantic Cod, *Gadus Morhua*, of Newfoundland and Labrador." *Canadian Journal of Fisheries and Aquatic Sciences* 51: 2,126-46.
–. 1995. "The Biological Collapse of Atlantic Cod off Newfoundland and Labrador: An Exploration of Historical Changes in Exploitation, Harvesting Technology, and Management." In Ragnar Arnason and Lawrence Felt, eds., *The North Atlantic Fisheries: Successes, Failures, and Challenges* (37-93). Charlottetown: Institute of Island Studies.
Mackay, R.A., ed. 1946. *Newfoundland Economic, Diplomatic, and Strategic Studies*. Toronto: University of Toronto Press.

Macpherson, Alan G. 1969. "Land Tenure, Social Structure, and Resource Use in the Scottish Highlands, 1747-1784." PhD diss., McGill University.

Mannion, John J., ed. 1977. *The Peopling of Newfoundland: Essays in Historical Geography*. St. John's: Institute of Social and Economic Research, Memorial University of Newfoundland.

Matthews, Keith. 1968. "A History of the West of England – Newfoundland Fishery." PhD diss., Oxford University.

Nemec, Thomas F. 1972. "I Fish with My Brother: The Structure and Behaviour of Agnatic-Based Fishing Crews in a Newfoundland Irish Outport." In R.R. Andersen and C. Wadel, eds., *North Atlantic Fishermen* (9-34). St. John's: Institute of Social and Economic Research, Memorial University of Newfoundland.

Newfoundland and Labrador. 1986. *Building on Our Strengths*. Final Report of the Royal Commission on Employment and Unemployment. St. John's: Queen's Printer.

Ommer, Rosemary E. 1989. "Merchant Credit and the Informal Economy: Newfoundland, 1919-1929." *Canadian Historical Papers* 1989: 167-89.

–, ed. 1990a. *Merchant Credit and Labour Strategies in Historical Perspective*. Fredericton: Acadiensis Press.

–. 1990b. Introduction. In Rosemary E. Ommer, ed., *Merchant Credit and Labour Strategies in Historical Perspective* (9-15). Fredericton: Acadiensis Press.

–. 1991. *From Outpost to Outport: A Structural Analysis of the Jersey Gaspé Codfishery, 1767-1886*. Montreal: McGill-Queen's University Press.

–. 1994. "One Hundred Years of Fishery Crisis." *Acadiensis* 23: 5-20.

Ommer, Rosemary E., and James K. Hiller. 1990. Canada-France Maritime Boundary Arbitration: Historical Framework. Report prepared for the Departments of Justice and External Affairs.

Oxaal, Ivaar, Tony Barnett, and David Booth. 1975. *Beyond the Sociology of Development*. London: Routledge and Kegan Paul.

Pahl, R.E. 1984. *Divisions of Labour*. Oxford: Blackwell.

Philbrook, Tom. 1966. *Fisherman, Logger, Merchant, Miner: Social Change and Industrialism in Three Newfoundland Communities*. St. John's: Institute of Social and Economic Research, Memorial University of Newfoundland.

Sinclair, Peter R. 1985. *From Traps to Draggers: Domestic Commodity Production in Northwest Newfoundland, 1850-1982*. St. John's: Institute of Social and Economic Research, Memorial University of Newfoundland.

–. 1987. *State Intervention and the Newfoundland Fisheries*. Aldershot: Avebury.

–. 1992. "Atlantic Canada's Fishing Communities: The Impact of Change." In G.S. Basran and D.A. Hay, eds., *Rural Sociology in Canada* (84-98). Don Mills, ON: Oxford University Press.

Templeman, Philip. 1918-28. Papers of Philip Templeman Limited, Bonavista, Newfoundland, Ledgers and Journals. Public Archives of Newfoundland and Labrador P71A/71.

Thornton, Patricia A. 1977. "The Demographic and Mercantile Bases of Initial Permanent Settlement in the Strait of Belle Isle." In J.J. Mannion, ed., *The Peopling of Newfoundland: Essays in Historical Geography* (152-83). St. John's: Institute of Social and Economic Research, Memorial University of Newfoundland.

–. 1978. "Dynamic Equilibrium: Settlement, Population, and Ecology in the Strait of Belle Isle, Newfoundland, 1840-1940." PhD diss., University of Aberdeen.

–. 1988. "The Problem of Out-Migration from Atlantic Canada, 1871-1921: A New Look." In P.A. Buckner and David Frank, eds., *Atlantic Canada after Confederation: The Acadiensis Reader* (34-65). Vol. 2. Fredericton: Acadiensis Press.

Wadel, Cato. 1969. *Marginal Adaptations and Modernization in Newfoundland*. St. John's: Institute of Social and Economic Research, Memorial University of Newfoundland.

Wright, Miriam. 1997. "Newfoundland and Canada: The Evolution of Fisheries Development Policies, 1940-1966." PhD diss., Memorial University of Newfoundland.

4
Community Change in Context
Christopher R. Bryant

Introduction

The adage "Think globally, act locally" nicely sums up both the central role that localities and, more specifically, communities must play in the overall quest for sustainable development on the one hand, and the challenge of integrating and reconciling local, community interests with the values and interests of the broader society, on the other hand. The role of localities – localized social action space (Marsden et al. 1993) – and, by extension, communities not only in influencing their own transformation but also in contributing to the overall changes in Canadian society has been increasingly recognized. This recognition is apparent both in the increased attention given to community-level involvement in the management of change through various federal (e.g., the Community Futures program) and provincial programs and bureaucracies devoted to community development (e.g., in Ontario, Saskatchewan, and British Columbia) and in various scholarly syntheses devoted to the issues and experiences of community development (e.g., Douglas 1994, 1995; Galaway and Hudson 1994; Vachon 1993). Increased involvement by, and attention given to, communities in Canada are part of a much broader trend that can be observed in many countries.

"Community" has different meanings, ranging from networks of social interactions and shared interests either associated with particular geographic spaces or independent of specific geographic spaces ("community of interests") to the geographic limits of various municipal and intermunicipal groupings (Bryant 1995a). The discussion here will focus on the geographic expressions of community, particularly as represented through formal municipal limits because municipalities are assuming greater responsibility in planning and managing their own spaces throughout the country (Douglas 1994). Furthermore, the population often identifies the modern community with the space within which services and infrastructure are provided in response to people's needs (Doucet and Favreau 1991).

However, this focus does not mean that the municipal organization must take the lead role (see below).

A common interpretation of sustainable development is that it originates from a twofold concern regarding the impacts of economic development, particularly economic growth, in relation to environmental degradation, on the one hand, and social marginalization, on the other hand. This interpretation emphasizes the importance of reconciling values associated with the ecological, economic, sociocultural, and political dimensions of society. When we acknowledge the multitude of interests and values associated with any particular locality, we also acknowledge the importance of some local involvement in identifying those interests and values. When we acknowledge the uncertainties involved in the transformation of our economy and society generally and the fact that as development changes, even within the context of a relatively advanced society such as Canada's, so do people's needs and interests, we also acknowledge that sustainable development at the community level involves the constant search for compatibilities between ecological, economic, sociocultural, and political values. That this intersection is dynamic and never totally attainable because of changing conditions and values has profound implications for how we go about planning (sustainable) community change.

The increased involvement by community (municipalities as well as various organizations and groups representing different interests and coalitions of interests in a community) in influencing and managing change has been accompanied by a shift away from simply managing change by using the various instruments of land-use planning and zoning. Today there is a greater variety of community activities that seek to influence economic and sociocultural activities and to contribute to the resolution of problems or impacts related to economic development. This shift effectively allows communities to begin to address the preoccupations associated with sustainable development. However, this shift has not occurred to the same extent in all communities, and truly coherent approaches to the range of preoccupations associated with sustainable development are not yet common.

In light of these introductory comments, two objectives are pursued in this chapter: (1) to explore the patterns of planned community change in Canada in terms of how they contribute to sustainable community development and sustainable development generally; and (2) to develop the theoretical basis for a set of actions at the community level aimed at sustainable community development. First, the nature of community change is considered using a simple framework to organize our thinking about the transformation of geographic space, be it at the community, regional, provincial, or national level. This framework builds upon the observable realities of any locality. It also sets the scene for understanding what sustainable community development needs to address. A framework is proposed for sustainable community development, in terms of both structure and process. Second, the dominant types of planned community change encountered across Canada are reviewed in relation to how they reflect the criteria for sustainable community development. And third, some prescriptions are made that respect the realities of the widely different geographic contexts in which communities find themselves. These prescriptions can help communities to move along a path of development that is more sustainable.

The Political Economy of Sustainable Development and Community Change

Finding a path of sustainable development is about finding strategies that balance the values and interests associated with the ecological, economic, sociocultural, and political dimensions of society in the context of achieving current and intergenerational equity. In addition, this search for, and construction of, a path of sustainable development must balance the interests and values of the local population with those of the broader society. Thus, in any planned change, there must be links between the local community and the broader sociocultural, economic, and political system. An essential starting point is to acknowledge that this search needs to be pragmatic. In the quest for sustainable development and in the context of Canadian society, it is difficult to argue for a rupture with past ways of doing things, even if we desire to achieve significantly different results. The majority of the population must be brought onside in order to achieve anything lasting. Thus, it is necessary to start with an understanding of the realities of actual development in a community and to use this understanding as a basis for providing courses of action that are likely to succeed.

Given the emphasis on values and interests, one logical place to start this analysis of (sustainable) community development is with the political economy approach that has been applied to localities in the United Kingdom (e.g., Marsden et al. 1990, 1992; Marsden et al. 1993) and in community development in Canada and France (e.g., Bryant 1995a, b; Bryant et al. 1996; Halseth 1996; Walker 1995).

In this approach, two fundamental ideas, expressed through a seven-component model, have been suggested (Bryant et al. 1996; Bryant et al. 1998). First, it is suggested that, at any particular point in time, a number of orientations characterize the development pattern in a community. Each orientation represents a bundle of initiatives, decisions, and actions; together the observed orientations define the community's development pattern. Each orientation is also associated with a set of identifiable interests and values, themselves linked in complex ways to the different actors present (Figure 4.1a). Examples of these orientations include the agricultural development orientation that is part of the makeup of many Prairie communities, the environmental industry orientation identified by the Triple S (Selkirk, St. Andrews, and St. Clements) "community" east of Winnipeg, and the tourism orientation that has emerged in Mont St.-Sauveur north of Montreal. Thus, these orientations characterize a community's socioeconomic development profile (Bryant 1995b, c, d, e). The mix of orientations in a particular community may reflect that community's general locational characteristics, its inherent attributes (resource mix, population composition, historical experiences), and the relative power of the actors whose interests are associated with different orientations.

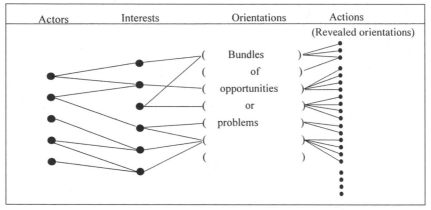

Figure 4.1a   The links between interests, actors, and orientations
Source: Bryant, Desroches, and Juneau (1998).

There are also latent orientations, such as potential bundles or clusters of initiatives and projects. They may be latent because the problems or opportunities associated with them have not yet been recognized as important to a community's development (e.g., lack of recognition of poverty in an area) or because the power structure in the community does not wish to acknowledge the importance of such orientations. In the latter case, "power structure" refers to entrenched interests that maintain their position by exerting influence through established networks, formal and especially informal, within the community (see below). This structure can constitute a significant barrier to the search for a path of sustainable development by retarding or even eliminating consideration of certain sets of values, interests, and therefore orientations.

In reality, there is a whole series of gradations between the fully emerged orientation and the completely latent one. In between the extremes can be bundles of initiatives and projects that are linked with an orientation, but the issues have not yet been given an important profile in the deliberations of the community leaders. For instance, we can talk about the "token" working group on the environment or on women's problems or about the city that supports community groups or organizations fighting poverty but that maintains those groups or organizations in a dependent relationship, thereby ensuring that they remain almost as marginalized as the population segments they are designed to serve.

Second, there is the issue of scale and networks (Figure 4.1b). People as agents of change operate in the context of various networks (Bryant et al. 1998). Through these networks, which may be political, social, and/or economic, they may exert influence on, and be influenced by, other actors. Networks can be relatively formal, as in decision-making structures with lines of command, or very informal. The informal networks are vital as means through which some actors can exert influence on other decision makers. Furthermore, these networks function at different geographic scales but are interconnected. Thus, local, regional, and national networks can sometimes be integrated because a particular actor is present in networks at each of these scales (see actor A, who is present in networks at all scales represented in Figure 4.1b). An example is a farmer who is the leader of a conservation group locally, a member of and an influential actor in a provincial agricultural association, and a member of a national association. Or the integration can occur simply because the relationship between actors in networks at two different scales allows pressure and influence, as well as information, to be passed from one to the other (see the relationship between actors E and D, C and B, H and G, and J and I in Figure 4.1b). This either enhances the power of an actor in his or her network or allows an actor from one scale to influence what happens in another scale, such as the influence of a senior federal politician in an area in which he or she has not been elected (H could be one such national politician in Figure 4.1b, whereas G could be the president of a regional development corporation with family or long-standing friendship ties to H).

There are some strong links between this framework and what Marsden et al. (1993) suggest as an appropriate approach to understanding the dynamic of locality: that is, the analysis of actors pursuing their interests by their actions within the broader economic, social, and political context. In an attempt to synthesize these various ideas and to build upon what we understand about the processes of community economic development (e.g., Beaudoin and Bryant 1993; Bryant and Preston 1987a, 1990; Douglas 1994, 1995; Douglas et al. 1992; Vachon 1993), a seven-component model has recently been suggested as a framework for analysis and action in community development (Bryant et al. 1998; Bryant et al. 1996) (Figure 4.2).

Essentially, actors (1) are seen as pursuing their interests and objectives (2) through their actions (3) while using the various networks (4) in which they operate or with which they have connections. An analysis of the networks reveals both their formal (5a) and their informal (5b) organizational structures. Networks provide ties between actors in the community envi-

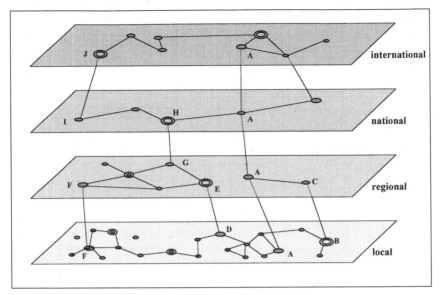

Figure 4.1b   Networks of actors and geographic scale
Source: Bryant, Desroches, and Juneau (1998).

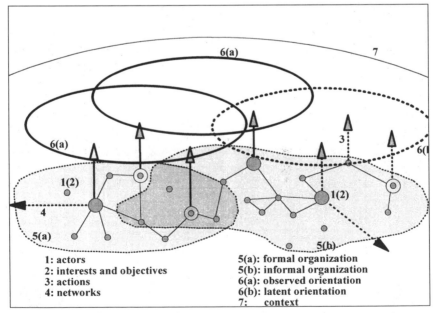

Figure 4.2   The dynamic of community transformation: A framework for analysis
Source: Bryant, Desroches, and Juneau (1998).

ronment and those in external environments. It is argued that understanding the networks of actors with their various interests, values, and relative weights together with the formal and the informal organizational structures helps us to understand why some orientations (6a) are dominant and clearly observed (see component [6a] identified with the solid lines in Figure 4.2) whereas others are much less prominent or do not even emerge at all – that is, they are truly latent orientations (see component [6b] identified with the dashed line in Figure 4.2). As argued above, these latent orientations may be prevented from emerging because the values and actions of the local power structure are stacked against them in a deliberate way. All of this evolves in a particular social, economic, and political context (7), itself dynamic. This broader context (e.g., as reflected in the provincial, regional, or federal context) can influence the dynamic of a particular community, while the dynamics of several communities may in turn have an impact on the broader context. An example of the latter would be lobbying by the various interests represented in the fishing communities in British Columbia and the progress made toward a new provincial-federal management agreement for the BC fishery in the spring of 1997.

From this framework, a number of salient points arise that are pertinent to sustainable development at the community level. First, the orientations that characterize the transformation of particular communities reflect multiple interests and values. Sometimes, in relation to a particular orientation, such as agricultural development and wildlife habitat, the interests involved are not necessarily convergent, but compatibility can be sought by bringing all the interested parties together. Furthermore, individual actors may have interests associated with several orientations, such as a farm family that may have an interest in an agricultural development orientation, a wildlife habitat conservation orientation, and possibly even an agritourism orientation. Interests and values can therefore overlap orientations and can change over time.

Second, the framework stresses the existence in most localities of multiple actors who function within various networks, many of which are informal. Thus, although the dynamic of change can be influenced through formal regulations, working through the informal networks and relationships is essential if paths of development are to be influenced. Development occurs through the decisions of a multitude of actors, including the individual, the family, the firm, the community organization, the municipal corporation, and so forth. Recognizing and then working through informal networks can provide much of the balance needed in the search for a path of sustainable development as well as offer a key to working with, influencing, and ultimately modifying the real power structure in a community at a particular point in time.

The framework can be used to analyze any locality. If we wish to pursue sustainable development, these first two points suggest the importance respectively of participation (not just consultation) and cooperation and partnership building. In addition, the framework emphasizes the many and complex values and interests of the different actors involved. Contradictions can even exist between the values espoused by an individual actor. Furthermore, this analysis is not fixed in time. Values and interests change, partly as socioeconomic conditions change, partly as actors receive and process additional information. A related point is that the capacity to identify issues and to influence and manage change varies between communities as well as between different segments of the population within a community. The configuration of this framework for a particular community will therefore change over time.

Can our formal institutional structures handle the sort of complex and dynamic situation that this analysis suggests? This is an important question because of the necessity in sustainable development to place all the legitimate needs and values associated with potential development in a community on the table – and this includes the legitimate values and interests of those not resident in the community. Sustainable community development can therefore be seen essentially as a democratic process in which people are able to express their legitimate needs and values and to modify their positions as uncertainties become certainties, new problems arise, and new information is assimilated. This is no trivial matter, because, in the earlier framework of analysis of the transformation of a community, it was emphasized that in the "natural" course of events (whether the processes of change are planned and managed by the community or whether it evolves without any collective intervention) orientations emerge as much because they represent the values and interests of actors who have the power and the influence to ensure that they are addressed and acted on as because they represent important bundles of challenges and opportunities "objectively" determined.

The ongoing creation and orchestration of open forums in which all legitimate views can be expressed represent a major way in which to validate the orientations pursued in a community and to encourage the discussion of latent orientations. Community forums, roundtables, and the like thus have the potential, as multistakeholder bodies, to play a critical role in sustainable development. To make this contribution, however, they must be recognized as important within the community, and they must be open and transparent, encouraging and affording accessibility to the individual citizen, not just to organized groups.

Further reflection on the framework from the perspective of sustainable development at the community level suggests a set of criteria for process and structure in planning and managing change. These criteria do not impose specific processes and structures for managing community change, for there are many different configurations that potentially meet them. This variety is critical if we are to adopt appropriate structures and processes that respect community, provincial, and regional specificities and the varying socioeconomic stages that communities and their populations have reached.

A basic set of criteria for assessing whether processes and structures of management in place move a community along a path toward sustainable development is suggested in Figure 4.3. The criteria have been established so that a community at its highest level of "readiness" and "awareness" regarding the economic, sociocultural, political, and ecological dimensions of sustainable development would score highest. There is nothing magical about such a checklist – it can be answered with yes or no or with a range of values; it can be modified as our understanding of sustainable development improves; and, because of the importance of varying perceptions about a community, it can even be administered to groups of citizens, professionals, and politicians to provide information about how "well" a community is performing.

The questions are divided into those that address issues of process and those that address issues of structure, although there is always some overlap. Process issues are important in that they refer to participation and communication, two critical dimensions that permit values and interests to be expressed (Bryant 1991a, 1994a; Cofsky 1995) and that provide for greater possibilities of integration of the ecological, economic, sociocultural, and political dimensions of sustainable development. Structure issues are important because, even though structure may have to change as conditions change, structural and formal relationships either provide or deny key "known" points of access to citizens and their organizations. Together the structure and the process of community change determine whether legitimate values and interests are represented and integrated in the community (Bryant 1994a). (Note that the term "community leaders" includes both formal elected or appointed leaders and informal leaders who are regarded as influential actors within the community.)

Where an unequivocally positive response is not obtained in relation to the questions in Figure 4.3, additional questions need to be posed. Is the less than completely positive response the result of the stage (or capacity) that the community has reached? The current structures and processes in place for managing change may be the most appropriate given the stage that the community is at, even though they do not address (all of) the criteria outlined in Figure 4.3. Or is the less than completely positive response the result of the evolution of processes and structures being retarded by particular groups in the community or by influences from outside the community? In the latter case, senior government involvement in a particular issue, such as forestry or the fishery, might make it difficult for people in

Process

1 Is participation by the population actively encouraged and sought out on a regular basis by community leaders?

2 Is effective communication maintained between the different organizations/groups in the economic development, social development and environmental domains?

3 Are environmental and social issues, as appropriate, considered by the community leaders systematically before major decisions are taken regarding economic development and infrastructural developments?

4 Does decision making in the community reflect reconciliation between the ecological, social, and economic imperatives for the community?

5 Is input from students in the community regarding directions for change regularly and systematically sought out by community leaders?

6 Do community leaders welcome input from nonresident interests in their deliberations?

7 Do community leaders actively seek to mobilize and enhance the capacity of groups in the community who have been marginalized or have not contributed to community debates about development issues?

8 Is there a continuous community planning process that ensures transparency and the ability of citizens to have input, participate, and take responsibility for different actions?

Structures

9 Are all the principal population and activity segments recognized by community leaders as being important to the community's well-being?

10 Are these population and activity segments either effectively represented on the different community organizations or adequately involved in communication with them?

11 Does the community have a permanent body (committee, agency, department, service, group) that debates issues in the domains of economic development, social development, and the environment?

12 Does the community through its formal representative body (e.g., municipal corporation, band council, neighbourhood council) encourage interaction with one or more neighbouring communities through some means such as formal observer status, etc.?

13 Do community leaders recognize the legitimacy of citizen groups and other organizations to organize and undertake their own development projects by supporting their existence (either morally or through resource contributions)?

14 Does the community (formal government structure, key community organizations) ensure someone has the responsibility for communicating with other groups and organizations?

15 Is there a community-level plan that reflects the planned actions of the various population and activity segments in the community?

16 Is it easy for the structure to change as conditions change?

Figure 4.3   Criteria for assessing community processes and structures from the perspective of sustainable development

the community to broaden their horizons and engage in the sort of free-ranging debate essential to their search for sustainable solutions to their predicament. For instance, government programs that maintain dependency on the government during crises (e.g., the cod crisis in Newfoundland) can contribute to retarding progress in the evolution of community structures for tackling change.

The framework for analysis introduced above incorporates the broader context as an important component. In relation to sustainable community development, this means that we have to take account of the provincial, regional, and national contexts – political, cultural, economic, and legislative – that influence what communities and their groups can do, the ease with which they can pursue their goals, and the role that they can play in representing broader collective interests in decisions that affect particular communities and localities.

Senior governments can thus play an important role in shaping the enabling environment within which communities can pursue their different trajectories of development. Municipalities, for instance, are the offspring of their respective provincial legislatures, and some differences exist between provinces regarding what municipal corporations can effectively undertake (Skelly 1995), whereas the governance of Canada's First Nations is structured under the federal Indian Act (Wolfe 1992). Senior governments can contribute to the reduction of long-term dependent relationships in community populations through their use of seed monies in, for example, setting up innovative community organizations (e.g., the Community Futures organizations) and building capacity through effective training programs. Provincial governments can recognize the need for community management to reflect local conditions by not insisting on specific structures, such as county reorganizations, without taking account of local conditions and how well the community already functions.

The Dynamic of Planned Community Change in Canada
Planned community change in Canada has a number of roots (Bryant 1991b), and the experiences that derive from each do not necessarily converge into a holistic and coherent process of planned change. Obviously, one major root involves the role of municipalities and other formal structures of local government in managing change. The most obvious form of this management has been the formal mechanisms of land-use planning in the different provinces, in which municipalities have different responsibilities conferred on them by the respective provincial legislation in areas such as the development of land-use plans and zoning bylaws, the responsibility for approving subdivisions (as with the regional municipalities in Ontario), the responsibility for managing certain types of infrastructure (e.g., some of the roads), and so on.

Municipalities have also been involved in other dimensions of "development," such as social assistance (e.g., municipal contributions to social welfare in Ontario). Furthermore, many municipalities in all provinces have helped to manage economic development in their communities through activities (depending on the province and the municipality) such as the servicing, ownership, and marketing of land in industrial and commercial business parks, the marketing of the community to nonresident and, increasingly, resident investors and entrepreneurs, local programs of business counselling, and so forth (Skelly 1995). Interestingly, much of this municipal involvement in economic development has not always been effectively integrated with the municipal involvement in land-use planning (Paparella 1987), even though the professionals involved have worked for the same employers.

Another major root of local involvement, which partly overlaps with the first one, is the many and varied local responses to conditions of distress or disadvantage created in the process of economic development. Sometimes municipalities have reacted to crisis conditions, such as in single-industry communities whose economic base has been threatened by the declining fortunes of their major source of employment. An example is the community of Elliot Lake in northern Ontario and its attempts to reorient its economy away from mining since the late 1980s. In other situations, community organizations have responded to the distressed situations of particular population groups in disadvantaged areas in the larger urban centres such as Montreal's Point-St.-Charles (Favreau and Ninacs 1994; Galaway and Hudson 1994). From the perspective of sustainable development, an important thrust of such organizations has been the empowerment of disadvantaged groups through capacity building and their integration into broader community processes of planned change (Pell 1994).

These local efforts, taking place in such a large range of geographic contexts in communities faced with such different development histories, preoccupations, and opportunities, have given rise to a tremendous variety of processes and structures. We can try to characterize them based on a number of dimensions, which can be interpreted from the perspective of sustainable development, particularly in light of the criteria outlined in Figure 4.3 that are presented as pertinent to the assessment of an individual community.

Five dimensions are suggested as differentiating between types of local community development (APEC and Bryant 1993; Douglas et al. 1992), and all five can be interpreted in terms of sustainable development practice.

1. Is there a long-term planning process in place that is continuous, holistic, and strategic?
Planning for development necessarily places the focus on the long term. However, the approach to planning in relation to development is far from

homogeneous and rarely holistic. The longest and most common experience with planning for development at the local level involves land use, particularly in urban municipalities. Land-use strategies often involve relatively sophisticated analyses, procedures, and some form of public consultation. However, while land use is very broad, land-use planning has not dealt adequately with the various activities on the land. Hence, it has been common for a municipal corporation to initiate land-use planning while at the same time pursuing economic development planning as a separate activity. Furthermore, other sectors have been subject to long-term processes of planning and reflection, such as social development, but rarely have all these sectoral efforts been systematically brought together to ensure effective communication.

In dealing with the uncertainties associated with development processes, it is useful to ask whether the planning process is strategic or not and whether it is continuous or periodic. Strategic planning became popular in many Canadian municipalities in the 1970s, especially in larger urban centres, in municipal economic development departments or development corporations. It was oriented toward economic development, particularly growth. Occasionally, strategic reflection took into account a broader array of issues, as in Brampton and Calgary (Bryant and Lemire 1993).

"Strategic planning" implies an effort that takes account of the dynamic environment, with all its uncertainties, and that attempts to position the community in question in this dynamic, open, and competitive environment. Ideally, it necessitates a continuous process of reflection and monitoring; this process, however, is often not present. Many efforts have been preoccupied with the preparation of a plan document rather than with process. This focus does not lend itself to continuous reflection and adjustment; rather, it lends itself to a periodic planning process, which unfortunately tends to get sidestepped because it is incapable of dealing with dynamic conditions.

In rural areas, some of the best and worst examples of strategic plans and strategic planning processes came out of the Community Futures program under the auspices of the federal government. In the first generation of these plans, the federal consultants often encouraged a noncontinuous process because of their focus on getting a plan document ready to use as the basis for project evaluation – and financial approval. In the 1990s, significant progress has been made, and many more Community Futures organizations have begun to pursue a more effective form of strategic planning.

2. Is there real community participation in the processes of community development planning and implementation and adequate representation of or communication with the various orientations in a community?
Community participation can take on a wide variety of forms. For some,

the least effective form of community participation is public consultation, in which the public is presented with what amounts to a limited range of alternatives (if any are indeed presented!) for comment and "input" (Cofsky 1995). Participation can go much further than this, however. It can be used to set objectives, provide ideas, assess needs and opportunities, and encourage some people to initiate and manage projects. From the perspective of sustainable community development, community participation in all its forms is an essential ingredient.

In many communities, such participation has not progressed very far. The community still functions under the control of an elite group of "leaders," such as the mayor, councillors, an economic development officer, and local businesspeople. This is not to denigrate the considerable efforts, good intentions, and many successes of such people. However, elitist management processes are vulnerable and depend too much on a small group of people for the assessment of needs and the evaluation of opportunities.

Furthermore, this elitist form of management is often associated with a lack of recognition of the multiple actors with legitimate interests in development in the community and who actually undertake development. Thus, even in a community coalition in which a range of elected representatives and other actors are present, some actors representing key strategic orientations may not be present. Are orientations representing marginalized segments of the population present? Are all the significant orientations of the economic sector present? Without effective representation or communication, it is too easy to put aside important sources of creativity in the community and to contribute to stress by creating images of closed shops and cliques. In some of the Community Futures organizations in Quebec, not only has there been a decided attempt to have representation from the different strategic orientations present in an area, but there have also been efforts to develop "electoral colleges" for the constituencies associated with those orientations in order to ensure more effective representation.

In the strategic planning for local development that spread initially in Canada, mainly in the domain of economic development, little community participation was present and management processes were dominated by an elite. This situation still exists in many communities, even though they and their leaders, through publications and training programs, have frequently been made aware of the significance of a community base for community development planning (e.g., Bryant and Preston 1987b, 1990; Douglas et al. 1992; Lewis and Green 1992). Interestingly, under the Eastern Ontario Development Program in the late 1980s, a subsequent evaluation suggested that the only plans that were "alive" and active were those in which the local population had had a significant role to play in identifying needs and opportunities (NGL Consulting 1991).

3. Are there effective links between the public, private, and voluntary (or "third")
sectors in planning and managing change?

This dimension deals with a particular aspect of participation and representation. The public sector, through formal municipal organizations,
band councils, and the like, has an important role to play in sustainable
community development because these are important institutions in our
democratic system. Municipal councils are duly elected to represent the
local populations, are accountable to those populations, and have access to
a financial resource base, despite the mounting pressures on it. However,
municipal councils, because of the electoral process, do not necessarily
reflect all the legitimate interests in the community. Furthermore, development is influenced in important ways by municipal councils, but a large
part of the development equation is accounted for by actors in the private
sector and the voluntary sector. Therefore, sustainable community development requires effective communication between all these sectors. One
way of achieving this communication is through organizations that represent a coalition of the various interests from all three sectors, such as the
RÉSO in the southwest neighbourhood of Montreal (Joyal 1995). In many
communities, however, such links have not been easy to achieve.

4. To what extent are the values and interests of nonresidents taken into account
in the process of planned change?

The values and interests of nonresidents can be taken into account in many
ways, ranging from input from provincial ministries and federal departments, to the development of formal intermunicipal organizations, to the
presence of external observers on various community committees, to various cooperative projects between adjacent communities. One example that
reflects this concern is the Community Futures "communities," which typically involve representatives from several municipalities in a regional
grouping, together with other segments of interests cutting across the
region, working together to plan and manage socioeconomic development.

5. To what extent are economic, social, and environmental values integrated into
the development planning process and the various projects and initiatives being
implemented?

It has never been easy to ensure effective communication between these
different interests, values, and organizations or groups that represent
them, despite the fact that "quality of life" is increasingly accepted as the
overriding goal of community development. Even with formal representation of the different interests and institutions in a community coalition, it
is a challenge to go from getting people to sit around the same discussion
table to deciding to engage in a truly sustainable path of development.

Despite all the obstacles alluded to, it is now generally agreed that the emerging form of planned community change in Canada that encapsulates all these dimensions (on the sustainable end of the scales) can be labelled "community economic development" (Douglas 1994, 1995) or "sustainable community development" (Bryant 1991b). It is much more broadly based than the brand of community economic development that had its roots in the "war on poverty" in the larger Canadian and American cities (Galaway and Hudson 1994). The common thread is a broader form of community involvement in setting the community's vision and objectives, in selecting strategies, and in providing resources than characterized many other experiences in local development in the 1970s and 1980s. It is also distinguished by a greater integration of economic, social, cultural, and environmental values and by a relatively decentralized approach to planning and management. The more decentralized approach, which can be encouraged by provincial and federal agencies in their dealings with communities, is centred on the strategic orientations of a community or group of communities. In the final section, these comments are drawn together to provide an agenda for action at the community level.

Ingredients of Sustainable Community Change and Policy Implications at the Local Level

The argument has been developed above that the emerging form of community economic development, based upon principles of participation, social justice, and the integration of values associated with the ecological, economic, sociocultural, and political dimensions of life, provides a theoretical basis upon which to develop paths of sustainable community development that contribute to sustainable development at the broader scale. However, there are many ways in which this community form of community development can take shape, ways that reflect varying community conditions and compositions as well as stages of community development.

Three basic ideas are reiterated, followed by a categorization of actions dealing with both process and structure in planned community change. First, sustainable community development is about development and not necessarily about growth. Even within a free-market economy and a capitalist framework, there is a major concern regarding control over the creation and distribution of "wealth" – social, economic, environmental, political. In discussing participation and cooperation in the context of community economic development, our fundamental concern has been with influencing the creation of wealth and its distribution. Second, development is the result of a large number of decisions in a community environment by many actors and not just the result of the decisions of the "state" – local, provincial, regional, or national. Thus, the community needs to be able to influence this multitude of decisions. How can we achieve this influence? Third, there are many legitimate interests present in most communities. How do we prevent exclusion and encourage effective participation? How can we avoid elitist structures over the long term?

One of the principal keys lies in the strategic orientations that represent the actual and potential challenges and driving forces in a community and that can shape its future (Beaudoin and Bryant 1993; Bryant 1994b, 1995a, b). Clearly, it is critical to be able to identify these strategic orientations, especially the latent ones. Doing so necessitates an important effort in community participation and reflection. Once identified through community forums or roundtables, the orientations can become the organizing vehicles around which, and within which, different interests interact and negotiate and undertake "development" (Bryant 1995b). For example, in the County of Haliburton in eastern Ontario, a community-based process of strategic planning was initiated in the summer of 1997. Through two events or community forums, a number of strategic orientations were identified. For some orientations, the discussions validated the work of an existing orientation working group (e.g., forestry, economic diversification), for others they involved recognizing a hitherto completely latent orientation (e.g., the roles of youth in the community), and for still others they involved activating an orientation previously acknowledged but rarely acted on (e.g., the use, management, conservation, and protection of the natural environment and its resources).

Finally, a number of generic actions that can be taken by communities are identified. Again, it is important to underline that the specific ways in which these actions are orchestrated in a community reflect specific community circumstances. As long as we recognize that sustainable development is a process, progress can be determined by asking the types of questions identified in Figure 4.3 over a period of time.

1. Openly Debating Community Orientations

Identifying the strategic orientations is an important first stage in community development, remembering that these orientations need to be reviewed and validated regularly to take account of changing conditions, new information, and different perceptions. This identification can be accomplished through various means such as community roundtables, town meetings, and brainstorming sessions, followed up by various processes of validation because such community events, even when well attended, rarely mobilize a large portion of the community.

Once identified, the orientations can be (and are increasingly) used as the basis for planning and managing change and for mobilizing actors and community residents generally (Bryant 1995d, 1995e). They also provide the basis upon which external interests and values can be integrated into the debates, even to the extent of involving outside actors in planning and implementation. Good examples are the many working groups focused on developing tourism, agriculture, small business, downtown cores, cultural activity, and the environment.

2. Building and Reinforcing a Team Mentality

The nature of the community environment discussed above points unequivocally to the importance of partnerships, functioning networks, and cooperative approaches in the quest for sustainable development. This can occur in the planning and management processes at the community level (e.g., the Steering Committee involving the City of Welland, Ontario, and the local Community Futures Committee), in an individual strategic orientation (e.g., the agricultural working group in the Mont-St. Hilaire region southeast of Montreal), or in relation to specific projects (e.g., partnerships between merchants, local residents' associations, and cultural associations in the many projects of downtown revitalization such as the Mainstreet program).

At the community level, the many efforts that contribute to building community identity, such as the hundreds of town festivals across the country, also influence positively the community environment for partnership building and cooperative approaches.

3. Communicating Effectively

To achieve sustainable community development, it is essential to maintain effective communication (1) generally to community residents, (2) between actors and interest groups working within a particular strategic orientation, (3) between the various planning and implementation processes within the different strategic orientations, and (4) between the community and external actors and networks. Given that much of the effort is volunteer, it is important that steps be taken to identify and utilize effectively the various networks of relationships within the community and between it and the external environment. This can become a major role for a community development officer or some other professional involved in one or more of the orientations. Not only are the networks important in influencing people's actions, but they are also extremely valuable as channels of communication.

4. Encouraging Innovation

Influencing community development often involves taking an innovative approach. Innovation is important not only in terms of economic development and business but also in terms of local and regional institutions and associations. It is not just about products but also about processes or different ways of doing things. For instance, an organization that pulls together different interests, groups, associations, and institutions can be a major innovation in an area.

Conclusion

Despite all the positives regarding local development, planned community change, even when the locus of control is in the community, does not necessarily take a community along a path of sustainable development. Management structures based upon a small group of people can represent the necessary first steps toward a broader-based process of sustainable community development – that is, a small group of initial leaders plans and proactively broadens the base of leadership in the community. Given human nature, this is no small challenge. Such management structures have often persisted in the long term. When they do, the danger is that the elitist approach creates exclusion, does not integrate values and interests associated with the ecological, sociocultural, economic, and political dimensions, and stifles creativity in the development of innovative solutions and ways of responding to people's diverse needs. However difficult it may be, the strongly recommended course of action involves democratizing the whole process of managing change. In a dynamic and uncertain environment, it is illusory to expect that the leaders or the "experts" can effectively know everything. Under these circumstances, pursuing and then managing more effective participation comprise the only reasonable approach in the long term to identifying a community's legitimate values, interests, and needs.

Senior governments have a major responsibility to create an enabling environment that encourages communities and community organizations to engage in more democratic practices. Indeed, despite periodic flashbacks to more centralized schemes, senior governments in Canada, as well as in many other countries, have rapidly been moving in this direction in the last quarter of the twentieth century. Further movement in this direction in the twenty-first century is likely as Canadian society becomes increasingly pluralistic and as technological change permits global communication and mobility on a scale and of a nature that will – and is already – shaking the foundations of the nation-state. Senior governments are moving away from their traditional roles – control, source of development capital, and even monitoring for the collective good – and toward roles that emphasize capacity building at community levels (e.g., through building awareness and supporting training, through seed financing to kick-start more effective management processes) and acting as a catalyst in the development of management processes at the most effective level of governance (i.e., local through regional levels), an endorsement of the principle of subsidiarity.

Acknowledgments

The author would like to acknowledge various research grants received from the Social Sciences and Humanities Research Council of Canada for research into the transformation of rural space, particularly in urban fringe environments, research that has given rise in part to the conceptual framework presented in this chapter.

References

APEC (Atlantic Provinces Economic Council), and C.R. Bryant. 1993. *Conditions for Successful Community Economic and Social Development: A Comparative Study in the Atlantic Provinces and Eastern Ontario.* Halifax: APEC, for Health and Welfare Canada.

Beaudoin, M., and C.R. Bryant. 1993. *Tools for Operationalizing Strategic Management for Community Futures Committees.* Ottawa: Employment and Immigration Canada.

Bryant, C.R. 1991a. "La Participation communautaire et le développement local: La Voie de l'avenir." *Les Cahiers du développement local* 1,1: 5-7.

–. 1991b. *Sustainable Community Development, Partnerships, and Winning Proposals.* The Good Idea Series in Sustainable Community Development 1. Sackville, NB: Mount Allison University, Rural and Small Towns Research and Studies Programme; St. Eugène, ON: Econotrends.

–. 1994a. *Working Together through Community Participation, Cooperation, and Partnerships.* Sustainable Community Analysis Workbook 1. St. Eugène, ON: Econotrends.

–. 1994b. "The Locational Dynamics of Community Economic Development." In D.J.A. Douglas, ed., *Community Economic Development in Canada: Integrated Readings* (203-36). Vol. 1. Toronto: McGraw-Hill Ryerson.

–. 1995a. "The Role of Local Actors in Transforming the Urban Fringe." *Journal of Rural Studies* 11,3: 255-67.

–. 1995b. "Interests, Interest Groups, and the Rural Environment: A Framework for Analysis." In J.F.T. Schoute et al., eds., *Scenario Studies for the Rural Environment* (599-607). Dordrecht, The Netherlands: Kluwer Academic Publishers.

–. 1995c. *Strategic Management and Planning for Local and Community Economic Development: I the Organization.* Sustainable Community Analysis Workbook 2. St. Eugène, ON: Econotrends.

–. 1995d. *Strategic Management and Planning for Local and Community Economic Development: I the Community.* Sustainable Community Analysis Workbook 3. St. Eugène, ON: Econotrends.

–. 1995e. *Mobilizing and Planning the Community's Strategic Orientations: Basic Tips.* Sustainable Community Analysis Workbook 4. St. Eugène, ON: Econotrends.

Bryant, C.R., S. Desroches, and P. Juneau. 1998. "Community Mobilisation and Power Structures: Potentially Contradictory Forces for Sustainable Rural Development." In I.R. Bowler, C.R. Bryant, and P.P.P. Huigen, eds., *Dimensions of Sustainable Rural Systems* (233-44). Netherlands Geographical Studies 244. Groningen, The Netherlands: Groningen University.

Bryant, C.R., P. Juneau, and S. Desroches. 1996. "Sustainability in Action: The Role of Local Actors in the Transformation and Conservation of Urban Fringe Environments." In I. Saito, A. Tabayashi, and T. Morimoto, eds., *Proceedings of the IGU Study Group on the Sustainable Development of Rural Systems, Tsukuba, Japan* (67-75). Tokyo: Kaisei Publications.

Bryant, C.R., and D. Lemire. 1993. *Population Distribution and the Management of Urban Growth in Six Selected Urban Regions in Canada.* Toronto: ICURR Press.

Bryant, C.R., and R.E. Preston. 1987a. *A Framework for Local Initiatives in Economic Development.* Economic Development Bulletin 1. Waterloo: Economic Development Program, University of Waterloo.

–. 1987b. *Strategic Economic Planning and Local Development.* Economic Development Bulletin 2. Waterloo: Economic Development Program, University of Waterloo.

–. 1990. *Economic Development in Small Town and Rural Environments.* Economic Development Bulletin 10. Waterloo: Economic Development Program, University of Waterloo.

Cofsky, S. 1995. "L'Influence de la participation dans la collectivité sur la réussite d'un développement local et communautaire: Comparaison entre milieux urbains et milieux ruraux." MA thesis, Département de Géographie, Université de Montréal.

Doucet, L., and L. Favreau. 1991. *Théorie et pratique en organisation communautaire, Sillery.* Québec: Presses de l'Université Laval.

Douglas, D.J.A. 1994. *Community Economic Development in Canada.* Vol. 1. Ed. D.J.A. Douglas. Toronto: McGraw-Hill.

–. 1995. *Community Economic Development in Canada*. Vol. 2. Ed. D.J.A Douglas. Toronto: McGraw-Hill.

Douglas, D.J.A., C.R. Bryant, and A. Joyal. 1992. *Community Economic Development and Strategic Planning: An Overview Course*. Ottawa: Employment and Immigration Canada.

Favreau, L., and W.A. Ninacs. 1994. "The Innovative Profile of Community Economic Development in Quebec." In B. Galaway and J. Hudson, eds., *Community Economic Development: Perspectives on Research and Policy* (153-65). Toronto: Thompson Educational Publishing.

Galaway, B., and J. Hudson, eds. 1994. *Community Economic Development: Perspectives on Research and Policy*. Toronto: Thompson Educational Publishing.

Halseth, G. 1996. "'Community' and Land-Use Planning Debate: An Example from Rural British Columbia." *Environment and Planning A* 28: 1,279-98.

Joyal, A. 1995. "Community Economic Development: The Montreal Example." In D.J.A. Douglas, ed., *Community Economic Development in Canada* (75-100). Vol. 2. Toronto: McGraw-Hill.

Lewis, M., and F. Green. 1992. *Strategic Planning for the Community Economic Development Practitioner*. Vancouver: Westcoast Development Group.

Marsden, T., P. Lowe, and S. Whatmore. 1990. *Rural Restructuring: Global Processes and Their Responses*. London: David Fulton Publishers.

–. 1992. "Introduction: Labour and Locality: Emerging Research Issues." In T. Marsden, P. Lowe, and S. Whatmore, eds., *Labour and Locality: Uneven Development and the Rural Labour Process* (1-18). London: David Fulton Publishers.

Marsden, T., J. Murdoch, P. Lowe, R. Munton, and A. Flynn. 1993. *Constructing the Countryside*. Boulder: Westview Press.

NGL Consulting. 1991. *Economic Development Strategic Plans for Eastern Ontario*. Ottawa: Ontario Ministry of Industry, Trade and Technology.

Paparella, G. 1987. "Planning and Economic Development." *Papers in Canadian Economic Development* 2: 59-66.

Pell, D. 1994. "The Third Sector, Sustainable Development, and Community Empowerment." In D.J.A. Douglas, ed., *Community Economic Development in Canada* (161-86). Vol. 1. Whitby, ON: McGraw-Hill Ryerson.

Skelly, M.J. 1995. *The Role of Canadian Municipalities in Economic Development*. Toronto: ICURR Press.

Vachon, B. 1993. *Le Développement local: Théorie et pratique*. Réintroduire l'humain dans la logique du développement. Montréal: Gaetan Morin.

Walker, G. 1995. "Social Mobilization in the City's Countryside: Rural Toronto Fights Waste Dump." *Journal of Rural Studies* 11,3: 243-54.

Wolfe, J. 1992. "Changing the Pattern of Self-Government in Canada." In I.R. Bowler, C.R. Bryant, and M.D. Nellis, eds., *Economy and Society* (294-306). Vol. 2 of *Contemporary Rural Systems in Transition*. Wallingford, Oxon, England: C.A.B. International.

5

Northern Communities and Sustainable Development in Canada's North

Timothy McTiernan

Northern Communities

There are shades of *north* in Canada. This is more than apparent from a browse through Revenue Canada's annual *Guide for Northern Residents Deductions* (e.g., 1995 guide). Sable Island is listed, as are Ear Falls, Ontario; Carrot River, Saskatchewan; and Chetwynd, British Columbia. These communities fall in a swath along a broad band of demarcation that touches the Queen Charlotte Islands and sweeps ashore by the BC-Alaska border. The swath cascades over the Rocky Mountains and across the Prairies in a line roughly from Grande Prairie through The Pas before swinging south through Red Lake, east past Matagami, out by the north-shore communities of Quebec, into the Strait of Belle Isle and the cold Labrador current flowing, past Greenland, out of Davis Strait.

People argue about what is truly northern, moving the demarcation line up or down the map of Canada, based on different weights given to different criteria of *northerness*. Polar, grizzly, and black bears, caribou, migrating birds, boreal forest, rock, tundra, water, ice, and snow are part of the essential image. So, too, are pictures of grey smoke rising from homes in small communities tucked among the shadows of mountains or along the edges of lakes, rivers, and the Arctic Ocean.

If there is a composite portrait of northern communities, and northerners would make the point vehemently that there is no true composite, then it would be of a small settlement, not much more than 100 years old, widely separated from its nearest neighbours, with a majority or predominant Aboriginal population. Common characteristics of these communities include long and easily fractured transportation and communication links to southern centres and narrow economic bases focused on natural resource extraction, traditional uses of the land, and, to a greater extent in recent years, seasonal tourism. Residents project a proud sense of distinctiveness, combined with an often overwrought sense of "not being listened to" by the powers-that-be in the rest of the country. The apparently widespread and sustained northern outcry throughout 1996 over proposed federal gun-control legislation is a case in point. And, while this is one of many instances in which Aboriginal and non-Aboriginal members of northern communities join voices in a common cause, it is equally often the case that the combined feelings of distinctiveness and of being dismissed, shared by northerners, manifest themselves differently in the Aboriginal and non-Aboriginal segments of the community (see Jull 1991).

The heartland of the North lies north of the sixtieth parallel. It encompasses two territories, the Yukon and the Northwest Territories (NWT). It covers a shade under 40 percent of Canada's land mass and reaches from the Alaskan border to within sight of Greenland. It sits across the top of British Columbia, the Prairies, Ontario – the islands in Hudson Bay are a part of the Northwest Territories – and Quebec. It has a total population of just under 100,000 people. By mid-1999, it will have been reshaped politically into three separate territories, a new Eastern Arctic territory of Nunavut coexisting with a smaller Northwest Territories and the Yukon. None of the territories, by that time, is likely to have a population over 50,000 people.

As of June 1996, the Yukon, with a geographic area of 483,450 square kilometres, had a population of 32,903. Over 23,500, or 71.5 percent, of all residents live in Whitehorse. The remaining 9,400 people are spread across fifteen smaller communities and a number of outlying settlements (Government of Yukon 1996c). More than 36 percent of resident Yukoners are under twenty-five years of age. The majority of the population, from 70 to 75 percent, depending on the criteria used in the assessment, is non-Aboriginal.

The Northwest Territories, at just under 3,380,000 square kilometres, is to the Yukon and the ten provinces what Alaska is to the other forty-nine states in the union. It covers 34 percent of Canada, from fossilized forests in the High Arctic Islands to sedge marshes in Wood Buffalo National Park. In January 1996, it had an estimated population of 66,100 (Government of the Northwest Territories 1996). Census figures from 1991 show over 50 percent of the population as being younger than twenty-five. The same census statistics listed 61 percent of those enumerated as being Aboriginal. Unlike the Yukon, where the Aboriginal population is almost entirely Athapaskan Indian, Aboriginal people in the Northwest Territories include Dene Indians, Métis, and Inuit. All of the sixty-one population centres listed in NWT statistical documents, except Yellowknife, Hay River, and Nanisivik, are predominantly Aboriginal.

The population of the Yukon has risen by over 25 percent in the last decade, with in-migration tending to exceed out-migration through most of that period (Government of Yukon 1996b). In only one year since 1985 has in-migration exceeded out-migration in the Northwest Territories (Government of the Northwest Territories 1996). The ten-year population increase of about 14,000 in the Northwest Territories is due, fundamentally, to the high birth rate, nearly twice the national average over each of the last twelve years.

Economic activities in communities in the North are pursued by a mix of small local businesses and branches of larger western Canadian or national firms with their head offices in southern ("outside" is still a frequently used term) centres. There are a few large homegrown operations and a few major sources of northern capital; however, with a growing number of comprehensive land claim settlements, First Nations are beginning to acquire and attract capital. Mining, oil and gas, tourism, construction, and telecommunications all have a strong "outside" presence. In the Yukon, tourism and Holland America Westours go hand in hand. Finning Tractor of Vancouver dominates the heavy-equipment market. NorthwestTel has become an arm of Bell Canada. Hard-rock mining is dependent on decisions made by Toronto financiers and companies based in Vancouver and Toronto. Whitehorse families get their fast food from local franchises of national and international chains, such as McDonald's, Pizza Hut, Tim Horton's, Dairy Queen, and A&W.

The federal government, through the Department of Indian Affairs and Northern Development (DIAND), still retains provincial-type responsibility over land and many of the natural resources in both northern territories. It continues to have a legal responsibility, based on the terms by which Rupert's Land was accessioned to Canada, to settle outstanding comprehensive land claims treaties with the region's First Nations. At the same time, it has offered to enter into self-government agreements with First Nations to allow Aboriginal people to move out from under the administrative shadow of the Indian Act and to set up their own duly constituted governmental decision-making processes. DIAND works with, and frequently clashes with, the elected territorial governments of the Yukon and the Northwest Territories. The Yukon government has been structured along party political lines since the Yukon legislature divided into organized political party groups in the 1978 general election. The NWT government is not party based, and the NWT legislature operates on a consensus model, unlike any other legislature in Canada. Regardless of the form of government and the structure of legislature, both territorial governments administer a full range of services to their citizens, from education and health to transportation and physical infrastructure. In some instances, the territorial governments work with established municipal governments in the delivery of services. In many more cases, the territorial governments end up delivering a number of community services to unorganized communities in the absence of community-level government. Likewise, the federal government delivers a number of services directly to communities when there are no alternative mechanisms of delivery and when it has ongoing provincial-type jurisdiction or Indian Act responsibilities.

The situation is a bit simpler in the northern regions of the provinces, where provincial and municipal governments deliver general programs and where DIAND has a presence, alongside First Nations government bodies, on Indian Act reserves.

In sum, any northern resident can end up dealing with three, if not four, levels of government in his or her day-to-day life. Nevertheless, it is possible, if somewhat ironic, to talk about sustainable development in the North without much reference to community input and involvement, because of the structure of government jurisdictions and authorities in the North and because of the substantial influence of external investment decisions on the regional economy. To do so, however, would be to miss the essential point that sustainable development is about more than just the careful use of resources and the management of our environment. It is fundamentally about how individuals, on their own and collectively, make choices and conduct their lives in relation to their locality, their region, and their feelings of connection with and responsibility to the world at large. This is an issue for Canada's north, in terms of both how northern residents define their own long-term prospects and how those outside the region react to northern residents as they go about their lives and articulate their sense of a future.

Northern residents live, work, and pursue their various lifestyle concerns in two different types of community: settlements and communities of interest. Both are important. Communities of interest reach across the North, and sometimes outside it, joining people with similar views on issues into recognizable groupings. Settlements define the locales of northern residents, the settings from which they react to the world. In many cases, an individual may identify as much with a group sharing a common set of values as with the settlement in which he or she lives. In a region with few residents, numbers count a lot. In a region where a large number of the residents are young people under the age of twenty-five, numbers count even more. A settlement of 600 people has to work hard to have its views heard in Ottawa, Yellowknife, Whitehorse, or Regina. A settlement of 600 people with differences of opinion has little chance of shaping regional decisions. A settlement of 600 people on the other side of an issue from a regional interest group of 600 or 700 or 800 people has to work hard to maintain a strong enough focus on the issue to have its views factored in to the final equation.

If any one circumstance convincingly demonstrates the powerful social dynamic created by small populations, then it is that of the local or regional election. Seats on municipal councils, on First Nations councils, and in territorial legislatures can be, and are, won by a couple of votes. In the October 1996 territorial election in the Yukon, one seat tied on election night, the seat for Vuntut Gwitchin (Old Crow); one seat was won by three votes, the

Lebarge seat, just north of Whitehorse; and one of the Whitehorse ridings was won by fewer than ten votes. Three votes, cast a different way, would have reduced a strong majority to a bare working majority with the speaker of the legislature having to cast the deciding vote on key legislative items.

A certain stridency is not unusual in public debates on issues when such small numbers can have significant impacts on matters in the region. At the same time, a certain stridency is common when the North wants to be heard on the national stage, again because of an understanding, even in an era of fast electronic communications, that northern voices are truly voices in the wilderness among 30,000,000 people. (One has to shout to be heard across the tundra, the boreal forest, and the Canadian Shield.) There are interesting differences and similarities between the styles of northern debate in the region and in broader national and international settings. The important common characteristic of these debates, for the purpose of discussing sustainable development, is their intensity.

Northern Settlements and Northern Communities of Interest

A community focus on sustainable development in northern Canada revolves around questions of population characteristics (including age and gender), growth patterns, links with other centres, uses of the hinterland, economic base, level of control over resource and economic issues, and prospects. In general terms, there are four different types of northern settlement, each with a different profile along these dimensions.

There is a handful of *major hubs* that function as key regional transportation and communication links with southern and, particularly, urban Canada. Whitehorse, Hay River, Yellowknife, and Iqualuit serve this purpose. They are the largest centres in their regions. With the exception of Hay River, they are major government centres. Their economies are heavily dependent on the transportation and service sectors. Whitehorse and Yellowknife together account for almost 40 percent of the population of the two northern territories. With the closing of the copper mine in Whitehorse in 1982, Yellowknife is the only one of these centres with a primary industry: gold mining. All four communities get tourism spin-offs because of their role as transportation and distribution centres.

There is another handful of *regional administrative centres*, which, like the major hubs, play an important role in the distribution of goods and services to surrounding communities and which have a substantial government presence. Administrative centres are essentially an NWT rather than a Yukon phenomenon, because the much larger Northwest Territories does not have the same intercommunity road links that exist in the Yukon. Towns such as Inuvik, Rankin Inlet, and Fort Smith are strongly connected to the social, economic, and political facets of life in their surrounding communities. Watson Lake, Dawson City, and Haines Junction, in the

Yukon, act to some extent as regional centres, but more in relation to activities in the surrounding area – exploration, mining, and tourism – than to the administration of a broad range of regionally consolidated government services.

Most settlements across the North are *traditional communities* in that they are focused on land-based harvesting activities that form part of both the wage and the nonwage economies. Many of these settlements are Aboriginal communities, but some have both Aboriginal and long-term non-Aboriginal residents. Old Crow, Sachs Harbour, Snare Lake, and Arviat are representative of traditional Aboriginal communities. Mayo and Carcross in the Yukon, and Fort Simpson and Cambridge Bay in the Northwest Territories, are settlements that have sizeable non-Aboriginal populations. Nonwage economic activities in these communities include harvesting fish, marine mammals, and game for meat. They also include informal social support networks for people in distress (see Waring 1988). Women play a significant role in the broad range of nonwage tasks and activities, particularly in managing them through their various roles in the informal social structures of the communities. Wage activities range from trapping, guiding, and selling artworks and crafts to road and airstrip maintenance, water delivery, and seasonal construction. Unlike the larger administrative centres, where salaries are a major source of monetary flow, residents of traditional settlements depend more on seasonal and short-term work for cash. Salaried positions tend to centre on the school, the police detachment, and the nursing station. Jobs are critical in these communities, however, because expenses in going out on the land are high, and traditional bases of income, such as fur sales, have been sharply eroded by urban antifur campaigns.

Faro, Norman Wells, and Nanisivik are three of a number of *resource extraction centres* that have grown up across the North since the dying days of the last century and, more often than not, have become ghost towns. Clinton Creek in the Yukon, and Cassiar in British Columbia, are two abandoned asbestos towns. Herschel Island was a short-term whaling community. Pine Point has stopped producing lead and zinc. Fewer such communities are being planned or built at present, because transportation has improved sufficiently and government policy has shifted fundamentally to support fly-in, fly-out camps rather than new settlements at any new mining or oil and gas production site. These communities have few natural connections with the traditional settlements in their regions. Indeed, people living in these communities vary as much from people in traditional settlements in their views on what constitutes sustainable development as residents in traditional settlements differ from businesspeople and administrators in the larger northern centres.

One thing that resource extraction communities now have in common with other types of communities in the North, which was not the case five years or a decade ago, is that *all* settlements have become vulnerable to outside economic forces. Historically, mining communities depended for their continuity not only on the richness and size of the ore bodies being mined but also on world commodity prices. As a case in point, the mine at Faro shut down three times in the past fifteen years due to low metal prices and high costs of production. Trapping also has long been affected by cycles in prices and is currently under threat as a viable source of income by sanctions from the European Community. Recently, federal actions in reducing the deficit have resulted in reductions to transfer payments to the provinces and territories and in reductions to the rate of growth of the federal budget for Aboriginal affairs. These reductions will have a marked impact over time on the operations and maintenance and capital expenditures of all levels of government in the North, affecting the types and levels of services available and affecting salary, wage, contract, and social service cash flows into both traditional settlements and government centres. Governments' long-term economic and land-use planning activities have already been affected in two ways. Within the past six years, proportionately more energy has been diverted to short-term crisis management than to long-term "vision" building. And, when long-term economic planning is considered, it is compromised by an inability to identify and establish certain, useful, and stable assumptions.

Expectations about future sources and rates of cash flow into the North, through government and the private sector, will have a growing influence on northerners' views about what constitutes sustainable development and will modify existing concepts of sustainability based on people's involvement in the current economic life of their home community. Changes to the financial base supporting northern communities will not only affect the range of short- and long-term economic opportunities available to residents but will also, in various ways, challenge some of the fundamental value systems of northerners.

Within and across northern communities, there are six different and often competing value perspectives that have as much influence on how people think and talk about sustainable development as where they live and what they do to earn a living.

First, there is an *administrative perspective* shared by many professionals and public servants that takes a rational – "policy and procedure" – approach to addressing problems and proposing options for resource management, allocation, and protection. People who share this perspective, more often than not, do not depend on a vibrant local economy for their income. They are relatively mobile and look outside the region as much as they look within the region for support for their value systems. Balance and trade-off are two central concepts in this point of view.

Second, associated with the administrative perspective, but driven by quite different pressures and operating styles, is the *local political perspective*. It is focused on short-term problem solving and the maintenance of advantage in the community or territorial political arena. Politics in the North are extremely intense and volatile. Short-term political fixes, often seen to be essential at the moment, are not always sustainable in the long term and are not always implemented according to principles of sustainable development. Minimizing political pressure and opposition, and setting the agenda on the issue in question, are twin pillars of this point of view. It is a mistake to think that only candidates for office subscribe to the political perspective. It is as strongly held by many political supporters who never appear on the public political stage but who are active organizers and campaigners in communities and who, as such, are influential.

Third, the *Aboriginal perspective* is by far the most complex of the key value systems that underlie thinking about sustainable development in northern Canada. It is founded on a way of looking at the world that is profoundly different than that of the non-Aboriginal population. It is based on a different sense of time (see Hall 1983), a different sense of relationships between people, and a different sense of relationship between people and the land (see Kassi 1987). There is both an individual component and a collective component of the perspective. In its collective manifestation, the perspective can be infused with many of the characteristics of the local political perspective and can be directed, intensely, at representing First Nations interests on issues of regional concern, from pipeline construction to the allocation of timber-harvesting agreements. In both its individual and its collective expressions, this perspective addresses aspirations for the future self-determination of Aboriginal people as well as a strong sense of the past.

Collectively, these three perspectives cut across the core of the political power structure in northern communities. Partially disengaged from the main course of political and administrative activities in the region, and directly disengaged from decision-making processes, are the three other perspectives, which speak to the lifestyles of their proponents.

Fourth, the *northern business perspective* centres on efforts to promote local economic activity, to diversify, and to attract capital. It is a conflicted mix of protectionism and boosterism, and it is founded on the notion that growth is essential for the future of northern communities.

Fifth, in contrast, there is a *northern environmental protection perspective*, which has strong support outside the region as well as considerable support within the region, particularly in the larger centres. This perspective puts the North into a global context and argues that northern resources and wilderness are valuable global assets that should not be squandered.

Sixth, there is what can best be called a *local pragmatic perspective*, most easily visible in the smaller communities, adhered to by men and women who have consciously chosen a northern lifestyle based on serial jobs, food and fuel-wood gathering from the land, fixed-up '82 Chevy trucks, and a well-tuned chainsaw.

Without being facetious, watching two or three episodes of CBC's *North of 60*, and perusing Doug Urquhart's (1994) collection of "Paws" cartoons, offer a more complete sketch of these quite diverse value systems.

The small population in northern Canada creates a level of interpersonal familiarity that, when factored across the different types of communities and the different values of people in these communities, promotes vigorous public discussion on issues. Out of the history of debate on development, wilderness protection, resource use, traditional values, and future options for northerners have emerged two competing visions of sustainable development. Neither vision is always well articulated. At times, they are alluded to simultaneously, with no clear recognition that they are essentially incompatible. On occasion, they underlie arguments on seemingly unconnected matters, such as the Western Arctic debate on structures of governance in the new Northwest Territories.

One vision of sustainable development in the North is a *stasis model*. It emphasizes the need for maximum protection of the North's renewable resources, privileges traditional activities on the land, and stresses the need for planning and regulatory processes to manage change. It is heavily endorsed by First Nations communities across the North. It embeds discussion of issues of northern environmental and resource use in both national and international contexts, giving significant weight to national and global interests. In its fundamental form, it views human populations as being a single component of a much larger, interlinked natural system that must be protected at all costs. It does not, in any strong way, address economic and employment pressures that result from a young and growing population or from the restructuring of the financial transfers to northern governments that account for over two-thirds of their revenues.

The alternative vision of sustainable development in the North is a *growth model*. It emphasizes the need for expanded business activity in the North to stabilize, diversify, and strengthen the regional economy. In this regard, it implicitly supports substantial population growth. It places a reliance on resource management processes to protect what is critical in the northern environment and to minimize the impact of development. It advocates clear, transparent, and timely decision making, with the emphasis on getting decisions, arguing that bureaucratic and political decision makers tend to embrace elaborate, costly, and time-consuming hearing processes catering to special interests and producing few conclusive results. It has, at heart, an optimistic – "let's build it and fix it" – view that almost all natural problems can be solved by appropriate kinds of active and properly conceived human intervention. This model does not account well for the collectively expressed social and political aspirations of First Nations in the North, but it has some First Nations adherents, especially among First Nations that have settled their comprehensive land claims. It is a model that emphasizes local control over decision making for the region. It does not do a good job of defining the demands or the markets for new business activities.

The see-saw for paramountcy between these different versions of a sustainable future for the North is taking place during a period when the North's relationship with the outside world is undergoing an intense transformation. Electoral redistribution, resulting from court decisions, is weakening the voice of individual northern communities, relative to the larger urban centres, in provincial and territorial legislatures. At the same time, groups of northern citizens from remote communities are familiar with and comfortable in the halls of power in Ottawa, Washington, and Brussels as they lobby for resource protection, for support for the fur industry, and for a greater share of political power in the North. Indigenous issues have a new measure of national attention. The Cree of James Bay are active players in the United Nations system. Since the late 1980s, the territorial governments have become active participants in all Canadian intergovernmental forums, from first ministers' conferences to federal-provincial-territorial meetings of ministers of the environment, transportation, trade, education, or tourism, and in the full range of interjurisdictional meetings beyond these forums. Cultural exchanges and conferences across the circumpolar north are becoming more common; third-level educational institutions in the North are developing; and Canada is attempting to refine a northern vision through its advocacy of the Arctic Council of circumpolar nations, through its appointment of an arctic ambassador, and through its establishment of a polar commission, which is paying attention to northern environmental issues. Regional governments, those of the Yukon and Alberta among them, are participating in activities of the Northern Forum, an organization of northern provincial and state governments with active participation from Alaska, Japan, China, and regional jurisdictions in Russia. In each of these arenas, for each of the topics being addressed at any particular time, the question of the future of northern communities is fundamental to both the discussion and its outcome.

Defining the Agenda for Sustainable Development in Canada's North

The relative merits and consequences of pursuing either the protection-oriented or the development-oriented model of sustainable development in the North have been debated vociferously, during the 1970s, in hearings on the proposed Mackenzie Valley Pipeline and on the proposed Alaska Highway Natural Gas Pipeline. The arguments in support of or opposition to each contrasting vision were repeated in the 1980s during the Beaufort environmental assessment review and during the Lancaster Sound regional-planning exercise. The debate continues, through the 1990s, in northern Quebec on extensions to the James Bay hydroelectric project, in Labrador on base-metal mining and on military-training overflights, in the Northwest Territories on diamond mining, and in Saskatchewan on uranium mining.

Starting in the early 1980s, discussions about the stasis and growth models of sustainable development in the North began to flow along two separate channels. The one channel involved a general attempt, at national and regional levels, to forge some type of integration and rapprochement between contrasting views of the appropriate balance between development and management of the environment and its resources. The other channel bumped from specific issue to specific issue, from placer mining regulations in the Yukon, to the Norman Wells pipeline in the Northwest Territories, to oil production test flows in the Beaufort and the High Arctic.

The work of the Task Force on Northern Conservation was the first in a series of efforts to define common ground between the different perspectives on northern sustainable development. Established by DIAND, and including a diverse range of northern voices, its 1984 report spoke to principles that would ensure integrated resource management, protected areas, and marine conservation in the North. This initiative was followed, over a five-year period, by northern-based efforts to develop a Sustainable Development Strategy for the Northwest Territories (Bastedo 1987), to complete a Yukon Conservation Strategy (McTiernan 1990), to implement a pilot Community Conservation Strategy in Old Crow (Fuller and McTiernan 1987), and to finalize a regional Inuit Conservation Strategy (Doubleday 1990). Work at the federal level on Arctic Marine Conservation Strategy (Snider 1990) and on the application of the UNESCO "Man and the Biosphere Programme" to northern Canada (Inglis 1990) was linked to the northern strategies. All of these projects owed a considerable intellectual debt to the World Conservation Strategy (International Union 1980), to professionals working in the IUCN arena (see Prescott-Allen and Prescott-Allen 1990), and to the work of the World Commission on Environment and Development (1987). The northern focus on conservation strategies as a tool in pursuing sustainable development was captured in the report of the National Task Force on Environment and Economy (1987). A number of the issues raised during development of the strategies were later addressed in detail through the Arctic Environmental Strategy (Sadler 1996). The workshops, meetings, and drafting sessions that shaped the strategies included community representatives and members of the northern business and environmental communities. Most of the participants were nominated by their respective organizations. Substantial efforts were made on all sides to achieve consensus in the preparation of the strategy documents. The key feature of these strategies, and to some extent their collective weakness, was that they spoke to all of the interests of all of the participants in the process. They embraced both the stasis model and the growth model of sustainable development without having to chose one model over the other (a criticism made about *Agenda 21*; see Sadler). The people involved in the process of strategy development made accommodations of inclusion, not of options. Rather than dismiss perspectives and views that they did not share, they were prepared to consider, accept, and endorse a range of environmental and developmental objectives. They were not asked to and did not attempt to weight, prioritize, or note a preference for any particular objective.

The work on northern regional strategies did not lead to subsequent efforts to develop a range of formal community-based strategies of conservation. However, it did set the stage for territorial environmental protection legislation, such as the Yukon's Environment Act, passed in 1992, and it did prepare the ground for community-based programs of waste management, recycling, and environmental education. The strategies, in this regard, injected the notion of sustainability into northerners' views of their communities and their future (see Olson 1995), and they facilitated community action on relevant issues.

Meanwhile, in the Yukon at least, over the same period, the debate between those advocating a stasis model of sustainable development and those promoting a growth model intensified on specific issues, which do involve choices, such as land-use regulations on mining claims, management plans for "heritage rivers," and forest-harvesting practices. DIAND's ministerial advisory committee of miners, environmentalists, government, and First Nations interests reached agreement on proposals for changes to Yukon mining legislation that would permit stronger environmental control over activities on mining claims. Later, at the point of the introduction of amending legislation, the proposals failed to get the support of the conservation group represented on the advisory body. A working group of mining industry, community, First Nations, conservation, and tourist interests deadlocked on the provisions of a draft heritage river management plan for the Bonnet Plume River. Disagreement over approaches to forest harvesting in southeast Yukon resulted in two blockades of the federal building in Whitehorse in 1996.

A convergence of opinion in northern communities on the generalities of sustainable development in the North, coexisting with continued friction between the different community interests over particular development proposals or specific resource management plans, suggests a number of things. It suggests that progress toward an integrated vision of sustainable development in the North, one that has widespread grassroots endorsement, is still in its early stages (see Hinkle et al. 1996). It suggests that, in spite of extensive consultation, motivation for conflict resolution and consensus building falls off as debate on sustainable development moves from the general to the specific, as people's vested interests are more directly affected by the issue at hand, and as strong contrasts between people's basic value systems are uncovered. In this regard, if consultation processes inadvertently highlight differences between the goals of the various participants, and underline the advantaged or the disadvantaged status of the different participant groups relative to each other, then they can intensify conflict rather than produce consensus (Hinkle et al.). Bissoondath (1994) has illustrated such unintended consequences at the national level in his thesis that, by failing to emphasize "common cause" among Canadians, government policies on multiculturalism, and the processes supported by these policies, have inadvertently created intergroup discomfort rather than tolerance for diversity. Politicians and public servants need to pay thoughtful attention not only to the ongoing need for consultation with community interests on issues of sustainable development but also to the format of such consultation. There is no single formula that works in all circumstances. Commitment to consultation does not abrogate responsibility for the careful design of the process. Consultation, to achieve its intended goal, needs to be seen to be fair, open, and goal oriented. Consultation seen to favour particular interests, hijacked by an agenda, or without a clear end point will fail.

Ultimately, the gap between being able to reach consensus on general objectives of sustainable development and being unable to avoid strident disagreement on specific issues suggests that value differences between residents in northern communities are strong enough and wide ranging enough to create significant barriers in any effort to solve disagreements and find common ground.

McTiernan (1982) reported some findings that partly address this question. As an element of a broader study, 240 respondents living at the time in the Yukon, British Columbia, and Alberta, were asked to complete the Environmental Response Inventory (McKechnie 1971), a personality assessment questionnaire. Half of the respondents had grown up in a small-town setting, half in a big-city setting. Within each of these two groups, half of the people described themselves as being conservation minded, half as being development minded. Of the 240 people, 153 were women and 87 were men.

The Environmental Response Inventory (ERI) measures environmental dispositions along eight different dimensions: *pastoralism*, for conservation and against development; *urbanism*, measuring the enjoyment of city settings; *environmental adaptation*, tapping a "bulldoze and be damned" attitude; *stimulus seeking; environmental trust*, the lack of fear of being alone or lost; *antiquarianism,* a preference for traditional designs and historical places; *need for privacy;* and *mechanical orientation,* an interest in machinery and technology. The small-town respondents differed from their big-city counterparts on three dimensions. They had higher pastoralism scores, lower urbanism scores, and somewhat lower environmental trust scores. In ordinary language, they were more laid back, more conservation oriented, and more cautious than people from big cities. There were no measurable differences on any of the other five dimensions. The conservation-minded respondents, however, differed from the development-minded people on every dimension except need for privacy and stimulus seeking. They had higher pastoralism, lower urbanism, lower environmental adaptation, lower environmental trust, higher antiquarianism, and lower mechanical orientation scores. Whether the conservation-minded and development-minded people had grown up in small towns or big cities made no difference to their scores on any of the eight dimensions. In terms of environmental dispositions, the conservation-minded and development-minded groups represented widely divergent worldviews and value systems. Such divergence makes it difficult to reach agreement on questions of environmental management or economic development. A final note: the women had lower stimulus seeking, lower environmental trust, higher antiquarianism, and lower mechanical orientation scores than the men.

Managing the formal, government-sponsored interpersonal and inter-group processes in the ongoing debate and dialogue on sustainable development in northern Canada is as important as defining the substantive issues and building an integrated and coherent vision of a sustainable future. However, the productive and effective management of formal processes is extraordinarily difficult because the management framework imposed by governments is a short-term one dictated by electoral cycles, whereas the natural evolution of the dialogue on sustainable development is long term and organic and does not fit well into a governmental frame of reference.

Foundations for Northern Sustainable Development

The long-standing debate between the adherents of a stasis model of sustainable development in the North and the proponents of a growth model has not impeded change in two key areas that provide the foundation for sustainable activities in northern Canada.

On one hand, on a formal level, governments in the North continue to refine policy on resource management, allocation, and protection and to address the challenges of creating employment and business opportunities in remote communities (see Pell and Wismer 1987). Much of this work in the territories is driven by the process of negotiating land claims. Across the North, the settlement of land claims contributes to sustainable development in four ways. First, it provides for certainty over land tenure, facilitating decisions about allocation, and it defines the ongoing rights of Aboriginal people to harvest resources and to have a voice in resource management. Second, it sets out requirements for integrated processes of resource management, allowing for new and stronger links between land, water, and renewable resource management, land-use planning, and the assessment of development proposals. Third, it establishes an interrelated web of advisory boards and committees, at local and regional levels, designed to facilitate community involvement in resource management processes and to vest substantial power and responsibility at a local level over management decisions. And fourth, it supports the implementation of self-government arrangements that vest jurisdiction for the management of their settlement lands and their citizens with formally established First Nations governments. In broad sustainable development terms, the land claims agreements that will ultimately blanket the North will legally entrench the resource management conditions necessary to support a stasis model of sustainable development. At the same time, they will ensure the establishment of the processes of land-use planning, environmental assessment, and resource-use licensing that will serve as platforms for debates on sustainable growth.

In essence, the structure of land claims agreements in the North, and the legal framework that emerges from land claims agreements, define the future course of the debate between the major competing visions of northern sustainable development. One vision cannot fully displace another without consensus on major amendments to Aboriginal rights and land management legislation. The web of legislation setting out resource management objectives and processes encourages a fusion between the disparate visions. General community support for any form of a fusion between visions will require the reorientation of values within a number of interest groups. Such a reorientation will take time and depend on circumstances (Mayton, Ball-Rokeach, and Loges 1994).

On the other hand, at an informal level, awareness about issues of environmental and sustainable development has increased among northern residents. This increase is reflected in the attention given by municipal councils and community advisory groups to waste management, water quality, sewage disposal, air quality, local employment opportunities, recycling, and the relationship between green space (figuratively speaking for many northern communities) and community recreational opportunities. Catch-and-release ethics in fishing, voluntary restrictions on wildlife harvesting by Aboriginal communities, and concerns about overuse and degradation of some wilderness areas all contribute to a common value of care about home communities and their surrounding environments, care that is reflected in turn in public discussion on a range of issues. There is growing attention in the non-Aboriginal northern community to the value of many of the traditional practices and beliefs of Aboriginal elders. New opportunities and ways of doing things get a respectful hearing. Children in schools produce myriads of classroom projects on resource management and environmental protection. School graduates consider the advantages of staying in their home community rather than leaving for the south.

Indicators of Sustainable Development

Progress on sustainable development in the North, for the North, depends as much on community values, activities, and aspirations as it does on the level of sophistication of resource management processes. Tracking progress in northern sustainable development requires paying attention both to indicators of environmental and resource well-being and to indicators of individual and community health (Hodge 1996). So far in this chapter, the generic discussion of sustainable development in the North has drawn on examples that invariably involved articulate, experienced, and economically comfortable community and interest group spokespeople. As any quick review of the media will confirm, this is not the only North. Statistically speaking, the North is bimodal. It has a high percentage of high school, university, and advanced-degree graduates. It has high levels of annual average income. It carries a national media profile far beyond what might be suggested solely on the basis of its population. However, it also has a high number of school dropouts; a high incidence of fetal alcohol syndrome; depressing statistics on substance abuse, family abuse, and suicide; extremely high levels of unemployment in smaller settlements; and poor housing stock. For some people, it is a region of hope, but for many it is one of despair. Hope and despair are balanced in each settlement across the North, from Beaver Creek in the west to Davis Inlet in the east.

Even with the most integrated and complete resource management regimes, sustainable development is not possible for northern communities if the general physical health and social well-being of individuals in the community is poor (Table 5.1). In counterpoint, the long-term viability of even the healthiest of communities in the North, outside of an artificial community like some of the Soviet-era scientific centres, is questionable if hinterland resources and resource management systems are absent. General poor health in the population and the absence of any consistent resource use are indicators of a community in crisis. It is only when comprehensive resource management systems are present with a well-adjusted community that the conditions exist for sustainable development at a local level.

For some communities in northern Canada, sustainable development will depend on building a stronger renewable resource base and resource management regime, combined with a search for nontraditional ways of earning an income and a search for alternative markets for products, such as seal fur, that are subject to boycotts. Nowhere is this more apparent than

Table 5.1

___

Indicators of sustainable development

	Low level of resource stewardship	High level of resource stewardship
Good community health and social well-being	Poor prospects for long-term sustainability; high likelihood of resident out-migration	Essential conditions for community opportunities that are beneficial and sustainable
Poor community health and social well-being	Circumstances that exacerbate personal and community dysfunction and limit the possibility of viable local economic activity in any sector	Potential for the development of a sense of community alienation from the formal institutions and agencies making decisions on resource use

___

in the east coast communities dependent on northern cod stocks and in the High Arctic and Eastern Arctic communities recovering from the economic impacts of ongoing antifur campaigns in Europe and North America. For other communities, sustainable development will exist only after substantial attention has been given to the ongoing social and physical health of their inhabitants. Investments in health, social services, education, training, and employment creation are no less important in sustainable development than investments in resource management, environmental monitoring, and protected areas.

Community Involvement in Sustainable Development
A healthy resource base and communities that have generally positive social indicators are preconditions for sustainable development in northern Canada. These preconditions do not guarantee community involvement in sustainable development, particularly in the area of economic development. It often takes substantial effort by the proponent of a project and by the community to ensure local involvement in decision making, project management, and monitoring. This is particularly the case when the proponent comes from outside the community, a normal state of affairs in the North, even when the proponent is some level of government. When developers and communities have worked together on the business and environmental management sides of development activities, benefits have accrued to communities in the forms of employment, business opportunities, and skills transfer. In the absence of such cooperation, little accrues in the form of lasting community advantage.

In community-proponent working relationships, this is not always an issue of awareness, attitude, and orientation, although it can be. It is likely to be more fundamental. Basic communication and transportation infrastructure is unevenly developed in the North, and it is often fragile or intermittent. Roads are closed seasonally or during freeze-up and breakup. For instance, the Dempster Highway, the only land link to the Mackenzie Delta, closes for four weeks during spring breakup and for four to five weeks at freeze-up. Community phone lines go down for periods of time because of few, if any, backup routes into communities. Air traffic is grounded because of weather. Shipping is seasonal. The Internet is a long way from "webbing" all communities. Communication costs are high (e.g., Government of the Northwest Territories 1995). Language and translation needs are an issue. Traffic, real and virtual, is light relative to the capital and operational expenditures needed to keep transportation and communication links open. For instance, it costs approximately $3.8 million to keep the 464-kilometre Yukon stretch of the Dempster Highway open on a year-round basis. The government of the Northwest Territories estimates an annual average of 1.6 trucks a day northbound. Yukon government estimates of traffic counts on the highway for 1994 and 1995 range from a low of twelve vehicles *for the month* of December 1995 to a high of 133 vehicles *for the month* of July 1994. The Yukon government traffic counter installed at kilometre 66 of the Dempster Highway recorded 615 vehicles for 1995, up from the annual total for the previous year (Government of Yukon 1996a). With cost-to-use ratios in this order all across the North, it takes substantial time for public infrastructure to be established and expanded. Private sector transportation operations are either limited to the relatively high-volume corridors or, in the absence of regularly scheduled service, chartered and contracted. East-west routes are thinner than north-south routes. According to the Air Canada timetable on the Internet, it takes six hours and twenty-five minutes to fly from Iqualuit to Cambridge Bay via Rankin Inlet and Yellowknife. The farther west across the North, the more extensive the highway system.

The fewer the transportation and communication connections between communities, the greater the effort needed to ensure opportunities for community residents to engage in the wage economy and to develop business prospects. The problem creates its own dynamic in the North. People are drawn out of smaller communities toward a larger range of job opportunities in the bigger centres, reducing the workforce in the smaller communities, limiting the focus on the community as a source of workers and business suppliers, and possibly affecting the development of community infrastructure services tied to population.

The North has developed its own systems to cope with the thin communication and transportation links. There are strong informal lines of communication between settlements. Conferences have become a major means through which people from different communities meet and exchange information. In many respects, conferences are to the North what the Internet is to global communication, an easy means of sharing a great deal of knowledge with a large audience in a short time and an easy means of introducing distant government and industry representatives to community residents, "up close and personal" as they say. Table 5.2 summarizes scenarios that can result from different combinations of circumstances in northern communities.

Communities that are not well linked to regional and southern centres and that do not attract many employment or business benefits from economic activities in their area are likely to manifest symptoms of political alienation and to express opposition to proposals for new ventures in their locality. The health and well-being of those residents who have not left for

Table 5.2

Potential for community involvement in sustainable development in the North

	Weak transportation/ communication connections	Strong transportation/ communication connections
High level of benefits to community associated with regional activity	Potential for dependence on narrow or single sectors (e.g., regional mine, seasonal tourism) for socioeconomic benefits; potential for booms and busts and population swings	Essential conditions for community to avail itself of opportunities to diversify activities and build sustainability through involvement in a web of different initiatives
Low level of benefits to community associated with regional activity	Circumstances that can contribute to a sense of community alienation from regional political institutions and from possible sources of new investment in the region — potentially resulting in a strong NIMBY sentiment and the danger of personal or community ill health	Circumstances that can result in a heavy reliance locally on government transfer payments into the community as a source of income, and the development of a migrant community workforce that earns a living outside the community but that returns at frequent intervals

employment elsewhere may be low. This pattern of alienation and personal distress can be countered in traditional settlements by a high level of involvement in land-based harvesting and cultural activities. In the past, sales of raw fur provided a significant measure of cash flow into traditional communities and provided the means and the incentive for people to spend significant periods of time on the land. However, 1994-5 fur production in the Northwest Territories was valued at $1.4 million, down from a ten-year high of $6.1 million in 1987-8 and substantially below averages throughout the 1980s (Government of the Northwest Territories, 1996). Government transfers are now an essential source of income in these communities.

There are communities in the North without good communication links that have benefited substantially from activities in their area. More often than not, the activities have been cyclical, single sector, or both. Tuktoyaktuk, heavily involved in oil exploration in the Beaufort, has ridden the same boom-and-bust wave as the oil industry. During down cycles, there is a high likelihood of skilled resident workers leaving such communities, particularly if there are no homegrown activities to take the place of the lost enterprise. The potential for the development of a migrant community workforce is even higher where there are good communication links but few local opportunities in the home community. As a case in point, the former chief of a First Nations band, whose home settlement is on one of the highways in the Yukon, has speculated that many of the younger members of his community may end up living and working in Whitehorse during the week, returning to their home community to pursue cultural activities on the weekend.

None of these conditions supports a community economic base that is resilient, that can diversify, or that can contribute to the long-term sustainability of the community.

The possibilities for the development of a community-based business sector, and a stable, skilled, community-based workforce involved in sustainable economic activities, increase exponentially in northern communities that have good transportation connections and a history of attracting business and employment opportunities from outside investment.

Indeed, as transportation links increase, so does access by community residents to educational and training opportunities. Over the years, by road and air, postsecondary students, in increasing numbers, have moved to and fro between northern home communities and training facilities in larger centres. For instance, Canadore College of Applied Arts and Technology in North Bay, Ontario, provides a range of long- and short-term training to Cree students from James Bay communities. Increasingly, building on successful partnership arrangements, more training programs are being established in communities through a combination of distance delivery, where access is available, and on-site classroom work, where equipment can

Table 5.3a

Potential for community contribution to sustainable development in the North given strong reciprocity in relationships with others

	Low level of involvement in decision making/ management	High level of involvement in decision making/ management
Strong, cohesive sense of community identity/ vision	Potential exists for community to play a strong advisory role in local management and development decisions, without any ultimate involvement in the decisions – in terms of either what they are or when they are made; strong community advocacy for community-initiated projects	Essential conditions for community to negotiate true partnerships in management and development activities, with a reciprocal exchange of commitments and responsibilities and with an equitable sharing of the benefits; active community initiation of projects and management initiatives
Weak, discordant sense of community identity/ vision	Potential exists for internal community dissent and competition to be "the community voice," destabilizing arrangements that have been negotiated by the appropriate community authority that is unable to maintain broad community support; weakening interest in participation in activities, resulting in economic uncertainty	Potential exists for decision-making gridlock within community, with different authorities and interests (e.g., municipal council, regional provincial/ territorial agencies, Chambers of Commerce, and First Nations agencies) unable to achieve consensus or a sense of workable approach; internally, this can intensify factiousness, and in relationships with others it can lead either to unwitting playoff between competing community interests or to withdrawal

Table 5.3b

Potential for community contribution to sustainable development in the North given weak reciprocity in relationships with others

	Low level of involvement in decision making/ management	High level of involvement in decision making/ management
Strong, cohesive sense of of community identity/ vision	Potential exists for community to ignore or actively campaign against activities or initiatives and to focus community energies on advocacy for community projects and on longer-term community-based political or cultural priorities	Potential exists for confrontation with outside-community interests over lack of a shared understanding of community objectives and priorities, resulting either in protracted negotiations over implementing initiatives or in the exercise of a tacit or explicit veto over initiatives that are not community generated and sponsored
Weak, discordant sense of community identity/ vision	Potential exists for substantial internal dissent within the community, with sharpened differences emerging between the different community groups with different visions; few community initiatives and little involvement in activities in the region	Potential exists for a condition of continuous instability in internal and external relationships regarding resource management and allocation and economic develop-ment, slowing down decision making, intensifying a focus on process at the expense of final decisions, and sharpening value differences within the community and between the commu-nity and regional and national interests

be moved in or is in place. Broadening the community skills base broadens the range of possibilities for locally based economic initiatives. Building a local economy moves a community from being involved in sustainable development to being a contributor to a sustainable future.

Potential for Community Contributions to Sustainable Development

There are social conditions that, if they exist in combination within any particular community, can enhance the potential for substantial contributions by the community to sustainable development. These conditions include a cohesive community vision of its future, a significant measure of community control over or input into decisions affecting service delivery and resource management, and a style in dealing with others that is predictable and constructive, with the expectation of the same treatment in return.

A cohesive community vision or sense of identity is possible when different community interests have a reason and a willingness to work together. This cooperation involves defining, understanding, and accepting the various aspirations of the different groups within the community – a process not unlike that used in the development of regional conservation strategies and much like that used by the City of Whitehorse in community planning. Many of the sharpest images of northern communities projecting a cohesive sense of identity come from the intense debates on issues such as the Meech Lake Accord or the Mackenzie Valley Pipeline hearings, when communities felt threatened and saw themselves as minority voices trying to influence more politically powerful players in the strongest possible fashion (see Moscovici and Nemeth 1974 for a discussion of factors contributing to minority influence). The challenge for northern communities is to articulate their aspirations for the future during the course of everyday business as clearly as they can under difficult and politically charged circumstances. The complementary challenge is to express a sense of community identity that defines the character of the community in terms that are more social than political. Without efforts to develop a widespread sense of community identity, the potential exists for division within the community on important questions of resource protection and economic development. At best, this can slow progress on resolving issues; at worst, it can result in a loss of opportunities and the unnecessary limiting of the economic potential of the community (see Tables 5.3a and b).

Local control of and community involvement in management decisions are made possible in northern communities through two different processes. First, self-government arrangements set out the jurisdiction of First Nations governments over treaty settlement land and resources. They also define the authority of First Nations governments to deliver a range of programs and services to their citizens, and to administer justice, as agreed upon with the federal government and the relevant provincial or territorial government. Second, land claim agreements provide for a linked array of resource management and resource allocation advisory bodies, from land-use planning commissions to local renewable resource councils. Each body provides a forum for input from both the Aboriginal and non-Aboriginal communities, and each one includes representation from both communities. Aboriginal communities with self-government agreements will have considerable autonomy over their own affairs. Non-Aboriginal communities and Aboriginal communities without self-government agreements will be drawn much closer to resource management decisions through the work of the management advisory boards and committees. The potential for the delegation of the delivery of social services, health care, and educational services, including third-level education, to local boards also increases options for community control over matters of critical importance to community well-being.

The extent to which these community-based arrangements for governance can be realized is limited practically by the current fiscal conditions of all levels of government in Canada. However, real means are available to enhance the say of communities in activities in their local areas. The effectiveness of resource management boards and committees in giving a voice to communities, and in advancing the process of sustainable development, depends to a great extent on the ability of the bodies themselves to clarify their respective roles and responsibilities, particularly as the function of one board relates to the responsibilities of another and to the respective government managing authority.

The perception and the reality of local control over matters affecting community sustainable development empower the community in its dealings with regional and national government agencies, with outside proponents of development proposals, and with outside interest groups trying to influence regional management decisions. Involvement in decision making moves the community from being an advocate of to being a partner in the initiative in question, whether it be the establishment of a park, the construction of a highway, the excavation of a mine, or the building of a sawmill.

Partnership is easier to achieve and maintain when there is mutual respect between the partners. This is a sensitive issue for northerners. Valid or not, there is a strong historical feeling among northerners in general that they are all too often overlooked or disregarded by the political and economic powers that be in the south. Northerners point to the Meech Lake Accord as an example, but each person has a private collection of stories of "sins" of omission and "sins" of commission. Next to the stories about bad flight experiences, stories about the many ways in which outsiders don't understand the North are the glue that unites northern residents in a common bond, especially waiting to board flights back home at departure lounges in

Vancouver, Edmonton, Winnipeg, Ottawa, and Dorval. So the question of relationships is fundamental to the prospects of sustainable development in northern communities. If there is a northern view about mutually respectful relationships between communities and others, then it is that they have to be built from the ground up over time and are few in number.

Reciprocity in the relationships between northern communities and others involved in activities in the region provides a measure of social stability and facilitates progress on initiatives. More importantly, reciprocity increases the probability that mutually acceptable solutions will be worked out when problems arise and when unforeseen circumstances warrant special attention. Reciprocity in a relationship is possible only when all parties bring something to the relationship and accept that they have responsibilities arising out of the relationship.

There are some general indicators of reciprocity in relationships, including regular formal and informal contact between the parties, arrangements for sharing information, procedures for joint issue identification and problem solving, and mechanisms to raise an alert over any matter of concern. When these indicators are evident in an analysis of working arrangements on economic, environmental, and social issues, they constitute a positive signal that the initiatives support rather than impede sustainable development.

The long-standing expectation about outside investors in the North is that they be attentive and sensitive to northern aspirations and that they provide capital, technical expertise, and a willingness to involve northerners in the project. The expectation about the federal, provincial, and territorial governments is that they consult with communities in a meaningful way before they act and that they work to support community priorities and aspirations, including the provision of community infrastructure and services. The expectation about communities themselves is an evolving one. Communities, clearly, can provide labour and business support to enterprises. More and more, they can be a source of some capital, especially First Nations communities with settled land claims. They can act as agents for the senior governments on specific programs or projects. In a more intangible way, they can inject a sense of cultural appropriateness into the ways in which activities are planned and implemented. Fundamentally, they can listen and respond respectfully, clearly, and in a timely manner to initiatives, in the same way that they expect to be treated. In the North, as much as anywhere else, sustainable development, at its most elemental, is about sustainable relationships.

Implications for Achieving Sustainable Development in Communities

Northern communities are distinctive. They are different from communities in the south. With respect to sustainable development, however, the differences are more a matter of degrees than of fundamentals. The institutional and social conditions that must exist in northern communities to facilitate sustainable development must also exist in rural communities in the other regions of Canada.

The institutional factors that set the foundations for sustainable development are beyond the direct control of the communities affected. The responsibility for resource management, protection, and allocation and for communication and transportation infrastructure is largely territorial, provincial, and federal in Canada. The ability to delegate authority to a local level and to provide mechanisms through which communities can have greater involvement in decision making rests with the higher orders of government. In essence, the potential for any community to contribute to sustainable development in the region, and to have a sustainable future, depends on the quality of attention and judgment made by government agencies at arm's length from the community in question. Regular and comprehensive communication between communities and these government agencies is important to ensure that the best relevant information is fed into the senior governments' decision-making processes.

However, vertical lines of communication between orders of government in Canada are not reliably strong. Moreover, horizontal lines of communication between agencies within governments are no stronger. The impact, if only in terms of delays in decisions and the management of the odd intergovernmental crisis, can be substantial when measured against progress on community sustainable development. In periods when the relationships between a community and other levels of government are problem laden, as they are currently, due to budget cutbacks, the absence of established lines of communication on matters of common concern makes the exchange of information between governments all the more difficult. Mechanisms need to be established to facilitate the exchange of information between orders of government on regional and local issues of sustainable development.

The social conditions necessary to support community sustainable development follow a developmental sequence. Health is a necessary precursor to ongoing income generation. Economic security is an important contributor to the development of a positive sense of identity and to the establishment of long-term social relationships. These conditions represent stages in both personal growth and community growth. The responsibility for addressing issues and resolving problems at each stage is entirely the community's. Community sustainable development requires grassroots as well as institutional involvement and commitment. Continuing work within the community, at a formal level and an informal level, is essential to ensure the long-term maintenance of community health, economic security, and relationships with others.

There is one responsibility of the higher orders of government that rural and remote northern communities depend on: the funding of education, health, and social services. That funding for services comes from the provincial or territorial governments and in some instances the federal government does not, however, abrogate the responsibility of each community and its residents to continue the ongoing process of community social development.

Recommendations

There are several levels at which institutional support can be directed to help northern communities and their residents invest in sustainable economic and social development.

The conditions necessary to encourage employment and economic diversification can be enhanced through continued emphasis on completing and implementing equitable land claims and self-government agreements in the North. Also to this end, progress should continue on the devolution of provincial-type resource management responsibilities from the federal to the territorial governments. The settlement of outstanding land claims, self-government, and devolution will mature and stabilize regional government systems and result, as a side benefit, in the injection of capital and a resident core of professional administrators into northern regions.

As government systems consolidate at a regional level, processes for the local control and management of natural resources should be built around a clear definition of the respective roles, responsibilities, and relationships between regional governments, community governments, and appointed management bodies. Without such clarification, there is an increased potential for competition, lack of coordination, and poor communication between the various advisory groups and agencies. This situation runs counter to the principle of constructive relationships that is at the heart of meaningful community involvement in sustainable development. Indeed, if the essential condition for the involvement of northern communities in regional sustainable development is a set of healthy relationships within communities and a set of constructive relationships between communities and economic and environmental interests, then a number of factors need to be addressed to ensure the nurturing of such relationships. These factors include the collection and exchange of information relevant to sustainable development decision making, the creation of mechanisms that support dialogue on sustainable development, the development of formal institutional perspectives on sustainable development, and formal and informal attention to integrity and a sense of community responsibility in relationships.

In terms of assembling and distributing relevant and comprehensive information, analytical frameworks are needed that highlight social factors in the analysis of sustainable development issues. Recommendations on actions toward sustainable development will be addressed and implemented only when they have relevance within the social circumstances of the people to whom the recommendations are directed. In this regard, indices of personal and community social and economic health should be defined and included in provincial and territorial state-of-the-environment reports. Ten-year regional infrastructure plans should be included in updates on northern conservation strategies and sustainable development plans. Social, economic, resource, and environmental data, where possible, should be aggregated regionally to better represent a community perspective on sustainable development. Monitoring reports on regional land-use plans, compiled by provincial and territorial agencies, are an appropriate means of assembling and distributing these data. If used for this purpose, such reports would help to maintain a human dimension to the implementation of regional land-use plans. On a broader level, territorial government statistical agencies should champion a project on qualitative and quantitative indicators of sustainable development for small populations, with specific attention to gender and age factors (see Human Development Index 1995).

Mechanisms that support dialogue on sustainable development require three characteristics: (1) they should be comprehensive in focus, (2) they should be inclusive regarding participation, and (3) they should be structured with care to address the specific circumstances at hand. In support of comprehensive and inclusive dialogue on local issues of sustainable development, resource management and resource allocation advisory committees should meet periodically with counterpart bodies in the social service, community service, and training fields to address and integrate perspectives on the community and social dimensions of sustainable development. Where specific consultation at a community level is necessary, as a part of the ongoing dialogue on sustainable development, it should be implemented with care and consideration to achieve a productive outcome. Multistakeholder groups, either ad hoc groups or standing bodies, could be used by government agencies to advise on consultation processes designed to minimize polarization when different interest groups clearly have divergent values and aspirations. In broader terms, as work in the North continues on implementing and refining regimes of resource and land management, community roles, involvement, and access points should be defined for regional land-use planning and for environmental assessment processes. Specific and well-understood community access points facilitate the engagement of community members in the debate.

Reams of information and extensive debate on issues can yield little progress without a set of viewpoints and organizing principles. Communities should incorporate, as a part of their community plans, a vision statement that sets out the social, economic, and environmental aspirations of the community and that defines the community in relation to its surrounding region. To give concrete expression to their general vision statements, communities, working with appropriate territorial and provincial government agencies, should sponsor ongoing community-based programs of sustainable development such as recycling, organic composting, and cleanup drives. The joint goals of these programs should be community awareness of and personal involvement in sustainable activities. To reinforce individual and collective visions at appropriate intervals, associations of municipalities should incorporate biannual workshops on community sustainable development into their annual general meeting programs. Relevant officials from senior government agencies should be encouraged to attend, as should representatives from First Nations and unorganized communities.

Ultimately, with all the planning, discussion, information gathering, and analysis, and when all the decisions about resource allocation have been made cautiously or carelessly, sustainable development depends on people acting with a sense of both personal integrity and collective responsibility that supersedes individual self-interest. The health of ecosystems requires the containment of egosystems! Politicians must act on principle as much as or more than on expediency. Bureaucrats must learn that people unschooled in systems analysis have worthwhile perspectives to offer. They must also learn that the world is not saved or lost on policy papers – the natural extension of the all-night term paper at graduate school. Advocacy groups must learn that victory comes more from understanding than from vilifying opposing perspectives. Community residents must understand that local interests are sometimes not the only interests that have a legitimate place at the table, especially when the outside interests are paying the freight. Academics and businesspeople must reject the nineteenth-century notion that the scarcely populated northern regions of the country are playgrounds to be enjoyed but not invested in. Collectively, we need to understand that true community sustainable development is about improving the human condition and enhancing connections between people.

References
Bastedo, J. 1987. "Framework for a Northwest Territories Conservation Strategy." *Canadian Society of Environmental Biologists Newsletter/Bulletin* 44,2: 47-55.
Bissoondath, N. 1994. *Selling Illusions: The Cult of Multiculturalism in Canada.* Toronto: Penguin Books.
Doubleday, N. 1990. "The Inuit Regional Conservation Strategy: Sustainable Development in the Circumpolar Region." In E. Smith, ed., *Sustainable Development through Northern Conservation Strategies* (83-90). Calgary: University of Calgary Press.
Fuller, S., and T. McTiernan. 1987. "Old Crow and the Northern Yukon: Achieving Sustainable Renewable Resource Utilization." *Alternatives* 14,1: 18-25.

Government of the Northwest Territories. 1995. Presentation to the Canadian Radio-television and Telecommunications Commission, Yellowknife, 15 March.

–. 1996. *Statistics Quarterly.* Vol. 18, no. 2. Yellowknife: Government of the Northwest Territories.

Government of Yukon. 1996a. *Discussions on Maintenance of Dempster Highway Continue.* News release 169. Whitehorse: Government of Yukon.

–. 1996b. *Yukon Annual Statistical Review: 1995.* Whitehorse: Government of Yukon.

–. 1996c. *Yukon Monthly Statistical Review: September 1996.* Whitehorse: Government of Yukon.

Hall, E.T. 1983. *The Dance of Life: The Other Dimension of Time.* New York: Anchor Books.

Hinkle, S., L. Fox-Cardamone, J.A. Haselau, R. Brown, and L.M. Irwin. 1996. "Grassroots Political Action as an Intergroup Phenomenon." *Journal of Social Issues* 52,1: 39-51.

Hodge, R.A. 1996. "A Systemic Approach to Assessing Progress toward Sustainability." In A. Dale and J.B. Robinson, eds., *Achieving Sustainable Development* (267-92). Vancouver: UBC Press.

Inglis, J. 1990. "The UNESCO Canada/Man and the Biosphere Program." In E. Smith, ed., *Sustainable Development through Northern Conservation Strategies* (141-48). Calgary: University of Calgary Press.

International Union for Conservation of Nature and Natural Resources. 1980. World Conservation Strategy. IUCN. Gland, Switzerland. 46 pages.

Jull, P. 1991. *The Politics of Northern Frontiers.* Darwin: North Australia Research Unit, Australian National University.

Kassi, N. 1987. "This Land Has Sustained Us." *Alternatives* 14,1: 20-1.

Mayton II, D.M., S.J. Ball-Rokeach, and W.E. Loges. 1994. "Human Values and Social Issues: An Introduction." *Journal of Social Issues* 50,4: 1-8.

McKechnie, G.E. 1971. *Environmental Response Inventory: Booklet.* Palo Alto, CA: Consulting Psychologists Press.

McTiernan, T. 1982. "An Examination of Some Referential and Causal Attributions Underlying Stereotype Content." PhD diss., University of British Columbia.

–. 1990. "A Conservation Strategy for the Yukon: Process and Products." In E. Smith, ed., *Sustainable Development through Northern Conservation Strategies* (27-42). Calgary: University of Calgary Press.

Moscovici, S., and C. Nemeth. 1974. "Social Influence II: Minority Influence." In C. Nemeth, ed., *Social Psychology: Classic and Contemporary Integrations.* Chicago: Rand McNally.

National Task Force on Environment and Economy. 1987. Report. Downsview, ON: Canadian Council of Resource and Environment Ministers.

Olson, R.L. 1995. "Sustainability as a Social Vision." *Journal of Social Issues* 51,4: 15-35.

Pell, D., and S. Wismer. 1987. "The Role and Limitations of Community-Based Economic Development in Canada's North." *Alternatives* 14,1: 31-4.

Prescott-Allen, R., and C. Prescott-Allen. 1990. "Circumpolar Conservation Priorities." In E. Smith, ed., *Sustainable Development through Northern Conservation Strategies* (119-33). Calgary: University of Calgary Press.

Revenue Canada. 1995. Form T4039(E) Rev. 95.

Sadler, B. 1996. "Sustainability Strategies and Green Planning: Recent Canadian and International Experience." In A. Dale and J.B. Robinson, eds., *Achieving Sustainable Development* (23-70). Vancouver: UBC Press.

Snider, E. 1990. "Arctic Marine Conservation Strategy." In E. Smith, ed., *Sustainable Development through Northern Conservation Strategies* (99-106). Calgary: University of Calgary Press.

Task Force on Northern Conservation. 1984. *Report of the Task Force on Northern Conservation.* Vancouver: Agency Press.

United Nations Development Programme. Human Development Index 1995. Human Development Report 1995. Cary, NC: Oxford University Press.

Urquhart, D. 1994. *Skookum's North: The "Paws" Collection.* Whitehorse: Lost Moose Publishing.

Waring, M. 1988. *If Women Counted: A New Feminist Economics.* San Francisco: Harper San Francisco.

World Commission on Environment and Development. 1987. *Our Common Future.* Oxford: Oxford University Press.

6
Sustainable Communities and Sustainable Agriculture on the Prairies
Michael E. Gertler

Introduction[1]

Farming and ranching shape the landscape, economy, and social life of the Prairies. Although there has been much debate about definitions of sustainability, and about the status and resiliency of agricultural resources, farms, and rural communities, there is no doubt that agriculture in the region faces multiple environmental, economic, and social challenges. These sustainable development challenges are often framed so as to focus on a small number of parameters, such as profitable returns to farming plus acceptable levels of soil loss. Broader questions of the human, cultural, and community implications of competing solutions are not addressed or are dealt with only rhetorically. In this chapter, such issues are accorded a greater importance. The goal of sustainable development in agriculture is taken to include cultural as well as ecological diversity. People – with their multiple concerns as workers, owners, producers, consumers, kin, neighbours, citizens, group members, and community members – are the agents and arbiters of a sustainable agriculture, and their well-being is the most important indicator.

Sustainable agriculture is viewed here as an appropriate set of resource-conserving farming practices but also as an orientation or approach that seeks to protect environmental values while pursuing broader social objectives related to health, emancipation, and democratic control. In this conception, sustainable agriculture hinges on appropriate relationships "between people *and people* and nature" (Allen 1993, 5). Community enters the equation both as a necessary condition and as a worthy goal. Can sustainable production systems be developed and can they endure without a community of concern that has more than an instrumental relationship with the working landscape? Does a system of production qualify as sustainable if it undermines the economies of local communities? Is sustainable production conceivable without sustainable communities? After reviewing important changes occurring in the organization of Prairie farming, in rural communities, and in the lives of rural residents, this chapter addresses the possible links between communities, organizational arrangements, and farming systems that promote sustainability. This discussion is followed by a critical evaluation of several major initiatives being taken in the name of agricultural sustainability. The chapter concludes with a discussion of pre-requisites for sustainable farming and sustainable rurality on the Prairies, including necessary institutional and organizational developments.

The Social and Economic Context

Farm-based rural economies on the Prairies have suffered the effects of depressed commodity prices since the early 1980s. Low grain and hog prices in the late 1990s have brought renewed threats of financial crisis. Reduced incomes combined with high debt loads have pushed many farmers toward bankruptcy. Compared with the survivors, the casualties of the crisis of the 1980s and early 1990s generally were guilty of little more than bad timing: they entered farming or expanded their operations when land prices and then interest rates hit record highs. Then grain prices sank to historic lows, and land values plummeted.

The agrarian crisis on the Prairies has social, economic, and ecological dimensions. Communities as well as individuals show signs of depression. Competitive pressures originating globally and locally promote rapid restructuring and new inequalities. Fiscal crises, free trade, and a penchant for market-oriented regulatory arrangements have all contributed to a redesign of government programs. Deregulation (or reregulation) in agri-culture, trade, and transportation has had significant impacts. Services and infrastructure are being reorganized in the context of funding cuts, rising costs, and new demands. Reduced support for farmers has been combined with significant public investments in major initiatives, such as agricul-tural biotechnology, that are argued to be essential to competitiveness. Farmers generally have increased their use of industrial inputs, but the industrial model of agriculture has come under unparalleled criticism for impacts on biodiversity, wildlife habitat, water quality, soil quality, human health, and animal welfare (Altieri 1998; Fox 1997). With increasing fre-quency, industrial approaches to agriculture are associated with health, environmental, and ethical problems that transcend local settings and the agrifood sector itself.

Farming has gone through continuous rationalization and restructuring. There is an increasing divergence between farmers who have managed to grow large in terms of acreage, capital, and production; those who have seen their farm operations grow at moderate rates; and those who have remained small-scale producers or have downsized as they rely more heav-ily on off-farm income. The largest farms tend to differ from their smaller neighbours in key respects: the large farm is more likely to be incorporated;

the land farmed is often spread over several jurisdictions; much of this land may be rented; the farm requires the labour of hired workers as well as several family members; and farm managers are strongly networked to extralocal sources of information, inputs, finance, and markets. Their size, wealth, and "reach" in terms of ability to make and use connections outside the immediate region give the larger farmers a different perspective on the rural community. They may travel widely on business and as members of organizations. Investments may be diversified outside agriculture and the local region.

Farming on the Prairies is increasingly specialized, though sometimes the new specialties contribute to regional diversification. Farmers may be quite different from their neighbours not only in terms of scale and wealth but also in terms of commodities produced, links to agribusiness firms, participation in agricultural organizations, and involvement with the local community. Attitudes and practices with respect to business management, neighbouring, and resource stewardship can also be widely divergent. Some of this variability indicates cultural diversity in farming and "room for manoeuvre" (Ploeg 1993, 248) that augurs well for alternative approaches to sustainable agriculture. On the other hand, there appear to be important structural barriers to the implementation of sustainable farming practices (Gertler 1992). The momentum continues to be with productivist visions, reductionist approaches to problem identification and resolution, simplified ecosystems, increased reliance on agrochemical inputs, substitution of capital for labour, and aggressive expansion.

The rural Prairies is one part of Canada where farm (and ranch) households still account for a substantial share of the population. Nevertheless, thanks to a reduced labour force in agriculture, and to the relative growth of other sectors and activities, farmers and farm families are now the minority even in areas considered predominantly agricultural. While farm people continue to play a large role in local communities, and farm operations are reproduced in the context of these communities, the culture and the politics of farm communities are changing as agriculture is transformed. Communities vary with respect to resource base and history, but new demographic, economic, social, and institutional conditions throw into doubt previous conceptions of rurality, what it means to be a farmer, and the very foundations of community. Like cities, rural communities have been affected by the growing emphasis on individual rights and needs; smaller families and households; greater geographic mobility combined with more time spent commuting to work, school, and other activities; increasing disparity in income and education; greater specialization in the workforce; greater participation of women in the wage labour force; and greater choice with respect to where and how to participate in communities or associations. Although many of these changes are not uniquely rural, some of them occur in forms without parallel in urban places.

The context for sustainable agriculture and sustainable communities has been fundamentally altered by changes within and outside local farming economies. The resilience of rural agricultural economies is challenged by the restructuring of farming and farm markets, demographic change, and narrow conceptual frameworks with respect to sustainable development. Agricultural abundance persists, but agricultural development is still pursued with little regard for social impacts, economic and ecological consequences, or critical connections between people and land (Gruchow 1995). Issues of equity and community are largely ignored. The multiple connections between sustainable communities and a sustainable agriculture are generally not examined.

Connecting Sustainable Farming and Sustainable Communities

In resource-based economies, there are obvious connections between sustainable resource use and community sustainability. If resources are depleted, then the foundations of the local economy are compromised. There are less obvious reciprocal links. In a sector based largely on private land ownership and moderate-scale firms, the widespread implementation of sustainable practices requires a shared vision and commitment. Communities can provide necessary motivations, supports, and social sanctions, along with the requisite collective memory and a long-term planning horizon (Gertler 1994). Sustainable production regimes also require appropriate organizational and institutional arrangements. These arrangements must be elaborated and negotiated both locally and regionally. Many of the organizational frameworks for pooling resources, sharing costs, and equitably distributing the gains of sustainable agricultural development will have to be worked out and set up at the local level. Communities are important as sites or contexts for the elaboration of institutional and organizational arrangements that reflect and promote long-term collective interests in sustainable development. Thus, it can be argued that a sustainable agriculture depends on a triangular linkage between mutually reinforcing components: community, appropriate organizations and institutions, and sustainable resource management practices.

Is this community necessarily local? Both local and extralocal communities are important. Although geographically extensive networks can provide information and support, locally rooted communities are critically important for the sustainable management of agricultural resources. Many of the required observations and actions are local, though not necessarily at the microscale of a single field or farm. Individuals acting alone cannot adequately monitor and manage watersheds, build economic infrastructure, influence the environmental behaviour of neighbours, or maintain a culture of sustainable living. Of course, the characteristics of the communities involved will matter a great deal. A community dominated by a few individuals cannot unite on common agendas for sustainable development. Equity is a crucial variable: equitable sharing of costs and gains and equitable participation in the ownership and control of resources. Community and collective interests must be reflected in key relationships, including those involving property.

What are the prospects for a robust and cosmopolitan localism that builds on historic strengths yet avoids common forms of inequality, discrimination, and oppression? Whether Prairie communities are experiencing expansion or contraction in population, business, and tax base, traditional forms of community life are passing. Nor are some proposed new forms of localism – for example, bioregionalism, "buy local" programs, or appeals to refocus on indigenous, endogenous, or local knowledge – likely to prevail in any pure form (Liodakis 1997). Still, local community remains important for maintaining local infrastructure, for neighbouring, and for resisting unwanted development. Local community, and the informal economy that it hosts, is important to the quality of life of most of us, especially to those with limited mobility.

Community on the Prairies has always meant a mix of short- and long-distance engagements. From the pioneering era, settlers on the Prairies went to cities to shop, trade, and find services. Many families migrated and resettled more than once in living memory. Many migrant workers worked on Prairie farms and railways or in mines and service industries. Relatives were scattered around the nation and the globe. Rural kids often left to find freedom and fortune or to fight overseas. The wealthy and the well connected travelled freely (Siggins 1991). Unlike the dairy-based farming economies of Ontario and Quebec, the Prairie agricultural economy has been heavily dependent on long-distance trade since the first sod was broken. This dependency engendered awareness of life outside the local setting and of political-economic relationships with other regions. Moreover, immigrants, teachers, preachers, peddlers, itinerant workers, and politicians brought the culture of the wider world into every part of rural western Canada.

Extreme forms of localism have never been a dominant characteristic of the social ecology of Prairie inhabitants (Gruchow 1995). Before and after European contact, Aboriginal peoples moved around a good deal. They traded, trapped, and followed herds. Those dwelling on the open prairie often left it in the winter in favour of forested areas offering shelter, fuel, fish, and game (Bennett 1969). The pattern of movement between zones and between settlements continues as those with primary residence in a city relocate to rural reserve communities for parts of the year or parts of their lives (and vice versa). Other Prairie people continue to partake in this tradition, farming and maintaining an urban residence, going to the southern United States for winter breaks, or retiring to British Columbia. Even among the Hutterites, the conservative Anabaptist farming communities whose kibbutz-like colonies now number over 200 on the Prairies, localism is far from complete. Men travel frequently for purposes of trade or to access services. All colony members are involved in periodic visits with other colonies. The heads of particular colony enterprises, such as the hog boss, typically maintain contact with a network of counterpart Hutterite producers to share market and technical information and to collaborate on volume purchases. Moreover, as with most of the farmers around them, local acquisitions are mixed with purchases made at a distance.

Localism should not be taken for granted, and historic aspects of rural community life that did revolve more around local relationships have been extensively transformed. If community is valuable or necessary for implementing sustainable production systems, then from whence is this community likely to come? This question remains open. Pessimists can point to evidence of individualism, disengagement, and disaffection. Indeed, one reaction to the exigencies of competitive survival is to withdraw from non-economic aspects of collective life and to refocus on networking with commercial contacts. Optimists can cite evidence of the resilience of community, its continual reconstruction, and the creative blending of localized forms with extremely long-range networks supported by improved communications and personal mobility.

A potential connection between sustainable farming movements and sustainable rural communities is illustrated by field evidence from the northern Great Plains (Flora 1995). This study suggests that, where a group of alternative agricultural practitioners has successfully established itself, its members can contribute to sustainable community development. Patterns of problem solving cultivated in the movement toward sustainable agriculture are transferable to other kinds of development. Skills developed by practitioners of organic farming – and other nonmainstream versions of sustainable agriculture – include researching and evaluating alternatives, mobilizing local resources, initiating inclusive processes of decision making, and building horizontal and vertical networks. The presence of a critical mass of alternative producers can lead to such practices being applied to a wider set of community development objectives and can result in enhanced well-being, greater economic security, and broader civic participation. Sustainable agriculture and its practitioners can promote the formation of social capital, leading to more sustainable rural communities (Bird, Bultena, and Gardner 1995; Flora 1995).

Many who are interested in alternative approaches to sustainable farming have had to search beyond the local to find an adequate community of support. Organic farmers form associations and share experiences, concerns, and strategies across provincial and national borders. The need for a community of support is recognized by many promoters of alternative approaches to farming. For example, families interested in the approach known as Holistic Resource Management receive a newsletter originating in New Mexico and are encouraged to meet regularly with other families who have adopted this model. They support one another in the development of new philosophies of farming and ranching and in learning new techniques for managing grasslands and livestock.

The need for some sort of community connection and shared identity is not lost on those who promote conventional farming technologies or their offshoots. Agribusiness firms selling machinery, seed, or agrochemical inputs provide caps with company logos – and farmers frequently wear them. As discussed below, input suppliers, extension experts, and scientists who have promoted zero-till agriculture have employed many strategies designed to build positive associations, social networks, and common understandings. They have sponsored soil conservation groups, field days, demonstration plots, and promotional literature. A farmer experimenting with this set of practices need never feel that he or she is in it alone.

The next section focuses on several significant initiatives pursued in the name of sustainable production. They include recent efforts to promote diversification of the agricultural economy, especially the expansion of hog production in large barns. Contemporary developments in tillage and crop protection practices are also examined, notably zero-till techniques and "precision farming." Agricultural biotechnology represents another major effort to apply high technology to farming. In each case, current developments are reviewed in light of environmental claims, risks, and possible implications for the social ecology of farming and rural communities.

Agricultural Diversification and Industrial Hog Production
Diversification of agriculturally based economies is a preoccupation of rural-development experts worldwide. This has also been a focus of much recent effort by federal, provincial, and regional/local agencies interested in the growth and stability of rural Prairie economies. Farmers have been encouraged to consider nontraditional crops and livestock, and many programs support entrepreneurs willing to establish a business that builds on local resources or provides employment. There have been notable successes, but the whole campaign lacks a holistic vision and a thorough commitment to sustainable development (Gertler 1998b).

In farming, diversification has often meant a new form of specialized production, not a return to the flexible regime of classical mixed farming, in which external input use was low. Moreover, the markets and technologies involved often reduce rather than increase local links between farm households. The producers involved join specialized trade groups, rely on nonfarm firms for key components or inputs, and market in niche markets or specialized channels rather than in general commodity markets. Cumulatively, this reorganization of cropping systems and commercial relations leads to significant changes in the politics and social dynamics of farm communities. Local processes of solidarity may be further weakened through the erosion of local interdependencies and linkages (Gertler et al. forthcoming 1999).

Where diversification of the agriculturally based rural economy has involved new ventures with multiple partners, it can contribute to the formation of social infrastructure that supports further development in the local economy. However, a broadly beneficial form of association and co-operation is not automatic. The farmer partners in new ventures, such as large seed-cleaning plants, grain-handling facilities, feedlots, or processing plants, tend to be drawn from among the well-heeled minority. Their investment portfolios may be strengthened, but the processes of polarization may also accelerate as they consolidate their dominance in the local farm economy. Moreover, larger farmers are not the only partners involved: these projects are often joint ventures with nonfarm corporations. These agribusiness firms have the upper hand in terms of market information, proprietary technology, and organizational resources (Gertler 1998b). The power differential is reflected in the character of agreements and contracts under which these new entities operate.[2]

Livestock production on the Prairies has increased in the case of beef cattle, but many other types of livestock have diminished in number over the longer term. This is true of dairy cattle, horses, sheep, and many kinds of fowl. Moreover, the number of herds and flocks has decreased even more rapidly than the number of farms. Livestock production has been consolidated, and farmers have specialized – sometimes getting out of animal production altogether to concentrate on crop production. The separation of crop and livestock production, and the concentration of livestock on a smaller number of farms, have important – and mostly negative – implications for sustainable resource management and environmental protection (Gertler 1992).

Given the removal of subsidies from grain transportation, and the need for value-added activities in rural areas, hog production is being actively promoted on the Prairies. Processors, consulting firms, provincial governments, agricultural scientists, marketing cooperatives, and economic developers are all promoting an industrial model of hog rearing involving large, specialized facilities (Moen 1997). This initiative has multiple and contradictory implications for the sustainability of farming and rural communities. Rural communities are often quite desperate for new investment and employment, and farmers are anxious to find local opportunities to market grain. Large hog barns may help to increase production in line with the needs of processors seeking to expand their operations and competing for retail market share.

Although there has been active promotion of the model, it is difficult to assess the full implications of a switch to larger-scale, more industrial hog production. There will be impacts on the social organization of farm communities. The diversity of local economies may be increased where there are net gains in the number of pigs produced, but diversity at the farm level will be reduced as small producers see themselves edged out of the hog business. The exit of small- and medium-sized producers may be accelerated by the demise of producer marketing boards that become problematic from the point of view of large producers and processors. On the positive side, where the new barns are set up as partnerships, they may also allow some grain farmers to invest in a profitable livestock operation and to create an outlet for their own feed-grain production without having to become directly involved in the management of a piggery. If the implications for the farm sector are mixed, then the impacts on local communities are also a mix of costs and benefits. Although some additional tax revenues will accrue, the siting and the tax treatment of new hog barns may mean that governments (at all levels) will have a hard time recouping the costs in terms of road maintenance and other infrastructure. Provided that skilled managers and dedicated staff can be recruited, these establishments can produce a standardized product meeting the specifications of packers, and local economies may also benefit. Where significant new employment is created, however, there may also be costs associated with providing a range of services to families that move into small towns.

A fuller evaluation of the implications of this industrial model of production reveals risks and limitations from the perspective of sustainability. Until recently, most Prairie pigs were raised in small herds, on mixed farms, without the use of specialized buildings. Pigs were part of a flexible strategy: production could be expanded when grain prices were low or when it was necessary to generate additional income from the farm. The profitability of the new specialized barns is sensitive to the relative prices of feed grains (e.g., barley) and hogs. This price ratio will fluctuate from year to year, and this is potentially bad news for those investing heavily in structures that have no other economic use. Some of the costs of new barns may be underwritten by the public treasury. Consulting firms and other investors involved have adopted an arrangement well known in the oil and gas industry: the limited partnership. Under this formula, losses in the pig operation can be used to offset income in other businesses. Investors with other sources of income can benefit from investments in hog barns even if they lose money.

Whether individually or jointly owned, the new barns involve major capital commitments. Well-established farmers with capital reserves are best able to avail themselves of opportunities of this sort. The various advantages favouring investors with substantial resources will speed the differentiation taking place in the livestock sector – with a minority of larger producers expanding rapidly to control a significant share of production and farm assets. Moreover, these barns are predicated on hired management and labour, and they imply the creation of another social group at the same time: the employer-investor farmer. The addition of such positions changes the social class structure of farming and will have implications for the character of farm politics and the social dynamics of rural communities.

In addition to cheap feed and inexpensive land, many parts of the Prairies are attractive as sites for intensive hog production precisely because of problems that have been encountered with industrial hog farming elsewhere. On the Prairies, sparse population reduces the potential for nuisance conflicts with neighbours, and (usually) dry landscapes reduce the problems associated with controlling pollution of surface water and wells. However, sparse population and a typically dry climate do not eliminate air and water pollution, truck traffic, or impacts on real estate values. Relatively relaxed environmental regulations reduce start-up and operating costs, but they may only be postponing the investments required to mitigate ecological impacts. Low density of pig populations combined with harsh winters limit the spread of pig diseases, but this is not a permanent exemption from the buildup of pathogens.

Whenever hundreds or thousands of animals are brought together in one complex, there are unavoidable impacts on human and herd health. The confined production of pigs is predicated on routine use of antibiotics, some of which are similar to products used in human medicine to fight closely related groups of organisms. The problem of antibiotic-resistant infections that is now taxing the hospitals of North America is bound to have repercussions for the use of related products in industrial livestock production (Khachatourians 1998). Moreover, these large hog facilities remain notoriously vulnerable to epidemics – witness the recent slaughter of nearly 3,000,000 pigs in Taiwan due to hoof-and-mouth disease and the slaughter of some 2,000,000 pigs in the Netherlands as a result of swine fever (Reuter 1997a, b; White 1997).

Although the animal welfare movement is not yet powerful in the region, the confined production of livestock has raised ethical questions for consumers in many parts of the world. This expanding social movement has strong links to other environmental and social movements. It would seem reasonable and prudent to incorporate "best practices" in terms of environmentally sound and humane systems of production into the design of any new structures. With a few honourable exceptions, this is not being done. The Prairies are missing an opportunity to build on an image of clean air and water and to capitalize on the chance to differentiate their products to supply the growing market for ecologically and ethically justifiable food production. Prairie farmers and other taxpayers may be investing in costly technology that is in danger of rapid obsolescence on ecological, economic, and ethical grounds.

Precision Farming and Zero-Tillage

High technology has come to Prairie farm communities via a number of routes. As part of an array of technologies known as "precision farming," satellite global positioning systems and ground relay stations have been married to computers on combines and tractors. This technology allows mapping of farm fields and the application of agrochemicals according to soil characteristics or crop conditions in specific areas within fields. The technology is expensive and at a fairly early stage of development, but already a few avid Prairie farmers have begun to use it. It is supposed to allow more precisely calibrated application of fertilizers and spot spraying of herbicides based on localized weed problems. This precision, it is argued, will lead to reduced pesticide use, reduced environmental impacts, and more efficient use of inputs.

The implications of precision farming for a sustainable agriculture are not all obvious, especially at this early stage.[3] This system is predicated on the use of high-value industrial inputs. It only makes sense as part of such a package. Moreover, it is most useful to those who are farming large acreages, and it will facilitate the financially efficient management of larger farms. It may give farmers increased information about localized field conditions and production, but it cannot reinforce an ethos of land stewardship. It is connected to an engineering mentality that presumes good farming practices can be reduced to algorithms dealing with a few variables. Finally, from the farmer's perspective, it puts tremendous amounts of data into the hands of traders and input suppliers – information that they will use to target markets, price their products, and more effectively promote their wares (Swihart 1997; Wolf and Wood 1997). Although it will lead to a new round of mechanization (Briere 1997), it is unlikely that the chief beneficiaries will be average farmers or the rural communities in which they live.

Precision farming is linked in a number of ways to another innovation in field operation and soil preparation: minimum- or zero-tillage technology. These systems involve new cultivation and planting equipment (especially air-seeders) and a new generation of crop protection (pesticide) products. Herbicides, particularly glyphosate (Roundup), are used in place of tillage operations to control weeds in fallow fields and in crops. The technological package is promoted as a conservation system because less tillage means less fuel consumption and associated pollution; less soil disturbance generally reduces the risk of soil loss through erosion; and less soil erosion reduces the chance of runoff and pollution. However, adoption of zero-till technology has generally been connected with expanded use of herbicides and other agrochemical inputs and thus with increases in some associated risks for water quality, air quality, and nontarget organisms. Zero-till is only effective under certain soil and climate conditions, and its adoption is connected to a growing problem of herbicide resistance in weeds (Duckworth 1997b).

Acceptance of zero-till equipment has been encouraged by the promise of soil conservation and, especially in recent years, because it speeds critical planting operations, increases labour productivity, and reduces some machinery-related costs (McMillan 1997). Like precision farming, it is therefore linked to a restructuring of the farm sector that involves further expansion of the farm operations that survive. Zero-till allows crop farmers to expand their acreage without adding more labour. Adoption of this cropping system involves the purchase of new and usually larger equipment. This equipment, in turn, promotes the expansion of farms and fields. Larger equipment and the pursuit of "field efficiency" encourage operators to consolidate fields, clear brush, drain wetlands, and bulldoze windbreaks. Large, costly equipment also encourages renting or buying additional acreage in order to use an implement's full capacities and to recoup the investment.

Like precision farming, zero-tillage has been championed by an alliance of machinery manufacturers, agrochemical firms, soil scientists, agricultural engineers, extension agronomists, innovative farmers, and (some) conservationists. It provides an opportunity to sell a new line of equipment and an expanded market for herbicides. Because it is conceived and marketed as a technological advance offering improved efficiency and resource management, it also provides a convenient response to critics who question the sustainability of conventional cropping systems. It becomes a useful means by which mainstream agricultural science can deflect criticism and undercut arguments for more fundamental and radical approaches to sustainable agriculture – such as organic farming.

Agricultural Biotechnology

Biotechnology or, more precisely, genetic engineering (GE) is the application of new tools of cellular biology to the creation of genetically modified crops and livestock, as well as new products for treating plants and animals. Agricultural biotechnology is supported by agrochemical firms, agricultural colleges, research agencies, and governments. It has been aggressively promoted in the name of productivity, efficiency, and environmental protection. To date, the most significant application of biotechnology to Prairie farming has been the development of canola varieties that tolerate herbicides. This advance allows the packaging of genetically modified seed with broad-spectrum herbicides, a commercially attractive proposition for the companies with proprietary rights to the seed, the herbicide, or both. The package promises effective weed suppression and fewer problems with herbicides in high-value crops. Other important products of biotechnology with application to Prairie farming include veterinary pharmaceuticals, such as cattle vaccines, and transgenic crop varieties with built-in insecticidal properties. An example of the latter is a potato cultivar with an introduced gene for the production of *Bacillus thuringensis* (Bt), a bacterium with insecticidal properties.

Some products of agricultural biotechnology will be profitable for farmers, and others will be useful to processors seeking new uses for farm commodities (or to replace farm commodities). The risks for farmers, farm communities, and the overall sustainability of agriculture are not all obvious. Genetically engineered inputs are costly but do not necessarily guarantee a profitable harvest given the challenges of weather, pests, and markets. In order to gain access to novel-trait and herbicide-tolerant varieties, such as Roundup Ready Canola, farmers must sign "gene agreements" and pay a technology fee to the patent holder – in this case, Monsanto. These contracts make it clear that power relations in the industry will be used to shift risks and costs down to the farm level. It is farmers who face the most immediate risks due to consumer backlash, unintended environmental impacts, and rapid evolution of herbicide-resistant weeds or Bt-resistant bugs (Levidow 1993; Snow and Palma 1997).[4]

Given the characteristics of many of these new technologies, and the secrecy surrounding their development, it seems unlikely that farmers will effectively participate in scientific agenda setting. The commercial success of certain biotechnologies may also contribute to the neglect of broader research agendas – to a lack of diversification in university, government, and private sector research portfolios. In the high-pressure marketplace of biotechnology, researchers focus on immediate, patentable results, while work and debate on alternative systems of production are postponed (Gertler 1998a).

Biotechnology can be viewed as one component of a drive toward a larger-scale, more industrial model of farming (Boehljë 1996). The real world of agricultural biotechnology is captured in the definition suggested by Hindmarsh (1991, 196): "the scientific manipulation of organisms at the cellular level in order to produce altered, or novel, organisms that carry 'desired' or 'programmed' functions, invariably to facilitate industrial production processes." The evaluation of these technologies therefore cannot be separated from wider debates about the restructuring and sustainability of agriculture. Biotechnology may serve to mask some of the environmental and ecological contradictions of an industrialized agriculture and may divert attention from the holistic redesign of systems of production (Hindmarsh

1991). Biotechnology promotes an engineering mentality with respect to complex agronomic problems, and it encourages productivist visions as a response to issues of sustainable rural and agricultural development.

Achieving Sustainable Development in Prairie Communities

The discussion above provides a brief evaluation of key initiatives taken in the name of sustainable agriculture on the Prairies. Each includes risks and biases that reduce the potential for economically, ecologically, and socially sustainable development. Agribusiness interests appear to be paramount in the development of new technological packages while basic research on agroecology is neglected (Busch 1994). Technologies developed for commercial reasons are then presented as exogenous factors that carry opportunities and challenges. There is little disinterested leadership from the leading institutions. Farmers have a hard time evaluating the competing claims of sustainability. Most go along with what appear to be the winning products, systems, and worldviews.

There are promising options for sustainable development of agriculture and the rural economy of the Prairies. Innovative organizational and institutional arrangements will be as critical as appropriate technologies. Those concerned with sustainability must address multiple issues simultaneously (Vail 1996). This is a political and cultural challenge as well as an agronomic and engineering test. It will be necessary to consider the diverse impacts of production and consumption. The ecological efficiency of economic activities must be assessed in terms of resource depletion, degradation, conservation, and restoration. This assessment is related to the idea of full-cost accounting, which includes the long-term and off-site environmental costs and benefits of farming systems. Another dimension of sustainable development is captured by the concept of the economic multiplier, which measures the extent to which economic activities provide a further stimulus to the local economy through payroll expenditures, procurement of goods and services, and reinvestment. The economic multiplier reflects the character of the particular industry, the organization and orientation of the firms involved, and the capacity of the local economy to capture upstream and downstream development opportunities associated with a specific subsector. Many rural businesses score low on indices of this type, in part because the local economy is poorly integrated with the activities that exist. The wider social impacts of economic activities should also be considered. These impacts include concerns such as equity, the quality of employment opportunities, the fostering of civic institutions, and the development of fully competent citizens. These important effects are components of what can be called the social multiplier (see Ketilson et al. 1998). This array of concerns is addressed in part in the related practices of social impact assessment and social audit (Fairbairn et al. 1991).

The sustainable development of agriculture and rural communities will require the mobilization of many allied forces: farmers, nonfarm rural residents, researchers, public servants, food industry workers, consumers, and environmentalists. Resource managers and conservationists will need to develop their knowledge with respect to sustainable agriculture. There must be a more genuine dialogue. Sustainable rurality on the Prairies will require new connections to informed and engaged urban communities. Farmers' markets, community shared agriculture, food cooperatives, community food councils, and community kitchens are a useful start (Fieldhouse 1996; Kloppenburg, Hendrickson, and Stevenson 1996). Along with chefs, food service managers, and retailers, professionals in nutrition, health, education, community development, and social services all have vital roles in achieving the potential for genuine agricultural diversification, added value, and sustainability.

Agricultural scientists and institutions will need to explicitly address the mandate to protect and develop agricultural resources, with all that this mandate implies for biological and (agri)cultural diversity. There is a continuing role for government in research geared to public interest. Production goals must be balanced with broader goals of system stability and food security. The diversified portfolio should include agricultural ecology, long-term studies of agricultural alternatives, the environmental and social impacts of new systems of production, and research on the efficacy of practices that have been developed and refined in the hands of experienced and observant farmers.

It will be necessary to reduce the economic and social barriers that inhibit entry into farming, especially for Aboriginal peoples, new immigrants, youth, and women (Sachs 1996). Farming communities will need to learn to welcome new Canadians, back-to-the-landers, activist retirees, and female farm managers at least as enthusiastically as they do new products, companies, and favourite sons. Breaking down barriers to entry into farming will also require experimentation with new organizational arrangements under which more people can participate in farming. Various models of multioperator, multifamily production cooperatives, partnerships, and joint ventures demonstrate the potential of organizational innovations beyond the single-family farm. Multioperator farms offer distinct advantages: savings in machinery and equipment; sharing of tasks, experience, and responsibilities; greater potential for diversification and experimentation; greater capacity to institute strategies for conservation; increased personal security; development of organizational and leadership skills; and time to apply these skills to other kinds of activities and interests (Gertler and Murphy 1987).

It seems probable that cooperation and collective entrepreneurship will be important features of many of the more enduring sustainable agricultural

arrangements (Vail 1996). The extent to which various forms of cooperation are crucial to the sustainability of Prairie farming communities has not
been adequately studied. The mythologies of the independent operator
("the self-made man") and the efficiency of competitive relations continue
to reign in explanations of the survival of family-based farms and small
communities. Sustainable rural development may require a reevaluation of
the relative contributions of cooperation and competition, women and
men, nonfarmers and farmers, critics and boosters.

There are some promising signs of organizational invention and renewal
in support of sustainable rural economies on the Prairies. Roundtables bringing together Aboriginal leaders and associations representing rural municipalities in Saskatchewan are developments that reflect the growing
economic and political importance of Aboriginal communities. Rural
women have provided leadership in many facets of political and economic
life. The importance of both agricultural sustainability and alternative
approaches has received increased recognition. The National Farmers Union
newsletter frequently carries articles focusing on organic farming. The
Western Producer, the most important farm newspaper on the Prairies, has a
regular column on organic production. Both the Canadian Wheat Board and
the Saskatchewan Wheat Pool have taken steps to become players in the marketing of organic commodities. The response has been positive and greater
than expected.[5]

Organic farmers represent some of the important cultural and agricultural
diversity in Prairie farming. Their efforts to develop ecologically sound farming practices provide important clues in designing sustainable farming systems. Lacking institutional support, organic farmers are nevertheless part of a
substantial grassroots movement with local and international links to the
environmental, health food, and alternative health care movements. Organic
farmers are growing in numbers and are entering new partnerships with
researchers. Farmers, environmental activists, and university researchers
organized the 1998 conference Exploring Organic Alternatives: Meeting the
Challenges of Agriculture, Health, and Community; more than 300 people
attended it in Saskatoon.

With Tri-Council Green Plan funding originating from Environment
Canada, Saskatchewan researchers have recently collaborated on the study
Sustainability of the Semi-Arid Prairie Ecosystem (PECOS). This interdisciplinary research focused on a dryland farming area in the southwest of
the province, a region that has faced many economic, ecological, and social
threats to sustainability. The work has linked resource management
concerns, community sustainability, and occupational health issues.
Researchers at the Lethbridge Research Centre, Agriculture and Agri-Food
Canada, recently inaugurated a comparative study of low-input and
organic cropping systems. With twenty farmers as an advisory committee,

the study evaluates soil quality, crop production, and economic returns under several alternative cropping systems (Duckworth 1997a).

Agricultural development on the Prairies has been a full-scale experiment without comprehensive planning or evaluation and without systematic assessment of alternatives. Production has been maintained, but at the cost of much-intensified input use. Government policies, commercial logic, and reigning philosophies have tended to promote specialization, simplified cropping systems, and larger production units without heeding potential risks. The arrangements and practices necessary for sustainability must be worked out both locally and regionally. Success will also depend on appropriate adjustments at provincial, national, and international levels. Taxation, trade, monetary, educational, environmental, labour, regional, and agricultural policies create the context in which sustainable solutions will either take root or fail. Agriculturalists, planners, community entrepreneurs, civil servants, scientists, educators, workers, and consumers are all "stakeholders" in this project. Resilient and productive agricultural economies, healthy ecological systems, and vibrant rural communities are closely interconnected. We must find ways to simultaneously address the cultural-agricultural and ecological-economic dimensions of sustainability. Arrangements that squander natural or social capital can only generate a temporary affluence – and only for a few people.

Notes

1 JoAnn Jaffe, the editors, and two anonymous reviewers provided useful recommendations on drafts of this chapter. Its limitations reflect my own.
2 New generation cooperatives (NGCs), in which farmers-investors buy shares and enter a mutual agreement to supply raw products to a cooperatively owned processing facility, represent a potentially more equitable arrangement. They are popular in the northern Great Plains states and have attracted some attention in the Prairie provinces (Harris, Stefanson, and Fulton 1996).
3 There is an eerie commonality with the military terminology of precision bombing popularized during the Gulf War. This is an agricultural application of some of the same technology of global positioning and mapping, but it likewise depends heavily on the operation of multiple high-tech systems and on the capacity to gather, store, interpret, and use certain kinds of "intelligence."
4 Many organic horticulturalists use Bt sprays to control susceptible pests. Bt is a naturally occurring bacterium and is acceptable for certified organic producers. Research evidence that widespread planting of crops with the Bt gene could lead to rapid development of resistant bug populations is thus of particular concern to organic farmers. They risk losing one of the most effective biological controls available.
5 On 8 May 1997, the *Western Producer* carried a full-page advertisement: "Attention Organic Producers, Saskatchewan Wheat Pool Is Going Green. Naturally." Many of the farmers who called in wanted information on how to gain certification as organic producers.

References

Allen, Patricia. 1993. "Connecting the Social and the Ecological in Sustainable Agriculture." In P. Allen, ed., *Food for the Future: Conditions and Contradictions of Sustainability* (1-16). New York: Wiley.

Altieri, Miguel A. 1998. "Ecological Impacts of Industrial Agriculture and the Possibilities for Truly Sustainable Farming." *Monthly Review* 50,3: 60-71.

Bennett, John W. 1969. *Northern Plainsmen: Adaptive Strategy and Agrarian Life*. Chicago: Aldine.

Bird, Elizabeth Ann R., Gordon L. Bultena, and J.C. Gardner, eds. 1995. *Planting the Future: Developing an Agriculture That Sustains Land and Community*. Ames: Iowa State University Press.

Boehlje, Michael. 1996. "Industrialization of Agriculture" *Choices* 11,1: 30-3.

Briere, Karen. 1997. "Precision Farming Shows Profit for Dealer." *Western Producer,* 8 May, 74.

Busch, Lawrence. 1994. "The State of Agricultural Science and the Agricultural Science of the State." In A. Bonanno et al., eds., *From Columbus to ConAgra: The Globalization of Agriculture and Food* (29-52). Lawrence: University Press of Kansas.

Duckworth, Barbara. 1997a. "Low Input/Organic Systems Are Studied." *Western Producer,* 26 June, 52.

–. 1997b. "Too Much Herbicide Use Big Cause of Resistant Weeds." *Western Producer,* 3 April, 94.

Fairbairn, Brett, June Bold, Murray Fulton, Lou Hammond Ketilson, and Daniel Ish. 1991. *Co-operatives and Community Development: Economics in Social Perspective*. Saskatoon: Centre for the Study of Co-operatives, University of Saskatchewan.

Fieldhouse, Paul. 1996. "Community Shared Agriculture." *Agriculture and Human Values* 13,3: 43-7.

Flora, Cornelia Butler. 1995. "Social Capital and Sustainability: Agriculture and Communities in the Great Plains and Corn Belt." *Research in Rural Sociology and Development* 6: 227-46.

Fox, Michael W. 1997. *Eating with a Conscience: The Bioethics of Food*. Troutdale, OR: New Sage Press.

Gertler, Michael E. 1992. "The Social Economy of Agricultural Sustainability." In D. Hay and G. Basran, eds., *Rural Sociology in Canada* (173-88). Toronto: Oxford University Press.

–. 1994. "Rural Communities and the Challenge of Sustainability." In J. Bryden, ed., *Towards Sustainable Rural Communities* (69-78). Guelph: University School of Rural Planning and Development, University of Guelph.

–. 1998a. "Biotechnology and Social Issues in Rural Agricultural Communities: Identifying the Issues." In Ralph W.H. Hardy, Jane B. Segelken, and Monica Voionmaa, eds., *Resource Management in Challenged Environments, NABC Report 9* (137-45). Ithaca, NY: National Agricultural Biotechnology Council.

–. 1998b. "Organizational, Institutional, and Social Factors in Agricultural Diversification: Observations from the Canadian Plains." *Canadian Journal of Agricultural Economics* 44: 435-48.

Gertler, M.E., J. Jaffe, and L. Swystun, with L. Hauser, J. Liggett, and L. Gatin. Forthcoming 1999. Beyond Beef and Barley: Organizational and Social Factors in Farm Diversification. Research Report Prepared for Saskatchewan Department of Agriculture and Food.

Gertler, Michael E., and Thomas Murphy. 1987. "The Social Economy of Sustainable Agriculture: Family Farming and Alternative Futures." In B. Galeski and E. Wilkening, eds., *Comparative Family Farming in Europe and North America* (239-69). Boulder, CO: Westview Press.

Gruchow, Paul. 1995. *Grass Roots: The Universe of Home*. Minneapolis: Milkweed Editions.

Harris, Andrea, Brenda Stefanson, and Murray Fulton. 1996. "New Generation Cooperatives and Cooperative Theory." *Journal of Cooperatives* 11: 15-28.

Hindmarsh, R. 1991. "The Flawed 'Sustainable' Promise of Genetic Engineering." *Ecologist* 21,5: 196-205.

Khachatourians, George G. 1998. "Agricultural Use of Antibiotics and the Evolution and Transfer of Antibiotic-Resistant Bacteria." *Canadian Medical Association Journal* 159,9: 129-36.

Ketilson, L.H., M. Gertler, M. Fulton, R. Dobson, and L. Polsom. 1998. The Social and Economic Importance of Co-operatives in Saskatchewan. Research Report Prepared for Saskatchewan Department of Economic and Co-operative Development.

Kloppenburg Jr., Jack, John Hendrickson, and G.W. Stevenson. 1996. "Coming in to the Foodshed." *Agriculture and Human Values* 13,3: 33-42.

Levidow, L. 1993. "Agricultural Biotechnology: Whose Efficiency?" *Science as Culture* 3,3: 453-68.

Liodakis, George. 1997. "Technical Change in Agriculture: A Marxist Critique." *Sociologia Ruralis* 37,1: 61-78.

McMillan, D'Arce. 1997. "Low, Zero-Till Farming Changing Prairie Landscape." *Western Producer*, 29 May, 60.

Moen, Keith. 1997. "Hog Wild." *Saskatchewan Business*, March-April, 25-33.

Ploeg, Jan Douwe van der. 1993. "Rural Sociology and the New Agrarian Question." *Sociologia Ruralis*, 33,2, 240-60.

Reuter. 1997a. "Dutch Swine Fever Still Rising." *Western Producer* 5 June: 15.

—. 1997b. "Taiwan Lifts Pork Ban but Permits Required." *Western Producer*, 24 April, 15.

Sachs, Carolyn. 1996. *Gendered Fields: Rural Women, Agriculture, and Environment*. Boulder, CO: Westview Press.

Siggins, Maggie. 1991. *Revenge of the Land: A Century of Greed, Tragedy, and Murder on a Saskatchewan Farm*. Toronto: McClelland and Stewart.

Snow, A.A., and P.M. Palma. 1997. "Commercialization of Transgenic Plants: Potential Ecological Risks." *BioScience* 47,2: 86-96.

Swihart, Ric. 1997. "Farmers Urged to Protect GPS Secrets." *Western Producer*, 6 February, 27.

Vail, David. 1996. "'*All Sweden* Shall Live!' Reinventing Community for Sustainable Rural Development." *Agriculture and Human Values* 13,1: 69-77.

White, Ed. 1997. "Saskatchewan Puts $250,000 into Boosting Hog Health." *Western Producer*, 5 June, 65.

Wolf, Steven A., and Spencer D. Wood. 1997. "Precision Farming: Environmental Legitimation, Commodification of Information, and Industrial Coordination." *Rural Sociology* 62,2: 180-206.

7

The Canadian Pacific Salmon Fishery: Issues in Resource and Community Sustainability

Richard Schwindt

Introduction

Canada's Pacific salmon fishery is once again in crisis. This is not new. Periodically, the alarm is raised over one or several issues involving the fishery, including the fragile state of the salmon resource, the economic condition of the commercial fishery, the state of the recreational fishery, and disputes between and within user groups. Although the current problems of the fishery are not new, there is a new urgency in the pursuit of solutions. The collapse of the Atlantic cod fishery in the early 1990s has provided stark testimony to the disastrous effects of flawed management policies on resource-dependent individuals and communities. And the experience of the Maritimes seems to be repeating itself on the Pacific coast: "In 1996, fishers and fishing communities up and down B.C.'s coast suffered severe economic hardship as a combined result of the poorest salmon returns in recent history, federal restructuring of the commercial fishery and failure to achieve a fair and workable *Pacific Salmon Treaty*" (British Columbia 1997a, 3).

As a result, there has been a call, recently explicated in a BC government strategy paper, for policies that will create "sustainable fisheries jobs and communities" (British Columbia 1997a, 7). This chapter is intended to add constructively to the debate. It assesses the sustainability of the current organization of the commercial salmon fishery, evaluates the recently initiated federal government program to rationalize the commercial fishery, summarizes studies of the regional employment impacts of reduced landings and fleet rationalization, and considers a redirection of policy away from maintenance of a capital-intensive, marine fishery and toward the encouragement of a land-based, terminal fishery.

State of the Salmon Fishery

The Resource: Basic Biology

There are five commercially important species of Pacific salmon: chinook, chum, coho, pink, and sockeye. They are anadromous fish. They are spawned in fresh water, move downstream to the ocean, and after a number of years (depending upon the species) reach maturity and return to their original spawning grounds to reproduce and die. Each species can be organized according to a hierarchy ranging from subspecies to subpopulations. Units at the bottom of the hierarchy (populations and subpopulations) are associated with specific spawning sites.[1] The return of individual populations is fairly predictable. The commercial fishery is organized to take advantage of this cycle. The salmon fleet targets the mature salmon as they make their way through coastal waters toward their freshwater spawning grounds. In any season, the fleet will harvest specific age classes of specific populations.

Human activity most directly influences the sustainability of the resource in two ways. First, the ability of fish to move to and from the spawning grounds and the fertility of the grounds are affected by the management and use of inland waterways. Second, the rate of harvesting directly affects the number of fish that reach the spawning grounds.

Development, such as hydroelectric projects and stream diversions for other purposes, can directly obstruct the upstream migration of spawners and the downstream migration of juvenile fish. Slides, both natural and development induced (e.g., the disastrous Hells Gate slides of 1913 and 1914 were attributable to construction work in the Fraser River Canyon), can also disrupt migrations. Human intrusion on spawning grounds can have both positive and negative effects. Physical destruction and environmental degradation of spawning beds reduce their productivity, whereas enhancement, such as the construction of spawning channels, increases their carrying capacity. Although many enhancement projects have been very successful, researchers have identified the loss of a substantial number of salmon populations due in part to degradation of spawning habitat (Slaney et al. 1996). The concerns are the loss of biodiversity and the risk of greater reliance on a small number of populations.

Harvesting directly affects the number of fish allowed to reach the spawning grounds (the escapements). If too few are let through, then future harvests suffer. If too many are let through, then they exceed the carrying capacity of the spawning grounds, so there are obvious current costs (a smaller harvest) and no incremental future benefits (in fact, there may be a deleterious impact on current reproduction).

A primary responsibility of resource managers is to ensure an optimal level of escapements. This is done by determining the carrying capacity of spawning beds, estimating the numbers of returning spawners, and setting the total allowable catch (TAC). This calculus is extremely difficult because it involves, among other things, predicting the number of returning fish that have spent several years "grazing" in the north Pacific. The task is further complicated by the problem of mixed stock. Salmon of different species or stocks mingle as they mass for the upstream migration to their spawning beds. For a number of reasons, the optimal escapement level differs between species and stocks. The number of offspring per spawning adults differs between species, and some species or stocks may be weak because of previous overfishing or degradation of spawning beds. The commercial net fleet (seine and gillnet) cannot effectively discriminate between stocks when harvesting.[2] If harvesting is geared to fully and efficiently exploit the strong stocks, then the weaker ones will be overharvested with deleterious impacts on future returns. Conversely, if regulations are imposed to protect the weak stocks, then the stronger ones will be underharvested.

The task of ensuring adequate escapements and thereby maintaining the biological health of the salmon resource is made more onerous by the fact that salmon are easy to catch on their homeward migration. Salmon do not have to be hunted. Fishers need only wait at the mouths of freshwater systems and then take the fish as they mass for their upstream journey. And improvements in fishing technology have increased the efficiency of harvesters and made the job of management even more difficult.

Given the biology of salmon, effective management of the resource is directly tied to the organization of the harvesting sector. Because salmon are easily caught, they are vulnerable. At issue is whether harvesters have incentives to restrain their catches, allow adequate escapements, and thereby ensure the long-run sustainability of the fishery. The answer involves property rights to the fish.

Common-Property Problems
For many years after European settlement, the Pacific salmon fishery was operated as an open-access fishery. With few constraints (e.g., Canadian citizenship), anyone could go fishing. This situation led to common-property problems.

Theory
The exploitation of many natural resources generates a surplus that is called resource rent. In simple terms, efficient extraction of the resource costs less, sometimes much less, than the market value of the resource. In the context of the fishery, an efficient harvesting sector could take the catch at a cost well below the landed value of the salmon (i.e., the amount paid by processors for the raw fish). When there is competition for this surplus (the difference between cost and value), complications arise.

A commercial fisher's decision to go fishing is based upon a simple calculus. Does the expected value of the catch exceed the expected cost of the effort? Unfortunately, the rational individual ignores the fact that increased fishing effort by one decreases the net returns expected by all others. The more competition for the fish, the lower the expected average returns. As a result, there will be far more effort expended on harvesting a given amount of fish than need be. At the extreme, so much effort is expended that costs equal landed value, the surplus is extinguished, and resource rents are said to be completely dissipated. Furthermore, the individual fisher, no matter how well intentioned, has no incentive to forgo current catches to ensure future harvests. A forgone landing will simply be caught by a competing fisher.

Unconstrained competition for the resource has two negative impacts. First, the cost of landing the fish is higher than need be, and this cost is mirrored in lower returns to fishers. Second, competition results in overharvesting, which can imperil the survival of the resource.

Policy

Policy makers have long recognized the problems with open-access, common-property fisheries.[3] In the case of Pacific salmon, early regulations were aimed at protecting the survival of the stocks. Well over a century ago, observers recognized that some fishing techniques were so lethal that they had to be constrained lest entire salmon runs be depleted.

Because salmon return to freshwater when mature, they are subjected to a gauntletlike harvest. Before European contact, Indians depended heavily upon terminal-fishing techniques whereby the salmon were trapped as they made their way upstream. In the US Pacific Northwest, early cannery operators improved these techniques with ruinous success. Some major salmon runs were obliterated. Presumably on account of the experience to the south, industrial traps were never allowed in British Columbia. From the outset, European exploitation of the resource was based upon small-boat technology.

Even a small-boat fishing fleet, if massed at the mouth of a river, can overharvest. Recognizing this possibility, authorities tried to impose entry restrictions at the turn of the century. These and other early attempts to control fishing were largely unsuccessful (Fraser 1977).

With time, the fleet expanded, and technological improvements dramatically increased the fishing power of vessels. Regulators countered this mounting pressure on the stocks by imposing increasingly restrictive regulations on gear, fishing locations, and fishing times. By the 1950s, it was widely recognized that excess fishing capacity had reached a crisis level. The federal government appointed an economist, Sol Sinclair, to examine the industry, diagnose the sources of problems, and recommend corrective policies.

Sinclair (1960) concluded that the fishery suffered from classic common-property market failures and outlined three solutions. First, competition for the resource rents, the root of the problem, could be extinguished by monopolizing the fishery. Doing so would correct both the problem of overinvestment and the propensity to overfish. The monopolist would maximize long-term profits by harvesting the fish in the most efficient manner and by ensuring adequate escapements for future harvests.

Second, the government could tax the resource rents out of the system. Doing so would remedy, or at least moderate, the problem of overcapacity because the incentive for further effort would be dampened. Regulators would have to continue to monitor and restrict the catch in order to guarantee adequate escapements.

Third, the government could curb entry through licence limitation. This solution would attack the symptom of the problem (excess fishing power) but not its cause (competition for the resource rents). The idea was to close access to the fishery to new entrants by limiting the right to fish through a system of fishing licences.

The federal government adopted the most politically expedient of these policy choices and in 1968 initiated the Davis Plan, named after the incumbent minister of fisheries. Rights to fish for salmon were "grandfathered." Those who had participated in the salmon fishery in previous years were allocated licences. Thereafter, entrants would have to purchase these rights from exiting incumbents. The plan also called for a government-funded buyback of vessels to reduce extant capacity.

The Davis Plan was largely ineffective for two reasons. First, the buyback program had a negligible impact on the size of the fleet. During the implementation of the program, the price of salmon increased substantially. Fishers rightfully recognized that higher landing values combined with less competition for the fish (as a result of licence limitation) increased the expected rents for those remaining in the fishery. The price demanded for leaving the industry escalated. With limited funding, the program was able to retire only a small proportion of harvesting capacity. Second, licence limitation did not stop expansion of harvesting capacity. The number of fishing vessels was limited, but the fishing power of each was not. Licensed fishers continued to compete for the resource rents by enhancing the catching capacity of their vessels. Initially, inferior vessels were simply replaced by superior ones; when this option was closed, existing vessels were dramatically improved. This practice, known as capital stuffing, involved increasing the speed and manoeuvrability of the boats, increasing the speed with which nets could be set and retrieved, and investing in sophisticated, electronic fish-finding devices. In the end, real capacity continued to expand. Incentives had not changed. "It is clear that the fundamental incentives to employ extra resources to compete are latent, strong, quickly triggered, and basically unaffected by limited entry" (Wilen 1988, 316-7).

During the 1970s, a period of substantial price increases for most commodities (including salmon), the fishing fleet, now fixed in number, prospered. Capital stuffing continued, the fleet's fishing power grew, and regulators protected escapements by tightening controls on fishing times, allowable gear, and fishing locations.

With the recession of the early 1980s, salmon prices fell, the value of landings plummeted (see Figure 7.1), and interest rates increased. Many fishers had borrowed heavily during the period – some to buy licences at very high prices and some to participate in the capital stuffing of the period. The financial position of the salmon fleet was precarious, and another commission of inquiry, chaired by Peter Pearse, was initiated.

The Pearse Commission was charged with inquiring into the state of the Pacific fisheries and making recommendations for policy changes. The 1982 report began with the following description of the state of the industry: "Canada's Pacific fisheries are at a crisis point. This year [1982], following two depressed years, the economic circumstances of the commercial fisheries are exceptionally bleak. In addition, there is a growing concern about the precarious condition of many of our fish stocks and increasing anxiety among Indians about their traditional fishing rights and among sport fishermen about their recreational opportunities. Although aggravated by current conditions, the economic problems and other concerns are rooted in fundamental deficiencies in fisheries policy" (Pearse 1982, vii).

The situation was not much different from what Sinclair had found in the 1960s. There was too much harvesting capacity chasing too few fish. Pearse recommended the implementation of two of Sinclair's three policy

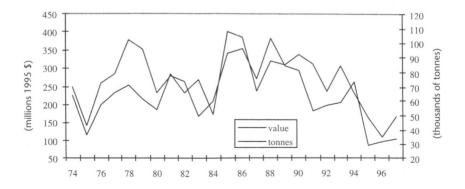

Figure 7.1 Salmon landings and landed value, 1974-97
Source: Derived from British Columbia, Ministry of Agriculture, Fisheries and Food, *Fisheries Production Statistics of British Columbia*, various years; and British Columbia, Ministry of Agriculture, Fisheries and Food, *British Columbia Seafood Industry Year in Review*, various years.

options. Licence limitation was to be continued, and the rents were to be taken out of the system through landing taxes and auctioning licences. Pearse also recommended a novel and complex system of fleet reduction. His idea was to reduce the size of the fleet by half over a ten-year period and to fund the retirement of vessels largely through the proposed scheme of auctioning licences (Devoretz and Schwindt 1985).

These proposals were not implemented. The recession ebbed, prices recovered (although not to the heights of the late 1970s), interest rates fell, and landings increased dramatically (see Figure 7.1). The improvement in the fleet's financial situation, combined with effective lobbying by the commercial fishing industry against any form of resource rent taxation, attenuated pressure for regulatory reform. This period of calm, however, was to be short-lived.

Now, in the latter part of the 1990s, the salmon fishery is once again in a state of crisis. In 1995, 1996, and 1997, landings and prices were low. The fishing power of the fleet is greater than ever, so great in fact that regulators have difficulty managing the harvest (vessels can take so many fish in so short a time that some openings are only minutes long). There is mounting evidence that a significant number of salmon populations have been lost through overfishing and habitat destruction. And disputes between the commercial fleet and other resource users have become more common and more acrimonious. Indians have seen their claims to a greater share of the resource reinforced by the courts, and sportfishing interests are increasingly effective in organizing their constituents and making their positions known. Finally, the recent collapse of the Atlantic cod fishery has increased public awareness of fishery problems and added a sense of urgency to the search for solutions. These pressures have led not just to proposals for policy reform but also to actual policy change. Before turning to a discussion of the initiatives introduced in early 1996, a brief review of the state of the salmon fishery is necessary.

The State of the Fishery
The state of the salmon fishery can be evaluated in a number of dimensions, including fish stocks, salmon markets, and financial viability.

Harvests and Stocks
The Pacific salmon fishery is not in danger of imminent collapse. Landings over the period 1974-97 are shown in Figure 7.1. There is no discernible long-term trend. Although there is considerable year-to-year variation (for biological reasons), landings in the first half of the 1990s were not much different from the twenty-year average. However, 1995, 1996, and 1997 landings were the lowest since 1975.

What is of great concern is the apparent loss or endangerment of specific salmon populations. Slaney et al. (1996) identified 9,663 salmon stocks in British Columbia.[4] The status of 57 percent of them could be classified.

Most were unthreatened. However, about 6 percent were in the category of high risk of extinction, 1 percent were at moderate risk, 2 percent were of concern, and 1 percent were extinct. Most recently, serious concerns have been raised over the state of coho stocks in both northern and southern British Columbia (Canada 1998c, 4).

The loss of specific populations raises two principal concerns. First, the eradication of individual stocks reduces biodiversity. This reduction leads to a dependence upon a smaller number of stocks and to great risk if those stocks are threatened by disease or a calamitous destruction of migratory paths or spawning beds (the impact of the 1913 Hells Gate rock slide on Fraser River sockeye is a case in point). As Walters (1995) notes, the fishery has become increasingly dependent upon a small number of stocks that have been the object of substantial efforts at enhancement. Second, when stocks are destroyed, the productivity of their spawning beds is lost because no other stock moves in to fill the unused capacity.

The threat to specific weak stocks is exacerbated by the mixed-stock problem. As noted above, seine and gillnet technologies (which account for most of the harvest) cannot accurately discriminate between species, much less stocks.

Markets
The financial health of the fishery depends upon the value of landings: a function of the quantity of fish landed and the prices received for them. Although there is no discernible long-term trend with respect to harvest volumes, landed prices have tended to decline over the past two decades. This decline is shown in Figure 7.2.

The demand for seafood generally, and salmon specifically, has increased over the recent past. However, the supply of salmon has also increased dramatically (see Figure 7.3). Indeed, world supply has nearly tripled since 1980, and a significant proportion of this increase is attributable to the rapid growth of salmon aquaculture. From negligible production in 1980, salmon aquaculture now accounts for 36 percent of world production.[5] By most accounts, world production of farmed salmon will continue to grow and put downward pressure on prices for both farmed and wild products. Farmed salmon targets the high end of the market and is primarily sold as fresh product, although some producing countries, Norway in particular, have marketed substantial volumes of frozen farmed salmon. The increased supply of farmed salmon has implications for requirements of quality in the fishery (they are discussed below).

Financial Sustainability of the Fishery
Historically, policy reform was called for when the commercial fleet was in financial difficulty. The current round of policy initiatives is no exception.

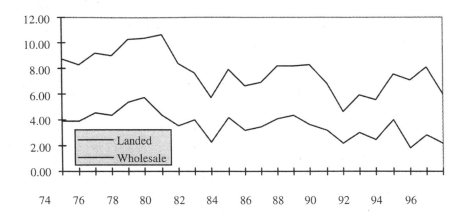

Figure 7.2   Landed and wholesale prices, 1974-97
Source: Derived from British Columbia, Ministry of Agriculture, Fisheries and Food, *Fisheries Production Statistics of British Columbia*, various years; and British Columbia, Ministry of Agriculture, Fisheries and Food, *British Columbia Seafood Industry Year in Review*, various years.

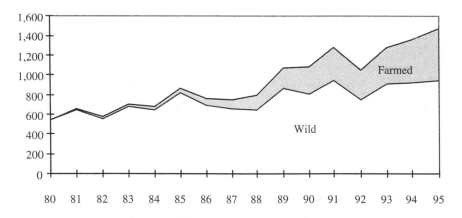

Figure 7.3   World production of wild and farmed salmon, 1980-95
Source: Bjorndal (1990); updates provided by Bjorndal in personal communication.

The 1995 landed value of the catch (in real terms) was at a twenty-year low, and the 1996 and 1997 results were only slightly better (see Figure 7.1). However, the fishery is subject to cycles, so conclusions about its financial sustainability cannot be based upon several years' experience. A more meaningful question is whether the fishery was financially viable over the cycle immediately preceding the most recent poor seasons.

Financial viability requires, in simple terms, that revenues exceed costs. At the harvest level, revenues are fairly easily determined. These are the landed values of the salmon catch. More complex is the identification and quantification of harvest costs. This is so for several reasons. Many vessels in the salmon fleet are "multiproduct" enterprises in that they also fish for roe herring, halibut, or other species. This versatility complicates calculation of the cost of the salmon harvest because certain common costs (e.g., vessel maintenance and depreciation) have to be attributed to the different fisheries.

More problematic are the costs incurred by the government to support the salmon fishery. The federal government, through its Department of Fisheries and Oceans (DFO), has primary responsibility for the salmon resource. It spends significantly to enhance the resource through investments in spawning-habitat rehabilitation, spawning channels, lake enrichment, salmon passages (e.g., fishways and fish ladders), and hatcheries. It also incurs considerable costs in managing the resource. Management involves determining optimal escapements; estimating return migrations; establishing the allowable catch; setting the rules on fishing times, locations, and gear to ensure that the allowable catch is not exceeded; and enforcing those rules.

Quantification of DFO expenditures on salmon enhancement is relatively easy because they are reported as a discrete item in the accounts. Estimating management and enforcement expenditures on salmon is more difficult because the DFO is responsible for a wide range of marine resources. It, too, can be viewed as a multiproduct operation.

Estimates of the private and public costs of the salmon harvest over the 1988-94 period are available (Schwindt, Vining, and Globerman 1998). The results (in constant 1995 dollars) are shown in Table 7.1. The first row

Table 7.1

BC salmon harvest: Landed values, public and private costs, net benefits (millions 1995$)

	1988	1989	1990	1991	1992	1993	1994	Avg.
Landed value	383.6	306.9	294.3	182.4	199.9	205.8	262.8	262.3
Total private cost	333.9	268.3	243.3	175.9	178.3	180.2	212.7	227.5
Private rents	49.7	38.6	51.0	6.5	21.6	25.6	50.1	34.7
Public costs	100.6	98.3	99.7	83.0	86.5	82.7	83.4	90.3
Social net benefit	-50.9	-59.7	-48.7	-74.6	-64.9	-57.1	-33.3	-55.6

Source: Schwindt et al. (1998).

shows the landed value of the salmon harvest. The second shows the costs incurred by the commercial fleet to harvest the salmon. These include operating costs such as fuel, labour, supplies, and vessel repairs and capital costs (for both depreciation and opportunity costs).[6] The row titled "private rents" shows the difference between the value of landings and the private costs of the harvests. These are essentially returns above the costs of bringing the resource to market. They are resource rents.

The engaged reader will recall that economic theory predicts that, when valuable natural resources are held as common property, unconstrained competition for available rents will drive up the costs of resource exploitation to the point where the rents are dissipated. In other words, fishers will invest so heavily in capital and expend so much effort in pursuit of a larger share of the catch that the cost of the harvest will equal its value. Apparently, this extreme situation has not yet been reached in the salmon fishery. It is likely that the policy of licence limitation, by imposing binding constraints on vessel size and type (e.g., gillnet licences cannot be converted to seine licences), has curbed capital stuffing to the extent that all rents have not been dissipated. Over this seven-year period, licensees received, on average, about $35 million above their actual costs (which include a normal profit) of harvesting.

The picture changes substantially when public costs are included in the accounting. Here public costs are limited to expenditures by the DFO's Pacific Region on the salmon resource.[7] Undoubtedly, they are an underestimate because other levels of the DFO (the Ottawa head office), other federal ministries, provincial ministries, and even local governments expend funds directly or indirectly on the resource.[8] Over the seven-year period, public costs averaged about $90 million per year.

When public costs are included in the accounting, net returns to the fishery are actually negative. Over the 1988-94 period, the annual average cost of enhancing, organizing, monitoring, and carrying out the harvest exceeded the value of landings by almost $56 million. As it is now organized, the salmon fishery is not financially viable. It could be sustained in its present form only if the government were willing to continue to expend large sums on its enhancement and management.

The Pacific Salmon Revitalization Strategy
Throughout 1994, it became increasingly clear that the federal government was no longer willing to support the extant structure of the salmon-harvesting sector. There were a number of forces at play. The recent collapse of the Atlantic cod fishery, with its considerable human and financial costs, was fresh in the ministry's mind. The introduction in 1992 of the Aboriginal Fishing Strategy, whereby the DFO allocated additional salmon to Indians, led to bitter complaints by the commercial fishery and allegations between

groups over responsibility for inadequate escapements, particularly of Fraser River stocks.[9] The federal government must have been sensitive to the costs – although not explicitly mentioned – of fisheries management (on both coasts) in an era of deficit reduction.

In early 1995, Minister of Fisheries and Oceans Brian Tobin announced that reform would be achieved with or without industry agreement: "The issue of fleet capacity has been discussed repeatedly over the years, with no success. I want to be absolutely clear that failure to reach consensus must not again be an excuse for inaction. In the absence of an industry consensus, I am fully prepared to make the final decisions arbitrarily and to implement unilateral changes in the 1996 fishery" (1995).

Tobin subsequently resigned. His successor, Fred Mifflin, continued the process of policy reform. In March 1996, he announced the Pacific Salmon Revitalization Strategy (the Mifflin Plan). The DFO stated that the strategy was necessary for four principal reasons: (1) changes in the ocean environment had led to lower salmon productivity; (2) the short, crowded, and highly competitive fishing openings made management difficult if not impossible; (3) the private costs of harvesting were increasing; and (4) world salmon prices had declined (Canada 1997).

There are three main elements to the Mifflin Plan. First, the DFO adopted a risk-averse program of fisheries management. This meant a more conservative approach when setting the allowable catch (i.e., a lower TAC) and more stock-selective fishing practices in an effort to attenuate the mixed-stock problem. Second, the fleet was to be reduced by half over several years. The process was initiated with a government-funded $80 million voluntary licence retirement program that was implemented in 1996. Third, area licensing was imposed. The programs of licence retirement and area licensing are alleged to have serious implications for fisheries-dependent coastal communities.

Licence Retirement

In the spring of 1996, eligible holders of salmon licences were invited to submit applications for vessel retirement to the Fleet Reduction Committee. The applications set out the asking price for the licence. Predictably, the announcement of the buyback precipitated an escalation in the market price of licences. Licensees correctly perceived that, as the number of vessels declined, the expected catch of each remaining vessel would increase and with it the expected rent capture. The private rents set out in Table 7.1 would now be shared by fewer licensees.[10] In the end, the program retired 48 seine, 444 gillnet, and 305 troll licences (see Table 7.2). The buyback retired 18 percent of the licensed vessels but considerably less capacity because a relatively small number of seine licences (the most efficient type of gear) were purchased (9 percent of the seine fleet was retired).

Table 7.2

BC Reduction of the salmon fleet under the Mifflin plan

	Initial no. of vessels	Buyback	Stacking	Total retired	Percent retired	Residual fleet
Seine	536	48	123	171	32	365
Gillnet	2,543	444	372	816	32	1,727
Troll	1,288	305	118	423	33	865
Total	4,367	797	613	1,410	32	2,957

Note: The initial fleet and buyback data are from ARA Consulting Group (1996:S-3). Stacking data were provided by DFO and are as of 14 September 1998. The total number of stacked licences is correct; however, vessel retirement by gear type was estimated. For example, it was assumed that when a vessel held both a seine and gillnet licence, a gillnet vessel had been retired, and when a vessel held both a gillnet and troll licence, a troll vessel had been retired. The total size of the fleet is not precise because some licences were "inventoried" by DFO (i.e., they were not attached to a vessel) prior to initiation of the Mifflin Plan but have since been released.

Area Licensing

Prior to the Mifflin Plan, licensed salmon vessels generally could range the entire BC coast in pursuit of fish. This freedom led to congestion in anticipation of openings and, in some cases, to very short openings (on occasion, the allowable catch for a specific opening was taken in minutes). Under the area-licensing policy, the coast was divided into two areas for seiners and three for gillnetters and trollers. Licensees had to commit to one of these areas for a four-year period. The goal was to reduce the number of vessels in any given location, thereby making management more tractable. With fewer boats on the fishing grounds, enforcement of catch constraints was more effective, which was more consistent with the risk-averse management strategy.

The program, however, did allow for licence stacking. Fishers licensed for one area or gear type could buy a licence for another. This policy was attractive to the more productive fishers, who recognized that the additional licence was more valuable to them than to the less efficient fishers. Stacking increased the demand for licences and put further upward pressure on their prices.

Stacking is ongoing. As of September 1998, 613 licences have been stacked, and the fleet has declined accordingly. Importantly, stacking removed a significant number of seiners (123) from the fleet.

The Rationalized Fleet

As a result of stacking and the buyback, the fleet was reduced by 1,410 vessels (32 percent). However, this number likely overstates the reduction in harvesting capacity. It is reasonable to assume that the least efficient fishers sold licences and that the most efficient fishers purchased them. Moreover, those who have stacked licences will likely be motivated to fish even harder to justify the acquisition. So far, the Mifflin Plan has done little to curb the "fundamental incentives to employ extra resources to compete" for the salmon resource identified by Wilen (1988).

Impacts on Fishery-Dependent Communities
Soon after its announcement, the Mifflin Plan was criticized on a number of grounds. Among them was the assertion that the plan would impose undue hardships on small, remote, fishery-dependent communities. This section identifies the role of fisheries in the BC economy and reviews the realized and potential impacts of the plan on those communities.

Fishery-Dependent Communities
The commercial salmon fishery plays a relatively unimportant role in overall economic activity in British Columbia. Over the decade 1986-95, primary fisheries (the commercial harvesting of all species) plus fish processing accounted for a little less than 1 percent of the provincial GDP.[11] This provincial share, however, belies the importance of fishing to a number of coastal communities.

In a 1995 study, Horne and Powell calculated the dependence of sixty-three local BC areas on what they defined as basic sectors.[12] They found that three local areas (comprised of nine communities) were highly dependent on fishing income in that more than 10 percent of basic income came from commercial fishing (excluding fish processing).

Impacts of Fleet Rationalization
In early 1998, the federal and BC governments engaged a group of consultants to study, among other things, the impacts on employment of fleet rationalization overall and on coastal communities (Gislason et al. 1998). The task was difficult because the researchers had a severe problem of simultaneity. Employment in salmon harvesting fell in the 1996-7 period because of vessel retirement (buyback and stacking) and because of very poor fishing seasons. To disentangle these influences, the researchers identified the type (by gear) of vessels retired and then estimated employment loss based upon survey estimates of average crewing by gear type (e.g., 5.2 jobs per seine vessel). To determine community impacts, the residence of the retiring licensee was determined, and it was assumed that skipper and crew resided in that community. Adjustments were made for processor-owned vessels.

On a provincial level, the effects of the rationalization were slight. Some 3,865 fleet-related jobs (i.e., captains and crew) were lost, less than 1 percent of the 1996 labour force. However, a number of communities were much more severely affected (see Table 7.3). A few small, fishery-dependent communities lost a significant number of jobs. What is striking about these communities is that most already suffered high unemployment rates and had relatively large Aboriginal populations. The income effects of the lost employment are difficult to determine for a number of reasons.

First, both skippers and crews are largely compensated on the basis of harvest results. That is, they are remunerated on the basis of a share of the vessel's catch. Fleet rationalization had no impact on the total value of landings. The allowable catch was taken with a smaller number of vessels, so presumably those fishers who remained in the industry earned more than they otherwise would have.

Second, skippers and crews that left the industry lost unemployment insurance entitlements, insofar as the entitlements were earned through fishing employment. In the past, a significant portion (up to 25 percent) of fishers' annual income came from this transfer.

Table 7.3

Community employment impacts of fleet rationalization

	Job loss as of 1991-4 community employment (percent)	1996 unemployment rate	Aboriginals as percent of population
Kyuquot	29	13	97
Ahousat	27	19	95
Alert Bay and area	15	24	68
Sointula and area	12	8	7
Hartley Bay	10	23	97
Sayward	9	15	5
Kitkatla	5	47	99
Central coast	5	17	59
Masset and area	5	11	38
Port Hardy	4	12	16
Ucluelet	4	13	20
Quadra Island and area	4	14	9
Tofino	3	8	27
Bamfield	3	8	16
Prince Rupert and area	3	17	30
British Columbia		10	3

Note: Calculations based on data in Gislason et al. (1998).

Third, it is impossible to determine what retiring licensees did with the proceeds of the sales of their licences. Many received substantial amounts of money. The federal government alone transferred $80 million to licensees through the buyback. Stacking involved significant intraindustry transfers. To the extent that these amounts of money stayed within the retiring licensees' communities, employment losses might have been attenuated.

Table 7.4

Federal and BC government transition funding (millions $)

Federal

	Habitat restoration	15.0
	Early retirement	7.7
	Gear payments	8.0
	Credit access	5.0
British Columbia		
	Habitat restoration	15.0
	Development projects	7.7
Total		58.4

Sources: Canada (1997), British Columbia (1997a).

Transitional Programs

Based in part upon the recommendations of a joint federal-provincial panel (Pacific Salmon Revitalization Plan Review Panel 1996), the federal and BC governments instituted a number of transitional policies with promised funding of $58.4 million (see Table 7.4).

The major component of the initiative is a program to restore and enhance salmon habitat. The goal is to restore or increase spawning-bed capacity. Priority is to be given to projects that provide employment to displaced fishers in or near their communities.

The federal government allocated $5 million to facilitate stacking through the access-to-credit component of the program. Fishers who have difficulty financing additional licences through conventional sources can turn to this fund. Any subsidy to purchasers will, of course, add upward pressure to licence prices.

A further $7.7 million was allocated to an early-retirement fund for fishers over fifty-five. The province committed a matching allocation for industry and community fisheries diversification and development projects (British Columbia 1997a, 15). Finally, $8 million was allocated to purchase redundant gear as fishers are limited to single gear licences. In the past, vessels were allowed to use both gillnet and troll gear. This is now prohibited.

Reform and Sustainability

In sum, the Mifflin Plan, including the transitional program, did little to enhance the sustainability of the salmon fishery. A 30 percent reduction in the salmon fleet might hinder, but would not arrest, the process of capital stuffing. The incentives for this type of behaviour remain. Nor did the plan ensure the sustainability of fishery-dependent coastal communities. The once-off contribution to habitat restoration would likely have a very transitory effect. The gear payments and early-retirement benefits simply facilitated the exit of those who had chosen to retire licences.

Apparently recognizing the inadequacy of the program, the federal government announced in June 1998 that it would allocate substantial, additional funds to the fishery (Canada 1998a, b). Program details remain sketchy, but the main elements include a further buyback of licences ($200 million), supplementary funds for habitat restoration and protection ($100 million), and additional funds for transitional policies ($100 million).

With these additional funds, the targeted halving of the fleet will likely be achieved and some relief provided to adversely affected communities. However, these programs will not likely solve the underlying problems of the fishery.

First, as the size of the fleet is reduced, the remaining fishers will continue to have incentives to increase fishing effort. Moreover, these buyback programs will make future reform more difficult. Buyback, stacking, and preferential access to credit for licence acquisition will all act to increase the value of the remaining licences. Furthermore, these policies entrench private rights to this public resource and will make future rationalization or reallocation of rights even more difficult. The government, through the buyback, has paid retiring fishers the value of the rents that they expected to receive during the rest of their fishing careers. But these rents have been left in the industry and are now capitalized in the value of the remaining licences. Thus, in any future buyback, the public will pay for resource rents for which it has already compensated retired licensees.

Second, although it will be easier to manage a smaller fleet, the mixed-stock problem will persist. Notwithstanding the introduction of more stock-selective fishing techniques (which become more feasible as the "race for the fish" is slowed), the problem will remain and threaten the maintenance of biodiversity.

Third, the program does little to sustain fishery-dependent communities. Transitional funds will assist those leaving the sector, but there will remain few employment alternatives in many of the coastal communities adversely affected by fleet rationalization. This is particularly true given the downturn in the forestry sector, which has traditionally provided some employment opportunities for many of these communities.

An Alternative, Extreme Strategy: Terminal Fisheries

In all of the recent debate over policy reform, one of the remedial options identified by Sinclair (1960) thirty-eight years ago has been ignored – monopolization of the resource. If exclusive rights to the resource (or to a discrete component of the resource, such as a specific salmon run) were allocated, the common-property problem would be resolved. The holder of the rights would have the incentive to take the optimal amount of fish at the lowest harvesting cost. A method of achieving this monopolization, on a piecemeal basis, is to create and allocate rights to terminal fisheries.

Terminal fisheries target the fish in the freshwater system. This approach includes fishing at the mouths of major river systems while the salmon school before the upriver migration, fishing in the river itself, in tributary streams, and at the terminus (spawning grounds) of the run. The potential advantages of terminal fishing were identified by Commissioner Pearse in his 1982 report: "Support for terminal fisheries generally rests on three grounds. First, they improve the economy of fishing by eliminating the need for a large offshore fleet. Second, they enable more discriminating management and harvesting of discrete stocks as they approach their spawning grounds. Third, they confine the catch to mature fish and hence, increase production" (44). Pearse noted that terminal fisheries create some management difficulties and that there were concerns about quality because some species deteriorate fairly rapidly as they move upstream. Nonetheless, he concluded that "terminal fishing appears to hold some promise for fisheries management. But surprisingly little study has been made of the opportunities" (44).[13]

Advantages

Pearse identified three advantages of a terminal fishery: low-cost harvesting, avoidance of the mixed-stock problem, and avoidance of the incidental catch of juvenile fish. A fourth advantage is the positive impact on the sustainability of remote coastal communities.

Cost-Efficient Harvesting

The current harvesting regime is clearly inefficient. There are too many boats chasing too few fish, and, even if the Mifflin Plan's goal of halving the fleet is achieved, there will still be too much harvesting capacity. Some observers estimate that the fleet is three or even four times what is required to take the catch.[14] Walters (1995, 24) notes the following: "From studies on the capture efficiency and working time allocation of commercial seine, troll, and gillnet fishermen, we estimate that current harvests could be taken by a small fraction of the existing fishing fleet."

Terminal fisheries rely on land-based techniques using devices such as weirs, traps, and wheels. In simple terms, as the fish move upstream, they can be guided with fences across the stream into "corrals" where they are easily harvested. Precontact Indians commonly used these techniques, and European settlers, recognizing their efficiency, adapted them to the early commercial salmon fishery in the US Pacific Northwest. In time, these devices were banned, ostensibly in the interest of conservation (Newall 1994).

There are some obvious advantages to terminal fishing. Hunting fish requires expenditures on pursuit and detection capabilities (e.g., fuel, engines, bow thrusters, and electronic fish finders). Waiting for fish in freshwater streams avoids these costs. Transporting fish from distant fishing grounds to processors requires investment in and maintenance of sophisticated refrigeration technologies. Land-based fishing can avoid some of these costs. Arguably, the level of human capital required for an offshore fishery is also higher. The safe and effective operation of seagoing vessels requires skilled mariners. Land-based technologies do not. Also, some terminal-fishing technologies, such as traps, reduce incidental-catch mortalities. Net harvesting, whether in freshwater or saltwater, is wasteful because some fish contact the nets but then escape. Some of them die from stress or net wounds, and some that are subsequently captured are net bruised.

Biologically Efficient Harvesting
Effective resource management requires determination and enforcement of the allowable catch. Given the current state of scientific knowledge, estimation of the size of a specific salmon run, the required number of escapements, and the residual (the allowable catch) is a difficult and imprecise exercise. It is further complicated by the mixed-stock problem (the mingling of weak and strong stocks before upriver migration). However, the job of determining the health of specific stocks becomes much easier as the fish get closer to the spawning grounds.

As discussed, the marine fishery contributes to the mixed-stock problem for several reasons. The commercial fleet targets the massing of fish when stock mingling is common. Net gear cannot easily discriminate between strong and weak stocks. And even when weaker stocks are identified and released, the survival rate is very low.

Terminal fishing does not obviate these problems, but it can lessen them. At the extreme, harvesting could take place at the terminus of the run, the spawning grounds. The number of returning spawners would be known with certainty, and harvesting allocations could be made with precision. The trade-off in terms of quality would, however, be untenable. More realistically, downstream harvesting could be organized to better protect weak stocks. More stock-selective gear could be employed, and, importantly, less lethal gear such as traps could be used to increase the survival rate of releases.

Community-Based Terminal Fisheries

A move to terminal fisheries could significantly enhance the sustainability both of the resource and of small, fishery-dependent communities. Terminal-fishery techniques are relatively less capital and more labour intensive than those of the marine fishery (particularly the seine fishery). There are obvious implications for employment in communities where there are few alternatives. Human capital requirements (e.g., education) are relatively modest, so major expenditures on training (or retraining) would not be required.

Additional benefits would accrue if comanagement responsibilities were attached to harvesting rights. Under such a regime, communities would be responsible for data collection, enforcement of catch limits, and protection and enhancement of spawning habitat. With regard to this last obligation, holders of downstream rights (who would have access to the highest-quality fish) would have to deal with upstream communities adjacent to spawning grounds.

The idea is to introduce a modicum of monopolization into the system in order to align private interests with the goal of wise resource management. Rights holders, in this case communities, would have incentives to properly manage the resource. Failure to do so would ultimately result in reduced harvests and incomes.

Disadvantages

There are a number of disadvantages associated with terminal fishing. Paramount among them is the potential problem of degradation of quality. It is also argued that legalization of commercial freshwater fishing will increase policing problems. Finally, from a policy perspective, there is the enormous problem of property rights.

Fish Quality

The argument against terminal fishing on the ground of quality is based on the fact that salmon deteriorate as they make their way upriver to the spawning grounds. This is particularly true for chum salmon. But the case against terminal fishing is not clear-cut in this regard.

First, the extent of deterioration depends upon species, race, and distance from the spawning grounds. Fish taken well downstream can be of premium quality (as good as sea caught), whereas those taken farther upstream may be of lesser but altogether acceptable quality (Slaney and Birch 1983).

Second, certain types of in-river harvesting and handling technologies have advantages from the perspective of quality over net technologies. For example, fish traps, combined with lift racks and on-site primary processing (butchering), can produce a very fresh, undamaged product. In contrast, offshore gillnetting involves harvesting drowned fish that have been caught in the net for varying periods of time, storing them on board until picked up by a packer or until the fishing trip is over, and then transporting them to port for processing.

Third, for certain types of processing, upstream fish are superior. For example, salmon flesh loses oil content as the fish moves upstream. This loss makes it less acceptable for canning but more appropriate for smoking.

The question of quality was considered in a study commissioned by the DFO of commercial sales made under the Aboriginal Fisheries Strategy. The findings suggest that a terminal, in-river fishery does not suffer a serious quality problem: "Most of the fish caught under the PSA [Pilot Sales Arrangement] are sockeye. In-river quality is generally slightly below that of ocean-caught fish due to location and timing; nonetheless, quality is sufficiently high that native fishers have experienced no difficulty selling their catches. Available data indicate that much of the 1993 catch was graded No. 1 or No. 2 (domestic) and was suitable for a broad range of fresh, smoked and canned products. There is scope for improvement in handling practices in the native fishery; this reportedly also contributes to minor quality differences" (Gardner Pinfold 1994, iii-iv).

It is worth considering future requirements of quality for wild-caught salmon. Figure 7.3 shows the rapid growth in the supply of farmed salmon. The salmon fishery is facing increasing competition from farmed products in the high-quality market segment. In the future, the fishery may enjoy a competitive advantage only in those products that can utilize lower-quality fish, such as canned salmon. If this is the case, then the emphasis will be on low-cost production and not on the maintenance of premium quality.

Policing
Once allowable catches are established, they must be enforced. Although no systematic study of policing costs exists, it is probably less difficult to monitor marine fishing than freshwater fishing. It is simply easier to observe, identify, and apprehend a vessel illegally fishing on open water than it is to monitor thousands of miles of freshwater streams.

In 1993, some $3.34 million was spent on policing the Indian fisheries, with 85 percent of the monitoring directed at the Fraser River (Gardner Pinfold 1994, vi). Whether or not commercial freshwater fishing is legalized, poaching has to be controlled. The question is whether monitoring is more difficult when a legal land-based fishery is in operation. The experience with the Indian fishery is instructive: "There is every reason to believe that enforcement costs would have been as high or higher [on the Fraser River] without legal sales. This observation is based on the widely-held view that the fisheries in some areas were already out of control. Enforcement costs would have increased substantially, with arguably much lower compliance levels, if DFO had attempted to impose the same degree of effort control and catch monitoring as it did under the PSA" (Gardner Pinfold 1994, vii).

It is not clear whether freshwater, terminal fisheries would result in higher policing costs. If these fisheries were community based, then as local property rights to the fish were strengthened there would be incentives for the local population to curb poaching by members of the community or by outsiders.

Redistribution of Rights
The thorniest problem in moving from marine to terminal fishing involves the redistribution of valuable property rights. Government policy has effectively entrenched the rights of incumbent licence holders. And, through its failure to extract the resource rents from the system, its policies of stock enhancement (which increase the rents), its preferential fisheries unemployment insurance policies (which make attachment to the fishery more valuable), and its policies of licence buyback, it has increased the value of each remaining licence (Schwindt and Globerman 1996). Given the precedent set by the buybacks, it would be difficult for the government not to offer compensation for retired licences. However, because the net losses imposed by the current organization of the industry are so high (and are likely to persist), a generous scheme of licence retirement might well be cost effective.[15]

Issues also arise over who should be the recipients of terminal-fishing rights. Aboriginal communities are, for a host of reasons, worthy candidates (Schwindt, Drost, and Crowley 1995). History, recent legal decisions, and the sorry economic state of many reserves provide rationales for redistribution in this direction. The finding that a number of Aboriginal communities have borne the brunt of job loss attributable to fleet rationalization (see Table 7.3) strengthens the case. Also, a larger role for Aboriginal people in the fishery is consistent with the recommendations of the Royal Commission on Aboriginal Peoples (1996, 652-6).[16]

Other observers report that examples of successful community-based schemes of fishery management include both Aboriginal and mixed communities (Pinkerton and Weinstein 1995). Probably the best approach would be to allocate rights on a watershed-by-watershed basis.

Finally, this suggested policy does not imply retirement of the entire fleet. As Walters (1995, 44) notes, there are a number of reasons for maintaining a marine fishery, including opportunities to take fish of the highest quality, to intercept fish of international origin (and thereby maintain bargaining strength in international negotiations over allocations), and to provide information early in the season on the size of the run, thereby facilitating effective management.

Conclusions

In 1996, the federal government spent $80 million and pledged to spend an additional $35.7 million on rationalization of the BC salmon fishery. In mid-1998, it committed an additional $400 million to this end. The BC government contributed $22.7 million to assist in the transitional period. Given the annual net social losses (which are estimated to average nearly $56 million per year) generated by this fishery, the money would be well spent if it resolved the chronic problems confronting this industry. Unfortunately, this resolution is unlikely because the programs do little to curb the incentive to overinvest in fishing capacity, to protect endangered stocks, or to sustain fishery-dependent coastal communities.

This chapter has argued that it is time to seriously consider an alternative organization of the salmon fishery. Community-oriented management and terminal harvesting could solve many of the problems that are endemic to the current regime. In large measure, the source of these problems is the absence of property rights to the resource. If rights to, and responsibility for, the resource were allocated to specific communities, then there would be incentives for the rights holders to manage the resource effectively. In this case, management would include both harvesting and habitat protection and enhancement. Rents generated at the harvesting stage could help to support efforts to maintain and expand the productivity of salmon habitat.

An analysis of policies to reallocate rights and responsibilities is beyond the scope of this chapter (there is a large body of literature dealing with the mechanics of successful community management or comanagement of fisheries; see, e.g., Pinkerton and Weinstein 1995). No doubt such a policy change would be resisted by those who benefit from the current organization of the fishery, and mollifying them would be expensive. However, current policies are very expensive and are not likely to ensure the sustainability of the fishery. A better solution would be to allocate rights and responsibilities to terminal fishers, thereby creating incentives for proper resource management. The result should be improved sustainability of the resource and the communities that depend upon it.

Notes

1   The hierarchy is as follows: species, subspecies, biological races, populations, subpopulations, demes. Stocks represent mixtures of biological races, populations, and subpopulations. Fisheries biologists define salmon stocks in different ways to accommodate scientific and management considerations (Slaney et al. 1996, 20). In other words, stocks refer to population units at the bottom of the hierarchy but might refer to races, populations, subpopulations, or a mix of all three.
2   This is not to say that fishers using net gear cannot mitigate impacts on the weaker stocks. Revival tanks, brailing seine catches, and hot-picking gillnets allow for the release (and survival) of weaker stocks (Copes 1998, 20).
3   A distinction is made between an open- and a limited-access common-property resource. Under open access, anyone can fish. Under limited access, entry is restricted, but the com-

mon-property characteristics persist. That is, the limited number of fishers continue to ignore the costs imposed upon other fishers when they increase their own efforts. At one time it was believed that limiting access to the fishery would solve the common-property problem. As will be discussed, this proved untrue.

4　See note 1 for the definition of stocks.

5　In 1996, British Columbia produced 33,100 tonnes (dressed weight) of farmed salmon. To put this amount in context, landings of wild salmon were 34,200 tonnes (round weight), although this was a low catch (British Columbia 1997b). Given the considerable debate about the potential impacts of salmon aquaculture on wild stocks and other marine life, it is not clear that the government will allow previous rates of growth to continue (see British Columbia 1997c; and Ellis 1996).

6　The private costs of the harvest were derived from the triennial surveys of fleet financial performance undertaken by the DFO (Canada 1992; unpublished updates). Corrections were made to account for the value of licences included in employed capital and for costs incurred in the pursuit of other species. For details of the methodology, see Schwindt, Vining, and Globerman (1998).

7　Expenditures by the DFO's Pacific Region were examined to identify items unrelated to the fishery. For example, there are considerable allocations to scientific research that is not in support of the fishery (e.g., hydrography, climate). Fishery-related expenditures were identified, administrative overheads were allocated between related and unrelated activities, and estimates of the salmon fishery's "share" of all fishery-related expenditures were made. For details of the methodology, see Schwindt, Vining, and Globerman (1998). These public costs refer only to federal government expenditures.

8　The provincial government claims to spend a significant and increasing amount on the protection of fish and fish habitat. These expenditures increased from $23 million in 1994-5 to $103 million in 1996-7 (British Columbia 1997a, 8). The province also incurs implicit costs. For example, the provincial Ministry of Forests sets and enforces rules governing logging in proximity to spawning beds. This activity costs the province in terms of both monitoring and forgone revenues for the unharvested timber along the streams.

9　The federal government interpreted the *Sparrow* decision (*Regina* v. *Sparrow* 1990) as meaning that Indians were entitled to greater participation in the salmon fishery. In June 1992, the DFO announced the Aboriginal Fisheries Strategy. Under this program, Indian groups entered into agreements whereby they accepted certain management responsibilities, such as policing the Indian fishery and habitat enhancement. The AFS also initiated special agreements with Indian groups on the lower Fraser River, the Skeena River, and at Port Alberni that set out explicit allocations to Indians and allowed for the sale of these fish. This part of the strategy was known as the Pilot Sale Arrangement.

10　More technically, the licence should reflect the present value of the stream of rents accruing to the licence holder. As the anticipated stream of rents increased due to less competition for the fish, the licence value increased.

11　Data from Province of British Columbia, Ministry of Government Services, BC Stats, personal communication.

12　Basic sectors bring income into the community from outside. Basic income results from payments for goods exported by the community, tourism expenditures within the community, transfers from senior governments (e.g., pensions, unemployment insurance benefits, and welfare payments), and investment income. Nonbasic sectors exist only to serve the community. Basic-sector dependence was calculated by dividing income in each basic sector by total community basic-sector income.

13　For a contemporary study dealing with the terminal fishery in the Skeena River area, see Copes and Reid (1995).

14　The DPA Group (1988, 1) suggests that the fleet is three times what is required. The head of the Fisheries Council of BC noted that Alaskan vessels are four times more productive because "their fleet is better matched to the size of the fishery" (Wilson 1994, A33).

15　Schwindt, Vining, and Globerman (1998) estimate that, prior to the 1996 policy reforms, the net present value of the fishery was -$784 million. In other words, if the future stream of annual losses is put into today's values, then the fishery is worth a negative $784 million.

It follows that, if reorganization of the fishery to achieve a break-even point cost society any amount less than this, then it would be worthwhile.

16   The commission recommended that the government buy up and turn over quotas for commercial fishing to Aboriginal people (1996, 654-5). It did not state the form that this reallocation was to take (i.e., it did not recommend that vessel licences be turned over to Aboriginal individuals or communities, although this has been the practice in British Columbia). Elsewhere (845-7) the commission agreed that the approach of community economic development (CED) should play a role in federal policy for Aboriginal economic development. The commission did not link fisheries policy with CED in a comprehensive manner.

References

ARA Consulting Group. 1996. Fishing for Answers: Coastal Communities and the BC Salmon Fishery. Report prepared for the BC Job Protection Commission.

Bjorndal, Trond. 1990. *The Economics of Salmon Aquaculture*. London: Blackwell Scientific Publications.

British Columbia. 1997a. *The B.C. Fisheries Strategy*. Victoria: Queen's Printer.

–. 1997b. *The British Columbia Seafood Industry Year in Review*. Victoria. N.p.

–. 1997c. *Salmon Aquaculture Review*. Victoria: Queen's Printer.

Canada. Department of Fisheries and Oceans, Pacific Region, Program Planning and Economics Branch. 1992. *Financial Performance of the British Columbia Salmon Fleet, 1986-1990*. Vancouver: DFO.

–. Department of Fisheries and Oceans. 1997. Backgrounder: The Pacific Salmon Revitalization Policy.

–. Department of Fisheries and Oceans. 1998a. Backgrounder: Helping People and Communities Adjust. Press release.

–. Department of Fisheries and Oceans. 1998b. Backgrounder: Restructuring the Pacific Fishery. Press release.

–. Department of Fisheries and Oceans. 1998c. *Coho Response Team, Final Report*. Vancouver: DFO.

Copes, Parzival. 1998. Coping with the Coho Crisis: A Conservation-Minded, Stakeholder-Sensitive, and Community-Oriented Strategy. Report prepared for the minister of fisheries of British Columbia.

Copes, Parzival, and Michael Reid. 1995. An Expanded Salmon Fishery for the Gitksan-Wet'suwet'en in the Upper Skeena Region: Equity Considerations and Management Implications. Discussion Paper 95-3, Simon Fraser University, Institute of Fisheries Analysis.

DPA Group. 1988. British Columbia Salmon Fleet Financial Performance, 1981-1985. Report prepared for the Department of Fisheries and Oceans, Vancouver.

Devoretz, Don, and Richard Schwindt. 1985. "Harvesting Fish and Rents: A Partial Review of the Report of the Commission on Canadian Fisheries Policy." *Marine Resource Economics* 2,4: 347-67.

Ellis, David. 1996. *Net Loss: The Salmon Netcage Industry in British Columbia*. Vancouver: The David Suzuki Foundation.

Fraser, G. Alex. 1977. Licence Limitation in the British Columbia Salmon Fishery. Environment Canada, Fisheries and Marine Service, Economics and Special Industry Services Directorate, Pacific Region, Technical Report PAC/T-77-13/.

Gardner Pinfold Consulting Economists Limited. 1994. An Evaluation of the Pilot Sale Arrangement of Aboriginal Fisheries Strategy. Report prepared for the Department of Fisheries and Oceans.

Gislason, Gordon, Marilyn Mohan, Edna Lam, Simon Anderson, and Ellen Battle. 1998. Fishing for Money: Challenges and Opportunities in the BC Salmon Fishery. Report prepared for the British Columbia Job Protection Commission, Victoria.

Horne, Garry, and Charlotte Powell. 1995. *British Columbia Local Area Economic Dependencies and Impact Ratios*. Victoria: Queen's Printer.

Newall, Dianne. 1994. *Tangled Webs of History: Indians and the Law in Canada's Pacific Coast Fisheries.* Toronto: University of Toronto Press.

Pacific Salmon Revitalization Plan Review Panel. 1996. Tangled Lines: A Federal-Provincial Review of the Mifflin Plan, Vancouver.

Pearse, Peter. 1982. *Turning the Tide: A New Policy for Canada's Pacific Fisheries.* Ottawa: Supply and Services Canada.

Pinkerton, Evelyn, and Martin Weinstein. 1995. *Fisheries that Work: Sustainability through Community-Based Management.* Vancouver: The David Suzuki Foundation.

Regina v. *Sparrow.* 1990. 4 WWR 410.

Royal Commission on Aboriginal Peoples. 1996. *Restructuring the Relationship.* Vol. 2 of the *Report of the Royal Commission on Aboriginal Peoples.* Ottawa: Royal Commission on Aboriginal Peoples.

Schwindt, R., H. Drost, and B.L. Crowley. 1995. *Market Solutions for Native Poverty.* Toronto: C.D. Howe Institute.

Schwindt, R., and Steven Globerman. 1996. "Takings of Private Rights to Public Natural Resources: A Policy Analysis." *Canadian Public Policy* 22,3: 205-24.

Schwindt, R., A. Vining, and S. Globerman. 1998. Net Loss: A Cost-Benefit Analysis of the British Columbia Salmon Fishery. Simon Fraser University discussion paper.

Sinclair, Sol. 1960. *Licence Limitation – British Columbia: A Method of Economic Fisheries Management.* Ottawa: Department of Fisheries.

Slaney, T., and G. Birch. 1983. "Commercial Quality of Sockeye Salmon Collected from the Skeena River." Vancouver: Aquatic Resources Limited.

Slaney, T., K.D. Hyatt, T.G. Northcote, and R.J. Fielden. 1996. "Status of Anadromous Salmon and Trout in British Columbia and Yukon." *Fisheries* 21,10: 20-34.

Tobin, Brian. 1995. Statement by Brian Tobin, Minister of Fisheries and Oceans, in Response to the Report of the Fraser River Sockeye Public Review Board. Speech delivered in Montreal, 7 March.

Walters, Carl. 1995. *Fish on the Line.* Vancouver: The David Suzuki Foundation.

Wilen, James. 1988. "Limited Entry Licensing: A Retrospective Assessment." *Marine Resources Economics* 5,4: 313-24.

Wilson, Mark. 1994. "Packers Pay Price." *Province* [Vancouver] 19 January: A33.

8
Incorporating Postproductivist Values into Sustainable Community Processes
Alison Gill and Maureen Reed

Introduction

Sustainable development poses particular difficulties for communities that have historically relied on natural resource extraction for their well-being. In many cases, these localities face a declining or degraded resource base upon which traditional productive modes of employment and wealth generation have relied. The effects of this decline have been exacerbated by capital movement and world trade relations, activism by networks of environmental nongovernmental organizations (ENGOs), and the affirmation of the rights of First Nations peoples. Changing societal values associated with land and resources have shifted priorities for land use from primary dependence on productive functions (e.g., timber harvesting) to incorporation of a more diverse set of values associated with consumptive purposes (e.g., housing, tourism, amenity). This shift has marked the emergence of a new "postproductive" landscape.

In British Columbia, land-use planning has been one means by which the provincial government has attempted to address these emergent values while promoting sustainability and introducing a level of certainty into land-allocation decisions. Accompanying this shift in priorities is a movement toward supporting participatory decision making through new advisory and/or decision-making processes designed to bring public stakeholders directly into environmental policy formulation and implementation (e.g., Pinkerton 1989; Reed 1995). These changes call for the establishment of new policy initiatives and processes of implementation.

Primary attention of policy advisors and decision makers has been focused on the implications of land-use changes for employment of resource workers within these places (e.g., regional land-use plans of the Commission on Resources and the Environment, timber supply area reviews, economic impact analyses). Less attention has been given to the social and political dynamics, especially as they relate to the ability of communities to direct their own development. For communities where resource extraction has been the primary economic base and where a significant proportion of the population continues to support the original resource sector (e.g., forestry, mining), there is an inherent tension between processes that allow these communities to direct their own development and planning processes that attempt to reallocate land uses for other purposes.

We argue here that, despite the emphasis on improving local autonomy and well-being, local communities still do not have the capacity to make effective contributions to land-use decisions concerning (re)allocation and management. More specifically, existing policy initiatives and institutional arrangements operating within local communities as well as those operating at larger regional and national scales render the contributions of local decision makers marginal. This insufficiency is particularly evident where land use is being transferred from productive functions associated with resource extraction (e.g., forestry, agriculture) to consumptive functions associated with tourism, recreation, amenity, and environmental protection (e.g., golf courses, wilderness parks). Existing institutional arrangements at various spatial scales (e.g., municipal, regional, provincial, and federal) associated with productive functions are not always congruent with the needs of new postproductive functions.

To examine this argument, we first pose a framework that depicts various policy arenas along a continuum of scales of institutional arrangements that affect local land-use decisions. Next we apply the framework with reference to land-use planning affecting Squamish, British Columbia, a forestry town experiencing a declining dependency on forestry extraction while simultaneously undergoing rapid population growth. Our purpose in using this case study is illustrative because institutional arrangements are context dependent and vary between communities. The case study highlights the constraints on local land-use decision making that have been imposed by the hierarchical nature of institutional arrangements resulting in agencies with potentially fragmented jurisdictions and overlapping mandates.

The Multijurisdictional Nature of Postproductive Land Allocations

Regions undergoing structural change in the local economy may be associated with a process of transformation described as postproductivism. The term implies that the intensive, industrially driven, state-supported resource production has given way to new forms of production and consumption (Urry 1995) and associated new institutional arrangements (Reed and Gill 1997). Postproductivism also suggests that these places attract new residents who are not as likely to be dependent on the traditional resource sector as long-standing residents (Cloke and Goodwin 1992) and who place demands on rural lands for space, infrastructure, and services to meet desires for amenity, recreation, conservation, and housing (Clark, Bowdler, and Ilbery 1995; Ward et al. 1995). As a consequence, these regions are characterized by new cultural interpretations of rurality (Clark, Bowdler, and Ilbery 1995; Halfacree 1995) and by a heightened differentiation of land uses (Lowe et al. 1993).

Whether defined as part of the "urban field" (Hodge 1974), the "regional city" (Bryant, Russwurm, and McLellan 1982), the "city's countryside" (Bryant and Johnston 1992), or the "accessible countryside" (Blunden and Curry 1988), these areas can be viewed as "a series of overlapping and more or less integrated systems of exchange that have developed between various functions" associated with home, work, and leisure whose boundaries have been extended "by improved communication and transportation" (Bryant and Johnston 1992, 7). Importantly, this environment is both a source and a receptor of multiple values and consequently the focus of attention by multiple jurisdictions and stakeholders. For example, new residents may view the recreational opportunities and associated amenity values as "positional goods" that secure their position in the good life of middle-class society. Visitors may perceive such areas as "idylls to which to escape from the pressures of modern urban-industrial society, as untamed wilderness which can rekindle the human spirit, or simply as large reserves of open area suitable for space-intensive recreational pursuits" (Shaw and Williams 1994, 223). Within and between these groups, individuals may seek varying levels of use and/or protection according to these preferences.

In many cases, because of these divergent values and common sites of use, landscapes managed for the production and consumption of tourism and environmental, recreational, and amenity values exhibit management problems of common-property resources where it is impossible to exclude users and where "consumption by one individual reduces the amount available for other users" (Healy 1994, 597). Authority for management is divided across public agencies as well as other stakeholders (Reed and Gill 1997). Public and private institutions (e.g., government agencies and property rights) have been created along preexisting priorities for resource exploitation and interpretation. Unlike productive activities such as forestry or agriculture, in which single institutions have historically had primary responsibility for resource allocation and management, the primary responsibilities associated with postproductive landscapes and associated tourism, recreation, environmental, and amenity values are split across several government agencies.

Furthermore, postproductive values cannot be neatly ascribed to fixed landscapes. They are often dependent on soft interpretations of aesthetics or amenity that are dynamic and contingent on local conditions. Yet, if such values are "soft," then there may be no obvious stakeholders assigned to protect them, only surrogates. Instead, elements of the landscape that reflect postproductive values may become part of a vision that is held by a loosely affiliated community of users. For example, a scenic land-mark may be attributed multiple values associated with cultural heritage, natural beauty, and recreational features. Designation as a "heritage site" may allow the landscape feature to become a signifier of community iden-tity, be it a social community (e.g., hikers), a cultural community (e.g., an ethnic group), a geographic community, or some combination of them. In short, these community interests reflect a broader and less defined range of public interests than that implied by the term "stakeholders." The problem for management becomes the absence of an obvious and effective regime of group management (or system of authority) necessary to allow sustained use of the landscape over time (Bromley 1992). Consequently, allocation and management decisions and policies are subject to the multiple agen-das and jurisdictions held at different levels of governance.

The Framework
The framework presented here organizes land-allocation policies into three arenas along a continuum of spatial scales (Figure 8.1). This framework allows us to consider differing levels of influence from different sources. It suggests that the influence that local communities have upon these processes may result from pressures both within and outside the communi-ties. The relative balance of these pressures is likely to differ from one set of circumstances to the next. This framework, therefore, can be considered a heuristic device, assisting us to identify the pressures, explore the implica-tions of those pressures, and target policy requirements to different actors within and across different levels of the decision-making process. The frame-work implies that power is held and contested and that change is welcomed and resisted across multiple policy arenas. Three such arenas are considered: development, allocation, and organization. Although they are considered separately, in practice they frequently overlap. By separating these issues, however, the framework can help to elucidate the nature of constraints on the local capacities of communities to determine reallocation of land uses.

Developmental Policy Arenas
Conventional developmental policies focus on provision of land and mar-keting efforts to stimulate economic growth. Historically, local develop-ment has been determined to a large extent by the primarily market-driven decisions of individual private entrepreneurs in the community (Douglas 1989). Conventional local elites include real estate developers, landowners, lending banks, and chambers of commerce or business associations. Local government is also a conventional player in developmental policy because it is responsible for land development within its boundaries, and it relies on local businesses to provide jobs and tax revenues. A local government may

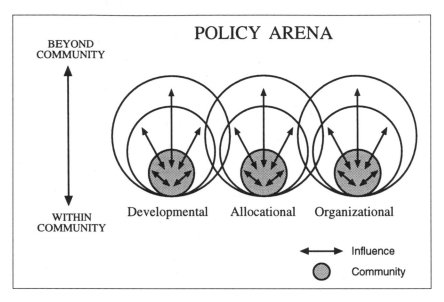

Figure 8.1 Conceptual diagram of policy arenas and policy scales affecting community-based land-use allocation

act on behalf of developers through favourable zoning or building bylaws or, if necessary, by mustering its energies and skills to lobby senior governments on behalf of developers.

Developmental policies affecting local municipalities, however, are also contested beyond their boundaries. In Canada, for example, local economic development is frequently shared because the provincial governments are responsible for the allocation of property rights and resources on public or Crown lands located primarily beyond municipal borders. In addition, new environmental regulations at the provincial or federal level may require that new proposals for development comply before they can be implemented. Regulation of labour agreements and corporate tax rates, for example, requires powers and financial resources that are simply not available to local governments (Markusen 1989). If development occurs beyond local boundaries, then powers to assign property rights, to regulate resource extraction rates and environmental standards, to administer taxation, and to oversee trade are held at provincial and federal levels. Furthermore, these levels of government across Canada have initiated programs and agencies to assist communities in identifying and implementing priorities for local economic development. Consequently, municipal governments frequently rely on the favourable discretion of provincial and federal policies and programs that may regulate land uses through agencies responsible for highways and transportation, parks and protected areas, resource extraction, and environmental management. Conflicts are likely to emerge between those who seek to maintain the status quo, or at least to encourage business starts that are consistent with it, and those who seek to change the nature of economic activities in the local community.

Allocational Policy Arenas

Allocational policies address which public or private groups/individuals will benefit from the distribution of resources associated with a particular developmental policy. Frequently, allocational policies include a broad range of public services that have traditionally been provided by government. In this arena, interest and activity, rather than economic resources, define who participates in these debates. Access to decisions is based upon information about the issues, knowledge of the political processes, and organizational and public relations skills. Elected officials frequently display sensitivity to the opinions of their constituents on allocational questions.

At the provincial or federal level, allocational issues may revolve around the need for strategic planning that provides a level of consistent regulation across broad geographic regions to ensure minimum standards of service (from environmental services to social services). This perspective may conflict with local interests that believe that, "because local governments are more knowledgeable about cultural and regional nuances, direct transfer payments or block grants to local governments might better achieve environmental quality objectives rather than more upper-level planning legislation, or regulation" (Dorney and Hoffman 1979, 151). The logic continues that priorities set at the local level will improve local conditions and, in aggregate, therefore improve conditions at higher orders.

At the local level, allocational issues may conflict with developmental policies if they require a redistribution of resources away from initiatives that support traditional elites. For example, where there are limited funds, politicians seek to provide services and infrastructure for developmental projects that they believe will contribute to overall employment and tax revenues. Yet local governments are also called upon to provide services for which there are no immediate economic returns (e.g., parks and public areas). In the latter scenario, it may not be politically palatable to reject proposals that provide such services. Rather, politicians may stall decision making in response to demands for funds funnelled toward specific initiatives. Politicians may also choose to do nothing, to thwart demands for change, or to adopt plans but imperfectly implement them (Bachrach and Baratz 1970; Debman 1975; Rees 1990; Wolfinger 1971). Funds may then be available for projects with more immediate and direct local economic benefits. In this way, conventional power elites may not appear to be actively involved in allocational issues; however, they may be instrumental to their outcomes.

Organizational Policy Arenas

Organizational policies deal with who will make decisions in the community and who will take responsibility for them. Authority for decision making is shared between different tiers of government as well as between different stakeholders within and beyond a local community. Centralized control directly affects the way in which local residents can use local resources and may interfere with efforts toward greater self-reliance. In contrast, those favouring more centralized control believe that environmental resources are too important to be managed by those at the local level who may lack management skills or the necessary ethic to protect the resources over the long term. With the rise of public involvement in all aspects of community development, it is no longer feasible for decisions to be left to elected representatives and their delegated officials. New players within developmental politics may question who should make the decisions without questioning the underlying premise of economic growth. Where the economic base and demographic characteristics of a community are changing, however, choices about who will be responsible for decisions may in fact be tied to different visions of the substance of economic development and community life (Blahna 1991).

Dimensions of Scale

The importance of scale in understanding land-use issues and in the sustainability of rural systems has been acknowledged by several authors (e.g., LeFroy, Salerian, and Hobbs 1991; Pierce 1993; Smit and Smithers 1993). The interrelationships between various scales of the spatial hierarchy are referred to by Lowrance, Hendrix, and Odum (1993) as a nested hierarchy and suggest that, at each level, decisions and actions are influenced by and have influence on the other levels of the hierarchy. Scale is seen as important because at different levels different values and constraints receive different emphases (LeFroy, Salerian, and Hobbs 1991). When a local economy moves away from productive values and toward consumptive values, such as tourism, there are several challenges within and across policy arenas and spatial scales. For example, despite grassroots support of tourism and environmental/recreational initiatives, local governments that have been supported through the traditional resource sector may attempt to co-opt or marginalize local support because they do not perceive its importance. Furthermore, although tourism establishments may be approved locally, the supportive infrastructure, marketing planning, and resulting allocations may only be accomplished by higher orders. As the cases below illustrate, local communities have little capacity (regulatory or practical) to control debates that touch on issues of development, allocation, or organization. Although developmental decisions within municipalities are frequently part of local government operations, the ability to resolve outstanding developmental debates is frequently beyond the capacities of municipal governments because of their dependency on agencies and resources beyond municipal boundaries. Their power is thus embedded within, and contingent upon, higher levels of authority.

At a broader spatial scale, a municipality may contribute to processes that have effects on the community but may not have final decision-making authority. Finally, planning processes that originate beyond the community often do so without explicit reference to the community itself. Although communities may have representatives within local forms of planning exercises, the model of planning, the definition of legitimate issues for discussion, and the identification of appropriate stakeholders are frequently predetermined. As a consequence, local municipalities may be marginalized. Their marginalization may be exacerbated by the lack of formal networking between local communities. Several outcomes may unfold. New initiatives may be juxtaposed, co-opted, embraced, or marginalized depending on their implications for power relations operating within, upon, and beyond local systems of governance. Therefore, the introduction of tourism to communities creates particular challenges to/for the substance of economic development, the allocation of funds and services, and the processes by which decisions are made.

Squamish: A Community in Transition

In this case study, discussion revolves around a community where the decline in dependence on the traditional economic base has been accompanied by growth in the population. This scenario is not uncommon where a resource-dependent community can no longer rely on its original economic base yet is located sufficiently close to urban areas to attract new residents who seek affordable housing and lifestyle changes associated with recreation, small-town atmosphere, et cetera (Bryant 1989; Rudzitis 1993). Our discussion of the community draws in part on results of a questionnaire survey administered to all households in July 1995 (Reed and Gill 1997; Gill and Reed 1997).

Squamish is located sixty kilometres north of Vancouver along Highway 99 (the "Sea to Sky Highway"), a scenic road leading to the resort of Whistler and beyond (Map 8.1). The economic backbone of the community has been the forest industry and associated activities. Major employers have been the pulp mill and the sawmill, with workers also employed in log cutting and sorting. Railway and port facilities linked primarily to the activities of the forestry sector have also provided jobs in the transportation sector, and until recently there was employment at a chemical plant.

Recession and restructuring in the forest industry of British Columbia (Hayter and Barnes 1997) began in the early 1980s, and employment opportunities in the forestry sector eroded during the next decade as

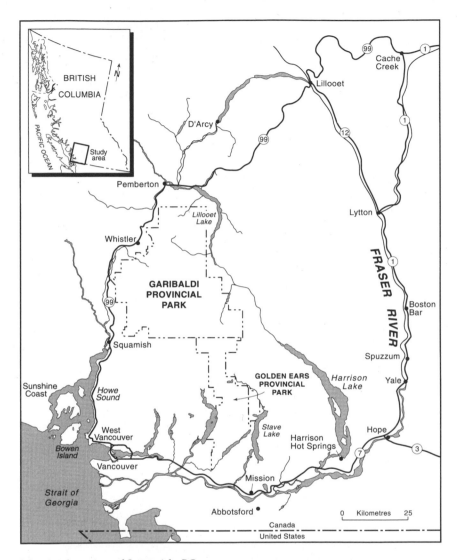

Map 8.1 Location of Squamish, BC

changing markets and technological advances resulted in job losses for
many workers. Squamish was no exception. Between 1981 and 1991, the
percentage of the labour force in Squamish dependent primarily on basic
forestry-related jobs declined from 27 to 18 percent respectively. In the
same period, the service sector increased its share of the labour force by 20
percent, to make up 47 percent of the force in 1991. The impacts of changing provincial forest policy to accommodate public demands for wilderness, recreation, and more environmentally sensitive forest practices
further reduced employment in the forest industry. In 1995, under the

review of timber supply areas, a 13 percent reduction in the annual timber harvest for the forest region in which Squamish is located was announced (Hamilton 1995). In the following year, the provincial government announced the establishment of twenty-three new parks in the broad region in which Squamish is located.

Although the traditional forestry-related industries have experienced cutbacks, the community as a whole began to experience population growth beginning around 1990. This growth was due primarily to the appeal of the community for residential purposes within commuting distances of Vancouver and Whistler, both of which have experienced skyrocketing land prices in recent years. Consequently, in 1995 Squamish had a population of 14,402, which represents a 16.5 percent increase since 1991.

Our survey revealed that new residents in Squamish are less likely to be as dependent on the traditional resource sector as the long-standing residents and have begun to place new demands on the community for the allocation of land and resources. For example, the influx of residents has corresponded with expanded strip development along the main highway and new housing subdivisions. Key issues associated with the rapid growth have revolved around the provision of appropriate housing and commercial services, the desirability and character of tourism and recreation, and the retention of cultural and natural heritage.

Squamish exhibits many characteristics of an emergent tourism setting. In 1996, the Chamber of Commerce reported that, of 350 local businesses in the chamber, 35 were related to tourism. This figure includes hotels, tour operators, and restaurants. Since 1985, the chamber has held a fee-for-service contract with the municipality to provide information for tourists. It also forms part of a joint tourism committee composed of members of the municipal council, the chamber, and a person from the local Parks and Recreation Board to oversee the contract. The chamber also retains the option to undertake marketing on behalf of the municipality. The marketing of Squamish as a tourist destination is currently hampered by its lack of a tourism infrastructure, the limited appeal of its town centre, the restricted access to foreshore areas, and a lack of local understanding of the current and potential impact of opportunities for tourism and recreation on the local economy. As we will discuss later, some members of the tourism sector would place the Chamber of Commerce among those who lack understanding of contemporary tourism opportunities.

The emergent character of tourism is also evident in residents' opinions of tourism development. Respondents to the 1995 survey agreed that dependency on forestry made Squamish vulnerable to economic changes (Reed and Gill 1997). Whereas all respondents supported diversification of the local economy, residents of five years or less (newcomers) showed stronger levels of agreement with statements concerning the benefits of tourism, and higher levels of disagreement with statements indicating the negative impacts of tourism, than did longer-term residents. In addition, longer-term residents were more pessimistic about the ability of long-term planning to manage the negative impacts of tourism (Gill and Reed 1997).

The major incentive for the municipality to engage in a community process of tourism planning was a proposal to develop a four-seasons resort at Brohm Ridge, located on Crown land adjacent to the municipal borders. To oversee the process, a Tourism Coordinating Committee was established, with representatives from the conventional power holders, including municipal and regional government agencies, the Chamber of Commerce, and BC Rail. A volunteer Citizens' Tourism Advisory Committee composed of nineteen residents worked for eighteen months to identify a vision for tourism in their community. Perhaps the most distinctive feature of this committee was the length of residence of the participants, with twelve of the nineteen members having lived in the community for five years or less. Notably absent were representatives of either the forest industry or environmental groups, although some environmental interests were represented by those advocating allocation of the local landscape for recreational use.

Whereas established institutions showed remarkable indifference to the community planning process, new local institutions provided key support to the committee during planning. Community Futures, a federally sponsored agency for community development, assumed a lead role by providing staff, facilitation skills, and logistical support. The Sea-to-Sky Economic Development Commission (EDC), an agency funded partially by the province and partially by area municipalities and private agencies, acted as an information resource and offered some logistical support.

It was in this transitional state of community development that we conducted the empirical research. Findings are drawn from two main data sources: observations made during meetings of the Citizens' Tourism Advisory Committee, and in-depth interviews conducted during the summer of 1995 with the nineteen ongoing members of the committee and three of its five resource people. In addition, media reports and informal discussions with local key informants provided corroborating evidence.

Implications of Selected Tourism Proposals

The plan drawn up by the Citizens' Tourism Advisory Committee was approved and adopted by the Squamish and District Municipal Council in December 1994. In addition to the development of a general vision statement, the committee identified thirty specific objectives for which action plans were developed. These plans addressed a wide spectrum of objectives, including specific projects, lobbying efforts, better tourism-planning information, and the achievement of social goals. The examples selected here illustrate that multiple agencies operating at various spatial scales will be involved in associated land allocations (Table 8.1). Although some of the associated decisions will occur within the municipal jurisdiction, they will not necessarily rely on local approval. Furthermore, policies established at provincial scales may be applied locally but be beyond the influence of the local municipality. Within the municipality, the goals of retaining small-town atmosphere and encouraging pedestrian access to the Squamish waterfront are considered, whereas recommendations dependent on land allocation primarily beyond the municipal boundaries are those associated with the development of winter tourism opportunities.

Retaining Small-Town Character

The rapid growth of Squamish is associated with growth throughout the region, which is growing at the fourth fastest rate in the province (Howe

Table 8.1

Agencies and organizations identified as possible lead support and/or regulatory agencies associated with the implementation of the three selected tourism proposals

Local/Municipal

Government Agency	District of Squamish; council and staff
	Squamish Estuary Coordinating Committee
	Squamish First Nation*
Non-governmental Organization	Squamish and District Chamber of Commerce
	Squamish Off Road Cycling Association
	Squamish Trail Network Society
	Squamish Yacht Club
	Brackendale Art Gallery
	Squamish Estuary Conservation Society
	Squamish Search and Rescue
	Squamish Rockclimbers' Association
Citizen Advisory Committee	Advisory Planning Commission
	Parks and Recreation Commission
	Tourism Coordinating Committee
	Winter Tourism Development Committee

Regional

Government Agency	Howe Sound Community Futures Society
	Squamish-Lillooet Regional District
Non-governmental Organization	Black Tusk Snowmobile Association
	North Vancouver Outdoor School
	SOO Coalition for Sustainable Forests
	Tourism Association of Southwestern BC
	Sea to Sky Economic Development Commission
	Sea to Sky Trail Society

▶

◄ *Table 8.1*

Agencies and organizations identified as possible lead support and/or regulatory agencies associated with the implementation of the three selected tourism proposals

Provincial

Government Agency	Ministry of Environment, Lands and Parks
	Ministry of Forests
	Ministry of Transportation and Highways
	Ministry of Small Business, Tourism and Culture
	BC Rail (Crown Corporation)
Non-governmental Organization	BC Federation of Mountain Clubs
	Festivals BC

Federal/National

Government Agency	Canada, Department of Fisheries and Oceans
	Canada, Transport Canada
Non-govermental Organization	Alpine Club of Canada
Private Company	Weldwood

Source: District of Squamish, Tourism Development Plan, 1994
* Squamish First Nation represents the Aboriginal interests. They own lands in the region and are negotiating further property rights and responsibilities.

Sound Roundtable 1996). Squamish is a favourable location for new residents due to its affordable housing close to both Whistler and Vancouver, its recreational attractions, and its health and educational services, which attract young families and retirees alike. In addition to physical changes in community form, newcomers have brought with them expectations of employment and lifestyle that do not always coincide with those of long-term residents. For example, our survey revealed that newcomers were more likely to be employed in the private service sector (e.g., business services and hospitality), whereas a higher proportion of longer-term residents were employed in resource production.

Recent attention has focused on the opportunities for and the implications of tourism and recreational development. In particular, there is some concern that future development will not threaten the "authentic" small-town atmosphere. Many residents contrast the "real" town of Squamish with the resort of Whistler to the north. For example, one resident stated, "The reason why I moved out of Whistler is because I did not like Tinsel Town North. So I think it can become too big and too all-consuming. And I don't like that any more than a lot of people in Squamish do. So I think, again, we have to look very carefully at what you want to do with this community, so we don't turn it into another sprawling place like Whistler, in my opinion." In supporting the decision to move, this resident stated, "I ... wanted to come to a real community, so I like the small-town atmosphere and lifestyle here in Squamish."

It is in this context that the Tourism Advisory Committee developed a vision statement that sought to "build and strengthen a diverse four-season tourism sector while maintaining our small-town character and retaining our heritage." The desire to maintain the small-town character was not uncontested, because (especially) longer-term residents on the committee did not necessarily view this feature as desirable. Newer residents, however, many of whom had moved to Squamish from the city, viewed this as a critical element of the residential amenities that they desired. One member of the committee noted that "There was a lot of fighting about it. The small-town character, people who had grown up in this town forever and had said 'You're joking, we don't want to be a small community, forget it'; people who had moved here from outside said 'Of course that's what we want to happen.'" There were also differences of view concerning the type of development compatible with retaining a small-town atmosphere. As one committee member observed, "So we had radically different ideas. I don't think that's surprising because you have some people who say 'Yes, we want to have a small community, but we want to have a Gulf Pacific [a retail mall] too." Indeed, the vision statement juxtaposed a diverse four-season tourism sector with a small-town atmosphere with relatively little debate about whether or not these two elements are compatible.

The issue of small-town atmosphere brings to light the extent to which the municipality is jurisdictionally and practically capable of guiding the rate and the character of its growth and development. In Canadian incorporated communities, the Official Community Plan (OCP) has been the means by which planning has included such visions. Some communities, such as Whistler, have incorporated growth management as part of their strategies. In Squamish, the pressures of new developments have precluded the allocation of time and resources to long-term planning, and thus only recently has the 1989 OCP been updated.

As Squamish moves to commodify the landscape for tourism development, however, the desire and ability to control the nature and pace of growth come to the fore. In this respect, Squamish remains dependent on other levels of government and on the independent decisions of individuals who want to live in the community. Two issues related to transportation and water supply reveal the limited ability of the community to retain its small-town atmosphere in the face of population growth.

The rapid development of Whistler and the paving of the Duffey Lake road to enhance a circular route for tourists, as well as the increasing commuter traffic to and from Whistler and Vancouver, have contributed to increased local traffic, which exhibits marked periods of daily, weekly, and seasonal congestion. These effects are beyond the control of the municipality and are managed by the provincial Ministry of Highways. As one key informant in the community observed, "We're frustrated with various levels of the provincial government and some cases federal government with what was perceived as a lack of cooperation for highway access. [A] hotel wanted to establish in Squamish. They couldn't get a 'right-in-right-out' off the highway, so it makes it less desirable for establishment. And various things as it relates to tourism, we weren't getting cooperation, they'd just say 'No, we want to fast-track everything to Whistler.'"

The issue of water supply is also closely linked to growth and development. Although constraints on water supply would obviously act to limit growth and retain a small-town atmosphere, the example given here demonstrates the nature of controls external to the community that impact on decisions about growth. Squamish is located on a floodplain, so developments located there must undertake adequate research into flood hazard. In particular, the estuary has been the focus of rising concern for environmentally sensitive development, and senior governments may be involved in assessing the environmental impacts of development. Domestic water and sewage cause some pollution in the estuary, and additional golf course and housing developments will have an effect on the ability of the municipality to deliver water. Squamish gets 90 percent of its water supply from the Stawamus River. The recent declaration of a new park located beyond the watershed may exacerbate the problems of providing a clean water supply as a result of increased recreational traffic going through the watershed to the park.

Concern over the quantity and quality of the domestic water supply is shared across a wide spectrum of public agencies and stakeholder groups both within and outside the community. They include, at the federal level, the Department of Fisheries and Oceans (DFO) and, at the provincial level, the Ministry of the Environment, Lands and Parks and the Ministry of Health. At the regional level, the Resort Municipality of Whistler, the Upper Squamish Valley Residents' Association, and Stop the Pipe (a lobby group now addressing issues of water quality) are stakeholder groups. At the local level, the Squamish First Nation, the Squamish-Lillooet Regional District (SLRD), and the District Municipality of Squamish are involved in issues relating to water supply. Community watershed plans for the Mashiter and Stawamus Rivers in the Squamish area have begun to address some of the issues through integrated committees. Ultimately, decision-making authority for water quality rests with the provincial and federal agencies that have regulatory requirements to protect waters for fish habitat and human consumption. Thus, community needs must be set within the context of broader regulatory requirements for overall watershed management held at higher orders of governance.

Managing issues such as mitigation of environmental impacts, research into natural hazards, or the incorporation of public input into decisions is exacerbated by the lack of systematic collection of information on growth. The rate of change is so fast that the census does not provide an adequate picture of the area. Monitoring of key indicators may be critical for identifying and addressing the effects of growth. Although a growth management strategy and an associated monitoring program have recently been established at the nearby resort of Whistler, Squamish, like most small towns, lacks the capacity to undertake such a venture. Lack of personnel and resources in the Municipal Planning Department results in a reliance on external agencies for expertise, yet data collected by other agencies often do not contain information at the scale that would be most useful locally. So, although the retention of the small-town character may appear to be an issue of local control, in practice it is almost impossible to guarantee, with or without a four-season product for tourists.

Pedestrian Access to the Waterfront

The recommendation to improve pedestrian access to the waterfront illustrates the significant limitations posed at the local level for implementing projects that are based on postproductive values, even when they are located within municipal boundaries. This proposal was brought forward by local interests and the tourism plan to allow for recreational and ecological benefits for residents as well as visitors. The need for greater access was also addressed implicitly in three other recommendations dealing with the development of windsurfing, trails, and outdoor attractions and the encouragement of wildlife viewing and interpretive activities.

Squamish has a large foreshore area, historically used for industrial purposes primarily related to forestry. The riparian zone is largely inaccessible because it is privately owned by local residents, the sawmill company, and BC Rail. In addition, there is one Aboriginal reserve located on part of the foreshore. Despite the location of the Squamish estuary within the municipality, its management is subject to provincial and federal jurisdiction. Deriving from the constitutional division of powers, the responsibilities for wildlife, fisheries, some elements of environmental quality and port facilities, as well as First Nations fall within federal jurisdiction. Policies related to economic development, some elements of environmental quality, lands and parks, forests, and highways fall within provincial jurisdiction.

Since 1980, planning and management of the estuary have been undertaken by the Squamish Estuary Management Committee (SEMC), composed of federal and provincial agencies, the municipal government, BC Rail, two community organizations, and the Squamish First Nation. By 1982, it had developed a plan to guide land-use decisions. From 1991 to 1993, through limited public consultation, SEMC reviewed its 1982 plan

(Avis 1995). It became clear that the earlier plan was insufficient to deal with new concerns, particularly the allocation of lands between environmental and compatible recreational values now attributed to the estuary and historically and economically important forestry-related uses.

Public meetings associated with the updating of the estuary plan revealed strong support for increased public access, particularly from residents (Avis 1995). The Squamish Estuary Conservation Society, a long-standing local environmental group, lobbied for more lands to be taken from log-handling activities and to be dedicated for ecological and recreational uses. In addition, the local newspaper was highly critical of the lack of sensitivity to local concerns. Forestry companies were officially silent, but their interests were represented through provincial forestry and economic development ministries as well as through a sympathetic municipal council (Avis 1995). Despite the rancorous debate, the updated estuary plan endorsed the need for improved public access. The plan was approved by participating agencies, including the municipal council and the Chamber of Commerce. As yet, only a small "art park," located near the waterfront, has been created for day use from existing municipal lands.

The waterfront proposal represents a mixed regime of private-property rights, residents, corporate landowners, and government agencies. Under a productive regime, land uses and associated property rights were allocated to private or state/public interests. In contrast, the common-property character of the proposal for a network of trails precludes an obvious allocation to individual users and reduces the incentive for either public or private investment. This element introduces a communal concern and raises the issue of who should be responsible for spearheading waterfront development. Diverse opinions expressed by members of the Citizens' Tourism Advisory Committee highlight the confusion. One member stated that "private enterprise has to decide if it makes sense," whereas another identified "people who are recreationally oriented." Furthermore, a representative of the Chamber of Commerce identified BC Rail (a Crown corporation) as a key player in the construction of a waterfront boardwalk while noting that "The perception of the public is 'When is the chamber going to do this?'"

The estuary also contributes to the community's self-definition, for it is highlighted in community educational events and in local walking and boating tours. It is also the site of an increasingly important eagle-watching festival each year as thousands of bald eagles congregate on their migratory route between Alaska and the contiguous United States. Finally, it is also considered important for wind surfing, which has a small but potentially significant following of recreation seekers. In combination, these common-property and community characteristics became features of implementation paralysis.

In this example, the proposed development is contained within the municipality but impinges upon several levels of government jurisdiction. The inability to implement the proposal lies in the lack of empowerment by those who actively sought support for the network of trails and the lack of commitment by government agencies that might be empowered to implement it. There is no obvious public agency to take a lead role in providing greater public access, and no agency was forthcoming.

In addition, the incentive to protect the estuary was limited by the perception of its local significance. Although greater access would be considered an asset for visitors as well as residents, to date the appeal for greater access has remained local. Its significance for ecological and recreational purposes has not yet reached a stage where extralocal advocacy groups (e.g., environmental or recreational nongovernmental organizations) have taken it up as a "cause" worth their lobbying efforts. Its regional and national significance, therefore, is still seen to lie in its values associated with productivism, such as its ability to provide for the sorting and transportation of resource commodities. Until postproductive values take on broader salience, access will likely continue to be of limited interest by higher-order government agencies that regulate land allocation.

Develop Winter Tourism Opportunities
The situation in which land allocation is dependent upon regulatory regimes operating upon the municipality is evident in a proposal to establish a ski-hill resort as an anchor for a four-seasons tourism product. In this case, the provincial government, as landowner, had clear jurisdiction to make a decision about this proposal. Because the land does not fall within the local timber supply area, the number of agencies at this stage is relatively small, restricted to two provincial ministries.

The Ministry of Environment, Lands and Parks is responsible for regulating both backcountry tourism and ski-hill development. Historically, this ministry served a gatekeeper role, regulating primarily by limitation and reacting to environmental changes (e.g., through zoning and penalties), rather than providing lands and incentives for economic development. In recent years, lobbying by ski-hill developers for a new provincial policy has drawn attention to the economic gains that ski hills might provide for the public purse. Consequently, the Ministry of Employment and Investment has become more involved in attracting investors and evaluating the economic aspects of such proposals provincewide. In 1994, the provincial government responded to these pressures and expressed tangible support for ski resorts by creating new legislation to facilitate their development.

It is in this context that the decision by the provincial government to seek a call for proposals for Brohm Ridge can be evaluated. This decision came primarily as a result of strategic policy changes at the provincial level rather than successful lobbying by the local government. The new provincial policy for ski resorts resulted in the advancement of several proposals throughout the province that are currently at different stages of review. Although local support clearly legitimizes the claim for a development near Squamish, it was not sufficient to draw the support of the provincial government initially. Indeed, one might argue that the requirement by the provincial government to undertake a provincially endorsed, community-based planning process is further evidence of the lack of faith in local mechanisms for identifying and articulating local interests.

Despite mixed public opinion, as soon as the tourism plan was completed, the municipal government and the original developer resumed lobbying for the ski hill at Brohm Ridge. Several Tourism Advisory Committee members commented that the plan was used by council as evidence of the public endorsement of a ski resort, particularly a resort as proposed by this proponent. After the summer of 1996, the proponent was successful in having his project accepted for the formulation of a master plan. As of October 1996, the provincial government and the proponent were negotiating an interim agreement for land occupation. Once the agreement and the plan are in place, the proposal will be forwarded to the provincial government for environmental assessment. The proponent is hoping to open the ski resort by Christmas 1999 (Enns 1996).

Conclusions and Recommendations

Thus far, communities have played a limited role in land-use planning for sustainable development. In large part, this limitation stems from the embedded nature of institutional and political structures. Communities are constrained in their ability to determine land allocations within municipal boundaries and even more so in their ability to influence decisions relating to land adjacent to the municipality on which the communities may be dependent. In this chapter, to help elucidate the complex nature of power relations, we employed a framework with a continuum of scales of institutional arrangements across three policy arenas: developmental, allocational, and organizational. This framework was used to examine the experience of one community, Squamish, British Columbia, as it reassesses land allocation in the face of changing economic dependencies. In particular, this case study emphasizes issues relating to changing community values in reallocations relating to the shift from productive to postproductive activities. These new societal values, which relate to a range of emergent consumptive uses of land for purposes of tourism, recreation, environmental conservation, and overall amenity, depend heavily on citizen participation as the mode of identifying, articulating, and influencing new policy directions. Indeed, the emergence of this reevaluation is integrally tied to the notion of sustainable communities that place social and environmental concerns alongside economic objectives and embody principles such as empowerment of people, integrated decision making, and consensus building as elements of the planning process (Brown 1996).

Although the diversity of conditions and processes at a local level limits the attempt to develop theoretical explanations, the suggestion from our research is that power relations are an integral element in understanding the characteristics and consequences of community-based planning. An understanding of such relationships offers insights into the constraints faced by communities in attempting to instigate processes and implement projects compatible with principles of sustainability. Contestation over land use is likely to occur at every level of the spatial hierarchy in response to differing values and objectives. Such conflict is especially evident when there is a reallocation of resources associated with the shift from productive to postproductive values and interests. In the case study, tourism-related interests challenged institutions and stakeholders whose dependencies were linked to the traditional mode of resource production.

In Squamish, the traditional elite represented by institutions such as the municipal council and the Chamber of Commerce were effective in diluting the efforts of the citizen-based tourism committee across all three policy arenas. In the developmental arena, for example, the conventional elites, the municipality along with the proponent of the ski-hill development, were partially successful in co-opting public participation in the planning process to their ends. Although the elites were able to ensure that the ski hill project remained on the agenda, they were not successful in derailing the entire planning process. As a result, the plan for tourism development presented a much broader vision than that held by the conventional power elites. Within the planning process, there was a shift from the development of a solely private project toward public goods and services that would be in keeping with community needs and desires. This is not to say that all members of the advisory committee spoke with one voice; rather, their input began to diversify the demands to which the traditional power brokers had to respond.

In the allocational arena, the traditional elites were successful in marginalizing the plan. Council approved the plan but subsequently did little to implement it. Instead, the plan was viewed as a document that could be taken forward by members of the private sector to advance specific projects. Council initially proposed to undertake a marketing strategy that would be in keeping with conventional viewpoints of tourism. When it was discovered that even this undertaking would require a larger allocation of funds than originally anticipated, the measure was not executed. Instead, council passed bylaws to allow for other developments (e.g., shopping centres) that contradicted elements of the tourism plan.

In the organizational arena, evidence of transition emerged with the juxtaposition of traditional and new models of organization. Within this arena, there was evidence that the traditional power elite, the Chamber of Commerce, was unwilling to relinquish its apparent hold on the organization and coordination of tourism in the municipality. Its opposition, and the resulting changes in the plan for tourism development, marked an attempt to render the plan marginal. However, the chamber has been unable to control all the players in tourism. New operators continue to organize apart from the chamber in order to promote their interests to the municipal council. Furthermore, since the tourism plan was completed, new people have been elected to council who are sensitive to the "next wave" of development. Although these members have not skewed the overall thrust of local development, their voices suggest that new visions for development will continue to be expressed. Juxtaposition of traditional and new modes of organization will likely continue throughout the period of transition to tourism.

Although there are constraints within a community to achieving desired outcomes based on sustainable values and processes, the embedded nature of power relations imposes further limitations on the ability of communities to determine their own futures. Even within municipal boundaries, local decisions are dependent on administrative and legislative authority at a more senior level. Although representatives of the local community will likely participate as members of the decision-making bodies, they will compete with the interests of other communities. Several examples from the Squamish case study illustrate this point. Squamish is dependent on provincially and/or federally managed resources such as water and transportation systems that it must share with other communities in the region. From an allocational perspective, Squamish frequently considers that agencies such as the Ministry of Highways exhibit favouritism toward Whistler. The proposal to develop the waterfront highlights the sometimes complex mix of stakeholders and the difficulties of coordinating the reallocation of land use for postproductive purposes.

The need for collaborative approaches that heighten the dialogue between all levels of decision making is critical if communities are to advance toward sustainable futures. There is a need for traditional elites to recognize the changing social and economic structures within their communities and to adopt new energies, insights, and initiatives. These changes would require explicit recognition of emergent businesses and collectives such as the new tourism association in ongoing government deliberations. Beyond the community level, improved mechanisms are needed to enhance communication between communities in order that they can move beyond the traditional competitive stances to recognize the benefits of collaboration. These mechanisms are especially necessary in the case of tourism initiatives because of the regional interdependencies associated with tourist activities. Furthermore, provincial policy makers need to ensure better dialogue with communities at the earliest stages of policy development.

The problems of complex jurisdictional issues and inefficiencies are endemic. An approach to these problems is suggested in the Crombie report on the Toronto waterfront; the Royal Commission on the Future of the Toronto Waterfront proposed a framework to "truly integrate environmental matters, provide a fair and consistent process and ensure that information, evaluation and decision-making are shared and accessible" (1992, 85). Specific recommendations included preparation of an integrated set of ecosystem policy statements, guidelines for municipalities and others in ecosystem planning practices, and requirements for environmental performance. Such approaches may lead to improved ecosystem protection, but we would argue that they do not necessarily resolve the embedded jurisdictional problems that hamper local communities.

Certain limitations of this case study pose challenges for future research. Community-based processes are complex. Their establishment implies the creation, destruction, and/or reinforcement of relations within and outside individual communities. The results will be processes of varying influence and efficacy over time and across different places. Further research in other localities would be required to help separate idiosyncratic elements from characteristic ones and to provide specific, if partial, understandings of the efficacy of community-based planning initiatives in shaping priorities for alternative economic development.

Notwithstanding these limitations, the suggestion from this research is that power relations along the continuum of various spatial scales are an integral element in understanding the characteristics and consequences of community-based planning where tourism is emergent. Attempts to balance or disperse power differences between stakeholders by selecting suitable structures may be contested. In this context, agencies such as municipal governments are not likely to be neutral conveners of power. They are more likely to be goal-oriented actors that may resist the redistribution of power and use their power for their own purposes. These relations are not simply hurdles to be overcome by creating better mechanisms and facilitating favourable conditions; rather, they are endemic to developmental processes. Thus, ultimately, power relations that favour tourism, recreation, environmental conservation, and amenity values will gain ascendancy as the nature and the structure of the community itself change through alterations to the demographic composition, economic base, and policies at higher tiers of government. The social justice of such changes has yet to be explored.

Acknowledgments
The authors gratefully acknowledge the financial support of the Social Sciences and Humanities Research Council of Canada and Forest Renewal British Columbia in conduct-

ing this research. Thanks are also due to members of the Citizens' Tourism Advisory Committee in Squamish and to various resource people who participated in our interviews.

References

Avis, W. 1995. "Women and Environmental Decision-Making: A Case Study of the Squamish Estuary Management Plan in British Columbia, Canada." MA thesis, Department of Geography, University of British Columbia, Vancouver.

Bachrach, P., and M.S. Baratz. 1970. *Power and Poverty: Theory and Practice*. Oxford: Oxford University Press.

Blahna, D.J. 1991. "Social Bases for Resource Conflicts in Areas of Reverse Migration." In R.G. Lee, D.R. Field, and W.R. Burch, eds., *Community and Forestry: Continuities in the Sociology of Natural Resources* (159-78). Boulder, CO: Westview Press.

Blunden, J., and N. Curry. 1988. *A Future for our Countryside*. Oxford: Blackwell.

Bromley, D. 1992. "The Commons, Property, and Common-Property Regimes." In D.W. Bromley, ed., *Making the Commons Work: Theory, Practice, and Policy* (3-16). San Francisco: ICS Press.

Brown, D.W. 1996. *Strategic Land-Use Planning Source Book*. Victoria: CORE.

Bryant, C.R. 1989. "Entrepreneurs in the Rural Environment." *Journal of Rural Studies* 5: 337-48.

Bryant, C.R., and T.R.R. Johnston. 1992. *Agriculture in the City's Countryside*. Toronto: University of Toronto Press.

Bryant C.R., L.H. Russwurm, and A.G. McLellan. 1982. *The City's Countryside: Land and Its Management in the Rural-Urban Fringe*. London: Longman.

Clark, G., I. Bowdler, and B. Ilbery. 1995. The Institutional Environment and the Development of Alternative Farming Systems. Paper presented to the American-British-Canadian Symposium on Rural Geography, Rural Systems, and Geographical Scale, North Carolina.

Cloke, P., and M. Goodwin. 1992. "Conceptualizing Countryside Change: From Post-Fordism to Rural Structured Coherence." *Transactions of the Institute of British Geographers* 17: 321-6.

Debman, G. 1975. "Nondecisions and Power." *American Political Science Review* 69: 889-904.

District of Squamish. 1994. Tourism Development Plan for the District of Squamish. Prepared by the Citizens' Tourism Advisory Committee and Howe Sound Community Futures Society, Squamish, BC.

Dorney, R.S., and D.W. Hoffman. 1979. "Development of Landscape Planning: Concepts and Management Strategies for an Urbanizing Agricultural Region." *Landscape Planning* 6: 151-77.

Douglas, D. 1989. "Community Economic Development in Rural Canada: A Critical Review." *Plan Canada* 29,2: 28-46.

Enns, R. 1996. "Developer Lands Brohm Ridge Ski Resort." *Squamish Chief*, 22 October: 1.

Gill A.M., and M.G. Reed. 1997. "The Re-Imaging of a Canadian Resource Town: Postproductivism in a North American Context." *Applied Geographic Studies* 1,2: 129-47.

Halfacree, K.H. 1995. A New Space or Spatial Effacement? Alternative Futures for the Post-Productivist Countryside. Paper presented to the American-British-Canadian Symposium on Rural Geography, Rural Systems, and Geographical Scale, North Carolina. (Text available from the author, University of Wales, Swansea, SA2 8PP, UK.)

Hamilton, G. 1995. "Reduced Harvest Hits Soo Hardest." *Vancouver Sun*, 12 October: C1-2.

Hayter, R., and T.J. Barnes. 1997. "The Restructuring of British Columbia's Coastal Forest Sector: Flexibility Perspectives." In T.J. Barnes and R. Hayter, eds., *Troubles in the Rainforest: British Columbia's Forest Economy in Transition* (181-203). Victoria: Western Geographical Press.

Healy, R.G. 1994. "The 'Common Pool' Problem in Tourism Landscapes." *Annals of Tourism Research* 21: 596-611.

Hodge, G. 1974. "The City and the Periphery." In L.S. Bourne et al., eds., *Urban Futures for*

Central Canada: Perspectives on Forecasting Urban Growth and Change (281-301). Toronto: University of Toronto Press.

Howe Sound Roundtable. 1996. *Howe Sound 20/20: Issues and Initiatives in Growth and Sustainability for Howe Sound.* Bowen Island, BC: Howe Sound Roundtable.

LeFroy, E., J. Salerian, and R. Hobbs. 1991. "Integrating Economic and Ecological Considerations: A Theoretical Framework." In R. Hobbs and D. Saunders, eds., *Reintegrating Fragmented Landscapes: Towards Sustainable Production and Nature Conservation* (209-44). New York: Springer Verlag.

Lowe, P., J. Murdoch, T. Marsden, R. Munton, and A. Flynn. 1993. "Regulating the New Rural Spaces: The Uneven Development of Land." *Journal of Rural Studies* 9: 205-22.

Lowrance, R., P. Hendrix, and E. Odum. 1986. "A Hierarchical Approach to Sustainable Agriculture." *American Journal of Alternative Agriculture* 1: 169-73.

Markusen, A.R. 1989. "Industrial Restructuring and Regional Politics." In R.A. Beauregard, ed., *Economic Restructuring and Political Response* (115-47). Vol. 34 of *Urban Affairs Annual Reviews.* Newbury Park: Sage.

Pierce, J. 1993. "Agriculture, Sustainability, and the Imperatives of Policy Reform." *Geoforum* 24,4: 381-96.

Pinkerton, E., ed. 1989. *Co-operative Management of Local Fisheries: New Directions for Improved Management and Community Development.* Vancouver: UBC Press.

Reed, M.G. 1995. "Cooperative Management of Environmental Resources: A Case Study from Northern Ontario, Canada." *Economic Geography* 71: 132-49.

Reed, M.G., and A.M. Gill. 1997. "Tourism, Recreational, and Amenity Values in Land Allocation: An Analysis of Institutional Arrangements in the Post-Productivist Era." *Environment and Planning A* 29: 2,019-40.

Rees, J. 1990. *Natural Resources: Allocation, Economics, and Policy.* 2nd ed. London: Routledge.

Royal Commission on the Future of the Toronto Waterfront. 1992. *1992 Regeneration: Toronto's Waterfront and the Sustainable City: Final Report.* Toronto: Royal Commission on the Future of the Toronto Waterfront.

Rudzitis, G. 1993. "Nonmetropolitan Geography: Migration, Sense of Place, and the American West." *Urban Geography* 14: 574-85.

Shaw, G., and A.M. Williams. 1994. *Critical Issues in Tourism: A Geographical Perspective.* Oxford: Blackwell.

Smit, B., and J. Smithers. 1993. "Sustainable Agriculture: Interpretations, Analyses, and Prospects." *Canadian Journal of Regional Science* 16,3: 499-524.

Urry, J. 1995. *Consuming Places.* London: Routledge.

Ward, N., P. Lowe, S. Seymour, and J. Clark. 1995. "Rural Restructuring and the Regulation of Farm Pollution." *Environment and Planning A* 27: 1,193-211.

Wolfinger, R. 1971. "Nondecisions and the Study of Local Politics." *American Political Science Review* 655: 1,063-80.

9

Natural Capital and Social Capital: Implications for Sustainable Community Development[1]

Mark Roseland

Introduction

Two of the most intriguing ideas to hit academic journals in recent years are natural capital and social capital. Natural capital is a term used primarily by ecological economists, themselves a relatively new breed, to further our understanding of sustainable development (e.g., Jansson et al. 1994; Wackernagel and Rees 1996). Social capital is a term used by progressive economists and other social scientists to further our understanding of society and community (e.g., Coleman 1988; Jacobs 1961; Ostrom 1993; Putnam 1995). This chapter examines the concepts of natural capital and social capital, whether (and, if so, how) they are linked, and their implications for sustainable development at the community level.

Natural Capital

Global resource depletion and pollution are forcing recognition that existing patterns of development and resource use are not sustainable. Since the publication of *Our Common Future*, intense debate has been generated in many countries over the meaning of the Brundtland Commission's call for "sustainable development" (World Commission on Environment and Development 1987).

Even conservative neoclassical economists are recognizing that the "sustainable" component of "development" requires that human activities today do not deplete natural or environmental capital. Natural capital refers to any stock of natural assets that yields a flow of valuable goods and services into the future. For example, a forest, a fish stock, or an aquifer can provide a harvest or flow that is potentially sustainable year after year. The forest or fish stock is "natural capital," and the sustainable harvest is "natural income."

The environmental assets that comprise this natural capital may usefully be divided into three categories:

1   nonrenewable resources, such as minerals and fossil fuels
2   the finite capacity of natural systems to produce renewable resources
    such as food crops, forestry products, and water supplies – which are
    renewable only if the natural systems from which they are drawn are
    not overexploited
3   the capacity of natural systems to absorb the emissions and pollutants
    that arise from human actions without side effects that imply heavy
    costs passed on to future generations (e.g., activities that release chem-
    icals that deplete the atmosphere's ozone layer and greenhouse gases
    that may cause serious climatic imbalances).

Natural capital also provides critical ecological services such as waste
assimilation, erosion and flood control, and protection from ultraviolet
radiation (the ozone layer is a form of natural capital). These life-support
systems are counted as natural income. Because the flow of services from
ecosystems often requires that they function as intact systems, the structure and diversity of the system may be an important component of natural capital (Wackernagel and Rees 1996).

Although natural capital is a relatively new way of framing choices for
social policy and action, it has helped considerably to refine the debate on
sustainability. For example, there is no doubt that the stock of nonrenewable resources is finite, nor is there any doubt that ecosystems (individually
and collectively within the biosphere) have limits in their capacities to
absorb pollutants. There is also agreement that some environmental assets,
such as areas of outstanding natural beauty, are irreplaceable. "The debate
centres on which environmental assets are irreplaceable and the extent to
which current (and projected) future levels of resource use degrade the capital stock of environmental assets for future generations, the extent to
which one resource can be substituted for another (for instance, a syn-
thetic substance replacing a natural one) and the extent to which pollutants derived from human activities are damaging the biosphere" (Mitlin
and Satterthwaite 1991).

Two Interpretations of Sustainability
Pearce, Barbier, and Markandya (1989) argue that "future generations
should be compensated for reductions in the endowments of resources
brought about by the actions of present generations," suggesting that each
generation should leave the next with a stock of assets at least as great as
that which it inherited. There are two possible interpretations of this condition: "weak sustainability," which aggregates all types of assets, and "strong
sustainability," which differentiates between natural and artificial assets,
arguing that, whatever the level of human-made assets, an adequate stock

of environmental (or natural) assets alone is critical in securing sustainability (Daly 1989).

The weak-sustainability interpretation reflects the neoclassical economic assumption that natural and nonnatural assets are substitutable and that natural assets can be liquidated as long as subsequent investment provides an equivalent endowment to the next generation (Rees 1992). Yet in some cases, natural and nonnatural assets are clearly not substitutable. For example, a sawmill cannot be substituted for a forest because the sawmill (nonnatural capital) needs the forest (natural capital) in order to function (Daly 1989). This interpretation also assumes that other forms of capital (e.g., manufactured, financial, or human) can be converted back into natural capital, but it does not take into account irreversible processes such as the extinction of species or the destruction of ecosystems.

All this suggests that the weak-sustainability interpretation is grossly insufficient; even Pearce, Barbier, and Markandya (1990) agree that natural capital stock should only be destroyed if the benefits of doing so are very large or if the social costs of conservation are unacceptably large. Yet this begs the key question: *are we capable of knowing the social costs and benefits of destroying or conserving natural capital stock?* Ecological economists can put a price on resources such as timber and fisheries, but the value of ecological-process resources such as carbon absorption or photosynthesis cannot easily be quantified and monetized (Rees 1991).

The very concept of econonomic "trade-offs" depends on being able to put *prices* on the items traded. Resources that cannot be quantified or monetized also cannot be priced. It may be theoretically possible to trade some value of a fishery for some value of a timber harvest, but it may not be possible to price the value of the ozone shield.

The economic benefits of destroying natural capital stock or the social costs of conserving such stocks may *seem* large, but only as a function of our inability to adequately assess such costs and benefits. So-called rational economic analysis has extended beyond its rational limits (Rees 1991). It is therefore time for a different kind of framework for planning and decision making, guided by the understanding that *natural capital stock should not be destroyed.*

The pace of global ecological change suggests that human activity may already be undermining essential ecosphere functions. In these circumstances, it would be a "sound risk-averse strategy" for society simply to accept, that while technically inestimable, the life support values of remaining stocks of natural capital are greater than any stock-depleting development values however large the latter might be. Given the threat to global security associated with irreversible disruptions of the ecosphere, and the increasing probability of such events under prevailing development approaches, we are confronting a category of strong catastrophic risk which "should, in the limit, not be undertaken at any price." In short, if the potential benefits of conservation can be shown to approach infinity, the costs are irrelevant. (Rees 1991)

In terms of the life-support functions of natural capital, destruction of any single significant natural asset can be likened to destruction of any single bodily organ or system. The destruction of the ozone layer may have the same consequences for the planet as the destruction of the immune system has for the human body; global warming may be analogous to a high fever. We do not ask those who suffer from heart disease to "trade" normal brain functioning for a healthier heart. Such choices are the stuff of literature's great tragedies; they only become more tragic if we insist on this approach to deciding complex societal choices. Like a thermometer registering a fever, the accumulating trends of ecological decline (e.g., decrease in stratospheric ozone, increase in greenhouse gases, extinction of species, loss of biodiversity, etc.) are the indicators of our condition: "The ecological bottom line for sustainable development can be stated as an economic metaphor: humankind must learn to live on the 'interest' generated by remaining stocks of living 'natural capital.' Any human activity dependent on the consumptive use of bioresources cannot be sustained indefinitely if it not only consumes annual production, but also cuts into capital stocks" (Rees 1991).[2]

Social Capital
Ostrom (1993) notes that all forms of capital are created by spending time and effort in transformational and transactional activities. Physical capital is the stock of material resources that can be used to produce a flow of future income. The origin of physical capital is the process of spending time and other resources constructing tools, plants, facilities, and other material resources that can, in turn, be used to produce other products. Human capital is the acquired knowledge and skills that individuals bring to productive activity. Human capital is formed consciously through training and education and unconsciously through experience.

The first significant appearance of the concept of social capital was in the work of Jacobs (1961), who used it to describe a norm of social responsibility, a corresponding atmosphere of social trust, and interconnecting networks of communication. Social capital is the shared knowledge, understandings, and patterns of interaction that a group of people bring to any productive activity (Coleman 1988; Putnam et al. 1993). Social capital refers to the organizations, structures, and social relations that people build up independently of the state or large corporations. It contributes to a stronger community fabric and, often as a by-product of other activities, builds bonds of information, trust, and interpersonal solidarity (Coleman 1990). The term also refers to features of social organization such as networks, norms, and trust that increase a society's productive potential (Putnam 1993). Social capital, as Putnam argues, although largely neglected in discussions of public policy, substantially enhances returns on investments in physical and human capital. However, unlike conventional capital, it is a public good – that is, it is not the private property of those who benefit from it. Thus, like other public goods, from clean air to safe streets, social capital tends to be underprovided by private agents. The ties, norms, and trust that constitute social capital are most often created as by-products of other social activities and then transferred from one social setting to another.

Social capital is created when individuals learn to trust one another so that they can make credible commitments and rely on generalized forms of reciprocity rather than on narrow sequences of specific quid pro quo relationships. Ostrom (1993) notes that the shared cognitive aspects of social capital help account for two unusual characteristics that differ from physical capital:

> First, social capital does not wear out upon being used more and more ... Using social capital for an initial purpose creates mutual understandings and ways of relating that can frequently be used to accomplish entirely different joint activities at much lower start-up costs ... Social capital that is well adapted to one broad set of joint activities may not be easily molded to activities that require vastly different patterns of expectation, authority, and distribution of rewards and costs than used in the initial sets of activities.
>
> Second, if unused, social capital deteriorates at a relatively rapid rate. Individuals who do not exercise their own skills can lose human capital relatively rapidly. When several individuals must all remember the same routine in the same manner, however, the probability that at least one of them forgets some aspect increases rapidly over time. Further, as time goes on, some individuals leave and others enter any social aggregation. If newcomers are not introduced to an established pattern of interaction as they enter (through job training, initiation, or any of the myriad other ways that social capital is passed from one generation to the next), social capital can dissipate through nonuse. No one is quite sure how they used to get a particular joint activity done. Either the group has to pay some of the start-up costs all over again, or forgo the joint advantages that they had achieved at an earlier time.

Social capital differs from other forms of capital in several significant ways – one is that it is not limited by material scarcity, meaning that its creative capacity is limited only by imagination. It thereby also suggests a route toward sustainability, by replacing the fundamentally illogical model of unlimited growth within a finite world with one of unlimited development[3] that is not bound by the availability of material resources.

However, social capital also has limitations that other forms of capital do not. It cannot be created instantly, and consciously trying to create it or direct it can lead to resistance. People resist being instrumentalized for even the best reasons. Social capital takes time to develop and is inherently nontransferable (Flora and Flora 1993). It is also fragile and subject to erosion not only by direct assault but also, more importantly, by neglect, if there are many or strong competitors for investment of emotional significance or time.

The modern conceptualization of social capital is associated with Coleman (1988), who describes it as the *relations between* individuals and groups. It can take several forms, some of which are mutually recognized bonds, channels of information, and norms and sanctions. For Coleman, the value of the concept is that it identifies aspects of the social structure by their functions: "The function identified by the concept of 'social capital' is the value of these aspects of the social structure to actors as resources that they can use to achieve their interests."

Measuring Social Capital

An obvious question about social capital is whether and how it can be measured. For example, Putnam (1995) argues that US social capital is declining. His "Bowling Alone: America's Declining Social Capital," published in the January 1995 issue of the *Journal of Democracy,* has had an impact far beyond the usual for academic writing. His thesis is that the vibrancy of American civil society "has notably declined over the past several decades." Putnam gets his title from the finding that from 1980 to 1993 league bowling declined by 40 percent while the number of individual bowlers rose by 10 percent. The rest of his evidence is less whimsical: voter turnout, church attendance, and union membership are down. The percentage of people who trust government and who attend community meetings has dropped, and membership in voluntary associations is down by roughly one-sixth from 1974 to 1989.

The significance of these changes, for Putnam, is not that they are inherently unfortunate so much as that they predict a broader decline in our society's economic vitality. Other analysts (e.g., Rose 1996) concur that the wealth of nations is likely to be highest where there is a large stock of social capital.

In "Kicking in Groups," Lemann (1996) wonders why Putnam's thesis that civic virtue is rapidly collapsing in the United States is being "so widely and instantly accepted as gospel." Lemann investigated several potential replacements for bowling leagues and found, for example, that the American Association of Retired Persons has 33 million members; US Youth

Soccer has 2.4 million members, up from 1.2 million ten years ago; individual donations to charity grew from $16.2 billion in 1970 to $101.8 billion in 1990; Little League membership has increased every year; and PTA membership has risen over the past decade.

In Canada, the number of charitable organizations registered with Revenue Canada more than tripled between 1967 and 1994, going from 22,556 to 71,414. Under federal law, registered charities are defined as nonprofit organizations established for the "relief of poverty, the advancement of religion, the advancement of education, and other purposes beneficial to the community as a whole in a way which the law regards as charitable." Revenue Canada classifies them under six broad categories: welfare, health, education, religion, benefits to the community, and other. Religious charitable organizations comprise the largest single group (42.3 percent), followed by welfare (17.3 percent), benefits to the community (17 percent), education (16 percent), and health (7.3 percent) (Browne 1996, 21-2).

Rose (1996) cautions that the number of formal organizations in a society, especially national organizations, is not an adequate indicator of social capital. Members of many organizations are not individuals but other organizations. Even when individuals are the constituent members, the number varies from one social activity to another, and so does the extent to which an association includes a high percentage of its potential members. Furthermore, people can put their names on a membership list and not attend meetings of their organization. The fundamental limitation of data about formal organizations is that it ignores informal social networks important in every society.

To use an instrumental definition, social capital is created when individuals form social networks to produce goods and services, nonmonetized as well as monetized. Networks are usually informal groups of people who know each other personally, such as villagers who help each other at harvest time or friends and neighbours who help each other cope with problems. "Even if networks have a formal institutional identity, such as a choir society or a rural cooperative, they remain face-to-face groups in which the reputation of individuals is known to its members. Informal face-to-face networks can be found not only in villages and urban neighbourhoods but also among economic and policy-making elites" (Rose 1996).

Social capital can add to human capital; for example, social networks provide many informal types of social security and health care to individuals within a collective "caring" network. It can also add to natural capital; for example, enhancing the use of natural resources, such as water for irrigation systems, requires collective action.

Social capital can take negative as well as positive forms. The development of natural resources can reduce the stock of social capital if, for example, villages are flooded and the social networks of the residents are broken up. Social capital can also distort the rule-bound market allocation of goods and services, as in mafia-type groups selling "insurance" to firms. In extreme cases, social capital can impose losses on individuals, such as when a strong social network effectively prevents girls from obtaining education and employment (Rose 1996).

Social Capital and Social Networks[4]

Coleman (1988) differentiates social networks into those with and those without closure and uses the difference to explain the presence or absence of social norms and their effectiveness or ineffectiveness. A network with closure is one in which most of the individuals in it know each other and the relationship of each to the others. Networks with closure can be highly effective in enforcing norms, but as discussed earlier the results can be positive or negative. Coleman uses the example of parents of students in a religious school, but a prison demonstrates the same principle at work.

A network without closure is one in which each individual's circle of acquaintances overlaps only partially or not at all with those of the others, and the degree of overlap is generally unknown. These networks can only weakly enforce informal norms and are forced to rely on formal structures – courts, police, lawsuits – to a much higher degree than networks with closure.

Coleman (1988) observes that the quality of public good of most social capital means that it is in a fundamentally different position with respect to purposeful action than are most other forms of capital. Because the benefits of actions that bring social capital into being are largely experienced by persons other than the actor, it is often not in the actor's interest to bring it into being. The result is that most forms of social capital are created or destroyed as by-products of other activities.

Another significant point is that, because social capital is located in relationships with specific individuals, that which is mobilized for one purpose can be readily appropriated for other purposes.

Beyond understanding the basic nature of social capital, one needs to know where it is located and how it can be mobilized and multiplied for sustainable community development.

Locating Social Capital

Formally organized groups are the necessary recourse of societies without closure. Organized groups have established procedures for adherence and keep membership lists, follow recognized procedures in conducting their affairs, and often administer budgets and own property. Examples are churches, ethnic associations, unions, trade associations, sports clubs, theatre societies, and environmental groups. However, a formal organization may also be a public representation of a society with more primary closure.

Churches, especially ethnically rooted ones, tend to fall into this category. Organizations that have survived intense struggles in a hostile social environment, such as some unions and environmental groups, can also take on characteristics of closure.

Informal groups can be regular customers of a shop, users of a park, sports fans, music fans, mothers of children who play together, or groups of street youth who mutually protect each other. Members of such groups may not necessarily know each other, or even that they constitute a group, yet they can be a useful resource for each other and an immense reservoir of energy and imagination if it can be accessed and organized.

Mobilizing and Multiplying Social Capital

Mobilization and use of social capital are not problem free. By nature, social capital can tend to mirror existing power structures. Marginalized people are sometimes marginalized exactly because they are unable to access social capital, as is often the case with the mentally ill or other people with poor social skills.

Even in a society with closure, social capital may be divided between different factions that regard each other as rivals or threats. Although there are tools to deal with this problem, their success is uncertain, and the difficulties are worse in larger Canadian cities, where there are many competing groups without closure, groups that may not even be able to communicate because of language barriers. This is to claim not that we should give up on prospects for sustainable community development in urban centres but that we should not deceive ourselves about the challenges involved.

If social capital is important, then classic liberal social policy, with its emphasis on enhancing the opportunities of individuals, is partially misplaced. Instead, argues Putnam et al. (1993), we must focus on community development, allowing space for religious organizations, choral societies, and Little Leagues. Whatever their intended effects, government policies should be vetted for their indirect effects on social capital. Government investment in social capital, from agricultural extension services to tax exemptions for community organizations, must be renewed and encouraged.

The role of education in facilitating social capital must also be reconsidered. Education should attempt to create integrated opportunities for both individual and collective learning, and students should understand and experience learning communities and learning organizations (e.g., Boggs 1990; Hamilton 1992; Schon 1983; Senge 1990).

Linking Natural Capital and Social Capital

From a sustainable development perspective, we must reinterpret our classical understanding of wealth and capital in terms of satisfying fundamental human and ecological needs. Thus, natural capital, human capital, social and organizational capital, and manufactured capital all contribute to the creation of wealth in its broadest sense (Ekins 1986).

Community "civicness" is key to maximizing the potential of communities as agents of sustainable development (Selman and Parker 1997). Putnam et al. (1993) suggest that civicness in a community will lubricate social life, enhance productivity, and facilitate action; in practice, it will then become a proxy for successful policy implementation. It is also an important component of the sense of place, which many authors have identified as critical for community sustainability (e.g., Aberley 1993, 1994; Hiss 1990; Roseland 1997; Sale 1985).

According to the UBC Task Force on Healthy and Sustainable Communities (1994), along with ecological carrying capacity, we also need an increase in the "social caring capacity" (SCC) of our communities. SCC, reflected by networks of social capital, is the prerequisite for sustainable development. Evidence from the Indian state of Kerala (McKibben 1996) suggests that quality of life can increase while industrial throughput decreases;[5] that is, social capital can substitute for manufactured capital. Furthermore, whereas natural capital diminishes with exploitation, social capital accumulates with regular use (Selman and Parker 1997).

Social Infrastructure and Sustainable Personalities
Flora and Flora (1993) have identified "social infrastructure" as the key to linking individual leadership to physical infrastructure and to facilitating community development. Social infrastructure is the group-level, interactive aspect of organizations or institutions. Swanson (1992) conceptualizes social infrastructure as having three parts: (1) social institutions, including local government, social service institutions, voluntary and civic organizations, and the like; (2) human resources, which include attributes of inhabitants such as their technical expertise, organizational skills, educational levels, and even social structure – class, race, ethnicity, gender, and so on; and (3) characteristics of social networks, including innovativeness, ability to mobilize resources within the community, ability to link up with outside expertise and information, and so on.

In the context of the Local Agenda 21 initiatives now being widely produced throughout Britain, Selman and Parker (1997) have identified three types of person – not mutually exclusive – that are essential to successful sustainable development processes at the community level. They argue that it is overwhelmingly important that strategies seek to ensure that the energies of these people are nurtured, stewarded, and sustained.

First are the "catalytic personalities," whose elemental presence speeds up the rate of a reaction in the social chemistry of community change. Although often thought to emerge spontaneously from the local community, they are actually often present in various quarters, including civil service, local government, and public agencies. They are willing and able to enthusiastically see a project through from conception to completion. They are also subject to feeling burned-out, exploited, or disillusioned, and if they leave in the course of a project then it can suffer a disastrous loss of momentum.

Second are "community champions," spokespeople who represent the views and interests of the community, often with unwelcome force, to otherwise impervious bureaucracies.

Third are the "supernetworkers." Although the role of networking is well established in community work, many people are not interested in, or able to comprehend, more than one aspect of sustainable development. Supernetworkers have the imagination, interest, time, and energy to take an active role in coordinating groups and to liaise with several parallel streams of interest. They not only underpin strategy synthesis, but they also typically bring their personal networking skills to bear on the mobilization of financial and personnel resources.

Implications for Achieving Sustainable Development in Communities

Much of the debate over the meaning of sustainable development focuses on the tension between the economic necessity for material growth and the ecological reality of limits. In the twenty-five years since *The Limits to Growth* was published (Meadows et al. 1972), few researchers have seriously explored the implications of this concept for social organization, work, and community economic development (e.g., see Meadows et al. 1992). Ryle (1988) notes that "ecological limits may limit political choices, but they do not determine them." The heart of the growth issue is simply that "underlying the social democratic advocacy of economic expansion is the fact that within a capitalist market framework, 'growth' is indeed the prerequisite of much else: especially, of the provision of welfare services and the creation of jobs, and of national economic status vis-à-vis other capitalist powers. Thus the critique of growth becomes a critique of capitalism and the market ... *An alternative would have to find new, non-market-based means of providing employment and of meeting welfare needs*" (italics added).

Just as sustainability has prompted a shift in our transportation and energy planning away from the traditional concerns with increasing supply and toward a new focus on managing demand, we must also shift our economic development emphasis from the traditional concern with increasing growth to *reducing social dependence on economic growth*, or what we might call economic demand management (Roseland 1992). This shift has distinct implications for sustainable community development, particularly regarding the future of work and community economic development.

The Future of Work

According to Statistics Canada, since the forty-hour work week became standard in the 1960s, Canadian workers' output per hour has more than doubled in many sectors. At the same time, unemployment, overtime hours, and incidents of health problems due to work-related stress have continued to rise (Karasek and Theorell 1990).

Harvard economist Juliet Schor (1992) argues that many North Americans are working themselves to death. Since the end of the Second World War, for example, labour productivity in the United States has almost tripled. Previously, workers gained leisure time as a result of increased productivity. In the postwar era, however, wage increases almost exclusively fuelled increased per capita consumption, which rose almost as much as productivity, rather than increasing free time. Consumption is an important motivator in modern society – that is, people work more to support a lifestyle in which material wealth is integral to happiness. The decline in "associational" activity observed by Putnam (1995) is tied in part to this time versus money trade-off. Most North Americans spend most of their recreational time watching television and shopping. These changes in the ways in which North Americans work and spend their time erode the extent and quality of community and of civil society (Schor 1992).

Much of the unrecognized work that maintains the social economy,[6] which in turn is the foundation of the market economy, is performed by women. This includes reproductive work, household work, parenting, caring for the old and the sick, home-based production for use, and subsistence agriculture (Brandt 1995; Henderson 1991, 1996; Korten 1995; Lerner 1994; Schor 1992).

Several proposals have been made for employment reform that helps to manage economic demand and more fairly distributes work and leisure. Key elements of these proposals include shorter work weeks and improved part-time employment options. Implementation of such alternatives brings forth a myriad of challenges, including improved employee benefits and incentives for volunteer and community service work for which there is social demand but no market demand.

The emerging literature on the future of work (see, e.g., Lerner 1994; O'Hara 1993, 1994; Rifkin 1995; Schor 1991, 1992) provides valuable insight into alternative work models and the sustainable development implications of employment. Much of this work, however, is highly theoretical and national or international in scope, ignoring community development implications and the challenges of implementing sustainable development at the community level.

Potentially significant employment opportunities, consistent with more sustainable patterns of development, exist in many economic sectors. Redesigned and improved infrastructure, knowledge-based services, environmental technologies, improved management and use of natural resources, and tourism are all rich areas for private sector investment, supportive government policies, and expanded training. Some of the most promising employment opportunities include (Shea 1994):

- upgrading energy efficiency in buildings, products, and transportation systems
- adopting and implementing sustainable forestry, fisheries, soil, and watershed management practices
- expanding delivery and use of information technologies
- centring sustainable tourism activities on areas of environmental, cultural, and historical significance
- recycling and remanufacturing of solid and hazardous wastes into marketable products
- accelerating and expanding development of marine and freshwater aquaculture
- adding value to fish, agricultural, and forest products
- developing, manufacturing, and marketing products, services, and technologies that reduce environmental burdens
- designing energy-efficient and people-friendly cities.

Community Economic Development
The concept of community economic development (CED) provides a means of addressing sustainable development at the community level. CED is also a constructive way to tap into the creative energies of the "sustainable people" described above that exist in most communities. The distinguishing features of CED, a rapidly evolving field, are characterized by the following working definition (SFU CEDC 1996): "Community Economic Development is a process by which communities can initiate and generate their own solutions to their common economic problems and thereby build long-term community capacity and foster the integration of economic, social and environmental objectives."[7]

Other observers describe CED in less flattering terms, arguing that, in response to external funding priorities, community development organizations have lost their original focus on the creation of local employment opportunities and local generation and control of capital in low-income communities (Surpin and Bettridge 1986). Examples of CED range from small-business counselling and import substitution ("buy local") to workers' cooperatives, community development corporations, and community land trusts. Boothroyd (1991) argues that, "Whether CED is practiced in hinterland resource towns, urban ghettos, obsolescent manufacturing cities, or Native communities' reserves, the general objective is the same: to take some measure of control of the local economy back from the markets and the state."

Achieving sustainable CED means emphasizing sustainable employment and economic demand management (EDM). Sustainable employment includes turning "wastes" into resources (e.g., recycling), improving efficiency with regard to energy and materials, converting to greater reliance on renewable energy sources, increasing community self-reliance (e.g., food and energy production), and sustainably managing natural resources (e.g., community forestry). EDM shifts the emphasis of economic development from the traditional concern with increasing growth to the new concern with reducing social dependence on economic growth.

Examples of sustainable CED include *car cooperatives* to reduce the cost and necessity of car ownership (Vancouver); *sustainable employment plans* to create jobs, spur private spending, and reduce pollution through public investment in energy conservation and audits (San Jose, CA); *new product development* to encourage manufacturers to develop environmentally friendly products through municipal assistance in research and development (Gothenberg, Sweden); *increased affordable housing supply* through zoning codes that promote a variety of housing types, including smaller and multifamily homes (Portland, OR); experiments with *local self-reliance* through closed-loop, self-sustaining economic networks (St. Paul, MN); *community-supported agriculture* to preserve farmland and help farmers while making fresh fruits and vegetables available in city neighbourhoods (Vancouver; London, ON; New York City); *local currencies* such as LETS: Local Employment and Trading Systems (Toronto); a *local ownership development project* with a revolving loan fund to encourage employee-owned businesses, considered more stable over the long term and more likely to hire, train, and promote local residents (Burlington, VT); and a community *recycling depot* for beverage containers that employs street people – "dumpster divers" – and provides them with skills, training, and self-esteem (Vancouver).

Conclusion

Four arguments have informed this chapter. First, the term "sustainable development" acquires tangible meaning when understood in terms of natural capital and natural income. The bottom line for sustainability is that we must learn to live on natural income rather than deplete natural capital. Economic growth with an ecological deficit is antieconomic and makes us poorer rather than richer in the long term (Daly and Cobb 1989).

Second, natural capital and social equity demand that North Americans, among the world's most inefficient and wasteful consumers of materials and energy (World Commission on Environment and Development 1987), find ways to live more lightly on the planet. At a minimum, we will have to increase the efficiency of our resource and energy use. More likely, we will have to reduce our present (not to speak of projected) levels of materials and energy consumption.

Third, reducing our materials and energy consumption need not diminish, and in fact would likely enhance, our quality of life and the public domain – in other words, our social capital. It is important to distinguish between "quality of life" and "standard of living" (Jacobs 1993). Standard of living generally refers to disposable income for things that we purchase individually, whereas quality of life can be considered as the sum of all things that people purchase collectively (e.g., the health care system, public education, policing) or things that are not purchased at all (e.g., air quality). Standard of living refers solely to the private domain, whereas quality of life refers to the public domain, the realm of social capital.

Fourth, the critical resource for enhancing social capital is not money – rather, the critical resources are trust, imagination, the relations between individuals and groups, and time, the literal currency of life. Many of the social issues that people relate to most intimately – family, neighbourhood, community, decompression from work, recreation, culture, et cetera – depend on these resources at least as much as on money. This is not to say that economic security isn't important – it is – but focusing solely on money to provide security is using nineteenth-century thinking to address twenty-first-century challenges.

The direction that these arguments collectively point in is clear. Economic and social policies must explicitly aim to nurture and enhance social capital not only to preserve our stock of natural capital but also to improve our economic and social well-being. Every government or corporate decision should be reviewed for its effect on both natural and social capital. Programs and policies need to be created at every level to ensure that natural capital and social capital are properly considered. Proposals such as the following need to be raised in debates about national public policy.

1   *A shorter work week* (e.g., a thirty-hour or four-day week) should become the standard for a majority of Canadians.

2   *Employee benefits reform* should be undertaken so that benefits are attached to workers and their families rather than to companies (like a registered retirement savings plan), allowing individuals and/or families to buy benefits and/or pension plans. This system would enable two distinct advantages: (a) a benefits system for *part-time work* could be created this way and would greatly expand the potential for *good* part-time work, shared jobs, et cetera; and (b) *a sabbatical system* could also be created this way, whereby people (besides tenured academics) could spread out their benefits to enable substantial time away from work for education, travel, family, et cetera.

3   *Community service and volunteer work*[8] should be encouraged by (a) *income vouchers for the permanently or chronically unemployed* (e.g., fishers, loggers) to do *community service work* for which there is social demand but not market demand (e.g., work with nonprofit organizations); and (b) *tax credits for volunteer work* with nongovernmental organizations.

4   *Income tax reform* should include (a) a guaranteed *minimum income*; and (b) perhaps a *maximum income.*[9]

None of the major political parties in the 1997 Canadian federal election paid any attention to these ideas. Yet these kinds of reform would enable individuals and families to become less dependent on both the market and the state; they would enable people to become more self-reliant in terms of providing their own economic security; and they would increase the ability of both men and women to provide time-dependent services such as day care and elder care. These are the *real* "family values" that we should encourage, values that contribute to the health and well-being of civil society. Indeed, these initiatives would vastly increase our social capital and simultaneously protect our natural capital.

Notes
1 Some material based upon this chapter also appears in Roseland (1998).
2 Rees (1991) also notes that "this shifts the emphasis of environmental policy from pollution control ... to managing consumption. In thermodynamic (rather than mechanical) terms, all material economic production is actually consumption."
3 In this context, "development" can be described as a process of social change for fulfilling human needs, advancing social equity, expanding organizational effectiveness, and building capacity toward sustainability.
4 I am grateful to Joan Fletcher for much of the analysis in this section.
5 Kerala, a state of 29 million people in southern India, has a per capita income estimated by various surveys to be between $298 and $350 US per year, about one-seventieth the US average. Yet data for life expectancy, literacy, and birth rates for Kerala are comparable to those for the United States. "One-seventieth the income means one-seventieth the damage to the planet. So, on balance, if Kerala and the United States manage to achieve the same physical quality of life, Kerala is the vastly more successful society" (McKibben 1996).
6 The social economy consists of "mutual, cooperative relationships" that "create a dense fabric of relationships based on long-term sharing and cooperation." It maintains "the ethical structure, social stability, and personal security on which the smooth function of a market depends" – a fact that is routinely overlooked by economic policy makers. It is not, therefore, counted in national income statistics, does not contribute to measured economic growth, and is undervalued by policy makers who count only activities in the market economy as productive contributions to national output. The social economy is founded on values of cooperation, sharing, trust, and mutual obligation. "Social economies are by nature local, non-waged, non-monetized, and non-market" (Korten 1995).
7 This definition is based on the founding report for the centre, written by David Ross and George McRobie in 1987. McRobie was a colleague of E.F. Schumacher. McRobie's *Small Is Possible* (1981) was inspired by Schumacher's *Small Is Beautiful: A Study of Economics as if People Mattered* (1973).
8 These two ideas are developed in Rifkin (1995).

9 Reflect a moment on this: the combined wealth of the world's 358 billionaires now equals the total income of the poorest 45 percent of the world's population, some 2.3 billion people (United Nations Development Program 1996). Then ask yourself how they could have *earned* that money in any realistic sense of the word.

References
Aberley, D. 1993. *Boundaries of Home: Mapping for Local Empowerment.* Gabriola Island, BC: New Society Publishers.
–, ed. 1994. *Futures by Design: The Practice of Ecological Planning.* Gabriola Island, BC: New Society Publishers.
Boggs, D. 1990. *Adult Civic Education.* Springfield, IL: Charles C. Thomas.
Boothroyd, P. 1991. *Community Economic Development: An Introduction for Planners.* Pamphlet. Vancouver: UBC Centre for Human Settlements.
Brandt, B. 1995. *Whole Life Economics: Revaluing Daily Life.* Gabriola Island, BC: New Society Publishers.
Browne, P.L. 1996. *Love in a Cold World: The Voluntary Sector in an Age of Cuts.* Ottawa: Canadian Centre for Policy Alternatives.
Coleman, J.S. 1988. "Social Capital in the Creation of Human Capital." *American Journal of Sociology* 94, supplement: S95-120.
–. 1990. *Foundations of Social Theory.* Cambridge: Harvard University Press.
Daly, H.E. 1989. "Sustainable Development: From Concept and Theory towards Operational Principles." *Population and Development Review.* Hoover Institution Conference.
Daly, H.E., and J.B. Cobb Jr. 1989. *For the Common Good: Redirecting the Economy toward Community, the Environment, and a Sustainable Future.* Boston: Beacon Press.
Ekins, P., ed. 1986. *The Living Economy: A New Economics in the Making.* London: Routledge.
Flora, C.B., and J.L. Flora. 1993. "Entrepreneurial Social Infrastructure: A Necessary Ingredient." *Annals of the American Academy of Political and Social Science* 529: 48-58.
Hamilton, E. 1992. *Adult Education for Community Development.* New York: Greenwood Press.
Henderson, H. 1991. *Paradigms in Progress: Life beyond Economics.* Indianapolis: Knowledge Systems.
–. 1996. *Building a Win-Win World: Life beyond Global Economic Warfare.* San Francisco: Berrett-Koehler Publishers.
Hiss, T. 1990. *The Experience of Place.* New York: Alfred A. Knopf.
Jansson, A-M., M. Hammer, C. Folke, and R. Costanza, eds. 1994. *Investing in Natural Capital: The Ecological Economics Approach to Sustainability.* Washington, DC: Island Press.
Jacobs, J. 1961. *The Death and Life of Great American Cities.* New York: Random House.
Jacobs, M. 1993. *The Green Economy: Environment, Sustainable Development, and the Politics of the Future.* Vancouver: UBC Press.
Karasek, R., and T. Theorell. 1990. *Healthy Work: Stress, Productivity, and the Reconstruction of Working Life.* New York: Basic Books.
Korten, D. 1995. *When Corporations Rule the World.* San Francisco: Berrett-Koehler Publishers.
Lemann, N. 1996. "Kicking in Groups." *Atlantic Monthly*, April, 22-6.
Lerner, S. 1994. "The Future of Work in North America: Good Jobs, Bad Jobs, beyond Jobs." *Futures* 26,2.
McKibben, B. 1996. "The Enigma of Kerala: One State in India Is Proving Development Experts Wrong." *Utne Reader*, March-April 1996, 102-12.
McRobie, G. 1981. *Small Is Possible.* London: Cape.
Meadows, D.H., D.L. Meadows, J. Randers, W.W. Behrens III. 1972. *The Limits to Growth.* New York: Signet.
Meadows, D.H., D.L. Meadows, J. Randers . 1992. *Beyond the Limits.* Post Mills, VT: Chelsea Green.
Mitlin, D., and D. Satterthwaite. 1991. Sustainable Development and Cities. Paper prepared for How Common Is Our Future? A Global NGO Forum, Habitat International Coalition, Mexico City, 4-7 March.
O'Hara, B. 1993. *Working Harder Isn't Working.* Vancouver: New Star Books.

–. 1994. *Put Work in Its Place*. Vancouver: New Star Books.

Ostrom, E. 1993. Social Capital and Development Projects. Paper prepared for workshop Social Capital and Economic Development, American Academy of Arts and Sciences, Cambridge, MA, July 30-1.

Pearce, D.W., E. Barbier, and A. Markandya. 1989. *Blueprint for a Green Economy*. London: Earthscan Publications.

–. 1990. *Sustainable Development: Economics and Environment in the Third World*. Brookfield, VT: Gower Publishing Company.

Putnam, R.D. 1995. "Bowling Alone: America's Declining Social Capital." *Journal of Democracy* 6,1: 65-78.

Putnam, R., R. Leonardi, and R. Nanetti. 1993. *Making Democracy Work: Civic Traditions in Modern Italy*. Princeton: Princeton University Press.

Rees, W.E. 1991. "Economics, Ecology, and the Limits of Conventional Analysis." *Journal of the Air and Waste Management Association* 41,10: 1,323-7.

–. 1992. *Understanding Sustainable Development: Natural Capital and the New World Order*. Pamphlet. Vancouver: UBC School of Community and Regional Planning.

Rifkin, J. 1995. *The End of Work: The Decline of the Global Labour Force and the Dawn of the Post-Market Era*. New York: G.P. Putnam's Sons.

Rose, K. 1996. Social Capital: Definition, Measure, Implications. Remarks at a World Bank Workshop on Social Capital, 16-17 April.

Roseland, M. 1992. *Toward Sustainable Communities: A Resource Book for Municipal and Local Governments*. Ottawa: National Roundtable on the Environment and the Economy.

–. 1997. *Eco-City Dimensions: Healthy Communities, Healthy Planet*. Gabriola Island, BC: New Society Publishers.

–. 1998. *Toward Sustainable Communities: Resources for Citizens and Their Governments*. Gabriola Island, BC: New Society Publishers.

Ryle, M. 1988. *Ecology and Socialism*. London: Radius.

Sale, K. 1985. *Dwellers in the Land: The Bioregional Vision*. San Francisco: Sierra Club.

Schon, D. 1983. *The Reflective Practitioner: How Professionals Think in Action*. New York: Basic Books.

Schor, J.B. 1991. "Global Equity and Environmental Crisis: An Argument for Reducing Working Hours in the North." *World Development* 19,1: 73-84.

–. 1992. *The Overworked American*. New York: Basic Books.

Schumacher, E.F. 1973. *Small Is Beautiful: A Study of Economics as if People Mattered*. New York: Harper and Row.

Selman, P., and J. Parker. 1997. "Citizenship, Civicness, and Social Capital in Local Agenda 21." *Local Environment* 2,2: 171-84.

Senge, P. 1990. *The Fifth Discipline*. New York: Double Day Currency.

SFU CEDC (Simon Fraser University, Community Economic Development Centre). "Our Working Definition of CED." SFU CEDC home page, http://www.sfu.ca/cedc/.

Shea, C.P. 1994. *Employment and Sustainable Development: Opportunities for Canada*. Winnipeg: International Institute for Sustainable Development.

Surpin, R., and T. Bettridge. 1986. "Refocusing Community Economic Development." *Economic Development and Law Center Report* (36-42).

Swanson, L. 1992. "Rural Social Infrastructure." In J.N. Reid et al., eds., *Foundations of Rural Development Policy*. Boulder, CO: Westview Press.

UBC Task Force on Healthy and Sustainable Communities. 1994. "Tools for Sustainability: Iteration and Implementation." In C. Chu and R. Simpson, eds., *The Ecological Public Health: From Vision to Practice*. Toronto: University of Toronto Centre for Health Promotion; Australia: Institute for Applied Environmental Research at Griffith University.

United Nations Development Program. 1996. *UN Development Report 1996*. New York: UNDP.

Wackernagel, M., and W. Rees. 1996. *Our Ecological Footprint: Reducing Human Impact on the Earth*. Gabriola Island, BC: New Society Publishers.

World Commission on Environment and Development. 1987. *Our Common Future*. New York: Oxford University Press.

10

The Civic State, Civil Society, and the Promotion of Sustainable Development

Bryan H. Massam and Jill Dickinson

Introduction

The prospects for sustainable development, as a worthy enterprise of collective action, to ensure inter alia stability and equity in economic, social, and environmental matters, are enhanced if citizens participate willingly, knowledgeably, and energetically in its promotion and governments work closely with citizens through regulatory processes and community practices. The brief case study of the small community of Field, British Columbia, presented at the end of this chapter seeks to elaborate these general assertions. Field is trying to become a sustainable community.

Although we strongly support initiatives to monitor, audit, and report objective and subjective conditions pertaining to the economic, social, and environmental milieu as promoted by Maclaren (1996), for example, unless citizens are cognizant of these initiatives and take steps to support policies that enhance sustainable development, the measurement exercises will serve little purpose. Prior, Stewart, and Walsh (1995, 1) demonstrate clearly that there is an important functional "relationship between the individual, the community and civil society, and the state" and that typically it is the set of rights, duties, and obligations of citizenship that define this relationship. Among the contemporary issues debated on this topic is the effect of the growing movement to recast the rights of citizenship into rights of individual consumers, and this movement is matched by a trend to view the obligations of government as management. "Both collective rights and individual obligations are secondary issues in this approach. The citizen moves from being a member of a community to being an agent in a public service market" (Prior, Stewart, and Walsh 1995, 1).

The Sustainable Development Research Institute at the University of British Columbia has published a summary of a series of workshops that it sponsored in 1994 and 1995 on reconciling human welfare and ecological carrying capacity (Dale, Robinson, and Massey 1995). Dale (1997) summarizes the three critical imperatives:

Sustainable development can be regarded as a process of reconciliation of three imperatives: (i) the ecological imperative to live within global bio-physical carrying capacity (ii) the social imperative to ensure the development of systems of governance that have "cultural sustainability" and (iii) the economic imperative to ensure a decent material standard of living for all. It is counter-productive to debate which is more fundamental. Meeting all three imperatives is both necessary and sufficient. Without satisfying ecological imperatives, we poison ourselves or run out of resources and destroy the basic life support systems so necessary for human and non-human survival. Without the economic imperative, our societies collapse into chaos. These three imperatives are causally interdependent. It is not possible to change the direction or nature of one without also paying attention to the other two. Given the interconnectedness, failure by any one, will make it impossible to address the other two.

In this chapter, we wish to focus on the civic state as the desired context to encourage a civil society to function effectively in order to enhance the prospects for sustainable development. Specifically, we argue that the civic state is a necessary condition for the reconciliation of the three imperatives and that within this state the gathering and dissemination of information are needed to help citizens develop legitimate public policies that yield outcomes that will protect both the current society and future generations.

The state as a context for the protection of consumer choices and for the promotion of individual values is revered by those who promote free enterprise and pure markets, yet those who value the protection of community argue that there is an important role for agencies of the state in finding a balance between individuals, vested interest groups, and collective rights and responsibilities. The search continues for the ideal balanced state. Furthermore, the case has been made that the gap between the roles played by individuals on the one hand and state agencies on the other should be filled by volunteer organizations functioning as a civil society that involves citizens in the promotion of civic pride and collective action. Clearly, sustainable development can be viewed as an exercise in which citizens can take pride, and it is worthy of their support through civic actions.

The second section of this chapter offers comments on sustainable development and community. This discussion is followed in the third section by an overview of the state and the variety of states that have been identified in the contemporary world. These include the nation-state and state-nation, the welfare state and the postwelfare state, the liberal state, the shadow state, the regulatory state, the local state, and the phantom state. The civic state is defined as the preferred one for the promotion of sustainable development, and some of the basic characteristics of this ideal type of state are identified. For the civic state to function effectively, we argue that a civil society must be promoted by the citizens of the state and be accepted by them as meaningful in the development and implementation of public policies. In the fourth section, we review the concept of the civil society and identify its critical elements. The fifth section offers suggestions for achieving the civic state, and it includes basic principles that can help to build legitimate public policies for a community that seeks to implement programs to promote sustainable development. Galbraith's (1996) comments on the good society are included in the final remarks in the sixth section. The case study of Field provides an example of a local state that is contending with the three imperatives of sustainable development.

Sustainable Development and Community

The current rates of economic development in the modern world cannot be sustained, especially in high-income areas where the ecological carrying capacity is being challenged. As Byrne and Hoffman (1996, 7) comment, "True sustainability requires the recognition that we cannot grow endlessly to meet our needs. We must, instead, develop within our ecological means, meeting the needs of the present and future equitably."

Each community approaches sustainability in a unique way, and this diversity leads to a spectrum of definitions of sustainable development. One common theme is the long-term protection of the natural environment. The definition may or may not include the concept of global sustainable development. Maclaren (1996, 1) cautions that using the word *development* implies "continuous physical or quantitative expansion of an urban area and the economy supporting it." Herkert, Farrell, and Winebrake (1996, 12-3) recognize that development also represents, among other things, "education, cultural and social activity, health, justice, peace, and security." The International Council for Local Environmental Initiatives (ICLEI) offers the following definition of sustainable development: "Sustainable development is development that delivers basic environmental, social and economic services to all, without threatening the viability of the ecological and community systems on which these services depend" (1996, 4).

At the local level, sustainable development embodies economical, ecological, and community development. "Ecological development reproduces the biological wealth and climatic conditions necessary for life on our planet," whereas community development "reproduces communities, families, educated and responsible citizens, and civilization itself" (ICLEI 1996, 1). Table 10.1 indicates the imperatives of these types of development according to ICLEI.

Contradictions arise between these types of development. Externalizing costs in the economic realm defeats the goal of conservation and waste reduction in ecological development. Similarly, the expansion of global markets and the integration of international economies through actions

Table 10.1

The imperatives of development

Economic development	Community development	Ecological development
Sustain economic growth, maximize private profit, expand markets, and externalize costs	Increase local self-reliance, satisfy basic human needs, increase equity, guarantee participation and accountability, and use appropriate technology	Respect carrying capacity, conserve and recycle resources, and reduce waste

Source: ICLEI, 1996: 2.

such as free trade undermine community self-reliance and the meeting of basic human needs.

Local levels of government are a key factor in promoting and maintaining sustainable development. "Local authorities construct, operate, and maintain economic, social and environmental infrastructure, oversee planning processes, establish local environmental policies and regulations, and assist in implementing national and sub-national environmental policies. As the level of governance closest to the people, they play a vital role in educating, mobilizing, and responding to the public to promote sustainable development" (ICLEI 1996, 4). Local levels of economic development need to utilize the talents and resources of local residents while ensuring the equitable distribution of benefits to all social groups over the long term. The case study of Field stresses the importance of directly involving citizens in the local state in government policy making to promote and legitimize actions for sustainable development.

It is the union of government, business enterprises, citizens, and the effects of their actions on the environment that will make sustainable development possible. Local municipalities rely on the ecosystem to supply items such as water, forestry products, and fisheries. As well, they rely on the social systems of families, neighbourhood organizations, and kinship networks to foster and maintain sustainable development. Its planning involves "stakeholders": residents, key institutional partners, and interest groups. The stakeholders need to be involved in the design and implementation of action plans so that planning becomes a collective action. Planning must be organized to reflect the "desires, values, and ideals of the various stakeholders within the community" (ICLEI 1996, 7). Accountability and consensus can probably be enhanced among the stakeholders if each group is involved in the entire planning process. Governments can play an important role in this planning process through the use of legislation to promote public participation and access to information via the Internet, for example.

Carr (1996, 3-4) argues that a strong sense of community and kinship is necessary for successful sustainability. He identifies the need to examine both consumption and production in order to achieve the social transformations necessary for sustainable development, and he offers five factors that define modes of production and consumption:

1   natural capital (not only land but also all natural goods and services)
2   human capital (skills and knowledge of labour and management)
3   physical capital (sometimes called "human-made" capital)
4   financial capital
5   social and cultural capital. (2)

Clearly, sustainable development requires assessing, monitoring, and regulating the biophysical environment in conjunction with Carr's anthropocentric forms of capital. With reference to environmental concerns, Dale and Hill (1996, 109-10) offer the concept of plural decision making, which "suggests that meaningful solutions for biodiversity conservation will be found in the 'untidy' multi-stakeholder and interdisciplinary interface between the academic, public policy, and non-government communities" (Dale and Robinson 1996, xiii). For them, conservation of biodiversity is essential for a healthy environment.

Social capital "refers to organizations, structures and social relations that are built up by people themselves, independently of the state or the large corporations ... [and it] refers to relationships and is manifested in the structure of relations between and among persons" (Coleman 1990, 300-18). Most importantly, social capital "builds bonds of information, trust, and solidarity between people," bonds that in turn create strong links of reciprocity, collaboration, and shared values throughout the community. Striving for sustainable development is more likely to succeed when these values are entrenched in a community.

Carr (1996, 3) defines cultural capital as the "interface between natural capital and human-made (often referred to as physical) capital." The concept of cultural capital includes "people's environmental philosophy, values, ethics, and religion; local/personal knowledge of the environment; traditional ecological knowledge; and traditional resource management institutions" (3-4). Carr believes that the harmonization of social, cultural, and natural capital results in an equilibrium between people and the environment. His analysis of the domestic mode of production in Kerala, India, shows that a high quality of life can be attained by citizens without a capitalist mode of production that often depletes the natural capital. Strong kinship relationships in Kerala resulted in "Norms of reciprocity, cooperation, pooling, sharing, and mutual aid that were everywhere associated with dense networks of intense horizontal interaction" (10).

According to Carr (1996), the same type of harmony is achieved at a regional scale in Mondragon in the Basque region of northern Spain through a two-tiered system that consists of individual cooperatives and a centralized working people's bank. The cooperatives are places where the human community is maximized under the principles of "openness, solidarity, and social responsibility" (Morrison 1991, 48-9). These cooperatives "support human capital in the form of socialized entrepreneurship and social and business planning" (Carr 1996, 22). The Mondragon example shows that social capital within the civil sphere, instead of being marginalized as it is in the capitalist mode of production, can be a bridge to the political and economic spheres. Such conditions of motivated community empowerment provide a viable structure through which sustainable development practices and programs can be implemented.

Global discussions regarding sustainable development have prompted state authorities to initiate goals for such development. Also, international lending agencies, such as the European Development Bank, are requiring state governments to have in place environmental policies as a necessary condition of eligibility for a loan. The realization of the goal of sustainable development is dependent on local communities and citizens and their willingness to participate, with pride and determination, fully and equitably in the planning process.

The State

In "The Shape of the World" (1995-6, 17), a recent article in the *Economist,* a state is defined simply as "a recognisable chunk of territory, recognisably under somebody's control," and, according to Dunn (1995, 3), "States consist of those who are fully subject to their own sovereign legal authority." Clearly, loyalty to a state is increased when the state provides security for its subjects. More broadly, the state can be conceived of as a de jure territorial political unit within which citizens feel bonds of attachment. Hutton (1995, 20) draws attention to the importance of the role of the state as a collectively organized institution that fosters trust, commitment, and cooperation. The state gives identity to individual members through citizenship.

In the modern world, the state is the basic territorial unit with the necessary political authority to raise and allocate funds for public uses. The state has the legitimate authority to offer opportunities to regulate, control, and generally manage the provision of goods and services to citizens, and all states are involved to a greater or lesser degree in the management of goods and services that are consumed collectively. Clearly, the state can play a major role in the promotion of the three imperatives of sustainable development at both local and national scales.

The state may or may not contain just a single nation. Examples of the nation-state are rare. Dunn (1995, 3) notes that "Nations consist of those who belong together by birth (genetically, lineally, through familiarly inherited language and culture)," and common birth is the course of allegiance that binds individuals into a collective. The Canadian philosopher Taylor (1995, x) agrees with this definition of the nation, and he asserts that the nation binds people together more so than the state. He refers to nations as "imagined communities," a phrase coined by Anderson (1983) in his book of the same title. For Taylor, a sense of nation emerges out of the "public," which refers to "what matters to the whole society, or belongs to this whole society, or pertains to the instruments, institutions, or loci by which the society comes together as a body and acts" (217). Public occurs in the loci of "public space." The public space from which a sense of nation emerges occurs through "the circulation of newspapers, reviews, and books among educated classes, and scattered, small-scale personal exchanges in salons, coffeehouses, and ... in political assemblies" (217).

Gwyn (1995, 20) argues that, although ethnic homogeneity and historical experience are obvious characteristics of many nations, they may not be as straightforward as we imagine. He reminds us that while Japan has the appearance of being a homogeneous society it has always included ethnically distinct aboriginals. Even though the shared histories of a nation may not be identical, Gwyn argues that a common history, an imagined history, is vital. It is this history that connects individuals and allows them to believe that they live in communion with other people whom they may or may not have known or been associated with. Another vital element of nations, according to Gwyn (20-1), is a shared printed language. He reinforces this point by noting that it was not the spoken language that joined Italy, because scarcely 5 percent of the population spoke Italian at the time of its unification.

The celebrated Canadian historian Cook (1995, 212) has identified three different ideologies concerning the definition of a nation. In the nineteenth century, Britain and France thought that a nation was a place defined politically, that it must be developed within the boundaries of sovereign states, and that loyalty to the state (nationalism) transcended cultural differences. Conversely, in Germany and eastern Europe, the notion was that the nation was "based on the idea of ethnic and cultural unity out of which a state should grow" (212). Finally, the German historian Meinicke claims that "The principle is not, whoever wants to be a nation is a nation. It is just the opposite, a nation simply is whether the individuals of which it is composed want to belong to that nation or not. A nation is not based on self-determination but on predetermination" (Berdahl 1972, 66). In Cook's (1996) opinion, the challenge in the 1990s is to decide, in the words of Finkielkraut, if Canada is an ethnic nation or a civic nation, *la nation-génie* or *la nation-con-*

trat. Cook notes that former prime minister "Trudeau rejected nationalism – French-Canadian, English-Canadian, Canadian – and sought to replace it with the ideal of a civic nation where the guarantee of individual freedom and cultural diversity was itself the tie binding a political community together" (93).

According to the entry for "nation" in *Webster's College Dictionary* (1991), nations consist of people defined as "1. persons indefinitely or collectively; persons in general. 2. persons considered as numerable individuals forming a group." In relation to nations and states, Huntington (1993) reported that, "when large masses of people join the common purpose, the primary link between them will be their shared heritage of language, history, tradition, and religion – that is, civilization," and he argued that these culture-based groupings will become the most powerful actors in world affairs (in Ohmae 1995, 10). Ohmae cautions that, although Huntington's observations may be true, we must be aware that hatred exists within cultural groups. It can and does engender violence on occasion, such as in Rwanda and the former Yugoslavia. These feelings of hatred may well negate the possibility of cultural groups becoming powerful actors in world affairs and active participants in sustainable development.

If a community wishes to promote sustainable development, then surely a prerequisite is that the community has some common history or cause that gives to each individual a vested interest in participating in the protection of collective rights and obligations.

Types of States

A basic understanding of the various types of states may help to guide us in the goal of sustainable development for a community that does have a common history or cause. This part of the third section briefly reviews the welfare and postwelfare states, the shadow state, the liberal state, the regulatory state, the local state, and the phantom state.

Bullock and Stallybrass (1980, 672-3) assert that the welfare state emerged after the Second World War and can be defined as "A political system assuming State responsibility for the protection and promotion of the social security and welfare of its citizens by universal medical care, insurance against sickness and unemployment, old age pensions, family allowances, public housing, etc., on a 'cradle to grave' basis."

The principles of a welfare state, according to Hutton (1995, 306), imply the existence of a just society where people have access to a higher quality of life, where the state symbolizes the ability of its citizens to act morally and to share in the rights and obligations of human association, including the transfer of funds between classes and generations. Each state employs a unique method of administering welfare programs. With respect to Canada, Gwyn (1995, 24-32) has argued that our welfare state uses top-down management as a method of combatting poverty, unemployment, sickness, illiteracy, and underdevelopment.

That welfare states around the world are in a state of crisis is now well documented. High inflation and recessions in the 1970s, along with substantial national debts, led to government restructuring within welfare states. Citizens continue to have high expectations in terms of the goods and services provided by the state, and welfare states are having considerable difficulty meeting these expectations. Opponents of the welfare state would agree that restructuring is necessary because the welfare state "is directly linked to social dependency and a diminution of self-sufficiency as well as the reduction of individual choice" (Barry 1990, xii), and Day and Klein (1987, xii) believe that welfare states are "excessively bureaucratic, paternalistic and ineffective."

The postwelfare state is driven in part by the belief that unfettered market forces are the solution to economic difficulties. Conservative policies such as the privatization of national industries, the reduction of financial regulations and public spending despite increased demand, and the reduction of private and corporate taxes, to name a few, are parts of this market solution. Despite the apparent shift toward reliance on nongovernmental sectors to provide social services (Hutton 1995, 11; Mishra 1990, 13-4), it is widely recognized that the free market is unwilling or unable to cater to the full range of needs at suitable levels for a society. This accentuates the need for the implementation of programs for sustainable development.

Myrdal's (1960) classic work on the welfare state made it abundantly clear that such a state will always be a work in progress, helping to bridge the gap between rich and poor within and between states, and as national and international economic policies and practices change. Innovations will never end. For example, in the fall of 1998, the Fabians in the United Kingdom published a pamphlet on *The Third Way,* which coincides with Giddens's (1998) book of the same title. In New York on 23 September 1998, Prime Minister Blair (UK), President Clinton (USA), and Prime Minister Prodi (Italy) announced their support for programs to deal with the five dilemmas identified by Giddens. A summary of these dilemmas is offered in the *Economist* for 19 September 1998 ("Third Way Revealed," 72):

(1) that globalization is changing the meanings of nation-hood, government and sovereignty. There exists (2) a "new individualism" that is not necessarily selfish but which means that social solidarity can no longer be imposed in a top-down way. Although distinctions between left and right keep changing, the left cares more about social justice and equality. However, (3) there is a category of problems – such as global warming, devolution, the future of the European Union – about which it is unhelpful to think in terms of left versus right. (4) Some jobs (defence, law mak-

ing) can be done only by governments, even though politicians are becoming less influential and pressure groups more effective. And do not forget (5) that while environmental dangers can be exaggerated, it is highly dangerous to be sanguine about them, not least because, as in the case of mad-cow disease, experts sometimes differ.

Critics of the Third Way, such as Cook (1998), point to the lack of explicit policies that can be implemented to handle the dilemmas. One alternative to the provision of social services by the free market is the mobilization of volunteer organizations. This provision of social services by a voluntary sector has been termed the shadow state by Wolch (1990). She defines the shadow state as "a para-state apparatus comprised of multiple voluntary sector organizations, administered outside of traditional democratic politics and charged with major collective service responsibilities previously shouldered by the public sector, yet remaining within the purview of state control" (xvi).

The formation of the shadow state varies geographically with the influence of key factors such as urban history, economic structure, prevailing welfare state characteristics, and the behaviour of local agents. Wolch (1990, 41) states that the shadow state "carries out welfare state functions, provides essential human services, financial and in-kind benefits, and surveillance of clients." Although the activities carried out by volunteer organizations are enabled, regulated, subsidized, and thus constrained by the state, they are not formally part of the state. According to Kramer (1990, x), West Germany and the Netherlands provide good examples of functioning shadow states.

Although volunteer organizations are cost effective, innovative, and more efficient at delivering services to those who need them, they are dependent on state contracts for funding and are thus hampered in their ability to criticize government policy. The creation of an excessive number of independently operating volunteer organizations, with overlapping initiatives, may lead to an ineffective and unaccountable system of social services.

Embodied in these various types of states is the concept of liberal democracy. Democracy is defined in *Webster's College Dictionary* (1991, 360) as "government by the people; a form of government in which the supreme power is vested in the free electoral system." Panitch (1993) argues that liberal democracy, when viewed normatively, should diminish the inequalities between people based on class, status, gender, and race, should put constitutional limits on arbitrary state authority, and should allow citizenship rights such as voting. He further suggests that one major criticism of Canada's liberal democracy is that groups such as single mothers, Natives, the poor, and the unemployed are compensated by the welfare state, but the causes of their situations are not remedied. It is evident that he wishes to promote a radical restructuring of the political and social system with the state – perhaps even the redefinition of the state – as the basic unit that caters to the needs of individuals within territorially defined communities. As Kettel remarks, sustainable development requires the possibility of sustainable livelihoods in which there is "secure and equitable access to basic needs, appropriate technology and income, and protection or enhancement of natural resources, all over both the short and long term" (1996, 160).

Although Canada has a democratic political system, by the early 1980s people were complaining about the federal government's inefficient management of the welfare state, and Panitch (1993, 4-5) argues that by the end of that decade conservative parties dominated most Western democracies, and their combined postwelfare state policies resulted in the privatization of public institutions and greater inequalities between rich and poor. In the early 1990s, the Spicer Commission showed that Canadian citizens wanted "more democratic forms of representation, accountability and control over public institutions" (Panitch 1993, 4). In a detailed and comprehensive report on values held by Canadians, Peters (1995, 6) notes that Canadians are dissatisfied with the current piecemeal approach to solving Canada's social and economic ills. Canadians want to be involved in the process of social policy restructuring, in which partnerships across sectors allow for systemic solutions and the promotion of collective well-being.

A recent survey by Ekos Research (1995) solicited opinions from citizens about governments in Canada. A series of key themes was identified, deep resentment and frustration described the current mood, and considerable ambivalence characterized the public's resolve to reduce the size of government in order to manage the public debt. The report notes that, although the country is a crucial source of identity and belonging, second only to the family, Canadians seem to be seeking a higher order of moral community. Canadians across a variety of regions, incomes, age groups, and educational levels share certain core values. Peters (1995, 5) identifies these core Canadian values as self-reliance, compassion leading to collective responsibility, investment (especially in children as the future generation), democracy, freedom, equality, and fiscal responsibility. While maintaining these values, Peters notes, Canadians "want to retain the social capital of this country, enhance social cohesion, and strengthen the social fabric" (1). Baum (1996, 6) agrees that "Canadians have not changed their basic sense of the need for a social contract – even though they recognize that the terms of this contract must change with the times." These values indicate a strong predisposition to a Canadian civil society and a desire for sustainable development within Canada.

The regulatory state has the advantage of encompassing both voluntarism and liberal democracy. Massam (1993, xii) has argued that the regulatory state is a political system that combines the advantages of the market while offering sufficient protection to accommodate the views of the collectivity. The effective functioning of the regulatory state requires cooperative action and shared responsibility. This type of state must embrace the concepts of choice, accountability, and consensus.

Choice is comprised of a number of imperatives, which include freedom, responsibility, and legitimacy. The onus for making decisions within a democratic regulatory state should rest with governments, businesses, and the public.

Accountability implies that decision makers will be held accountable for their decisions. Governments can promote cooperation and responsibility by establishing clear lines of accountability and authority. Attention needs to be focused on monitoring, auditing, and inspecting so that services are provided at the right time and the best cost. Precise guidelines and operational definitions that are credible, legitimate, and traceable would allow the public to scrutinize services quickly and efficiently. A greater quantity of services does not necessarily guarantee greater quality.

Consensus represents a degree of congruence that embraces individual positions and opinions to allow a collectivity to function. To permit consensus to operate freely in centralized decision-making environments, the regulatory state should not be authoritarian. Consensus is a legitimate and credible method of making choices in which there is acceptance and shared responsibility for a collectively chosen decision.

Massam (1993, 5) asserts that choice, accountability, and consensus in the provision of public goods and services within a regulatory state promote confidence and trust in government processes. Legitimacy is established. Shared responsibility by all stakeholders encourages participation in and acceptance of the final decisions. A consequence of not sharing responsibility for decisions is that inequities between groups are accentuated. Gaps increase, for example, between the rich and the poor, the needy and the cared for, the healthy and educated and the sick and uneducated. With the growth of impoverished groups, such as poor women, there exists "a condition of insecurity of access to the fundamentals of life in basic needs, technology, income, and a healthy environment" (Kettel 1996, 160). Consequently, the prospects for sustainable development are diminished.

The regulatory state provides a contemporary context within which bureaucratic, legislative, and political procedures operate to include technical evaluations and opinions of stakeholders in the search for responsible solutions. This type of state perhaps offers a viable option for transforming the classic welfare state into a civic state.

At a smaller scale is the local state. Simply defined, it is "The state apparatus that deals with localities" (Taylor 1993, 331). More explicitly, it is "any government entity having a political and spatial jurisdiction at less than the scale of (for example) a Canadian Province or one of the 50 States of the USA, and having authority to raise revenues from, and make expenditures on behalf of, its constituents ... The local state may therefore take many forms and more than one type of local state may exist" (Clark and Dear 1984, 133). (We can envisage the community of Field in British Columbia as a local state.)

The term "local state" was introduced by Cockburn (1977). "It is simply an administrative apparatus of the national and federal states" that serves the interests of capital (Clark and Dear 1984, 133). It is "an instrument of class domination managing the social needs of households for the ultimate benefit of capital" (Taylor 1993, 317-8). Saunders (1984) conceptualizes the local state as the notion of a "dual-state thesis" (Taylor 1993, 318) in which "At the centre a class politics based upon issues of production is to be found whereas in the local state a politics of consumption cuts across class lines" (Taylor 1993, 318).

The functions of a local state, according to Taylor (1993, 317), typically involve "education, housing provision, public transport and land-use planning," and it is often considered the most effective method for providing public goods and services. The local state serves many purposes: it decentralizes state functions to increase administrative efficiency, it ensures that "local needs are anticipated and answered, and national state legitimacy is ensured," it allows for "social and ideological control of a spatially extensive and heterogeneous national political system," and it provides "long-term crisis avoidance at the local level" (Clark and Dear 1984, 133).

Local states are administered by and depend on federal governments. Local economies provide additional funding, yet the overall political processes are initiated at the federal level, and they vary with the context of the politics. This situation reduces the discretion and autonomy of the local state and results in competition and tension between the various tiers of government.

The strength of the local state emerges "in its efforts at crisis avoidance, [and] the local state may develop citizen participation channels in order to reduce uncertainty by learning the demands of its electorate. Local state actions are thereby legitimized and facilitated" (Clark and Dear 1984, 137). Local groups can then use the local state to oppose central state policies. Local states also derive power from their ability to choose individual levels of expenditure while adhering to federal policy (Taylor 1993, 317, 322). The local state is an important mechanism for providing a voice for localities, it gives the state a link to the locality, and it promotes state legitimacy. The local state may be the best arena in which community action and multi-stakeholder processes can be encouraged in order to promote a civil society.

Globalization is another aspect of our modern world influencing the functioning of welfare states. Thrift (1995, 18) defines globalization as a world where "economies, societies and cultures are becoming ever more closely intertwined." He notes that new technologies transcend place and have compressed the time and space required to make transactions in the global economy. The speed with which information and capital are transferred globally is hyperactive. Our ability to understand the connections between economies, societies, and cultures is decreasing as the complexity of those interconnections increases. As Thrift notes, this new socioeconomic atmosphere has created a place where organizations are no longer concerned about "the social constraints of cultural identities and local societies" (20). Yet communities and individuals derive a strong sense of purpose from attachment to locality, as is clear in the Field case study. This community attachment surely must be protected by government actions on public participation and nurtured as part of the enterprise of encouraging sustainable development.

Thrift (1995) has identified international money as the "phantom state" within the new global economic system. Residing in a series of transient sites in a few global cities, the phantom state is nomadic. Because money in constant motion makes profits, the phantom state has the advantage of being difficult to tie down. It is at a disadvantage when money is trapped within a nation-state that has rules and regulations regarding the movement of money. The limitations of this type of state lie in the realization that technological transactions rely on human networks that may not be fully developed globally. Organizations committed to local and global sustainable development must be aware of the benefits and limitations of the monetary phantom state.

Civic State

The role of the state, at all political levels, has been shifting from one that protects and improves the life chances of the individuals within the state to one that manages the consumers, the citizens. In this consumer form, citizens begin to lose their sense of obligation to society and community. The reliance on the unfettered market system to meet all the needs of the public for social goods and services may prove unsuccessful. Services such as roads, street lighting, defence, and law and order would not be provided equitably by the market, and education and health care could not be supplied at current subsidized quantities. Governments surely have a responsibility to define the quantity and quality of social and environmental outcomes and acceptable levels while seeking the appropriate mix of public and private enterprise to deliver the outcomes and levels.

Citizens in Canada are feeling a growing sense of dismay about the inequalities between regions, between the haves and the have-nots. Citizens feel unempowered, detached from the levers that seem to control their lives, and as a consequence they are frustrated, worried, and unsettled.

The civic state's goal is to provide a place where citizens feel secure, protected, and satisfied. Within the civic state, markets must be embedded in cultural and political institutions that capitalize and enhance mutual trust, sharing, and obligations that go beyond formal contracts.

We suggest that the civic state challenges individuals to accept a covenant to cooperate, share, sacrifice, and celebrate together, to become citizens in a community with a recognized collective identity. This type of state demands the promotion of all aspects of civility, civil institutions, and civil practices, including, in a measured and regulated way, the effective and efficient functioning of a strong market-driven economic system. A major concern of the civic state must be providing identity and recognition to support "imagined communities," to use Anderson's (1983) term, comprised of individuals, albeit often as strangers to each other, with full and equal rights and obligations of citizenship. The civic state that does not respect the rights of citizens in other states will not be an acceptable member of the global community of states. The civic state does not require construction de novo of a state; rather, what is needed is explicit recognition, by government agencies via their policies and practices, of the merit of promoting identity for their citizens at local as well as national levels so that pride, respect, and self-esteem become hallmarks of statehood. We subscribe to the view of Hutton (1995) and others that the welfare state is a good and appropriate place to begin construction of the civic state. If public and private initiatives and energies can be marshalled to provide and enhance all those elements of culture, as well as of health and general welfare, education, and environmental responsibility, that stimulate and promote civic virtues and identity, then a civic state may emerge. A clear cultural identity appears to be a necessary condition for the establishment of a strong and free state, and this surely must be a major focal point for governments, as Griffiths (1996) has forcefully argued with respect to the contemporary scene in Canada. In his words, "To be able to look after ourselves as a people, we need first to assert Canada's political culture of civility. In turn, for civility to thrive, we must look anew to the needs of popular culture and communications in this country" (37). A strong case can be made for the promotion of the civic state to enhance the human condition.

According to Spinner (1994, 170), the civic state or the liberal state is eclectic, pragmatic, fair, just, and reasonable; it stresses identity and recognition while working for egalitarian, democratic institutional arrangements for individuals, voluntary groupings, and state agencies to cater to all the needs of all the citizens. Cook (1995, 1996) has identified three essential principles for the civic state's role. First, the state must not be aligned with one particular cultural group. Such alignment fosters the notions of elitism, other, insiders and outsiders, inferiority, and varying degrees of access to power, influence, control, and resources, particularly information. Second, the defence of basic personal rights for every person is to be supported by law. Third, the individual should not fear the state; the latter must serve the former. Ideally, the civic state includes a legitimate government as produced through fair electoral procedures, a free press, the rule of law, the promotion and protection of human rights, the acceptance of dissent by minorities, and meaningful public participation in all aspects of state activity, including environmental concerns. In a word, a well-functioning civic state can contribute mightily to sustainable development.

Trust is essential to the success of a civic state. The purpose of this type of state is to provide a place where citizens feel secure, protected, and satisfied. Through the equitable provision of public goods and services, the state can assure for all of its citizens an improved quality of life, in which their needs are met from birth until death. The most effective method of achieving these goals is through collective decision making by individuals and communities, all the way up to and including state political officials. The critical role of trust in the growth of successful and responsible communities is well argued by Fukuyama (1995).

The Social Planning Council of Metropolitan Toronto (1995) asserts that a civic state is one where all people have the right to expect certain types of support from the government and the community and where these individuals have certain responsibilities and obligations to fulfil for their community. The council's vision for a civic state includes five core principles to which society needs to adhere:

1 All people should have security – a stable home life, a safe community, a decent standard of living, and a connection with other people.
2 All community members should recognize their interdependence – individual lives are linked with a community, and we must accept that each of us is responsible for improving our community and that we can cooperate to solve problems in the best interests of the community.
3 Fairness should govern social and economic relationships – greater economic viability will result when all people have equal access to health care, education, and representation in government and under the law. There will be less of a gap between the haves and the have-nots, work will be shared more fairly, and all people will participate in decisions affecting their lives.
4 Many ways of participating and contributing should be valued – a greater sense of belonging to and ownership of communities occurs if both paid and unpaid work is valued, if government structures accommodate all citizens' participation in decision making, and if political representatives listen and respond to the needs of the people.

5   Diversity should be respected and celebrated – we need to celebrate the fact that in Canada there coexists many people from various parts of the world who want to work together to build a better future.

The focus of these five core principles is on the economic and social well-being of citizens. It must be recognized, as stated in the three imperatives of sustainable development, that ecological and environmental issues must be given due consideration if a civic state is to thrive.

Although we recognize that the role of the civic state is to foster a collective, cooperative, and trustworthy environment for its citizens, we suggest that this environment can be accomplished in large measure by creating a civil society.

Civil Society

In the contemporary world, the state provides a fundamental and significant regulatory context for controlling, influencing, and shaping the human condition via a range of political, economic, social, and environmental policies and practices situated within evolving values, mores, and ideologies within the state and beyond its borders. However, the state is not a fixed category of sociopolitical phenomena; rather, it is an evolving set of arrangements that necessitates its being viewed in the context of time and space.

Birth, life opportunities, death, inheritance, and beliefs about the meaning of human life and purpose are woven into public policies, activities, and patterns of behaviour of individuals within the state. Unfortunately, the state falls short in the eyes of many citizens because it lacks the ability to guarantee decent life chances for all its citizens.

Today it is increasingly evident that states are often too small to act alone in the world of global finance and communication, or they are typically too large and complex to give to all their citizens a unified sense of identity, solidarity, and control over events.

The world is divided not only into states. Gender, language, ethnicity, religion, and class can each be used to promote group solidarity that cuts across territorial boundaries, and, within a world of production and consumption of private and public goods, citizens as consumers can be viewed as stateless entities with productive and purchasing potential.

In the foreword to Massam (1996, iii), Pierce reminds us that:

As we approach the third millennium, the process of globalization is in full swing, a process which has its own imperative for fundamental change and which confronts societies with a number of difficult choices. On the one hand there is growing pressure to remain competitive and flexible to ensure economic growth, and on the other to maintain/enhance political freedom and social cohesion. This is a difficult balancing act in light of the insecurity and instability engendered by the push to flexibility. Increasing emphasis is placed upon expanding physical and financial capital without a commensurate concern for social capital. The decline in the welfare state, in a sense of community, increasing unemployment and income inequities and a re-emergence of social Darwinism are clear manifestations of the atrophy of social capital, social cohesion and a weakening of the civil society. And, in those cultures which have maintained social cohesion in the face of economic growth, it is often at the expense of civility and political freedom.

In Western democracies, the space between the individual and the state has historically been filled, albeit only partly, by the civil society, and – although the term is more suggestive than precise – the core meaning of the concept, according to Dahrendorf (1995, 23), is precise: "Civil society describes the associations in which we conduct our lives, and that owe their existence to our needs and initiatives, rather than to the state." Agnew (1995) observes that liberal democracy is in a state of arrested development, and the uncritical adoption of simple market or state models to cater to human needs carries much cachet. The role of civil society as the third pole of economic development in reviving flagging economies is drawing considerable attention according to Johnston, Taylor, and Watts (1995) in their overview of global changes and contemporary society.

Arguments have been made suggesting that the promotion of a civil society within a state, to fill the gaps between individuals, families, and the state, will go a long way toward improving quality of life by giving citizens a greater sense of control over and responsibility for their lives, while recognizing that globalization as manifest by international capital flows and transnational corporations can be successfully regulated if cooperation between civic states is secured by legitimate treaties and sanctions.

Historically, there has been a range of justifications for a civil society. Compliant, dependent, cooperative linkages have existed within societies for reasons such as desire to abide by God's wishes, determination to survive military rule, or adherence to a cultural history of respect for authority. Currently, in many modern Western societies, human needs are handled by individuals, families, state intervention, and political action via appointed and elected officials.

There is a growing and disturbing phenomenon evident in modern Canadian society. According to Valpy (1995), we have become a "society of strangers" in which the fortunate people no longer know who the unfortunate people are. He argues that the state has been intervening between these two groups for so long that eventually the haves will no longer want to pay the way for the have-nots.

Social interaction between disparate groups has been declining, and

Putnam (1995, 1996) offers empirical evidence drawn from the United States of the many volunteer activities, ranging from the PTA to socializing with a neighbour, that have reduced social engagement. Individualism is on the rise, and people are engaging in many more isolating activities, many of them technologically motivated. Putnam claims that television alone, not to mention the gadgetry associated with it, has a negative impact on social trust and group membership. He states that frequent television viewers are "unusually sceptical about the benevolence of other people – overestimating crime rates for example" (1996). He also comments that older generations are more socially active, often through extended family relationships, than younger generations consisting of single-family households and the like.

Low self-esteem, according to a report from the California Task Force to Promote Self-Esteem and Personal and Social Responsibility in 1990, appears to be central to many of the societal problems experienced today (including crime, violence, drugs, poverty, and chronic welfare dependency). Self-esteem is a self-feeding loop in that, when an individual's personal and social responsibility increases, so does his or her self-esteem. In general, higher self-esteem in turn leads to greater personal and social responsibility. The expansion of these factors in individuals' lives probably predisposes them to honesty, charity, dignity, faith, intellectual energy, optimism, self-acceptance, courage, and love. The results of successful sustainable development will surely include these fine human qualities.

Human beings require security in their daily lives in order to function without fear. Social trust and cooperation are enhanced as social relations between people increase. Axelrod (1984) shows that trust, more so than formal contracts, promotes cooperation and optimal outcomes for competing parties.

The method of creating a civil society is neither easy nor completely understood. Global agendas may or may not have positive effects on the creation of civil societies. At the World Summit for Social Development held in March 1995, the first global pledge toward a civil society was presented: "We the people of the world solemnly pledge to build a new global civil society, based on the principles of equality of opportunity, rule of law, global democratic governance and a new partnership among all nations and all people" (Massam 1996, 29). Pledges of this type may act as guides for policy making at all levels.

The use of common goals such as environmental concerns may stimulate social engagement, especially if it is carried out by nongovernmental organizations (NGOs). For example, the Regional Environmental Centre (REC) established in 1990 by Hungary, the United States, and the Communion of the European Communities functions as an independent, nonadvocacy, not-for-profit foundation to establish NGOs that focus on environmental matters. The overall agenda is to create a functioning civil society, to promote public participation in environmental decision making, to support grassroots organizations, and to cooperate with local authorities, national governments, academic institutions, the media, and the private sector (Massam and Goulet 1996).

In contemporary Canada, we must recognize that we have a society with a mixture of individual values. A civil society needs to accommodate the fact that there exists in Canada both individualistic, libertarian values and collectivist, conservative values. More specifically, a civil society will have certain basic characteristics. Shils (1991) states that there are three main components of a civil society:

1   a complex of autonomous economic, religious, intellectual, and political institutions distinguishable from family, clan, locality, or state
2   a complex of relationships with formal and informal rules, procedures, and practices to safeguard the separation of state and civil society yet to maintain effective ties between them
3   a widespread pattern of refined or civil manners.

The benefits to be derived from a social connection in a civil society are numerous, including a reduction in mortality rates as individuals realize a greater sense of belonging and control over their lives; a reduction in crime as more people practise surveillance of their neighbourhoods; an increase in the quality of education as parent-teacher interaction is expanded; and, finally, the networking possibilities with others in relation to job opportunities (Putnam 1993, 1995, 1996; Zinberg 1994).

A civil society of connections and exchanges between people is vital to social capital and economic wealth. Novick (1995), in his address on civic solidarity, stated that "wealth is created by people with talents and assets finding patterns of trust through which they can generate enterprises and activities." He mentioned that civic mobilization would "preserve essential public goods, and defend the quality of social life which people can understand." The focus should be on shared environments at the community, city, and regional levels. Organizations such as the Social Planning Council of Metropolitan Toronto can act as catalysts in movements of civic mobilization in which connections can be made and information, research, and policy perspectives can be shared.

A civil society is not comprised of citizens pitted against the state. Rather, it is a civic state that promotes the interconnectedness of social groups and the state apparatus. It is a celebration of human linkages that share in the responsibility for the fair distribution of the necessary goods that ensure for each person a life of dignity within the sustainable limits of his or her environment.

Achieving the Civic State

The civic state is more than a set of institutions, agencies, and general claims about civility; it also evinces a mind-set that cherishes and protects individuality and measures it using a calculus that yields shared values of strong identity, connection, and collective responsibility not only for the present but also for future generations. This is the rhetoric of the ideal civic state. The world must acknowledge the existence of de facto and de jure territorial units that are noncongruent. These spaces are occupied by individuals, agents of the state, and informal groupings of citizens with shifting alliances, who simultaneously try to pursue a variety of goals and objectives. Complete information is absent. The community that comprises a civic state is a highly complex organization, and there is an impressive body of literature developed by workers in many disciplines that seeks to explain and evaluate complex social organization. For the purposes of this chapter, we focus on a single aspect of the civic state drawn from this literature. Specifically, we identify the concept of legitimacy as the defining characteristic of an actual civic state and argue that to achieve legitimacy it is necessary to adhere to the five general conditions referred to earlier, as enunciated by the Social Planning Council of Metropolitan Toronto. Also, we support the proposition that legitimacy comprises explicit elements of a process of collective choice that includes the concepts of fairness, fullness, and thoroughness in plans for sustainable development within a civic state. Table 10.2 summarizes the fundamental characteristics of the three concepts and the notion of legitimacy.

The search for formal rules to define the constitution that leads to an ideal civic state continues to yield only abstract results. Perhaps the best-known work is that of Arrow (1951), which is based on a set of axioms to characterize a democratic constitution. The axioms are reasonable and indeed civil; for example, all voters are equally important, and the rule of the majority should obtain. However, when combined, the axioms that he identifies contain contradictions. Other work in a similar abstract style has been undertaken by Axelrod (1984). He wonders under which conditions self-interested individuals would cooperate in the absence of a central authority. And, while the format of his project falls within a narrowly defined context of two interest groups, each with the option to cooperate or not, the general conclusions are satisfying from both the purely theoretical viewpoint and the intuitive, practical standpoint. Essentially, the key to developing cooperation without resorting to a powerful dictator-style central authority is to stress the relationships of reciprocal dependency between the interest groups that stretch into the future. This is an important element in developing a functioning civic state that will seek to achieve sustainable development. Stakeholders and all citizens need to feel connected and share a cause. However, how to achieve this happy condi-

Table 10.2

Basic principles for evaluating public policy making

Fairness	Central to the rule of law. *Nemo judex in causa sua:* rule against bias. *Audi alterem partem:* right to a fair hearing. Refers to form of investigation and the substance of investigation and the dissemination of information.
Fullness	Refers to the scope of the inquiry, the evaluation and the needs assessment process, i.e., the variety and breadth of issues covered and the relevancy of issues.
Thoroughness	Refers to the depth of examination of the issues: the detail, accuracy, use of professional advice, good instrumentation, good sampling procedures, replication and traceability.
Legitimacy	Refers to sanctioning of actions by the populace. A legitimate process is one that is normatively sanctioned by the population. Ideal normative conditions include: a) Access to argument: gain access to argument and ability to follow up responses. b) Intelligibility: be authentically understood and comprehensible. c) Honesty and sincerity: ability to express feelings and intentions. d) Creative: development of a case based on evidence and full justification.

---

tion remains a problem. No doubt an important step is to empower citizens via a constitution or set of well-established rights seen to serve the interests of both individuals and the community. Clearly, there is a necessity to define territorial units with sovereign boundaries within which rules and regulations acceptable to the citizens actually apply. This situation must recognize that the sovereign boundaries are not impermeable but interfaces between complementary jurisdictions.

Finally, we assert that in order to achieve the civic state there is a clear need to provide information to all citizens about the conditions of their society. This exercise must focus on monitoring, auditing, inspecting, and reporting economic, social, and environmental conditions. Essentially, there are two dimensions of such measurement exercises: the magnitudes of the selected indicators that describe a component of the society, such as unemployment level, air pollution, or family violence; and the significance that individuals and communities attach to the magnitudes. The loss of 100 trees in a region may or may not be important depending on the scarcity of the species being cut down. The exercise to measure magnitude is, to a certain extent, technical and fairly objective, whereas the determination of significance is primarily a complex political activity that demands active citizen participation and access to reliable information.

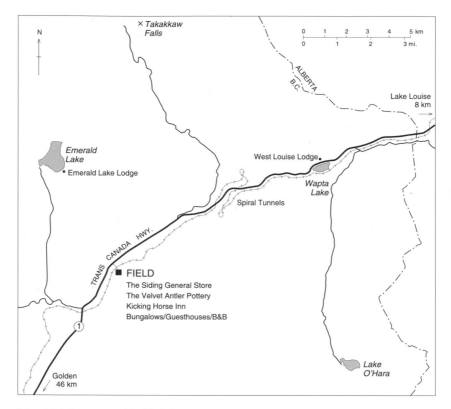

Map 10.1 Location of Field, BC

Perhaps the single most important element of a civic state is trust, as noted earlier. Fukuyama (1995) would subscribe to this view even though the precise ways to achieve it defy neat and simple definition. This *projet de société* to build a civic state can lead understandably to a discussion of the need for, and to the search for, meaningful definitions of the good life, the humane agenda for purposeful existence, and the moral standards that uphold correct behaviours. Without even scratching the surfaces of these topics, we conclude this section with the comment that we subscribe to the view that the civic state has a duty to promote discussion of and debate on these matters. There is a need to do so to address questions regarding the importance of the data collected via formal measurement exercises on the conditions of the civic state, and good, clear data collection will contribute to sustainable development.

A Beginning, Not the Conclusion

Recently, Galbraith (1996) posed important questions of concern to those who seek to promote sustainable development. Basically, he asked, what is the nature of and what are the requirements of the good and achievable economy and polity? The emphasis is on practice rather than on the recital of rhetoric. Galbraith argues that the basic dialectic between capital and labour has to be replaced by acknowledging the emergence of modern corporate bureaucracy and managers. To achieve sustainable development, all citizens must feel empowered to influence public and private policy making. Furthermore, among the necessary conditions of the good and achievable society, there cannot, must not, be a deprived and excluded underclass. The inference is clear: all members of society must feel that they have the rights and obligations of citizenship to participate in political processes. Galbraith goes on to argue for a basic source of income, educational opportunities, low-cost housing, and health care for the needful, as well as for the provision of those public goods and services such as parks and recreational facilities, emergency services, libraries, and the arts that are often needed more by the underclass than by the affluent.

Sustainable development is appropriately situated as the overarching outcome of efforts by individuals acting within civil societies in regulated civic states. Such development, with its clear emphasis on reconciling the ecological, social, and economic imperatives, demands specific initiatives by governments to monitor outcomes, assess the quality of life, and make information available and accessible to citizens. Through legislative and regulatory practices, governments should also promote public participation in the planning of projects. A more humane sustainable world is achievable if we shed today's conventional wisdom about inflation, the deficit, taxes, and immigration, for example, and if we actively recognize and support the immense value of education and environmental responsibility and the political action that the good society demands. Can we do less than support such an agenda?

The case study that concludes this chapter offers an overview of the activities of citizens and groups in the local state of Field, British Columbia, in trying to cooperate with government agencies outside the community and the private sector to establish a sustainable community. Field is a work in progress.

Case Study

Field, British Columbia: A Local State Struggles for Sustainable Development

In the mid-1880s, Field was constructed as a divisional point for the Canadian Pacific Railway (CPR). The location of Field is shown in Map 10.1. Originally settled by CPR employees, squatters, and construction camp followers, the town developed into a tourist centre with the construction of the imposing Mount Stephen House (1886) as well as the construction of tea houses and lodges in several nearby valleys. The spiral tunnels were completed in 1909, and the need for a first-class railway hotel on a year-round basis came into question. By 1953, most of Mount Stephen House was torn down, and ten years later its removal was complete. Forestry and mining operations occurred in the vicinity until the 1950s, when the population reached about 1,300 persons. The closure of the Base Metals Mining Corporation and the shift from steam to diesel locomotives some forty years ago began a trend of population decline. Today the community continues its CPR function, and it serves as the administrative headquarters for Yoho National Park. Tourism is an important activity for the community. The current population is about 300 people living in about 110 houses and mobile homes. Field is a relatively young community, with about 60 percent of residents being between twenty-five and forty-three years of age.

Field no longer has its own power generator using diesel fuel (approximately 360,000 gallons per year). This facility closed in 1997, and the power supply is now provided via a hydro grid system. There is also a water plant and a wastewater treatment facility in Field. Solid-waste handling, fire protection, and ambulance service for all of Yoho National Park are provided from Field, and the community is a response centre to deal with spills and accidents along the rail and highway corridors. Almost half the working residents of Field are employed for at least some portion of the year in Lake Louise – about fifteen kilometres away. Lake Louise prohibits privately owned residential leases, so Field offers the nearest opportunity for those who wish to develop equity in housing. The CPR is a major local employer, and some seasonal work occurs in the one hotel. There is one general store, a local craft shop (pottery), and a post office in the village. On the edge of the settlement, next to the information office of Parks Canada, a gift shop and snack bar has recently been opened. The school in Field currently has fewer than twenty pupils.

There are several local sports and arts clubs and councils that operate in the community, as well as a number of community organizations, which include the following:

- *The Field Advisory Board* is a volunteer group of residents who advise the parks superintendent on local matters of concern to citizens. Parks Canada regulates and controls land use in Field.
- *The Field Recreation Advisory Association* is a locally elected body with the mandate to develop and improve recreational opportunities for Field's residents.
- *The Golden School District (GSD) (18)* owns and operates the school.
- *The Yoho-Burgess Shale Research Foundation* promotes fund-raising and plans to construct a new school learning centre and museum for Field (in cooperation with the GSD) to encourage tourism and scientific activities

related to the spectacular local fossil beds. This is a nonprofit organization.
- *The Friends of Yoho* is a self-funding cooperative agency that promotes the park and assists in interpretation, education, and communication.
- *The Columbia Shuswap Regional District* is the regional government that levies taxes based on assessed land values.

In essence, the components of a civil society exist, and over the past few years this community has begun to struggle with the development of a plan that seeks to promote sustainable development.

In July 1994, Parks Canada, in the Department of Canadian Heritage, published a report that outlined alternate scenarios for the administration and cost-effective operation of the six national park communities in Canada's western parks. This review was prompted by the recognition that the average annual deficit over the period 1991-4 was $6.4 million for these communities. A series of recommendations was proposed "to reduce or eliminate subsidies, increase efficiencies and operate the communities with reduced impact on federal appropriations. The recommendations proposed would ensure the long term protection of the parks" (1). The publication of this report provoked a series of actions by the residents of Field, and perhaps the most significant one was the development of a Vision Statement for the Village of Field during the early part of 1995. This statement is shown in Figure 10.1.

There are two major stakeholders with which residents of Field must contend: Parks Canada, and the CPR. To the citizens of this small community, this is a formidable task because both organizations have access to considerable resources not readily available to Field residents as well as complex bureaucratic and legal structures embedded in local, provincial, and national politics. A number of individual citizens have worked long and hard to mobilize residents in Field to support the vision statement and to work with consultants on the preparation of budgetary plans to raise appropriate revenues via rate structures to provide local services, especially water, sewage, and garbage collection. The first year for the local budgeting of roads, stormwater management, and administration was 1997-8. The basic question is one of affordability, and there is continuing debate in the community on this issue. Closely related to it is the land-use plan that has been developed. This plan has been presented to Minister of Canadian Heritage Sheila Copps, but as of October 1998 she has not signed and approved it. In essence, by changing land-use zoning regulations, more private investment in property and commercial development may occur and would enhance revenue generation. Of course, an increase in the need for basic services such as water and sewage would also occur, and an acceptable balance that matches the spirit of the vision statement is being sought to preserve the identity of the community and the sustainability of the

The Village of Field will be a safe, economically self-sustaining, family-oriented community, where quality of life is paramount. Residents will actively participate in a partnership with Yoho National Park to maintain ecological and environmental integrity.

The residents are proud to share their special place in Yoho National Park, a World Heritage site: a place where visitors are able to meet the residents and share in the pride of Field's tranquil beauty.

Field, the gateway to British Columbia, was established in 1885 and reflects a history of the Canadian Pacific Railway, Logging and Mining activities. It is located in the Main Ranges of the Canadian Rockies and is nestled at the base of Mount Stephen, beside the Canadian Heritage Kicking Horse River.

An eclectic assortment of small affordable houses defines a unique character of architecture, which compliments its surroundings. Select heritage buildings will be protected and maintained. The style of new buildings will reflect the architectural motif designed by the Field Community Council. Residential ownership will be encouraged. The character of Field will not be sacrificed.

Field will encourage pedestrian access. Commercial development will consist of locally-owned cottage industry and home businesses that will provide the visitor and residents with high quality personal experiences. The village will evolve to a size that enables it to achieve optimum economic viability, within its physical limits. It will provide essential community services and assist Yoho National Park in sharing these costs.

Field will actively support interaction with visitors and share the services with the neighbouring communities of Lake Louise and Golden.

The Village will commit to providing recreational and educational facilities for residents and visitors that will continually encourage a strong representation of all age groups to visit and reside in Field.

Figure 10.1 Vision statement for the Village of Field, 1995
Source: Field residents during the spring of 1995.

village while following the primary mandate of Parks Canada to maintain ecological integrity. Resurfacing of the roads began in the summer of 1998 and will be completed by the fall of 1999. Burial of the overhead lines will also be completed by this time, and a tidier Field will result from these infrastructure improvements and aesthetic changes.

On the basis of our reading of reports and minutes of meetings in Field, discussions with the townsite manager, the townsite assistant, and the executive director of the Yoho-Burgess Shale Research Foundation, and informal interviews with residents in June and July 1995, 1996, 1997,

1998, October 1996, and January 1999, we believe that Field is at an important junction in its community life.

On 30 November 1996, the community held an open house to discuss a concept land-use plan for the townsite. This fourteen-page community plan (draft sections) had been prepared by a private planning company (Olson and Olson, Calgary) in collaboration with Steve Whittingham (townsite manager of Waterton). Consultations with the Field Community Council had been ongoing for months. Comment sheets were distributed to Field residents, and opinions were sought on the following questions:

• What did you like?
• What didn't you like?
• What changes would you make?

The deadline for receipt of comments was 10 December 1996, and a set of forty-nine detailed replies was received. These replies were summarized by Cathy Jenkins (townsite assistant). The range of comments was considerable and addressed a wide variety of items, including:

• potential conflicts of interest between residents, park employees, and business owners
• lack of early consultation with the residents and the general opinion that "this is a done deal"
• removal of the trailer park, viewed as social segregation and detrimental to low-income earners
• lack of attention to current sewer/water/infrastructure problems, including parking and snow removal
• lack of facts and figures to support proposed changes, especially concerning the ability of the village to pay for improvements
• expansion as a contradiction of the main purpose of a national park – to preserve ecological integrity.

It is naïve to understate a count of the responses and conclude that a majority of residents favoured or objected to the draft plan. Rather, the comments provided clear indications of matters of substance: what to locate where, the process of soliciting views from residents, the procedures for selecting a strategy for the community, as well as requests for information on costs and benefits over the long and short runs of alternative plans. Overall, with such a high level of response, the citizens of Field are actively engaged in making operational the vision statement for their community.

A revised version of the Field Community Plan was developed in early January 1997, and it was presented to the community in February. This version incorporated a number of changes, such as the removal of the trailer park and the unfinished skating arena/community centre, the relocation of the school, a slight reduction in the amount of residential and commercial growth, and the encouragement of community dialogue by delaying the time frame for completing the plan. Late in 1997, the plan was submitted to the minister of Canadian heritage.

One issue special to Field that has direct bearing on land-use planning and the tax base is the residency code. Although property in Field can be bought and sold on the open market, there is a strict occupancy regulation. Specifically, a "need to reside" condition must be satisfied before an individual can take up permanent residency in Field. Both Parks Canada and local residents strongly support such a regulation while they struggle to control changes to land use that will address community needs that have to be funded from a local tax base. Without continuing subsidies to Field from the federal and provincial governments, it is hard to envisage that the village can generate sufficient public funds to provide services such as road and sidewalk maintenance, garbage collection, clean water, a village school, street cleaning, lighting, snow removal, and recreational spaces while restricting the amount of residential and commercial development and maintaining the residency regulation.

Clearly, there is a limit to the carrying capacity of the infrastructure in Field. The seasonal fluctuations are accommodated at the moment; however, if more seasonal rental facilities are provided and/or residency requirements are relaxed, then the population is likely to grow, need will provide economic competition, land and property prices will rise, and the social character of the community will change dramatically. No longer will Field be a community with residents who earn very modest incomes. Such individuals will be forced out by market competition. The purpose and the role of Yoho National Park will be jeopardized. Plans are in progress to privatize Parks Canada, and this development will have an effect on employment opportunities.

Some people whom we spoke to believed that the circumstances surrounding the preparation of the vision statement and the community plan provide an opportunity for Field to become a model of sustainable community development within the national parks system. To implement this vision or plan will require continuing leadership in the community and the support of residents to legitimize public policy actions. To this end, it seems to us that considerable energy is being devoted to the promotion of the four principles enunciated earlier in this chapter: ensuring that the process is fair, full, thorough, and legitimate. Also, the five core principles identified earlier as necessary conditions of a civic state are implicitly adhered to in the development of the community plan. There is no simple way to measure explicitly the adherence to specific principles other than in general terms with respect to the final outcome. But we believe that progress is being made in Field's attempt to become a sustainable community. The residents of Field are citizens-clients, and it is they who are being encouraged to take responsibility for implementing their vision statement. The pressures of work and family life, as well as the pursuit of private interests, militate against full-time involvement in voluntary activities by all residents. This case study has been offered to whet the appetite and to suggest the merits of undertaking similar projects for sustainable community development.

Acknowledgments
Funds in support of this project were provided by SSHRCC, Ottawa, and the Faculty of Arts, York University. We would like to thank Randle Robertson (executive director, Yoho-Burgess Shale Research Foundation, Field), Caroline Marion (townsite manager), and Cathy Jenkins (townsite assistant) for providing reports on community development in Field and for the time that they devoted to explaining planning in this community. They are not responsible for our interpretations.

References
Agnew, J. 1995. "Democracy and Human Rights after the Cold Wars." In R. Johnston, P. Taylor, and M. Watts, eds., *Geographies of Global Change* (82-96). Oxford: Blackwell.
Anderson, B. 1983. *Imagined Communities*. London: Verso.
Arrow, K. 1951. *Social Choice and Individual Values*. New York: John Wiley.
Axelrod, R. 1984. *The Evolution of Co-operation*. London: Penguin.
Barry, N. 1990. *Welfare*. Milton Keynes: Open University Press.
Baum, G. 1996. The Practice of Citizenship in Today's Society. Paper presented at the Annual General Meeting of the Social Planning Council of Metropolitan Toronto, 25 May, Toronto.
Bullock, A., and O. Stallybrass, eds. 1980. *The Fontana Dictionary of Modern Thought*. London: Fontana Books.
Byrne, J., and S. Hoffman. 1996. "Sustainability: From Concept to Practice." *IEEE Technology and Society Magazine* 15,2: 6-7.
Carr, M. 1996. Social Capital, Civil Society, and the Informal Economy: Moving to Sustainable Society. Paper presented at the ACSP/AESOP Conference, 25-28 July, University of British Columbia, Vancouver.
Clark, G., and Dear, M. 1984. *State Apparatus, Structures, and Language of Legitimacy*. London: Allen and Unwin.
Cockburn, C. 1977. *The Local State*. London: Pluto Press.
Coleman, J. 1990. *Foundations of Social Theory*. Cambridge: Harvard University Press.
Cook, P. 1998. "How the Third Way Gets in the Way." *Globe and Mail*, 23 September, A2.
Cook, R. 1995. *Canada, Quebec, and the Uses of Nationalism*. 2nd ed. Toronto: McClelland and Stewart.
–. 1996. "Challenges to Canadian Federalism in the 1990s." In J. Littleton, ed., *Clash of Identities: Media, Manipulation, and Politics of the Self* (89-100). Toronto: Canadian Broadcasting Corporation.
Dahrendorf, R. 1995. "A Precarious Balance: Economic Opportunity, Civil Society, and Political Liberty." *Responsive Community* 5,3: 13-39.
Dale, A. 1997. Private communication to authors.
Dale, A., and S. Hill. 1996. "Biodiversity Conservation: A Decision-Making Context." In A. Dale and J. Robinson, eds., *Achieving Sustainable Development* (97-118). Vancouver: UBC Press.
Dale, A., and J. Robinson, eds. 1996. *Achieving Sustainable Development*. Vancouver: UBC Press.

Dale, A., J. Robinson, and C. Massey. 1995. Reconciling Human Welfare and Ecological Carrying Capacity. Workshop reports, Sustainable Development Research Institute, University of British Columbia.

Day, P., and R. Klein. 1987. "The Business of Welfare." *New Society* 19: 11-3.

Dunn, J., ed. 1995. *Contemporary Crisis of the Nation State*. Cambridge, UK: Blackwell.

Ekos Research Associates Inc. 1995. *Rethinking Government '94*. Ottawa: Ekos Research Associates.

Fukuyama, F. 1995. *Trust: The Social Virtues and the Creation of Prosperity*. Toronto: Simon and Schuster.

Giddens, A. 1998. *The Third Way*. London: Polity Press.

Galbraith, J.K. 1996. *The Good Society: The Humane Agenda*. New York: Houghton Mifflin.

Griffiths, F. 1996. *Strong and Free*. Toronto: Stoddart.

Gwyn, R. 1995. *Nationalism without Walls: The Unbearable Lightness of Being Canadian*. Toronto: McClelland and Stewart.

Herkert, J., A. Farrell, and J. Winebrake. 1996. "Technology Choice for Sustainable Development." *IEEE Technology and Society Magazine* 15,2: 12-20.

Huntington, S. 1993. *The Clash of Civilizations and the Remaking of World Order*. New York: Simon and Shuster.

Hutton, W. 1995. *The State We're In*. London: Jonathan Cape.

ICLEI (International Council for Local Environmental Initiatives). 1996. *The Local Agenda 21 Planning Guide*. Toronto: ICLEI, IDRC, UNEP.

Johnston, R., P. Taylor, and M. Watts, eds. 1995. *Geographies of Global Change*. Oxford: Blackwell.

Kettel, B. 1996. "Putting Women and the Environment First: Poverty Alleviation and Sustainable Development." In A. Dale and S. Robinson, eds., *Achieving Sustainable Development* (160-81). Vancouver: UBC Press.

Kramer, R. 1990. Foreword. In J. Wolch, *The Shadow State: Government and Voluntary Sector in Transition* (i-iii). New York: Foundation Center.

Maclaren, V.W. 1996. *Developing Indicators of Urban Sustainability: A Focus on the Canadian Experience*. Toronto: ICURR Press.

Massam, B.H. 1993. *The Right Place: Shared Responsibility and the Location of Public Facilities*. London: Longman.

–. 1996. "An Essay on Civil Society." *Community Economic Development Centre* (66). Burnaby, BC: Simon Fraser University.

Massam, B.H., and R. Goulet. 1996. "Environmental Nongovernmental Organizations in Central and Eastern Europe: Contributions to Civil Society." *International Environmental Affairs* 9,2: 127-47.

Mishra, R. 1990. *The Welfare State in Capitalist Society*. Toronto: University of Toronto Press.

Morrison, R. 1991. *We Build the Road as We Travel*. Philadelphia: New Society Publishers.

Myrdal, G. 1960. *Beyond the Welfare State*. New Haven: Yale University Press.

Novick, M. 1995. Civic Solidarity: Foundations of Social Development for the 21st Century. Paper presented at the Annual General Meeting of the Social Planning Council of Metropolitan Toronto, 18 May, Toronto.

Ohmae, K. 1995. *The End of the Nation State, the Rise of Regional Economies*. Toronto: Free Press.

Panitch, L. 1993. "A Different Kind of State." In G. Albo, D. Langille, and L. Panitch, eds., *A Different Kind of State?* (2-16). Toronto: Oxford University Press.

Parks Canada. 1994. *Operational Review #29: Communities*. Ottawa: Department of Canadian Heritage.

Peters, S. 1995. *Exploring Canadian Values: Foundations for Well-Being*. Canadian Policy Research Networks Study F-01. Ottawa: Renouf Publishing.

Prior, D., J. Stewart, and K. Walsh. 1995. *Citizenship: Rights, Community, and Participation*. London: Pitman.

Putnam, R.D. 1993. *Making Democracy Work: Civic Traditions in Modern Italy*. Princeton: Princeton University Press.

–. 1995. "Bowling Alone: America's Declining Social Capital." *Journal of Democracy* 6,1: 65-78.

–. 1996. "The Strange Disappearance of Civic America." *The American Prospect* no. 24 (winter) <http://epn.org/prospect/24/24putn.html>.

Saunders, P. 1984. "Rethinking Local Politics." In M. Boddy and C. Fudge, eds., *Local Socialism?* (22-48). London: Macmillan.

"The Shape of the World." 1995-6. *Economist.* 23 December 1995-5 January 1996: 15-8.

Shils, E. 1991. "The Virtue of Civil Society." *Journal of Government* 26: 3-20.

Social Planning Council of Metropolitan Toronto. 1995. *SPC News* July. Newsletter.

Spinner, J. 1994. *The Boundaries of Citizenship: Race, Ethnicity, and Nationality in the Liberal State.* Baltimore: Johns Hopkins University Press.

Taylor, C. 1995. *Philosophical Arguments.* Cambridge: Harvard University Press.

Taylor, P. 1993. *Political Geography: World-Economy, Nation-State, and Locality.* London: Longman.

"The Third Way Revealed." 1998. *Economist.* 19 September: 72.

Thrift, N. 1995. "A Hyperactive World." In R.J. Johnston, P.J. Taylor, and M.J. Watts, eds., *Geographies of Global Change* (18-35). Oxford: Blackwell.

Valpy, M. 1995. *Globe and Mail*, 28 June: A3.

Webster's College Dictionary. 1991. Toronto: Random House.

Wolch, J.R. 1990. *The Shadow State: Government and Voluntary Sector in Transition.* New York: Foundation Center.

Zinberg, D.S. 1994. "Drop Out and Tag On." *Times Higher Education Supplement*, 7 October: 16.

Assessing Progress

11
Concepts, Cosmologies, and Commitment: Using Biodiversity Indicators in Critical Zones Models
Thomas C. Meredith

Introduction

Life is change. Ecosystems are living complexes characterized by a perpetual and dynamic tessellation of niches. Survival, therefore, is adaptation, and, in the ever-shifting matrix of species interactions, the capacity to be ecologically flexible and responsive is vital. Human ecology is no different in this regard, though we humans are unique in the extent of our capacity to analyze change and anticipate consequences. This chapter is about our capacity for analysis and anticipation and about the relevance of these abilities to the quality of our future. The chapter argues that we have the tools at our disposal to ensure our future but that we do not appear yet to have the motivation to use them.

This argument is developed in two parts. The first part posits that our capacity to resolve our current crisis resides not simply in throwing more of the same (science, technology, money, policy, rhetoric) at the problem but also in continuing to ask the basic questions of where (or who) we are and where we want to go. The concepts of *socioecosystem* and of *critical environmental zones* are considered as two means of exploring those questions. The discussion addresses theories of cybernetic or "self-steering" systems from critical zones research. These systems are characterized by *perceive-interpret-respond* sequences that define thresholds of *perception, action,* and *intolerance.* The second part of the argument considers agriculture, forestry, and fisheries, three economic sectors that determine core elements of Canadian well-being, our culture, our prosperity, and our ecological viability. These are industries based on ecological resources but are generally considered to be distinct from the noncommercial ecological resource collectively referred to as biodiversity. Biodiversity management is considered as a fourth sector. This section assesses how the concepts from critical environmental zones research can be, and are being, applied to land management in each of these sectors. It shows that (1) for commercial sectors there are few incentives for constructing sector-specific cybernetic systems that are inherently selective of ecosystem-viability outcomes and that (2) for non-commercial objectives (e.g., biodiversity protection) it is unlikely that cybernetic response mechanisms will prove effective unless positive outcomes are conspicuously linked to economic productivity in other sectors.

It is argued that biodiversity is a sound measure of ecosystem sustainability and can be used more effectively as a measure of adaptive human activity. Biodiversity is currently valued as either a commercial resource or a good in its own right. Neither is sufficient to ensure adequate protection. This chapter argues that its conservation requires that it be used as a metric – that is, as a means of assessing progress toward sustainability in other sectors. Substantiating this argument involves three tests. Is it needed? Would it work? Is it possible? More explicitly, the questions are:

1   Without indicators such as biodiversity as feedback, is it probable that resource systems (including environmental life-support systems) will be drawn down to critical levels?
2   Can biodiversity, used as an indicator, prevent criticality in economic resource sectors (e.g., can biodiversity information prevent crises in agriculture, forestry, fisheries)?
3   Is biodiversity a measure of performance that is supportive of human well-being increases and therefore "marketable" as a decision-making criterion?

The answers, of course, are determined in part by normative issues rooted in the visions and the values – the conceptualization – of the decision makers. Conceptualization is therefore an integral part of the process of adaptation and must be addressed in both theoretical and management studies of human adaptation. This, for reasons considered below, raises questions of scale. The chapter continues with a discussion of the role of conceptualization, an appraisal of the issue of scale, and an assessment of critical zones theories as tools for effecting the required change at the appropriate scale. The chapter then applies these ideas as it compares and contrasts the four resource sectors. It concludes with an assessment of the implications for sustainable development in rural, ecological resource-based communities.

Why Conceptual Scale Is Important

> The greatest barrier to progress is not ignorance, but the illusion of knowledge.
>
> – Daniel Boorstin (1993)

Picture the angst-ridden commute by private car to a meeting downtown at 8 a.m. on a snow-snarled morning. Desperate anger mounts in exhaust fumes as minutes tick past deadlines. The search for parking is explosive. Such problems demand responses at least at two scales: the first is the obvious scale of the immediate crisis; the second is at the level of the system that permits these crises (and therefore makes them inevitable). Why do such crises arise, given that there is no outside, higher authority who constrained us to a dependence on urban agglomerations, commuter traffic, private automobiles, and the pigheaded inability to honour the power of weather by adjusting our fetish for punctuality? First-scale problems do get solved, but if we fail even to see the questions at the second scale when confronted by them, we may walk away smug and satisfied once we have parked our cars and miss an opportunity to amend the system that creates the crisis. Blindness to the meaning of cues dooms us to being victims of endemic dysfunctions. It cripples the mechanism of adaptation. The real challenges of sustainability are to find, and to act on, second-scale questions.

In the first volume of the SDRI series, *Achieving Sustainable Development*, Dale and Hill (1996, 103) quote Schneider and Kay (1994): "Given that living systems go through a constant cycle ... at many temporal and spatial scales, a way of preserving information about what works and what doesn't so as to constrain the self-organization process is crucial for the continuance of life. This is the role of the gene. At the larger scale, it is the role of biodiversity." Dale and Hill use the quotation to underscore the value of biodiversity as a record of evolution's success (measured, tautologically, only as individual species' *fitness* or propensity to survive). It is used again here not simply to reemphasize that but also to raise the question of records of evolution's success at yet another scale – that is, at the level of social organization. If the gene is the record of individual species' "achievement," and the pool of genes is the record of a community's, then what, or where, is the record of the intricacy of the noosphere – the complex of social organization and human competence? It is obviously not in any written encyclopedia; like dictionaries, encyclopedias are limited by the peculiarity that they have to assume infinitely more than they convey. In *One Hundred Years of Solitude*, Márquez (1967) celebrates this paradox as his characters respond to a fog of collective amnesia that seeps into their village. Every article in the village is first labelled. As the fog thickens and concern mounts, each article's purpose and the means of its use are written on the label. But as it becomes apparent that the labels will also need to contain descriptions of the meanings of the words used, the task is given up as absurd. There can be no comprehensive text of the noosphere.

Nonetheless, the information that defines the accumulated history of our survival and success obviously does have a real – if unrecognized –

existence. Embedded in custom, perception, and value is the vast and irreplaceable open "text" of how we survive. This is like the genetic code of a
species – it may be at least as self-unintelligible, and it is certainly as irreplaceable if lost or destroyed. But unlike genetic codes, it has no significant
physical presence. It does not exist in physical artifacts such as a sym-
phonic score; rather, it exists in the knowledge of how to read the score and
in the vision of what the score represents in sound sequences. It is the
aggregate of what is thought or remembered in human minds; it is what
gives the physical world meaning, purpose, utility, continuity, and value
(for humans).

What has this to do with critical environmental zones and sustainable
development? Everything. It is the "expression" of these ethereal "codes"
that has led us into the present crisis, and the fact that these codes are
dynamic gives us hope that the crisis can, indeed will, be resolved. Whatever
more we as a species may be, or believe ourselves to be, we are first ecological
beings, embedded in our ecosystems in a way that is unique only in the
extent to which it is dependent on cultural invention. We live in what
Colinveau (1983) called invented niches. Because they must conform to all
ecological limitations, they are indisputably ecological niches. But because
cultural invention is implicated in the definition of human niches, the
noosphere must be central in studies of human responses to niche crises.
Our conceptualization affects the pragmatics of our survival. Cosmology
does matter.

We have historically defined species in isolation and accepted specimens
in zoos or museums as representative of their species. Understanding that a
dead organism is significantly different from a live organism – though perhaps identical in weight and chemistry – is no greater a step than recognizing that an organism outside its ecological system is not the same
organism as one within it. The Darwinian revolution includes the recognition that organisms are elements of environments that shape and are
shaped by other organisms. Any organism can be defined as legitimately
by its niche functions as by its mass or chemistry (as, say, an organ is more
likely to be defined by what it does than by its composition). For humans,
as for other species, it is at best meaningless and at worst counterproduc-
tive to think of ourselves as other than part of an ecological system. But
because of the inextricable association between human culture and the
autecology of our invented niches, because it is necessary to characterize
human ecology by cultural attributes, ideas are part of the system. As much
as an oak tree's shade and an eagle's appetite are definitive though intangible parts of an ecosystem, so are human ideas. And because ideas reside in
language, human adaptation must involve linguistic adaptation. For example, there have been convincing criticisms of the use of the word *environment* because it implies an isolation of humans from "that which

surrounds" (reviewed in Meredith 1991). What we think of as "the environment" is a dynamic ecosystem that includes – even in the most sterile space – interactions between many species. It perhaps makes sense to talk of urban environments – if by them we mean inert buildings and pavements – but because outside the built environment what surrounds is alive, constantly changing and indivisibly connected to human activity, the term "ecosystem" is accurate. "Socioecosystem" has been proposed as more accurate still because it includes the recognition of culture and concepts in defining the ecological links of human niches. What we live in is an ecosystem defined by societal attributes; any simpler conceptualization misses the truth as surely as did the pre-Copernican geocentric cosmology. And if we don't understand our socioecosystem, then we are as blindly linked to our life-support system as are the members of a "cargo cult" – who prayed to the gods for another crashed plane to refill the cornucopia that the previous crash brought.

Humanity has successfully reinvented itself several times in the past. Our success as a species may be, in fact, a precise and direct consequence of our capacity to do so. The cultural geographers' inquiry into reinvented relationships between cultures and landscapes addresses one dimension of this reinvention – that is, the changes from local subsistence economies based on naturally regulated ecosystems to global interlinked market economies grounded in engineered landscapes. There are physical differences between these radically altered socioecosystems. But there are also profound differences between notions of how we fit into the universe. In Western philosophy, the worldview has changed from an ostensibly theosophic or theocratic base, through the Copernican dislocation, the Cartesian and Newtonian roots of positivism, to existentialism and to Fregean and Wittgensteinian speculation about cosmology as a linguistic artifact (Schulte 1992). This transition is certainly of second-scale concerns, and the impacts have been, and will continue to be, profound.

In the crises of human sustainability, there are many first-scale issues being dealt with, from emergency food aid to cod-fishery collapses. But there also appears to be a convergence of understandings that may help to define urgent second-scale questions. Sacks (1995, 113), a neurologist, writes, "We are not given the world, we make our world through incessant experience, categorizations, memory, reconnection." He is talking about the extreme difficulty of literally learning to see as a previously blind adult, but the relevance is more than metaphorical. Pickles (1995), a geographer, notes the inefficiencies that arise from the assumption that words can be mapped onto the world. They can't. Chomsky (1996), a linguist, points out that our definition of the geographic term "river" is grounded in nothing that is consistent – neither substance nor shape, genesis, morphology, dynamics, or topology. And he argues that there is nothing we can do (or need to do) about this imprecision except, perhaps, recognize it. But together these observations have profound implications for how we think about, and how we act in respect of, that which we consider to be our "environment." We can only act purposefully in response to our conception of the environment; where that conception has proven maladaptive, it must change. The "conventional wisdom" or "common sense" that led us into the ecological crisis is proving maladaptive and will almost certainly come to be seen as just as quaint as the worldview of a flat Earth. What will replace it may now seem as peripheral, bizarre, or revolutionary as did the restrictions on child labour that, say, Marx proposed little more than a century ago.

We have made great strides in recent centuries; we have come from a time when the common person felt that, although she or he did not personally understand the overall situation, someone else – chiefs, priests, rulers – did. Many people now accept that, at least on these issues, probably no one does. This is empowering, not only because it puts responsibility and accountability for decision making where it belongs (in everyone's hands), but also because overcoming the illusion of knowledge is the first step toward progress.

Why Spatial Scale Is Important

> Our understandable wish to preserve the planet must somehow
> be reduced to our scale of competence - that is, to the wish to
> preserve all of its humble households and neighbourhoods.
>
>   – Wendell Berry (1991, 153)

Questions of the relationship between human well-being and ecosystem viability cannot be considered without addressing the issue of spatial scales. It is, in folk terms, embedded in "think globally, act locally." Short of cataclysmic events such as nuclear war, the stresses that threaten the viability of human systems are aggregate in nature – that is, negative impacts arise from the sum of actions that in themselves may appear benign or trivial. Likewise, negative consequences are experienced differentially across both space and time; some regions, some sites, some individuals confront negative consequences more directly and more immediately than others. Environmental crises – whether resulting from local or remote causes – are experienced at specific sites, by specific groups, at specific times, as if in some (rigged?) ecological "lottery" in which the real costs of individual action are diluted in the pool of actions taken by others, and in which the accumulated consequences fall to individuals in no fixed relationship to needs, vulnerabilities, or deserts. Lessons about human ecology drawn from nonhuman survival strategies might suggest that global sustainability can be achieved through spatial variability that includes alternations of local booms (population increases) and busts (local extinctions). But for humans survival without equity is (argued to be) unacceptable. Hence, "global sustainability" is not merely a numbers game or a measure of survival. It is an abstract and subjective concept; ultimately, it is the aggregate of individual human experiences in local ecosystems. Given that each human being is attached to some specific local environment in the matrix, and that consciousness of sustainability resides only at the level of the individual, concerns about, degrees of satisfaction with, and motivation for progress toward sustainability will be rooted in the local. Even in the face of global change, sustainability will be won or lost on a case-by-case basis.

Underlying the logic of the phrase "think globally, act locally" is the knowledge of the importance of domestic environmental stewardship. A community confronting crisis looks for solutions, which may include attempts to influence institutions, policies, and international accords. Adaptive community response requires a degree of empowerment but also a clear framework for measures of progress. As Hammond et al. (1995, vii) note, "Policy makers and pundits sit up and take notice when the Dow Jones inches up – and millions of Americans rethink personal financial decisions. These economic indicators show the power of a single number ... Yet, no remotely similar numbers exist to indicate how the environment is faring." "Indicators have two defining characteristics: they quantify and simplify" (1). "Experience in public policy [illustrates several] characteristics of successful indicators: [they must be] user-driven, policy-relevant, [and] highly aggregated" (2).

Daly and Cobb (1994) proposed an innovative Index of Sustainable Economic Welfare that appears to be capable of capturing important variations but that, perhaps because of its complexity, has not been widely adopted. Hodge (1996, 267) discusses the importance of a framework being "honed to the needs of a given locale." To the extent that people can influence the evolution of their local landscape, *they* are the critical decision makers. Indicators of change must appear useful to them: "In the end, only users know what information they need – the bedrock principle for those who structure the data collection, analysis, interpretation and aggregation that results in indicators" (Hammond et al. 1995, 33). Despite global environmental trends, the stewardship role of local communities and resource users needs to be acknowledged.

The World Resources Institute (WRI) report on indicators develops a pressure-state-response model with four linkages between human activity and the environment: sources (material taken from the environment), sink (material put in the environment), life-support (what Westman [1977] called "nature's services," such as provision of clean water and oxygen production), and impact on human welfare (direct impacts of, say, water or food contamination). On this basis, WRI proposes four indicators: pollution, resource depletion, ecosystem risks, impact on human welfare. These indicators, if widely adopted, can have a beneficial impact on the self-regulating cybernetics of socioecosystems. But they tell us much more about ourselves than they do about our ecological linkages. A pollution index is obviously a valuable tool even though it fails to acknowledge that what constitutes pollution is defined not by innate characteristics but by consequences (such as are addressed in the third and fourth indicators). Nitrogen added to a field is not pollution (despite the fact that it may have devastating effects for some species), but it is when it runs into an adjacent stream. The resource depletion indicator, for example, is really just a (timely) rationalization, along the lines proposed by Pearce et al. (1991), of fundamentally flawed economic accounting systems that fail to distinguish wealth "creation" from asset transfer and liquidation. The fourth category of indicator is not developed or even discussed in any detail because of fundamental (indeed, profound) methodological problems related to equity issues, but the objective is to develop a way of indicating "impact on human welfare" as an aggregate of the number of people exposed to risk and the intensity of that risk. Nor, for similar reasons, is the third indicator developed at any length, but the discussion there moves quickly from the general scale of environmental risk to the consideration of biodiversity as a measure of ecological pressure and to habitat protection as a measure of biodiversity protection.

The pressure referred to by WRI is referred to elsewhere as stress (Rapport 1990). Following the logic of the WRI report, then, sustainable development can be seen as development that minimizes ecological stress or pressure associated with human activity. But does this conceptualization reflect accurately the complex and dynamic nature of ecosystems? The uniqueness of many specific natural landscapes is determined by what humans would describe as harsh environmental conditions (deserts, salt marshes, etc.), whereas actions that are ecologically destructive may come from eliminating that stress (irrigating deserts or draining salt marshes eliminates endemic plants). Clearly, the idea of stress is not as straightforward as we might like it to be. As a measure of environmental quality, it derives its value not from the concept of stress per se but from the ability to distinguish natural from anthropogenic stress. This suggests that what is thought (by humans) to be implicitly "good," in environmental terms, is determined by its degree of naturalness. That notion of purely natural sites as benchmarks is of marginal value because (1) they may not exist – humans are part of nature and of many if not most landscapes, so these landscapes (even in their "natural" state) bear human imprints; (2) they may be impossible to define if they do exist – because ecosystems are constantly dynamic, any human attempt to isolate, observe, or "freeze" them will modify them and, at best, produce a record of some arbitrary point in a process; and (3) they may not be what we want anyway – no species exists without modifying its environment, and no credible human development proposal would envision unaltered landscapes. Moreover, (4) any sustainability strategy based primarily on sequestration of land from human activity is doomed to failure because the amount of available land is inadequate, and, in any case, sequestered land would continue to be vulnerable as human needs increase. Ecosystem alteration and anthropogenic stress are prior conditions of most ecosystems. But, in considering sustainable development, human inhabitants of ecosystems do need means of both detecting and evaluating changes in their systems. And, clearly, it is not sufficient that the criterion be simply what we humans think is "good" for us.

The Concepts of Critical Zones

Sites of local ecological crisis can be thought of as "critical environmental zones." They are defined as areas where biophysical change threatens the well-being of the human community. These communities bear the brunt of the cost of imposed change (Kasperson, Kasperson, and Turner 1996) and so may be the first to recognize the real meaning of the challenges of sustainability. They may also have the deepest insight into causes and processes of environmental degradation, the strongest commitment to finding solutions, and the greatest sense of the real feasibility of restorative strategies. Hence, it is not surprising that, along with governments, institutions, and academics, community groups have mobilized to address the challenges of achieving sustainability. Residents of critical zones may live, rather than observe, the crisis.

A motivating hypothesis of critical zones research is that the processes leading to environmental degradation at a specific site are not idiosyncratic but characterized by elements that are common to different sites and different sources of degradation. The identification of these elements will provide an important second-scale tool for halting or reversing the trend toward degradation. The approach is based on a model in which human users of ecological resources *perceive, interpret,* and *respond to* environmental cues (Meredith et al. 1994). The perceptions of individuals are based on the array of cues that they receive, some directly from within their ecosystem, some in the form of data and information from outside actors. The analytic paradigms used to give it meaning determine the interpretation. Responses depend on values, priorities, and degrees of empowerment, as well as on technical, institutional, and financial factors. Mechanisms and structures of response are also part of human adaptation. The critical zones approach draws on the hazards research of Burton, Kates, and White (1993) in

which, as environmental cues become more conspicuous and consequences more onerous, individuals cross thresholds of *awareness, action,*
and *intolerance.*

The challenges of sustainability are related to differential responses to
two critical axes that can be used to describe socioecosystems (Figure 11.1).
We respond to one – perceived well-being – but depend on the other – ecological sustainability. When the signals from each are consonant (upper
right or lower left), the difference is immaterial. When they are discordant,
the difference is critical. Where choices exist, and information about consequences is available and understood, critical conditions will arise from
unwillingness to sacrifice perceived human well-being for ecosystem viability or, conversely, from the willingness to accept improvements in
human well-being without accounting for full costs in loss of ecosystem
viability. In a generic sense, what planning and management for sustainability require is a merging or colinearity of the two axes such that what *is*
required for ecological sustainability becomes part of what we respond to
in deciding on actions.

The impact of environmental degradation on the *human* population of a
socioecosystem is central to the concept of critical environmental zones.

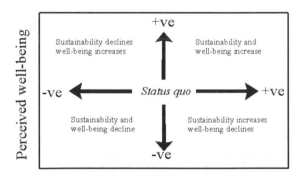

Sustainability

Figure 11.1 **Evaluating the consequences of environmental change**
Much of human activity is undertaken to increase net perceived human well-being,
but most actions also have implications for ecological sustainability. There is little
debate arising from the lower left or upper right quadrants in the diagram. The interesting quadrants are the upper left, which describes activities characteristic of the
crisis of sustainability, and the lower left, which reflects apparent sacrifices made
for ecological sustainability. These two quadrants are where the most difficult
analysis and management issues lie. Perhaps the most interesting questions are:
how orthogonal are the axes to one another, over what scales of evaluation, and
within what paradigms or value sets? Accepting biodiversity as a measure of human
well-being could demonstrate that the axes are, ultimately, parallel.

Successful development of predictive models and evaluation of the effectiveness of information systems are dependent on developing a clear understanding of the role of "human factors." The ability of modern human systems to compensate for local environmental stress can arise from the ability to import carrying capacity (food, energy, natural resources) and to export or defer negative impacts (shipping hazardous wastes to other places, leaving environmental costs of nuclear storage to another generation). One problem with an early attempt to develop a paradigm for the analysis of criticality was the assumption that environmental degradation would necessarily be reflected in levels of prosperity or of human well-being (Kasperson, Kasperson, and Turner 1996). This is clearly not the case. Farm yields may increase, even as soil is degraded, as long as technical inputs increase.

The concept of well-being is sometimes thought of in narrow terms – basic human needs or economic returns – but Maslow's (1954) hierarchy of needs suggests that humans are motivated by a range of factors. His hierarchy extends from the fundamental, first-level need for self-preservation through the procuration of adequate food, water, clothing, and shelter to second-level safety needs, third-level belonging needs, fourth-level self-esteem needs, and to the pinnacle, self-actualization needs, including the appreciation of justice, ethics, and aesthetics. Ecological change may impinge on one's well-being at any level of this hierarchy. For example, the loss of arable land may threaten food supply, and the destruction of a local wilderness pocket may compromise aesthetic appreciation. These are the cues that determine the pattern of perception and response to ecological change. Becoming more sensitive to the cues, or – as Burton (1991, 121) suggests – "making the invisible visible," is a first step in shifting thresholds of awareness and action.

Critical zones studies are concerned with the *processes* that lead to degradation and the *responses* within human-ecosystem relations. Because of the focus on process, they must deal with *variations*, both in patterns of human activities (the cultural base) and in the nature of the resources used (the ecological base). Canadian communities dependent on single, depleting, biological resources are informative microcosms of the processes of both environmental degradation and societal reaction. Although each community is affected, of course, by external forces largely beyond immediate local control (from climate change to market variation), there are also determining forces of which each is a part and can influence. Canadian forest, agricultural, and coastal ecosystems provide contrasts in the relationship between resources and users. Moreover, they dominate the Canadian landscape, contain the bulk of our endowment of biodiversity, and regulate much of our water supply; they embody quality-of-life parameters that are important in the Canadian cultural identity, and they are of great importance to the Canadian economy.

Three Questions

Are New Feedback Signals Needed?

The critical zones model recognizes that much of human activity is determined by consequences for perceived well-being. Without feedback to the human behaviours system that is independent of conventionally defined human well-being, are ecological resource systems (including environmental health systems) likely to be drawn down to critical levels?

The three commercial sectors are considered along with a fourth, biodiversity protection. The reason for including it as a "sector" is to facilitate comparison of feedback cues and management systems across sectors. The inherent differences between this and the other sectors are discussed later in the chapter. Intuitively and historically, the four sectors are distinct. A microscale view supports this perception, but a macroscale view shows them to be structurally similar: humans exploit natural systems to improve their own well-being. And, in fact, as they become more intensively exploited, they become more similar: Christmas-tree farming, short-rotation plantation forestry, and aquaculture are organizationally very similar to intensive agriculture. The transition of the socioecosystems can be viewed along a spectrum of changing control from unmanaged to managed ecosystems. In unmanaged systems, humans assume no responsibility for regulating the system, and all benefits from it are "delivered" to humans and to other species through self-regulating ecological linkages (which include humans but not their purposive management actions). The fisheries have traditionally depended on unmanaged ecosystems. More intense management may involve creating dependencies on human inputs for, say, nutrients, water, seed stock; for protection from competition, disease, and predation; for temperature control; and even for substrate. Hydroponic greenhouse agriculture is near the most intensely managed end of the spectrum. In part, this process of assuming increasing responsibility for the state of resource systems is a wilful demonstration of human ingenuity undertaken for predicted benefits. But at the same time, it is a process that increases dependence and vulnerability: dependence on the capacity to maintain inputs (e.g., the consequences of a power failure to a greenhouse operator), and vulnerability to the loss of inherent stabilizing mechanisms (e.g., pest outbreaks).

Where the choice of increased management is made consciously and with full information, it must be deemed, at least in the eyes of the decision maker, a wise choice. Others may see it as foolhardy if they disagree with the assessment of risks, or they may see it as inequitable if there are costs or hazards that are not borne by the beneficiary. These are problems of the decision-making context but not of the decision-making process. On the other hand, where choices are made on the basis of incomplete information and the risk assessment is incomplete, the decision-making process itself is flawed. If it is flawed simply because available information is not used, then the problem is in communication (or motivation), but the flaw is inherent if the information is simply not available. Innovations in land use are novel, real-time experiments with complex systems. Full information is simply not available, so contingencies must be built into the planning-response process. This is Holling's (1978) adaptive management and science of surprise. In each of the sectors, all else being equal, the desirability of sustainability is implicit.

Globally, the problems and challenges are similar in each sector; locally, however, decisions are made and systems are managed from a microscale perspective. The cybernetic sequence for each is different. Uniform elements are user, resource, means of adding to the productivity of the resource, and means of subtracting from negative impacts on the resource (Table 11.1). Variability comes from permutations of possible states in each of these categories: users can be individual or aggregate; the resource base can have restricted or open access; the system can be more or less responsive to productivity inputs; and impacts of harvest per se can be more or less easily regulated. Agricultural systems can be viewed as most manageable (hence no limits on harvest), but agriculture is also the most highly modified system and the one that may be least affected by public policy. But because management units are relatively small, because the beneficiaries/managers are in direct contact with the environment, and because they are connected to the specific site, a responsive, site-specific system of feedback is possible. The same factors may ensure greater knowledge of local conditions but make access to outside information more difficult (a single farmer cannot be expected to dedicate the same effort to research as a corporation). Likewise, these factors may limit flexibility of response (e.g., because of restricted capital to invest in alternative technologies). These very different linkages represent the management "physiology" of the different resource systems. It is clear that no single strategy will work for all. The following section looks briefly at the sectors and considers, for each, the importance of the sector (ecologically, economically, and societally), the socioecological problems, and the societal responses, including goals articulated in recent sector-specific policy papers.

Agriculture
The recent Agriculture and Agri-Food Canada (AAFC) reports on environmental sustainability provide a window on a vitally important industry. The production and handling of food comprise one of Canada's main economic activities, with agriculture and agrifood accounting for 8 percent of the GDP, 15 percent of employment, and generating about $75 billion in retail sales and $17 billion in exports (AAFC 1996b). Many communities are reliant on agriculture for their character and prosperity, but the

Table 11.1

**Some management characteristics of the selected resource sectors/
ecosystems**

Sector	Users	Tenure/ usufruct	Management of inputs	Management of harvest
Agro-systems (cultivated and improved pasture)	individual users	private resource	responsive to management inputs	no regulated harvest limits
Agro-systems (open pasture)	individual users	public resource, shared access	not (readily) responsive to management inputs	harvest limited by stocking density
Forests	corporate users	public resource, single access	responsive to management inputs	harvest limited by space
Coastal	individual users	public resource, open access	not (readily) responsive to management inputs	harvest limited by time or volume
Biodiversity	non-specific	resource	not (readily) responsive to management inputs	no conventional harvest

Aquatic resources are anomalous because their physical habitat is not shared by humans — we do not live in the same space — and so concerns about aesthetics are less likely to be significant. Biodiversity resources are anomalous because there is no major financial dimension. Thus, while for each of the commercial sectors a threshold of intolerance is contingent on the balance between market conditions and production costs (including the costs of actions required to compensate for environmental deterioration), the threshold of intolerance for biodiversity is defined entirely innately.

---

long-term viability of Canadian agriculture, and hence of these communities, is threatened by a number of widespread environmental problems, including soil degradation and inefficient recycling of nutrients. The changes that result from these problems tend to be cumulative, affecting the productivity of agroecosystems gradually over many years. They may be less "in the news" or in public consciousness than the obvious impacts of bad weather, market fluctuations, or agricultural policy, and they may go unnoticed or be masked by increased inputs.

A major trend in the industry is toward fewer but larger farms with corporate rather than family ownership. The number of farms in Canada diminished by almost half a million (733,000 to 280,043) from 1941 to 1991, but between 1971 and 1991 the average farm increased in size from 96 hectares to 242 hectares. Although overall the amount of agricultural land in Canada has remained about the same, there has been a dramatic shift toward more intensive use of the land, with a loss of woodlots, wetlands (-41 percent from 1971 to 1991), and croplands left fallow (-27 percent), and an increase in cropland (+20 percent) (AAFC 1996b, 18).

Apart from these direct habitat changes, the most obvious environmental threat resulting from current practices in Canadian agriculture is soil degradation. This degradation results from salinization, wind and water erosion, the depletion of organic matter, compaction, and acidification. Soil degradation takes place in nearly every farming community of the nation and reduces the availability and productivity of the soil resource upon which agriculture is based. The "environmental outlook" for agriculture describes major "new challenges" related to water pollution, solid-waste management, climate change, and impacts on biodiversity (AAFC 1996b, 45). But the challenges cannot be met with simple solutions: "production is affected by physical, technological, economic and social factors. The nature of these factors varies tremendously across the country" (AAFC 1996a, iii). This variability reveals a need for local adaptation. At the same time, the sector is linked to global forces and is driven by the vision that "production will need to significantly increase ... to meet the growing world demand" (iv). In other words, an array of site-specific procedures must be found to increase total production while reducing local impacts. Not an easy task!

Given the importance of agriculture in the Canadian landscape, it is all but understatement to say that "environmentally sustainable agriculture is an important part of overall sustainability" (AAFC 1996a, 7). The AAFC report suggests that "achieving environmentally sustainable agriculture will be a process of trial and error, energized and carried out by members of the agriculture and agri-food sector and government" (1). This statement is noteworthy for three reasons: its implicit acknowledgment of need, its assertion that the process will be trial and error rather than systematic or purposive, and its implication that the operative constituency is restricted to members of the sector and government. The report suggests that "the environmental future [of the sector] will be shaped by social and economic forces," including demand, prices, policy, international agreements, technology, and research (8). That said, the report goes on to define six principles – partnerships, integration, ecosystem approach, pollution prevention and stewardship, intergenerational equity, and competitiveness (4-5) – that do reflect recognition of systemic interactions. Four strategic directions are defined in some detail (10, passim): increasing understanding, promoting stewardship, developing innovation, and seizing market opportunities. The emphasis on understanding is important because this is the mechanism by which values and objectives will change. This is closely linked to the second objective, which addresses a stewardship ethic, noting that "wise stewardship ... is at the very heart of the survival of agriculture" and that "there are clear signs that a stewardship ethic has grown" (17). The third objective describes practical strategies dealing primarily with the technology of production, and the fourth objective demonstrates the relevance of public attitudes in noting that innovation in the agricultural sector will, in part, be driven by consumer awareness and demand. This document lists actions according to time lines of what has been or is being done or is proposed.

Forestry

The forest industry is the largest resource-based industrial sector in the Canadian economy, directly or indirectly generating almost 730,000 jobs, producing goods valued at $47 billion (1990), and providing the primary source of employment in over 350 communities across the country. Forestry contributed $19 billion to the export income of the country in 1991 and contributed more to Canada's balance of trade than agriculture, fisheries, mining, and energy combined (Forestry Canada 1990, 1993).

Canada is a forest nation. The Canadian forest industry has traditionally been supported by the harvest of forests that have not previously been cut, and current wood supply continues to be cut primarily (more than 90 percent) from such "first growth" forests. The "Canadian Commitment" to sustainable forestry is one manifestation of change in the approach to forest management (National Forest Strategy 1992). Its extensive list of specific actions for specific sectors begs two questions. First, how much is new? (An example is point 4.15: "Industry will upgrade ... to meet national standards" [21].) Second, how much is significant? (An example is point 9.2: "Canada will practice sustainable forest management" [49].) This document reflects "in broad terms what is needed to achieve our goal" and acknowledges that "Precisely how this goal is achieved is largely up to the forest community" (51). Its importance is that it does acknowledge that the status quo will not lead to the goal, and it advances the rhetoric that may assist in a shift of public values and, hence, perceptions, interpretations, and responses. The forest conflicts in British Columbia over the past decade show how interlinked ecological, social, and economic forces are.

At the level of the forest communities, one initiative that holds promise for enhanced forest management is the Model Forest Program. "A common feature of each model forest is the building of partnerships ... Each model forest commits itself to a set of objectives that reflect the environmental, socio-economic, cultural and political context of the area" (Natural Resources Canada 1996, 5). Each model forest is a socioecological experiment, and each successful experiment will offer lessons applicable in other situations. The promising element comes not from the fact that economic measures of success have been displaced – they haven't – but from the fact that there is a discourse that will allow some of the interdependence of human and ecological well-being to be assessed. In an economic sector so dominated by large economic interests, institutional ossification will make significant change impossible without profound restructuring (Francis and Learner 1996), but an opportunity exists in the dialogue on model forests to demonstrate that this interdependence matters.

Fisheries
Although the number of people employed in the fishery sector has declined (from 130,000 in 1990 to 100,000 in 1994 [Biodiversity Convention Office 1995]), there is perhaps no industry that gives a stronger imprint to the culture of people involved in the sector. The current management crisis regarding West Coast salmon stocks has affected many communities, but the impact is not (yet) comparable to the East Coast cod-fishery collapse. The fishery in Newfoundland has been the most important industry, accounting for approximately 17 per cent of the province's gross domestic product (Sinclair 1988; Wells 1992). In Nova Scotia, the fishery contributed to 3.6 percent of the provincial GDP but accounted for over one-third of its exports, more than all other industrial sectors within the province (Vardy 1992). Furthermore, the Atlantic fisheries directly employed 10 percent of that region's workforce, 15 percent within Newfoundland, and provided further employment in related sectors, supply industries, and businesses (Wells 1992).

On 31 August 1993, the minister of fisheries and oceans at the time announced fishery closures and cutbacks in response to the Atlantic fisheries crisis. "We are facing an unprecedented ecological crisis in Atlantic groundfish stocks" (Government of Canada 1993, 1). The northern cod stocks had reached their lowest levels in recorded history (Government of Newfoundland 1993). However, the closures and cutbacks were announced in response to a resource crisis that had been forthcoming and recognized for some time. "Unfortunately, the suggestion that the once prolific northern cod and important flatfish fisheries off Canada's Atlantic coast could end in two or three years is not rhetorical. It is a stark reality" (Wells 1992, 1).

The causes of this decline include overestimation of biomass levels, inadequate quota enforcement, below-average recruitment and growth rates, environmental and predation factors, and excessive fishing pressure (Government of Newfoundland 1993). Despite the nearly steady decline in the biomass since the 1970s, the harvesting and processing sectors of the industry expanded, and the number of jobs in the fisheries increased by more than 20,000 between the 1970s and 1990 (Government of Newfoundland 1993). Expansion within this period was based on available information regarding future stock estimations. "The primary basis for industry expansion and the redundant capacity now present in both the harvesting and processing sectors of the industry were the projections provided by the Federal Department of Fisheries and Oceans since 1977" (Government of Newfoundland 1993, 23). Government of Canada projections for the Atlantic fisheries resources were consistently inaccurate. "Since 1977 the Federal Department of Fisheries and Oceans (DFO) has produced three resource projections for Canada's Atlantic fisheries resources, all of which have proven to have been overly optimistic in projecting the future level of fishery resources" (Government of Newfoundland 1993, 23). Thus, industry expansion and quotas were established on inaccurate projections rather than on available information regarding actual biomass levels. Furthermore, fisheries management "has focused on a species-by-species application of catch limits or quotas. The focus on single species quota management has been at the expense of gaining a better understanding of the marine ecosystem as a whole and providing adequate protection for fish habitat and ensuring the sustainability of the fishery" (Vardy 1992, 36).

Biodiversity
To speak of the value of biodiversity is to speak of the value of life. Conventional concepts of mensuration are ultimately irrelevant. Nonetheless, because of our vulnerability to economic decision making, a market value for biodiversity is sometimes sought. A 1991 study showed that in Canada almost $6 billion was spent on nature-based recreational activities (Biodiversity Convention Office 1995, 21).

The Canadian Biodiversity Strategy, "developed as a guide to implementing the Biodiversity Convention ... and addressing the difficult issues posed by the loss of biodiversity" (Biodiversity Convention Office 1995, 3), defines five goals: conserve biodiversity, understand its dynamics better, promote that understanding, develop supportive incentives in legislation, and work internationally. Are these first-scale or second-scale goals? Goal 1 is self-evident – and it is under this heading that the specific strategies for the ecosystem-based economic sectors are considered. Given the mandate and the authority of the report ("governments ... will pursue the strategic directions ... according to their policies, plans, priorities and fiscal capabilities" [9]), it is not surprising that many of the specific recommendations have remained almost at the level of platitudes, such as "assess current ... policies ... to ensure that ecological, economic, social and cultural objectives are considered" or "use objective criteria to select sites" (35). Goals 3,

4, and 5 are only scantily treated in the report, but in essence they describe means of building the constituency of those who act in support of goal 1. Goal 2 involves three steps: the first is to conduct more strategic research, the second is to ensure that information is available to, and better used by, those who need it (52), and the third is to monitor outcomes. These steps can be seen in relation to the *perceive-interpret-respond* dimension of the critical zones mode. The call for further research and better access to information is aimed at our knowledge and understanding of the biodiversity system. The call for monitoring recognizes the cybernetic feedback mechanism required to keep the perception current and relevant. Goal 2, then, represents the opportunity for getting new information into the cybernetic system and redefining, as necessary, the practical objectives of conservation management. The importance of the report lies not in its contents – given their generality, conformity to existing perceptions, and understandable deference to "policies plans, priorities and capabilities" of existing governments – but in the fact that it exists at all. It signals that what was outside the consciousness of government actors decades ago has now risen above the horizon. It demonstrates that a threshold of awareness is being crossed. This is a first step on the way to a threshold of action. To the extent that this report, and other facets of the rhetoric of biodiversity conservation, stimulate concrete action under goal 2, and dissemination of new ideas under goals 3a and 4, there are grounds for believing that the conceptual retooling and the reinvention of the socioecosystem that is necessary may occur.

Although reports on sustainability in the three commercial sectors do mention biodiversity as an objective, only in the CBS report is there any real discussion of the role of biodiversity as an indicator of system well-being rather than as an end in itself. The AAFC analysis is perhaps the most exhaustive.

AAFC's Concern about Biodiversity   Selecting the issue of biodiversity to examine in more detail, AAFC has produced three documents – the first is an inventory of current activities (NIVA 1996) under ten headings that include gene conservation, information management, indicators and monitoring, policy assessment, and communication. Three of the remaining headings deal with the specific issues of alien species, pests, and genetic "living modified organisms" (LMO), and the remaining two deal generally with research and ecosystem management. The scope of these activities is noteworthy; it does not restrict itself to technical issues of farm management but recognizes the upward and downward links to aspects such as policy and consumer choice. The importance of research, information management, and monitoring is evident at this level.

A second overview document describes the biodiversity initiatives of producers (Greenfield and Richer 1996, 6). Its mandate is to assess the contributions to biodiversity action, not the net effects, so, naturally, the report has a very positive tenor. On the other hand, the projects reported are mostly those that include government partners, so it is possible to conjecture that many positive initiatives undertaken at a small scale by independent local landholders are unreported.

The third document proposes a three-year action plan (AAFC 1996c). This report identifies seven key issues: habitat fragmentation, agricultural practices, wild species, diversity of domesticated crops and animals, exotic species, living modified organisms, and atmospheric change. This report spells out five principle and four specific goals. The principles are precaution, shared responsibility, competitiveness, integration, and adaptability. The goals are (1) to promote sustainable agriculture while respecting natural ecosystems, (2) to increase awareness and understanding, (3) to ensure equity in access to genetic and information resources, and (4) to integrate biodiversity objectives into AAFC activities. These are not trivial or ill-informed discussions. They do reflect a considerable level of thought, awareness, and expertise in dealing with the issues. The recurrent references to knowledge and understanding, access to information, policy assessment, and sensitivity to external socioeconomic process demonstrate the extent to which farm management must be seen in a "socioecosystem" framework. Conservation activities will not be undertaken in isolation; they must be compatible with consumer or taxpayer willingness to support them (in real dollar terms). Thus, the viability of the land depends, ultimately, on choices that may be made by people who will never see the land. Information becomes the stimulant that will make the change, and information networks are the central nervous system of the cybernetic mechanisms.

The Need for New Feedback Signals
It is clear from the above discussion that there is a recognized need to change the way that these important sectors are managed. This means changing something in the *perceive-interpret-respond* process. It suggests that new feedback signals *are* needed. The great spatial and circumstantial variability within the sectors is recognized by industry analysts, and, implicitly for this reason and explicitly for reasons of equity, the role of local participation in decision making must be stressed. Therefore, a new feedback system must be local and accessible. Biodiversity protection is described as a worthwhile goal in each sector, although it is never cited as sine qua non; rather, it appears as one of many multiple-use objectives. It is not clear whether it is addressed merely because biodiversity protection is known to be appropriate rhetorically or whether the value of biodiversity as the measure of local environmental integrity is accepted. Biodiversity change, as a metric, is local and accessible and is consistent with the notion of a dynamic

socioecosystem model. Moreover, if biodiversity stability is taken as an integrator of significant impacts, then it is not necessary to model complex systems, only to monitor the outcomes (although value judgments are required to distinguish socially beneficial outcomes such as better crop returns from disasters such as oil spills). This leads to the second question.

Can It Work?
There is an evident need to change management strategies. Would a higher emphasis on, and a different conceptualization of, the value of biodiversity address this need? Does the "cybernetic" life-support model of adaptive communities help to make this value clearer? Does the "critical zones" analytic paradigm help? Could biodiversity change, used as the measure of change in socioecosystems, prevent criticality in economic resource sectors?

Communities do cross thresholds of awareness, action, and intolerance. Those approaching the threshold of intolerance are most active in seeking to interpret and respond to ecosystem change, but often individual cases are seen to be entirely anomalous. Second-scale analyses – for example, based on questions about system feedback that reflects sustainability rather than immediate perceived human well-being – seem to be lost in the urgency of the first-scale crisis. Recognizing ecological cues for what they are will shift the thresholds of awareness and thence of action and intolerance. Recognizing the sequence of thresholds and responses as part of a cybernetic, adaptive, life-support process will change the willingness to acknowledge, indeed to search for, ecological cues.

The three thresholds – awareness, action, and intolerance – are marked by differences in both degree and kind. Thresholds of awareness are related to knowledge of prior conditions – where things appear to be getting worse, more difficult, more expensive, less predictable, people will begin to question the sustainability of exploitative practices. The actual threshold of awareness is qualified by degrees of clarity and certainty and is modified by faulty recollections of how things "used to be," so it is perhaps the most difficult to define. Thresholds of action will be marked by overt activity that will include, but not be restricted to, steps taken to influence productivity. These steps may be obscured by the practical impossibility of attributing motive: in a complex and variable system of resource production, it may be difficult to determine with certainty that a given action is taken to offset productivity declines rather than to increase gross productivity. On the other hand, actions that have no direct implications for productivity – such as those taken to conform to environmental regulations, to avert public pressure, or to meet personal aesthetic or ethical standards – can be taken as direct evidence of a motivating concern.

The thresholds are defined by responses to ecosystem cues. What are the cues in the respective systems (Table 11.2)? In agricultural systems, because they are so highly modified and therefore so responsive to input management, the cues are likely to be in the nature of increased technical inputs to the system: fertilizers, pest controls, irrigation, engineered crops, pharmacologically altered feeds. These may well be steps undertaken simply to increase profitability and may not indicate a need to compensate for a decline in productivity. Moreover, because of market variability, policy impacts, and miscellaneous other system linkages, such as subsidies to various costs of production, market board decisions, international trade agreements, and crop insurance systems, the real economic impacts of productivity changes may be difficult to detect. Therefore, changes in input intensity are a possible but not a necessary sign of increasing stress in the system and of a drift toward criticality. Nonetheless, a case-by-case assessment of increasing technological dependencies should reveal thresholds of action in potential critical zones.

In forestry and fisheries, symptoms of increasing criticality will include increased inputs (for forestry, nurseries, planting, genetic selection, site preparation, thinning, and fertilizing; for fisheries, hatcheries and fish farming), but they will also include, probably first include, increased harvest effort (for forestry, accessing places farther from markets or in more difficult terrain; for fisheries, longer times to meet quotas, greater distances travelled, more nets/lines, and more sophisticated tracking equipment). But the trends may also show shifts along three important environmental gradients: age classes, successional stages, and trophic levels. Harvests from virgin old-growth forests involve removal of *objects* that are elements of complex, established, and to some degree homeostatic *processes*. The implications of removing the physical objects must be understood in terms of the objects' roles in the processes. Harvested trees are likely to be mature, simply because age is related to size, and size or volume is what is sought by the harvesters, and the processes are likely to be those of late-successional communities – that is, more trophic levels, more niche interdependencies, and more metabolic efforts going into maintenance rather than biomass accumulation. Depending on the harvest cycle relative to the rate of succession in the area, second-growth forests may approximate virgin forests, but as the cycle shortens harvested trees are likely to be younger (and therefore smaller), the stands are likely to contain fewer species, and the ecological linkages and niche patterns are likely to be less diverse and complex. Increased management inputs tend to reduce species and genetic diversity, and increasing economic need tends to shorten the harvest cycle. Thus, evidence that younger and smaller trees, of fewer species and of pioneer rather than climax species, are being harvested can be taken as a possible warning sign that system productivity is declining. In the fishing industry, evidence from age classes is similar; however, because habitat modification may be less, evidence from successional status is also likely to

Table 11.2

Critical zones thresholds

Sector	Threshold of awareness	Threshold of action	Threshold of intolerance
Agrosystems	input cost increase, yield decline, public or legal constraints	economic, regulatory, ethical/aesthetic	Contingent: market loss, productivity collapse, environmental incompatibilities
Forests	harvest effort increases (distance or difficulty), age structure and species composition changes, public or legal constraints	economic, regulatory, public pressure, ethical/aesthetic	Contingent: market loss, age structure and species composition changes, public or legal constraints
Coastal	harvest effort increases, yield decline, age structure, species composition changes, public or legal constraints	economic, regulatory	Contingent: market loss, age structure and species composition changes, public or legal constraints
Biodiversity	pest species change, charismatic species change	regulatory, public pressure, ethical/ aesthetic	Absolute: site destruction

The critical zones model describes the capacity within resource systems for users to buffer the initial stresses acting on an ecosystem (see Table 11.3) This, for example, includes such things as using chemical fertilizer to compensate for natural losses in soil fertility. Buffers may also serve to lessen the personal or societal costs of environmental change that is nonsustainable. This includes, for example, insurance that covers crop failure or state subsidies that cover otherwise uneconomic harvest activities. These buffers mask the cybernetic cues that should stabilize the system. The delinking of system state (e.g., reduced fertility) and feedback signals (e.g., productivity) permits wider and more erratic oscillations within the system because, generally, it permits the increase in apparent human well-being while ecosystem sustainability is being decreased (depleting natural capital). However, if the actions that are taken to compensate for system deterioration are themselves seen as cues, then the sensitivity of the cybernetic system can be restored *even though* the immediate costs of system deterioration are averted.

be less. But the third gradient, trophic level, may be important. If excessive harvest of one fish species (say cod) reduces predatory pressure on a food species (say capelin), then a simultaneous decline in the profitability of traditional catches and an increasing abundance of alternative catches may lead to a shifting of harvest effort. If the effect is to reduce the prey species through increased harvest, then the potential for rebound of the preferred species, at a higher trophic level, may be precluded.

These transitions – lower age classes, earlier successional stages, lower trophic levels – are *toward* higher bioproductive efficiency, and they are precisely the steps taken in intensively managed systems to maximize yield. Battery hens, veal feedlots, and industrial pork production are examples in agriculture. Short-rotation monocultural forests and fish farms are the analogues in the other industries. This intensification is not inherently undesirable – indeed, at a local scale, it can be beneficial to sustainability if, for example, it concentrates production in highly modified areas and reduces or eliminates harvest pressures in other areas. But the trends, particularly where they are driven by desperation, should be assessed as warning signs. Resource communities that value the option of remaining as resource communities have the responsibility of being aware of these trends and knowing what the implications of the transitions are.

The critical zones model describes the capacity within resource systems for users to buffer the initial stresses acting on an ecosystem (Table 11.3). This includes, for example, using chemical fertilizer to compensate for natural losses in soil fertility. Buffers may also serve to lessen the personal or societal costs of environmental change that is nonsustainable. This includes, for example, insurance that covers crop failure or state subsidies that cover otherwise uneconomic harvest activities. These buffers mask the cybernetic cues that should stabilize the system. The delinking of system state (e.g., reduced fertility) and feedback signals (e.g., productivity) permits wider and more erratic oscillations within the system, because it generally permits the increase in apparent human well-being while ecosystem sustainability is being decreased (depleting natural capital). However, if the actions taken to compensate for system deterioration are themselves seen as cues, then the sensitivity of the cybernetic system can be restored *even though* the immediate costs of system deterioration are averted.

The Effectiveness of Critical Zones Models and Biodiversity Indicators
A critical zones conceptualization may be more consistent with the ecological dynamics of the socioecosystems that we are inhabiting than the static view of the world or the view of an infinitely "forgiving" environmental resource base. If the critical zones model were adopted, then cues that do presage the threshold of intolerance – local socioecosystem criticality –

Table 11.3

Societal responses

Sector	Threshold buffers	Community consequences	Relation to habitat
Agro- systems	added inputs, product substitution, subsidies, and insurance	farm loss or consolidation, agricultural community transition	Contingent: habitat is highly modified (management is habitat modification). (Practice displaces habitat.)
Forests	harvest "efficiency," product substitution, subsidies	unemployment, forest community transition	Contingent: habitat less modified but what is harvested is critical structural element of habitat. (Harvest is habitat.)
Coastal	harvest "efficiency," subsidies	unemployment, fishing community transition	Not contingent: harvest does not require habitat modification.
Biodiversity	more nuanced appreciation	loss of aesthetic, recreational, ecological stability	Not contingent: harvest does not modify habitat.

would be recognized as interpretable feedback. That, in turn, would identify both maladaptive practices and the costs associated with those practices. If these cues were acknowledged and heeded, then the crises of damaged ecological resource systems would, in most cases, be avoided. The answer to the original question – "Would it work?" – is yes: to the extent that biodiversity changes signal changes in the ecosystem, a measure of biodiversity change would function effectively as an indicator of ecosystem sustainability. But this requires a reconceptualization of human ecology and a willingness to inventory other species that are part of the socioecosystem and to monitor their performance (e.g., through monitoring changes in abundance). This leads to the last question. Is it reasonable to propose these changes and/or to expect them to occur?

Is It Possible?

Some benefits would arise from a shift to understanding human communities as ecological entities with indissoluble links to other dynamic elements. Biodiversity is a direct measure of the performance (of the fitness) of other living members of the ecosystem and an indirect measure of physical processes. However, given that perceived well-being is the factor most likely to shape human decisions, can biodiversity changes be shown to be "marketable" as a decision-making criterion?

Perhaps we first need to consider the community consequences of failure to respond to cues of environmental criticality as described above. Because of the complexity of socioecosystems, there are no definitive diagnostics: for example, sectoral unemployment, farm bankruptcies, farm sales and consolidation, and land abandonment can all arise from a variety of factors. Increasing criticality is only one. But these factors, which are characteristics of decreasing human well-being, must be viewed as being part of the real costs of increasing criticality. Avoiding these costs must be seen as one of the benefits of taking action to protect or restore system viability. Human well-being in "invented niches" must be conceptually linked to ecological requisites and thus to environmental systems that support them. The spectre of unacceptable future outcomes must be factored into the present net value of alternative actions. This requires not only a conceptual framework within which transitions can be understood but also some indicators that can provide the personal-level motivational feedback that WRI advocates. Is an index of biodiversity change appropriate?

Why Biodiversity Is a Uniquely Valuable Indicator

> Biodiversity supports human societies ecologically, economically, culturally and spiritually. Despite its importance, however, ecosystems are being degraded and species and genetic diversity reduced at an alarming rate.
>
> – Biodiversity Convention Office
> (1995, 2)

What objective external criterion can there be? Biodiversity maintenance can be posited as one, and not simply for the utilitarian, aesthetic, or ethical reasons. Biodiversity changes are the aggregate of changes in the performance of individual species that, in turn, are the most dynamic non-human elements of the socioecosystem. To the extent that our activities are compatible with the long-run viability of existing species, those activities can be taken as benign. To the extent that they eliminate other species, they must be seen as being disruptive to the socioecosystem that supports the invented niche. This is true whether it describes a site in which a human activity evolved from being sustainable to being nonsustainable or a site to which a new, nonsustainable activity has been transferred.

If fitness is the measure of the success of species that Dale and Hill (1996) are concerned about, then preserving ecological conditions in which fitness can be maintained is an indication that, from the perspective of the implicated species, the ecosystem condition is "good." Of course, there will be instances in which we, as a species, will decide that the loss of fitness (local extinction) of other species is either sufficiently beneficial to justify or sufficiently trivial to ignore. For example, we know when we are clearing land for a house, farm, or parking lot that we are causing local extinction. We can, if we choose, ignore evidence of decreasing local, nonhuman fitness; still, the human impact is objectively "measured" by the viability of other species. In fact, given the philosophical difficulties of defining desirable ecological states, this may be the only index of ecosystem well-being that is consistent. Nonetheless, the index has been largely ignored; in fact, the dominant industrial paradigm of "multiply and subdue the Earth" is essentially one in which success is synonymous with driving the index down. But as the crisis of sustainability mounts, we should reexamine biodiversity as an index and determine what it offers for and implies about planning for sustainability.

In the above array of resource systems, biodiversity is clearly anomalous – it is not habitat specific, and it does not have a cash significance that leads to pressures of harvest and to a constituency with an economic interest in its preservation. It is not a resource sector for which there are many strong and functional cybernetic conservation links. Biodiversity can be seen as a resource in its own right, but it can also be seen as an indicator of overall ecosystem well-being. In attempts to monitor environmental change, two alternatives are possible: the first is to define specific, measurable parameters of change (e.g., changes in phosphate loading of lakes or of ozone level in air); the second is to look for integrators that reveal the consequences of various forms of change. The former is necessary to manage specific environmental impacts (e.g., emissions) that may not be distinguishable in the "black-box" measurement of the latter. But the latter has the advantage of showing consequences rather than precursors or intermediaries. Biodiversity will probably be designated as a specific primary management objective only in very restricted sites. It will be designated as a subsidiary objective in more sites to the extent that it is (1) compatible with primary objectives (e.g., wood harvest) and (2) believed to have positive consequences (either direct, such as through reduced cost of pest control, or indirect, such as through improved public relations). But if biodiversity resource protection can be seen not as an isolated objective but as an integrated measure of impact, then biodiversity protection will occur incidentally through its role as an indicator of sustainability. That is, if we accept that we cannot define all the aspects of human activity that will affect our ecological linkages, and cannot successfully model consequences for all those that we do define, then we must look to some end-of-the-pipe indicator of our net impacts.

This is not to suggest that local biodiversity protection should become an absolute barrier to noncompatible land uses: obviously, at one scale, no species, human or otherwise, occupies a site without eliminating others from it. Urban development, for example, is precisely the elimination of natural habitat and the superimposition of built or artificial habitat. It is also clear that the management of commercial ecosystems is operationalized through shifting biodiversity balances and selecting for target species: a wheat field is as ecologically interesting as a parking lot. But if we learn to measure our activities in terms of biodiversity impacts, and if we reconceptualize our socioecosystem in a way that biodiversity losses matter to us as much as a shift in the balance of trade or in inflation rates, then we will begin to get signals back from the systems we are part of that will provide stabilizing feedback. Species loss will not be seen as the costless consequence that it is now seen as; rather, it will be seen as a warning sign that the system we are part of is destabilizing. If this is a cost that we choose to pay, as in the case of intensively managed agricultural landscapes of monocultural forests, then we will at least be aware of it as a cost.

The Feasibility of Critical Zones Conceptualization
and Biodiversity Awareness
Conditionally at least, there may be no inherent barriers to making the concept of socioecosystem sustainability a more significant, pragmatic, routine, and personal factor in decision making. Supportable reasons for adopting the view can be provided, and biodiversity change can be proposed as a practical metric. This may happen by itself, but it is far more likely to happen, or to happen sooner, if those who are across the threshold of awareness at present take action to help shift the threshold so that people who have adopted either a "business-as-usual" or an "end-game" complacency will also be motivated. This shift requires active promotion of concepts, education about the meaning of environmental cues, and dissemination of useful and meaningful indices of progress or decline. What does this mean at the community level?

Implications for Achieving Sustainable Development in Communities
This chapter has argued for the use of critical zones models with biodiversity-based indicators of change. The relevance for policy is evident. Policy intended to meet the goals of sustainable development will require clear

ideas about the nature of change in Canada's ecological resource sectors and about the process by which stakeholders respond to perceived change. Critical zones studies can provide both specific markers that can be used to evaluate the state of socioecosystems and a general theory about the nature of the perception, interpretation, and response process. Better markers and better theories will lead to increased awareness of the processes affecting vast areas of our landscape. The critical zones approach is incisive because it focuses on crisis areas where the causes and consequences of nonsustainability should be most visible. It is highly relevant for policy because it works with the very stakeholders who are the targets of policy. Anthropogenic stress elicits a socioecosystem response, and, as the stress increases, the probability that the "threshold of action" (see Burton, Kates, and White 1993) will be reached also increases. Therefore, the communities most active in addressing environmental degradation may also be among those most in need of doing so. Working with local groups concerned about ecosystem change may be the most effective way of defining needs and achieving success. Doing so ensures adaptability to the spatial and temporal particulars of a given site in the highly variable Canadian landscape mosaic.

If one accepts that communities do not deliberately self-destruct, and that community members do have, alone and in aggregate, some control over many of the processes that affect (both causally and melioratively) the viability of their local socioecosystem, then one can conclude that, when maladaptive practices are widely accepted or seemingly condoned, it is for some combination of the following reasons: (1) critical information is lacking, (2) information is misinterpreted, and (3) an appropriate response cannot be formulated – that is, the adaptive *perceive-interpret-response* mechanism of the critical zones model of societal adaptation has been thwarted. The first-scale problem is local and immediate, perhaps related to fish stock collapse, forest industry closures, or soil salinization. The second-scale problem is one of information flow, interpretive ability, and empowerment. The Canadian legacy of jurisdictional disputes between levels of government, of impeded information flow between central decision-making bodies and affected end-users, of confusion over policy objectives, and of short-term versus long-term planning creates obstacles to redirecting our socioecosystem strategies. But it is not insurmountable.

A model that organizes information in a new way changes the meaning of what is observed. Ideas and concepts are important elements of human niches and of the noosphere. A socioecosystem model of critical environmental zones will change the meaning attributed to what is observed in a trend toward criticality. The concept of human systems as ecological systems needs to evolve to keep pace with our capacity to modify ecosystem elements. This is a fundamental shift (for Western industrial society at least) in cosmology. The shift, which might be identified with Darwin's contribution to science, is as fundamental as that identified with Copernicus. Analytical tools are already available to recharacterize evident trends within socioecosystems. For example, biophysical trends can be described in terms of accepted natural science models, such as the systematic categorization of environmental impacts described by Beanlands and Duinker (1983); economic trends can be elaborated in terms such as those of Pearce et al.'s (1991) concepts of natural capital – including the value of commercial and noncommercial resources and the value of nature's "services"; and trends in social attributes can be monitored by parameters such as those discussed by Daly and Cobb (1994). What seems to be lacking is the degree of commitment required to make the change. New commitment brings an openness to concepts that change the way in which the world is viewed. New perspectives aggregate into new cosmologies, and new cosmologies, in turn, spawn new commitments.

The third Canadian report to the United Nations on sustainable development (Canada 1996) notes the central importance of education and public awareness (11, 16, 39). Support for sustainable action must be embedded in the public consciousness. The same report notes that 69 percent of Canadian industries and institutions have environmental management systems in place (44), and, although it does not evaluate the effectiveness of these systems, the fact that they exist is evidence of change. The report is a political document and should not, then, be looked to for anything other than a general understanding of the government's ability to define relevant topics and present appropriate interpretations. Credit is due, for example, simply because the Canadian Environmental Assessment Agency exists. It is better than nothing and can be as effective as those directing the process choose to make it (as this is being written, debate is mounting about the federal decision to bypass impact assessment regulations for the $1.5 billion sale of CANDU reactors to China!). There is, in fact, nothing *in* the report that suggests profound change. But, again, the fact *of* the report suggests that profound change is taking place.

The trend toward criticality may arise from a lack of awareness of the cues of transition or of the significance of cues that are perceived. Providing appropriate information to overcome that lack of awareness will change the response. In cases where the trend toward criticality arises from the inability to formulate an appropriate response, a clearer perception of the model of transition will help to identify obstacles to action. A model accurately describing the antecedents to crisis will be an effective tool in overcoming limitations of perception or interpretation within the community and in identifying barriers to remedial action. As we begin to take the steps required to address sustainability, we begin to look at second-scale issues. Pivotal concepts are available if not widely known or used; the sum of our ecological crises imposes on us a need to adopt a more adaptive cosmology; the barrier at this point appears to be lack of commitment. But as the magnitude and pervasiveness of socioecological problems mount, more people will cross the threshold of awareness, and concepts, cosmologies, and commitments will continue to change. Either way, our conditions of life will change. How much we like what they become depends in part on how quickly and how adaptively we respond to the changes.

Acknowledgments

This chapter is based on ideas discussed and developed with the Critical Environment Zones Panel of the Canadian Global Change Program, with the IGU Commission on Critical Environmental Zones, and with research partners whom I have met through projects supported by SSHRCC, CIDA, CONACYT (Mexico), USIA (USA), and Foreign Affairs (Canada). These contacts and the research support are gratefully acknowledged.

References

Agriculture and Agri-Food Canada. 1996a. Environmentally Sustainable Agriculture and Agri-Food Development in Canada (Draft). Ottawa: Agriculture and Agri-Food Canada.
–. 1996b. Profile of Production Trends and Environmental Issues (Draft). Ottawa: Agriculture and Agri-Food Canada.
–. 1996c. Three-Year Action Plan for Biodiversity (Draft). Ottawa: Agriculture and Agri-Food Canada.
Beanlands, G.E., and P.N. Duinker. 1983. *An Ecological Framework for Environmental Impact Assessment in Canada.* Halifax: Institute for Resource and Environmental Studies, Dalhousie University.
Berry, Wendell. 1991. "The Futility of Thinking Globally." In Bill Willers, ed., *Learning to Live with the Land* (150-6). Washington: Island Press.
Biodiversity Convention Office. 1995. *Canadian Biodiversity Strategy.* Ottawa: Supply and Services Canada.
Boorstin, Daniel. 1993. *The Listen Earth.* Beaty Lecture Series. Presentation. Montreal: McGill University.
Burton, I. 1991. "On Making the Invisible Visible." In T.C. Meredith et al., eds., *Defining and Mapping Critical Environmental Zones for Policy Formulation and Public Awareness* (121-2). Montreal: Department of Geography, McGill University.
Burton, I., R.W. Kates, and G.F. White. 1993. *The Environment as Hazard.* 2nd ed. New York: Guilford Press.
Canada. Department of Foreign Affairs. 1996. *Report to the United Nations Commission on Sustainable Development.* Ottawa: Supply and Services Canada.
Colinveau, Paul. 1983. *The Fate of Nations: A Biological Theory of History.* Harmondsworth, Eng.: Pelican Books.
Chomsky, Noam. 1996. *Power and Prospects: Reflections on Human Nature and the Social Order.* Boston: South End Press.
Dale, Ann, and Stuart Hill. 1996. "Biodiversity Conservation: A Decision-Making Context." In Ann Dale and John Robinson, eds., *Achieving Sustainable Development* (97-118). Vancouver: UBC Press.
Daly, Herman, and John B. Cobb. 1994. *For the Common Good.* Boston: Beacon Press.
Forestry Canada. 1990. *Forestry Facts.* Ottawa: Natural Resources Canada.
–. 1993. *The State of Canada's Forests.* Ottawa: Natural Resources Canada.
Francis, George, and Sally Learner. 1996. "Making Sustainable Development Happen: Institutional Transformation." In Ann Dale and John Robinson, eds., *Achieving Sustainable Development* (146-59). Vancouver: UBC Press.
Government of Canada. 1993. *Additional Conservation and Assistance Measures for Atlantic Fisheries.* News release, 31 August.

Government of Newfoundland. 1993. *Changing Tides: A Consultative Document on the Fishery of the Future*. St. Johns: Department of Fisheries.

Greenfield, Joyce, and Nicole Richer. 1996. *Biodiversity Initiatives Involving Canadian Agricultural Producers*. Ottawa: Agriculture and Agri-Food Canada.

Hammond, Allen, Albert Adriaanse, Eric Rodenburg, Dirk Bryant, and Richard Woodward. 1995. *Environmental Indicators: A Systematic Approach to Measuring and Reporting on Environmental Policy Performance in the Context of Sustainable Development*. Washington, DC: World Resources Institute.

Hodge, Tony. 1996. "A Systemic Approach to Assessing Progress toward Sustainability." In Ann Dale and John Robinson, eds., *Achieving Sustainable Development* (267-92). Vancouver: UBC Press.

Holling, C.S. 1978. *Adaptive Environmental Assessment and Management*. New York: John Wiley.

Kasperson, Jeanne X., Roger E. Kasperson, and B.L. Turner II. 1996. "Regions at Risk: Exploring Environmental Criticality." *Environment* 38,10: 4-12.

Márquez, Gabriel García. 1967. *One Hundred Years of Solitude*. New York: Harper and Row.

Maslow, A. 1954. *Motivation and Personality*. New York: Harper.

Meredith, T.C. 1991. "Environmental Impact Assessment and Monitoring." In Bruce Mitchell, ed., *Resource Management and Development* (224-45). Toronto: Oxford University Press.

Meredith, Thomas C., Catherine Moore, Laura Gartner, and Wynet Smith. 1994. *Canadian Critical Environmental Zones: Concepts, Goals, and Resources*. Canadian Global Change Program, Technical Report Series 94-1. Ottawa: Royal Society of Canada.

National Forest Strategy. 1992. *Sustainable Forests: A Canadian Commitment*. Hull, PQ: Canadian Council of Forest Ministers.

Natural Resources Canada. 1996. *Model Forest Network: Year in Review*. Ottawa: Canadian Forest Services.

NIVA Inc. 1996. Agriculture and Agri-Food Canada (AAFC) Initiatives Relating to Biodiversity (Draft). Ottawa: Agriculture and Agri-Food Canada.

Pearce, D.W. 1991. *Blueprint 2: Greening the World Economy*. London: Earthscan.

Pearce, D.W., and R.K. Turner. 1990. *Economics of Natural Resources and the Environment*. Baltimore: Johns Hopkins University Press.

Pickles, John, ed. 1995. *Ground Truth: The Social Implications of Geographic Information Systems*. New York: Guilford Press.

Rapport, D.J. 1990. "Criteria for Ecological Indicators." *Environmental Monitoring and Assessment* 15: 273-5.

Sacks, Oliver. 1995. *An Anthropologist on Mars*. Toronto: Vintage Canada.

Schneider, E.D., and J.J. Kay. 1994. "Complexity and Thermodynamics: Towards a New Ecology." *Future* 24,6: 626-47.

Schulte, Joachim. 1992. *Wittgenstein*. Albany: State University of New York Press.

Sinclair, P.R. 1988. Introduction. In P.R. Sinclair, ed., *A Question of Survival: The Fisheries and Newfoundland Society* (1-19). Institute of Social and Economic Research.

Vardy, D. 1992. "Biodiversity: In the Context of the Newfoundland and Labrador Fishery." *National Round Table Review* (11, 28). Ottawa: NRTEE.

Wells, Clyde K. 1992. Address to the Royal Institute for International Affairs, Brussels.

Westman, Walter E. 1977. "How Much Are Nature's Services Worth?" *Science* 197: 960-4.

Conclusion

12
Making Communities the Strong Link in Sustainable Development
John T. Pierce

Introduction
George Bernard Shaw once remarked that "The reasonable man adapts himself to the world; the unreasonable one persists in trying to adapt the world to himself. Therefore all progress depends on the unreasonable man" (quoted in Kronenberger 1972, 224). Clearly, our "progress" to date has been based upon adapting the world to ourselves. Whether this means that we are unreasonable or simply short-sighted I leave to others to decide. The compelling and necessary point, however, is that our development models of the past and present must change. We must embrace a new paradigm that emphasizes adapting ourselves to the world. Nowhere is this more important and necessary than at the local/community level.

The intersection of community and sustainable development reinforces certain common bonds between the two terms – their symbolism, their elusive character, and their dynamic properties. Communities are as much imagined entities as they are networks of common interests and boundaried spaces (Cohen 1985). The dynamics of community sustainability require that we recognize the interface between the complex and changing dimensions of community, real and imagined, and the equally complex dimensions of sustainability, an amorphous but integrative paradigm that offers the possibility of reorienting our attention away from simple mechanistic/reductionist approaches and toward a broader and better understanding of the relation of parts to the whole within and beyond communities.

The evolution in our understanding of the multidimensionality of sustainable development and the importance of the local are important themes that lend unity to the diverse contributions in this volume. In discussing sustainable development in the North, McTiernen notes that "It is fundamentally about how individuals, on their own and collectively, make choices and conduct their lives in relation to their locality, their region, and their feelings of connection with and responsibility to the world at large."

Meredith reinforced this view by arguing that global sustainability is ultimately the aggregate of human experiences embedded in local ecosystems.

In developing a coda for this assemblage, I have chosen to synthesize the
key arguments, concepts, and issues according to three dimensions – economic, social, and ecological imperatives to sustainable development – discussed in the previous volume of this series (Dale and Robinson 1996) as
well as by a number of authors in this volume. Each imperative has a number of spatial and hierarchical expressions and, of course, interpretations.
Cutting across this assemblage of imperatives with a diversity of spatial
expressions (i.e., from the local to the global) are recurring issues specific to
this volume relating to community, value systems, actors, policies, governance, and indicators (Figure 12.1). Together these dimensions provide a
framework for situating specific examples important to developing this
synthesis.

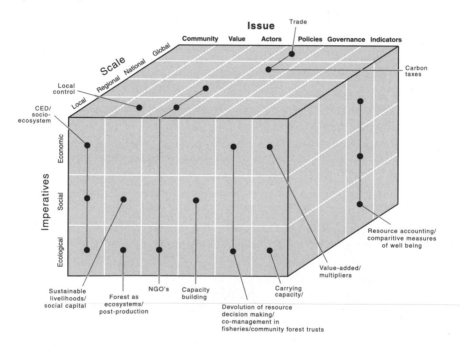

Figure 12.1 A situational framework of sustainability: Summary of key issues

Before proceeding with a brief discussion of the three dimensions of sustainability as framed by the local and the community, it is important that I
bring to the foreground not only the very interconnected nature of all three
but also the very real challenge of understanding them across different spatial and temporal scales. Gertler, in his chapter on the link between sustainable agriculture and sustainable communities on the Prairies, observes that

"Healthy rural communities and resilient agricultural economies are closely interconnected. Arrangements that squander or cannibalize natural and social capital can only generate a temporary affluence – and only for a few." The legacy of mismanagement of resources and the trend toward globalization, including the formation of "phantom states" that restructure labour and economic relations into a process of "creative destruction," threaten the ability of communities to be sustainable. And these threats are not manifested simply at the local level in small to midsize communities. They are common to communities of all sizes, with the exception that larger urban centres, found in European societies of the nineteenth and early twentieth centuries, had the advantage of possessing a number of safety valves and adaptive strategies. Diminishing marginal productivities of labour were compensated, in part, by emigration to the Americas and other colonial possessions. More recently, major urban centres have become adept, as Woollard and Rees point out, at importing carrying capacity and exporting environmental contaminants. The existence and persistence of unsustainable practices can be understood as a problem of the disconnection between action and consequence, both of which have complex and overlapping spatial and temporal scales that make identification of the problem, let alone solutions, difficult at best.

Despite this complexity, communities are microcosms of the larger world. Their experiences provide important and timely reminders of what is in store for society at a larger scale unless adaptive strategies and policies are formulated to assist in reconciling ecological, economic, and social imperatives. The knowledge gained by academics, practitioners, and policy makers at the smaller scale now will likely be invaluable at a later date for solving these larger-scale problems.

The Three Imperatives

Social Dimension

Throughout this volume, reference has been made to various forms of capital: natural, human, physical, cultural, financial, and social. Development is implicitly seen as the product of various combinations of capital, each with different implications for social welfare, community stability, and long-term sustainability. Economists frequently describe and model output as a function of various inputs: typically, land, labour, and capital. Much has been made of the ability of the market to encourage substitution of less scarce for more scarce factors at the microscale and by analogy at the macroscale where technological change (or innovation) and factor substitution become critical processes for growing economies adapting to scarcity and limits imposed by source and sink functions. If factor substitution is infinite, then so is the potential for economic growth. Daly (1993) has been highly critical of this paradigm or conceptualization of development and our ability to overcome natural limits through technological changes, arguing that in many cases these factors are complements, not substitutes.

Roseland also takes issue with this neoclassical conceptualization, agreeing with Daly and Cobb (1989). He persuasively points to the need to recognize the importance of social capital as an ingredient for sustainable development. Because social capital "is not limited by material scarcity," he argues that this form of capital can be "a route toward sustainability, by replacing the fundamentally illogical model of unlimited growth within a finite world with one of unlimited complexity, which is not bound by the availability of material resources."

One way to better understand the interrelations of capital and the potential to recombine them, not as factor substitutes but as complements with different emphases, is to imagine four broad categories of capital as illustrated in Figure 12.2. Combined here, for the sake of simplicity, are social and cultural capital, related but different phenomena (as Carr [1996] notes) and physical and financial capital (also related but different). Traditional approaches to development, certainly in Canada, have heavily emphasized the exploitation of natural capital, perhaps first clearly identified and understood by Innis (1930) in his staples thesis and further elaborated by Watkins in his staples trap in terms of a reliance on physical/financial capital (Barnes and Hayter 1992).

Roseland argues that much more attention needs to be placed on social capital. He and others, such as Putnam (1996), rightly observe that investment in social capital enhances returns to investment in physical and human capital. This interpretation, further supported by Gertler, Ommer and Sinclair, Massam and Dickinson, and Woollard and Rees, would require a redrafting of Figure 12.2a to "downplay" the reliance on natural capital and to "up-play" the role and importance accorded to social/cultural and human capital – a shift, in other words, from the top left to the lower right (Figure 12.2b). This shift represents a key condition for a sustainable society, decoupling development from its historical attachment to economic growth as the basic engine for the improvement of human welfare.

Of course, one of the difficulties, if not dilemmas, in this revisioning of society is that social capital is a public good independent of the market, so that its provision and maintenance are very dependent on public service investment and consensus building and shared values – that is, the development of a civil society within a civic state. Regarding a civil society, a number of authors have pointed to a decline in the role and commitment of the state in intervening in its traditional manner in the economy and in providing public services (Robinson and Tinker 1995; Robinson and Van Bers 1996). As McTiernan rightly observes, "Investments in health, social

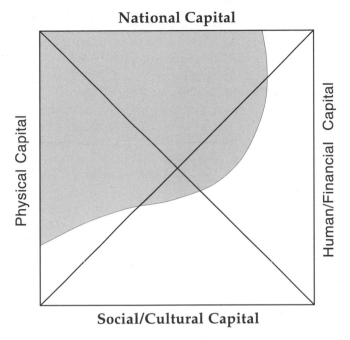

Figure 12.2a Capital mixes under traditional development

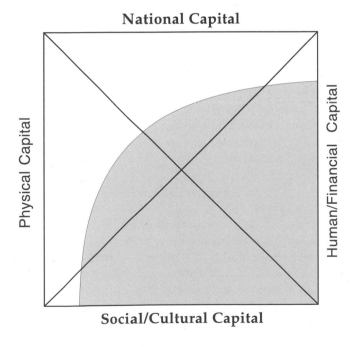

Figure 12.2b Capital mixes under sustainable development

services, education, training, and employment creation are no less important in sustainable development than investments in resource management, environmental monitoring, and protected areas." The rise of the welfare state, its role as a counterbalance to the hegemony of the market and international capitalism, provided for the promotion of social, cultural, and human capital. Yet this model is changing as much for practical and ideological reasons as for fiscal ones. As Nozick observes, and these views are echoed by both Bryant and Massam and Dickinson, traditional top-down approaches to decision making and power sharing are giving way to new community-based formal and informal associations, enterprises, and networks in which a greater degree of the economic and sociocultural development is determined locally. Bryant notes that there is, of course, tremendous variation in the "readiness" of communities to undertake this form of development, which is firmly tied to a complex process of participation and cooperation and partnership building, an issue pursued in more detail below.

The context for these formal and informal associations and networks is grounded in the notion of a civil society and civic state. Massam and Dickinson note that a "civil society of connections and exchanges between people is vital to social capital and economic wealth." Yet "A civil society is not comprised of citizens pitted against the state. Rather, it is a civic state that promotes the interconnectedness of social groups and the state apparatus." The dilemma is that globalization and the push toward flexibility create an environment of insecurity and instability that threatens social cohesion and our ability and willingness to maintain and protect civil associations and a civil society.

If we are to promote the notion of social capital as a touchstone for sustaining development, then we need to pay far more attention to how, in the face of numerous external threats to stability, we can foster a civil and cohesive society. That process takes as its point of departure the way in which we have "refashioned nature" or the ecological dimensions of our lives.

Ecological Imperatives

Woollard and Rees eloquently make the point that "human carrying capacity is at the heart of the sustainability crisis." As they observe, this is a controversial premise that, arguably, can be questioned on conceptual grounds – the viability of the concept of ecological footprint or ecological deficit – and/or on analytical grounds – the feasibility of measuring our maximum load. However, this should not sideline the inherent logic of their position: (1) there are limits to source and sink functions, (2) our impacts are cumulative, and (3) our inability to recognize a crisis lies in our modes of human habitation (cities) and exchange (trade). The separation of actions and consequences is clearly a major source of our inability to fully appreciate our impact on the integrity of our ecosystems. Although urban systems are increasingly exceeding their carrying capacity as defined by what is required to sustain consumption within a given geographical area, the authors identify from the literature on evolution ways for these systems to live more closely within their means. These are important sources of adaptation that can assist in what Robinson and Tinker (1995) have referred to as reconciling ecological carrying capacity and human welfare.

The theme of ecosystem evolution and integrity is central to Meredith's discussion of critical zones. His premise is that the human socioecosystem is dependent on ecosystem health – one measure of which is biodiversity. Sites of local ecological crisis can be thought of as critical environmental zones in which biodiversity is threatened – in fact, Meredith suggests that biodiversity can become a very useful surrogate measure or "end-of-pipe" indicator for sustainability. The chapters by Gertler, Schwindt, Ommer and Sinclair, McTiernan, and Gill and Reed underscore the validity of Meredith's framework, in which increasing criticality of the resource is a sign of the decline in biodiversity that, in the absence of other countervailing forces, leads to the decline of the socioecosystem.

The discussions by both Meredith and Woollard and Rees of countervailing forces/actions are rooted in local action. For Meredith, the priority for communities should be domestic environmental stewardship and an adaptive community response – specific indicators of progress required to make the "invisible visible." Woollard and Rees, like Roseland, argue for the need for a paradigm shift (perhaps the need for what I would term "homo sustinens" [Pierce 1992]) in which significant efficiency gains and a move toward greater investment in social capital achieve a "factor 10" economy and avoid ecological collapse. Other authors have identified as an underlying source of the environmental problematic, particularly as it applies to managed ecosystems for fishing, forestry, and agriculture, a process of intense capitalization and industrialization of the modes of production – removing management from a process of "natural accountability."

I have written elsewhere (Pierce 1992) that sustainable development can be viewed as a "self-enforcing process," meaning that ecological imperatives combined with an increasing scale of human activity could combine to create an equilibrium in welfare far lower than if society consciously chooses to recognize those imperatives and structure consumption accordingly. This is why local knowledge and local appreciation of environmental problems are so critical. As Meredith observes, "Given that each human being is attached to some specific local environment in the matrix, and that consciousness of sustainability resides only at the level of the individual, concerns about degrees of satisfaction with, and motivation for, progress toward sustainability will be rooted in the local."

Economic Imperatives

Resource-dependent communities and single-industry towns are more prone than cities to economic instability, higher unemployment, lower incomes, and, arguably, overall lower levels of social welfare. A number of persistent conditions – including economies based on primary, largely undifferentiated, low-value products that in agriculture and fisheries have experienced real price decreases; technological change, which continues to lower the price of capital relative to labour, favouring "capital stuffing" and intensification; and the increasing need for flexibility in capitalist economies – have created a difficult circle to square for resource-based economies. Their high fixed-capital investments and their immobility of resources have combined with an increasingly deregulated trade environment and increasing economic and demographic pressures to push the envelope on harvesting rates and resource extraction. Making more self-reliant communities that can control their local resource bases (as Nozick has identified) and be less susceptible to the instabilities engendered by flexible accumulation is a real challenge that has defied a litany of well-meaning federal and provincial government initiatives that attempt to alleviate regional disparities.

Ommer and Sinclair, in their history of the sustainability of the outport, make it clear that before the modernization of the fisheries (beginning around 1950) "the interconnection of global and local, formal and informal, economic activities sustained life in the outports, though not without hardship and periodic local resource crises." The pluralism that characterized the traditional economy, incorporating both subsistence and exchange hallmarks, was gradually reduced through modernization to exchange for profit and a wage economy that lost most of its resilience and its ability to adapt to vagaries in the cod harvest. The collapse of the cod fisheries in the early 1990s left the coastal communities of Newfoundland with physical capital (e.g., fishing boats) but little natural capital to exploit – a disastrous situation because these two forms of capital are complements and not substitutes.

West Coast fishers are going through a similar process of industrialization/capitalization and, like their East Coast counterparts, are faced with declining stocks as a result of overfishing, intense competition, habitat loss, and the spectre of large-scale environmental change. These factors, as Schwindt documents, combined with declining economic value, will undermine the livelihoods of many individuals and coastal communities dependent on the fisheries.

A similar process and fate await many agriculturally based Prairie communities. Gertler exposes dramatic structural changes to farming resulting largely from industrialization and capital intensification of production. The retrenchment in the number of farms, population base, and community stability attests to the necessity for, and the importance of, increasing scale and concentration of operators. Ecosystems, although already simplified, are becoming more so with commensurate declines in diversity.

Interestingly, the agricultural and fisheries ameliorative and response strategies, such as "precision farming" and "aquaculture," do little to improve the viability of the ecosystem or the collective economic health of a community. A possible shortcoming of these strategies is their failure to acknowledge, much less act on, the need to integrate economic, social, and ecological dimensions. In the case of comanagement strategies in fisheries, there is promise of a greater degree of integration (Pinkerton and Weinstein 1995).

The spectre of a significant shift from a productivist to a postproductivist landscape raises a variety of questions regarding opportunities for economic renewal, stakeholder involvement, shared decision making, and the vision of what a community will become. The work by Gill and Reed in particular makes it clear that as economic restructuring occurs (in their case, the downsizing of forest-based industries combined with an influx of new residents with different sets of values or new cultural capital) competitive tensions emerge between the old and the new. In discussing the importance of these new societal values as they relate to the development of emergent consumptive uses of the land, the authors contend that "the emergence of this reevaluation is integrally tied to the notion of sustainable communities that place social and environmental concerns alongside economic objectives and embody principles such as empowerment of people, integrated decision making, and consensus building as elements of the planning process." Although these new values provide a platform for sustainability, Gill and Reed's work also highlights the real difficulties of community-based planning because of a variety of factors, including (1) the authority for management divided across public agencies, (2) the failure of provincial governments to "empower" local planning, (3) the lack of obvious stakeholders, and (4) the conflicts over land use "at every level of the spatial hierarchy in response to differing values and objectives." Not surprisingly, many communities feel marginalized and disempowered when it comes to redirecting local economic development.

Bryant notes that, historically, community change was frequently organized through land-use planning, various forms of remedial action and economic crisis management (often with higher levels of government), various forms of social assistance, and infrastructure improvement. There was insufficient attention paid to the important differences between growth and development – the former clearly being the preoccupation of most municipal governments.

Today many communities place more emphasis on development in the sense of a genuine improvement in "quality of life." Sustainable community development is distinguished from earlier forms of economic development by virtue of its broader involvement of the community in setting a vision and objectives. Bryant goes on to say that "It is also distinguished by a greater integration of economic, social, cultural, and environmental values and by a relatively decentralized approach to planning and management." Clearly, communities have different potentials and strategic orientations, "especially latent ones," so that an important ingredient differentiating communities and placing them on paths to sustainable change is the degree to which they are able to identify and capitalize on these strategic orientations. In a similar vein, Gertler reminds us of the importance of recognizing needs and possibilities in communities and of the significance of more carefully weighing effects from economic and social multipliers that result from different strategies and tools used to foster economic development.

Policy Implications of the Three Imperatives

If we accept the notion that there are three interrelated imperatives to the achievement of sustainable development, and if we accept that both problems and sources for change are rooted in the local, then what policy and political/governance changes are required to recognize these fundamental realities and move society closer to sustainability? The discussion that follows is premised on the belief that, while the market will remain an important instrument in shaping social choices, social action, both formal and informal, governmental and nongovernmental, will represent a pivotal counterbalance, widening the array of development possibilities and reducing the emphasis on simple growth formulas to fulfil our "needs."

To fuse and rebalance the various forms of capital discussed and illustrated earlier (Figure 12.2) will require social action at various scales, directed at key problems (e.g., second-scale problems as discussed by Meredith), based on ecosystem principles, and involving a large number of participants in an agenda for change. An important issue here is that governments not enter into agreements, such as the OECD's Multilateral Agreement on Investment (MAI), that effectively preclude local action and control of people and their environments. At the same time, we must, to paraphrase Bryant, be pragmatic, given the current social milieu, about the scope and makeup of planned change, if we are to have a "significant chance of succeeding." And this nadir of pragmatism must reflect the need to balance the interests and values of the local population with those of the broader society.

There are many ways in which government can devise and implement policies that assist communities in coping with change and integrating the social, economic, and ecological dimensions of sustainability. Canada has a long history of government involvement in development, most of which can be classed as a top-down "industrial model." Regulation theory that offers "a systematic conceptualization of the state" (Moran, Blunden, and

Lewis 1996, 3), with both economic and social imperatives, sees the act of regulation as a mediating function, in which nation-states attempt to counteract the negative effects, spatially and temporally, stemming from modern and postmodern capitalism. And, of course, governments in the past quarter-century have become increasingly preoccupied with the environment as an object of regulation. In most cases, there has been very little devolution of powers to local and regional constituents. This traditional and top-down approach to "regulation" needs to be replaced in favour of a more reflexive approach that recognizes a number of current shortcomings and emergent processes:

1   Many government policies have numerous unintended and unantici-
    pated consequences that aggravate structural changes in communities.
2   The shift from a productivist to a postproductivist landscape dictates
    innovative policies.
3   Current government structures are too small to deal with global prob-
    lems but too large to deal with local problems.
4   Local knowledge and informal groups and actors have much to offer
    in the resolution of problems.
5   Ecosystem planning and its relationship to the socioecosystem have
    been almost totally absent.
6   Although efficiency and equity concerns have preoccupied economists
    and influenced government policy, there is, in the view of Daly (1993),
    a need to consider issues of scale and, more specifically, the optimal
    scale of economic activity.

This last issue is critical because federal and provincial governments have been in charge of determining access to resources, harvest rates, and overall sustainability of various ecological sectors. We know from the examples presented in this volume that conservation in fisheries, forestry, and agriculture has not been adequate, with the scale of economic activities often far in excess of what a given ecosystem can support.

Both federal and provincial governments need to recast their policy agendas so that they are more in tune with local realities and ecological processes. Following are five roles of macrogovernmental policy that can greatly assist in improving the conditions for sustainability at the community level.

1. Policies of integration, coordination, and delegation. Recognizing multiple and changing uses of the land, improving information flow between ministries, and empowering communities are at the heart of reconciling the parts to the whole. Both British Columbia and Alberta are particularly advanced with respect to this form of planning. As McTiernan notes, "the potential for any community to contribute to sustainable development in the region, and to have a sustainable future, depends on the quality of attention and judgment made by government agencies at arm's length from the community in question." Clearly, delegation is a critical function that rests with higher levels of government. It has been proposed, for example, by M'Gonigle (1996) that British Columbia create a "Community Forest Trust Act" in which Crown lands are shifted to ecosystem-based "trust" status. A designated communiy would act as a permanent trust manager. Equally radical is Schwindt's suggestion that British Columbia should consider the development of a terminal fishery to reduce waste, improve management of a scarce resource, and distribute the rewards to communities.

2. *Capacity building.* An important theme throughout this volume is the need to provide necessary and sufficient conditions for sustainable development. Communities across Canada need investment in social/human capital if they are to weather economic uncertainties and become more self-reliant. If Rifkin (1995) is correct that the "third" or informal sector is becoming an important source for meaningful work and sustainable livelihoods, then governments still have a vital role to play in supporting the basic investments needed to maintain these nonmarket and nonpriced activities. A significant component of capacity building is improving communications and access to information. Research conducted by Halseth and Arnold (1997) and Jespersen (1997) makes it clear that expanding access to the Internet and the World Wide Web and creating community networks, which the federal government has already begun to do across Canada, is a necessary condition for reducing the barriers to development imposed by remoteness and ultimately strengthening local economies.

3. *Indicators.* Governments have played an important role in providing information on economic indicators and basic social trends. This role needs to be expanded to include resource accounting or more complete accounting that incorporates environmental measures in the system of national accounts and/or in providing alternative measures of welfare/progress gains. Measures of changes to biodiversity, ecosystem health, and human health would assist in closing the circle on the interface between environment and economy.

4. *Efficiency.* Decreasing throughput by means of gains in efficiency is a necessary condition for reducing per capita consumption of resources. Taxation policy to date has favoured the substitution of capital for labour and has done little to reduce our reliance on fossil fuels, to expand our use of renewable energy sources, and to make more meaningful use of labour resources. Targeting both material and energy intensities through taxation (e.g., carbon taxes) is a simple yet effective means of representing the "truer" or fuller costs of growth and encouraging new technologies and modes of development.

5. *Conservation strategies.* In the late 1980s and early 1990s, the National Roundtable on the Environment and Economy proposed the adoption of conservation strategies by communities and regions to assist in more closely integrating environment and economy in decision making. Although roundtables continue, their potential has not been realized. A rejuvenation of these strategic plans could greatly assist communities in meeting their objectives and plans for the future.

If governments have an important facilitating role to play, then what, in turn, needs to be done at the community level to contribute to sustainable development? A number of common conditions and responses have been identified in this volume. Perhaps the greatest overlap of and consensus on ingredients for successful community-based sustainable development initiatives rest with the contributions of Nozick, Bryant, and McTiernan. They explore the themes of cohesive community vision, promotion of shared values, community control over resources, resource stewardship, participation and input of stakeholders, recognition of and debate on various "orientations," emphasis on quality of life and sustainable livelihoods, effective communication within and between communities, individual and community health, and strategic plans that are innovative and recognize the importance of integrating economic, social, and ecological dimensions. What is also clear is that to pursue these themes will require a different role of government, which, as previously discussed, will mean sharing or devolving powers and redefining development in such a way that the new model is more broadly based, recognizes and incorporates diverse interests, and, in short, places greater emphasis on development as opposed to growth. In a number of instances, the operative word will be on *redevelopment* of the resource base to compensate for years of mismanagement.

Bryant (1995) has argued that community economic development (CED) is the cornerstone of sustainable community development: "In the involvement of 'community' in the definition of its own vision and objectives, in the choice and evaluation of alternative strategies and in the use of local and community resources, the stress is placed on the involvement of as wide a range of legitimate interests as possible" (10). He goes on to say that this form of CED contributes to the "redemocratisation of our local and regional institutions" and may, in fact, lead to the "redefinition of the roles of government specifically and society generally."

Our willingness to explore these alternative models of development, including alternative resource management practices and strategies, rests with the understanding that, just as sustainable CED is people based, barriers to its adoption and promotion are also people based. Decentralized approaches to development will require the promotion of a community culture for the management of change. The authors of this book hope that it extends our understanding of the next steps and the ultimate directions that societies and the communities in which they are embedded must take.

References

Barnes, T.J., and Hayter, R. 1992. "'The Little Town That Did': Flexible Accumulation and Community Response in Chemainus, British Columbia." *Regional Studies* 26,7: 647-63.

Bryant, C.R. 1995. Community Economic Development: Changing the Shape of the Future through the Power of the People. Paper presented at the Preparing for Now Conference, June, Simon Fraser University, Burnaby.

Carr, M. 1996. Social Capital, Civil Society, and the Informal Economy: Moving to Sustainable Society. Paper presented at the ACSP/AESOP Conference, 25-8 July, University of British Columbia, Vancouver.

Cohen, A.P. 1985. *The Symbolic Construction of Community*. London: Tavistock Publications.

Dale, A., and J. Robinson, eds. 1996. *Achieving Sustainable Development*. Vancouver: UBC Press.

Daly, H. 1993. "The Perils of Free Trade." *Scientific American*, November, 50-7.

Daly, H., and J. Cobb. 1989. *For the Common Good*. Boston: Beacon Press.

Halseth, G., and D. Arnold. 1997. *Community Internet Access Groups: Case Studies from Rural and Small Town British Columbia, Canada*. Burnaby: Community Economic Development Centre, Simon Fraser University.

Innis, H. 1930. *The Fur Trade in Canada: An Introduction to Canadian Economic History*. Toronto: University of Toronto Press.

Jespersen, J. 1997. *Establishing a Community Computer Network: A Review of Issues and Process for Organizations in Canada*. Burnaby: Community Economic Development Centre, Simon Fraser University.

Kronenberger, L. 1972. *The Last Word*. New York: Macmillan.

M'Gonigle, M. 1996. Living Communities in a Living Forest: Towards an Alternative Structure of Local Tenure and Management. Discussion paper D96-3b. Eco-Research Chair, Faculty of Law, and Environmental Studies Program, University of Victoria.

Moran, W., G. Blunden, and N. Lewis. 1996. Regulating Sustainable Rural Systems: Political Rhetoric and Reality. Paper presented at the International Geographical Conference, August, Den Haag.

Pierce, J.T. 1992. "Progress and the Biosphere: The Dialectics of Sustainable Development." *Canadian Geographer* 36,4: 306-20.

Pinkerton, E., and M. Weinstein. 1995. *Fisheries That Work: Sustainability through Community Based Management*. Vancouver: The David Suzuki Foundation.

Putnam, R.D. 1996. "The Decline of Civil Society: How Come? So What?" *Optimum: The Journal of Public Sector Management* 27,1: 27-35.

Rifkin, J. 1995. *The End of Work*. New York: Putnam's Sons.

Robinson, J., and J. Tinker. 1995. Reconciling Ecological, Economic, and Social Imperatives: Towards an Analytical Framework. SDRI Discussion Paper Series. Sustainable Development Research Institute, University of British Columbia.

Robinson, J.B., and C. Van Bers. 1996. *Living within Our Means: The Foundations of Sustainability*. Vancouver: The David Suzuki Foundation

Contributors

Christopher Bryant is a Professor in the Department of Geography at the Université de Montréal. Formerly, he was with the University of Waterloo, where he was Director of the Economic Development Program. He has written extensively on community economic development and has had substantial experience in capacity building with communities, particularly in terms of accompanying communities in mobilizing citizen participation and helping community development organizations undertake strategic planning.

Ann Dale is a Senior Associate with the Sustainable Development Research Institute at the University of British Columbia and Vice-President of Research for the Canadian Biodiversity Institute.

Jill Dickinson is a graduate of the York University geography program. She is currently working for the Regional Municipality of Waterloo in Kitchener, Ontario.

Michael Gertler is an Assistant Professor in the Department of Sociology and Research Fellow at the Centre for the Study of Co-operatives, University of Saskatchewan. With a background in regional planning, agriculture, and development sociology, he has studied organic farming both as a researcher and practitioner. His current work focuses on resource communities, cooperatives, and related organizational innovations supporting sustainable rural development.

Alison M. Gill is an Associate Professor at Simon Fraser University with a joint appointment in the Department of Geography and the School of Resource and Environmental Management. She joined the faculty in 1984 after completing her PhD at the University of Manitoba. Her recent research has focused on mountain resort communities and the role of tourism in community economic development.

Clifford Lincoln was elected to the House of Commons in 1993. He is now the Chairman of the Standing Committee on Canadian Heritage and represents Canada on the Standing Committee of Parliamentarians of Arctic Nations. Long interested in the integration of environment and economy, he has led Canadian delegations at several international conferences, notably those of the Commission on Sustainable Development, the UNEP Governing Council, the Biodiversity Convention, and the UNEP/UNCTAD Conference on Trade and Environment.

Bryan H. Massam, FRSC, is a Professor at York University in the Department of Geography and the Social Science Division. He has served as Dean of Research at York University and President of the Canadian Association of Geographers. He has a long-standing interest in the provision of public goods and services, and the use of computer models for tackling complex location problems.

Timothy McTiernan is President of Canadore College of Applied Arts and Technology in North Bay, Ontario. He lived for eighteen years in the Yukon, where he worked for the territorial government, taught briefly at Yukon College, and consulted. Major areas of interest are sustainable development, Aboriginal governance, and intergovernmental relations. He has a PhD in psychology from the University of British Columbia.

Thom Meredith completed a Bachelor of Environmental Studies (geography) at the University of Waterloo in 1974. After a year of travel in Africa, he completed an MSc (botany, geography, zoology) and a Diploma in Conservation at University College London, and then proceeded to PhD research in conservation biology at the University of Cambridge. In 1979 he joined the Department of Geography at McGill University and, from 1981 to 1993, was Director of McGill's Environmental Studies Program. He has since been involved in research on community-based environmental conservation in Canada and Mexico.

Marcia Nozick is the author of *No Place Like Home: Building Sustainable Communities* (1992). She is the former coordinator for Healthy Communities Winnipeg and past editor of *City Magazine*. An activist and researcher in community economic development for fifteen years, she is currently an Associate of and Instructor at the Community Economic Development Centre at Simon Fraser University.

John T. Pierce is Dean of Arts and Professor of Geography at Simon Fraser University. He is the former director of the Community Economic Development Centre at SFU. His current research interests include investigations into structural change in resource-dependent communities, best practice in community economic development, and models for the reconciliation of environment and economy.

Maureen G. Reed is an Associate Professor in the Department of Geography at the University of British Columbia. Her research is focused on community development and sustainability, particularly on resource-dependent communities that are experiencing economic and social restructuring as well as changes in environmental conditions and policies.

William Rees is Professor and Director of the School of Community and Regional Planning at the University of British Columbia. As a human ecologist, his teaching and research focus is on the policy and planning implications of global ecological change. In this context, he is perhaps best known for his invention of "ecological footprint analysis," a method to measure progress toward sustainability. Professor Rees is also currently President of the Canadian Society for Ecological Economics.

Mark Roseland is Director of the Community Economic Development Centre at Simon Fraser University and an Associate Professor in SFU's Department of Geography. Dr. Roseland's books include *Eco-City Dimensions: Healthy Communities, Healthy Planet* (1997) and *Toward Sustainable Communities: Resources for Citizens and Their Governments* (1998). He is also the North American editor of the international journal *Local Environment*. Dr. Roseland lectures internationally and advises communities and governments on sustainable development policy and planning.

Richard Schwindt holds a joint appointment in the Department of Economics and the Faculty of Business Administration at Simon Fraser University. His research focuses on the industrial economics of renewable resource industries, with particular emphasis on forestry, fisheries, and agriculture. In 1992 he headed a provincial Commission of Inquiry into the expropriation of private rights to Crown natural resources.

Peter R. Sinclair is a Professor in the Department of Sociology at Memorial University in Newfoundland. His current research includes formal and informal economic practices in rural Newfoundland, marine biology and its relationship to fisheries policy, and timber dependency in rural Alabama. He is the author of *From Traps to Draggers* (1985) and *State Intervention and the Newfoundland Fisheries* (1987), and the coauthor of *Village in Crisis* (1974), *A Question of Survival* (1988), *Living on the Edge* (1995), *Aquacultural Development* (1996), and *When the Fish Are Gone* (1997).

Bob Woollard is Royal Canadian Legion Professor and Head, Department of Family Practice, Faculty of Medicine, University of British Columbia. He is Cochair of the UBC Task Force on Healthy and Sustainable Communities, an interdisciplinary research group publishing on the interrelationship between human and ecological health. He holds national organizational positions in environmental health and medical education.

Index

The Sustainable Development Research Institute at UBC was established in 1991 to initiate and contribute to interdisciplinary research on linkages between the environment, the economy, and society. The Institute develops and coordinates sustainable development research activities that are policy-relevant, encourage interdisciplinary collaboration, and involve non-academic partners including government, the private sector, and other institutions across Canada.

This second volume in the series would not have been possible without the support of the staff of the Environment Canada Departmental Library, and the editors would particularly like to thank Judy Patterson, Marie Jetten, and Claire Paquet for their unfailing courtesy and professionalism.

The first volume in the series, *Achieving Sustainable Development*, edited by Ann Dale and John B. Robinson, was published by UBC Press in 1996.

David V.J. Bell, Faculty of Environmental Studies, York Centre for Applied Sustainability, York University

Philippe J. Crabbé, Institute for Research on Environment and Economy, University of Ottawa

Jessie Davies, Environment and Sustainable Development Research Centre, University of New Brunswick

Terence Day, Atlantic Canada Centre for Environmental Science, Saint Mary's University

Jim Fulton, Executive Director, David Suzuki Foundation

Louis Guay, Sociologie, Université Laval

Arthur Hanson, International Institute for Sustainable Development

Thom Meredith, Centre for Society, Technology and Development , McGill University

John Middleton, Environmental Policy Institute, Brock University

Paul Painchaud, Studies and Research Center on Environmental Policy (GERPE), Laval University

Bill Ross, Faculty of Environmental Design, University of Calgary

Jim Robinson, Department of Environment and Resource Studies, University of Waterloo

John Robinson, Sustainable Development Research Institute, University of British Columbia

Mark Roseland, Community and Economic Development Centre, Simon Fraser University

Slobodan P. Simonovic, Natural Resources Institute, University of Manitoba

Peter Victor, Environmental Studies, York University

Jeffrey Watson, Canadian Global Change Program, Royal Society of Canada

Rodney White, Institute for Environmental Studies, University of Toronto

Peter N. Duinker, School for Resource and Environmental Studies, Dalhousie University